W9-BYJ-423

JOHN F. KERRY

PublicAffairs

New York

JOHN F. KERRY

THE COMPLETE BIOGRAPHY

BY THE BOSTON GLOBE REPORTERS

WHO KNOW HIM BEST

★ ★ ★ ★ ★

Michael Kranish,

Brian C. Mooney & Nina J. Easton

Published in the United States by PublicAffairs™, a member of the Perseus Books Group.

Book design and composition by Mark McGarry
Set in Caslon 540

ISBN 1-58648-273-4

FIRST EDITION
10 9 8 7 6 5 4 3 2 1

MICHAEL KRANISH:
*To my wife, Sylvia, daughters Jessica and Laura,
and Mom; and, in memory of Dad.*

NINA J. EASTON:
To my sons, Taylor and Danny.

BRIAN C. MOONEY:
To my wife Rosemary and daughter Meredith.

CONTENTS

PREFACE

With the *Boston Globe* having spent six months relentlessly digging into the life and record of Senator John F. Kerry for a newspaper profile, campaign operatives were chafing at what seemed like a journalistic enterprise without end. Relations with the campaign had turned downright toxic by June 2003, however, when our reporters began double- and triple-checking the most sensitive facts they had unearthed.

Our goal was to publish nothing less than the definitive portrait of a man who was seen early that summer as the favored Democratic nominee for president. Within three days, the first of seven installments was to appear, and Kerry's campaign manager, Jim Jordan, apparently had heard enough from us. Jordan fired off a searing message from his Blackberry, all but calling us liars for having pledged to be as fair as we were thorough.

JORDAN: It's becoming increasingly obvious that the profile is, in fact, going to be a seven day rip job. That's been the buzz out of both newsrooms for some time, but we'd hoped for better. However, from everything we can divine from our end of the project wrap ups, this doesn't look to be a fair, contextual look at a long, good life but, instead, a collection of gaffes, controversies, disputations.

MY RESPONSE: Oh please.

Why don't you just wait and read it? Then you can complain, if you feel it's warranted, rather than rely on "buzz." What's obvious to you, having read not a word, doesn't seem obvious to me, having actually read it.

JORDAN: Because nothing is more impotent than bitching about a story once it's run.

Sorry that you find my concerns old lady-ish. Of course we haven't read the piece in toto, but we've lived with this f——r every day for six months, and there isn't [any] mystery left.

And it's become increasingly clear that this thing, despite your assurances to the contrary a couple of months ago, has lurched into a predictable direction. Small bore, snarky, cynical. Nothing taken at face value, no benefit of any doubt, no explanation accepted without challenge. A preoccupation with finding scandal where none exists. Everything interpreted through an entirely political lens ...

Here's hoping I have to eat these words.

Jordan (fired by Kerry in November as his campaign was faltering) was mostly wrong, but on one important point he was right. Wrong, because the *Boston Globe*'s seven-part series last June was absolutely fair, and the campaign would later acknowledge that. And right, because we never did take anything at face value. We checked every assertion. We assumed nothing. Nor should we have settled for less than exhaustive documentation and verification. John Kerry was seeking the most powerful position in the world, and the *Boston Globe* aimed to cover him better than anyone else.

In December 2002, our editors and political reporters began conferring about the need for a portrait of John Kerry. He was already collecting more financial support than any other prospective candidate for the Democratic nomination. He was leading in early polls. We determined then that the *Boston Globe* should be the point of reference for anyone seeking to know John Kerry. No one should discover material about him that we hadn't identified and vetted first.

Not surprisingly, there were some skeptics in our newsroom. They wondered whether revelations were possible, no matter how long we searched. Our archives already bulged with stories about Kerry, reflecting unwavering attention to a man who had served in the U.S. Senate for two decades and who first entered Massachusetts politics in 1972. Our appetite was both for new insights and new information about John Kerry, and in the end we could claim both.

The *Boston Globe*'s major advantage was the trio of reporters we had assembled for the challenge. Each had deep experience covering Kerry over the course of his political career. They knew enough about him to appreciate what was yet unknown, and they had the skills to fill in the gaps.

Michael Kranish was assigned to examine Kerry's early years, his upbringing, and his combat in Vietnam. Kranish has followed the senator closely since his first interview in 1986 about oil industry tax breaks and in 1987 on the Iran-contra investigation. As early as 1988, Kranish interviewed Kerry for a lengthy piece about how he had worked to change his image from liberal senator to a hard-charging investigator of drug running. "It all seemed so far from Kerry's far-left image," Kranish wrote, touching on a theme as fitting today as it was then, "and that was exactly what Kerry wanted: mainstream credibility."

John Kerry's record in Congress fell to John Aloysius Farrell, now with the *Denver Post*. It was familiar territory for Farrell, who arrived in 1990 at the *Boston Globe*'s Washington, D.C., bureau with the mission of covering the Massachusetts delegation in Congress. He has followed him ever since. He chronicled the 1992 speech at Yale University when Kerry labeled affirmative action an "inherently limited and divisive program," remarks that would later dog him during the South Carolina primary. He recorded as well what is now regarded as Kerry's signature legislative achievement, resolving the POW issue and bringing about rapprochement with Vietnam.

No one on the reporting team has kept an eye on Kerry longer than Brian C. Mooney. He has known and covered him for more than twenty-six years. His first contact dated back to 1977, when Kerry was first assistant district attorney in Middlesex County and Mooney was a cub reporter at the Medford (Massachusetts) *Daily Mercury*. He has covered his campaigns since for the *Sun* in Lowell, the *Boston*

Herald, and the *Boston Globe*. Mooney was asked to delve into the period of John Kerry's life that had received the least attention—his job as a prosecutor, his short tenure as lieutenant governor, and the period of relative obscurity when he served as a lawyer in the private sector. Also under Mooney's microscope were Kerry's political relationships and campaigns in Massachusetts.

Despite all the stories written about Kerry over the years, research by these reporters quickly produced astonishing results. Working with an Austrian genealogist, Kranish turned up family history that had been hidden from Kerry himself—his paternal grandfather's Jewish heritage and the story that in 1921, apparently broke, Kerry's grandfather had shot himself in the washroom of the ornate Copley Plaza Hotel in the center of Boston.

Later, in studying Kerry's post-Vietnam years, Kranish found previously unpublicized tapes of President Richard Nixon's remarks about a young antiwar protester he derided as "sort of a phony," despite his harrowing combat experience.

Mooney, too, was poring through documents that had never before caught the attention of reporters. None had ever possessed Mooney's curiosity. Nor had they shown Mooney's patience at inspecting papers from Kerry's brief stint as lieutenant governor of Massachusetts. And so Mooney was the first to disclose Kerry's costly courtship with an exotic tax shelter, a transaction he abandoned because of potential embarrassment as he prepared to run for the U.S. Senate.

Piece by piece, these reporters assembled the most

comprehensive look ever at the man who would be president. Journalists on the campaign trail considered it required reading.

The strength of the series and its narrative force was due in large part to the exacting and elegant editing by Nina J. Easton, deputy bureau chief in Washington. Easton came to the task with her own history of distinguished accomplishment in covering politics and public policy. As an award-winning staff writer for the *Los Angeles Times Magazine* in the 1990s, those were her beats. During the 2000 presidential campaign, Simon and Schuster published her book on the rise to power of a new generation of conservatives who became central to the election of George W. Bush. In reviewing her book *Gang of Five: Leaders at the Center of the Conservative Crusade*, the *Washington Post* said she told the story of post-Reagan conservatism "more inventively, exhaustively, and entertainingly than anyone else." Easton set aside her editing responsibilities to do reporting for this book on Kerry, concentrating on his legislative record.

Both the *Boston Globe* series and this book involved, like so much at newspapers, a large team. Editors on the series included John Yemma, a deputy managing editor; and Kenneth Cooper, national editor. Patrick Healy, who reported on Kerry throughout the presidential primaries, made major contributions to the chapter on the presidential campaign, as did reporter Glen Johnson, who covered Kerry through the early stages of his candidacy. Research by the *Boston Globe*'s Richard Pennington has been critical at every stage to the entire effort.

As ambitious as the seven-part series was, there remained much more to tell about John Kerry. This book significantly expands upon the articles published in June of 2003.

During the presidential campaign, even Kerry's closest allies have commented in frustration on the candidate's discomfort at revealing himself and how difficult it can be for voters to get to know him. With this book and the newspaper series that preceded it, we have sought to help voters understand the real John Kerry. By all accounts, he is a complex man. There is no question he has led an intriguing life.

If a newspaper is doing its job, its relationship with leading politicians is bound to be testy. Adulation is not in our mission statement. Serving as public watchdog is. Politicians, for their part, often view the watchdogs more as cynics, with agendas of their own and portfolios of unfairness.

The *Boston Globe*'s relationship with John Kerry has been marked by rocky moments, and he has not infrequently conveyed, directly or through surrogates, a feeling that the newspaper was out to get him.

We are not ideally positioned to impartially assess its our own newspaper's history with Kerry, but it seems only proper that we at least mention here the observations of others. A *New Yorker* profile in December 2002 touched on what writer Joe Klein seemed to regard as harsh treatment by the newspaper. "We were pretty rough on him over the years," former *Boston Globe* political writer Martin Nolan told Klein, who identified Nolan as "a recently retired member of the *Boston Globe*'s mostly Irish and extremely raucous stable of political writers."

Klein related Kerry's distress over coverage of his 1984 race to become the Democratic nominee for Senate, when he perceived the *Boston Globe* as favoring his opponent, U.S. representative James Shannon of Lawrence. Michael Janeway, then the newspaper's editor, told Klein: "He wanted to know why we were so rough on him. I reminded him about Sam Rayburn's classic political categories. I said, 'John, there are workhorses and show horses, and I guess our staff considers you a show horse.'"

In his 1996 Senate race, Kerry faced off against Massachusetts governor William Weld. "With a shock of strawberry hair and irony to burn," Klein wrote in the *New Yorker*, Weld "seemed an honorary Hibernian"—an opponent "bound to be favored by the reportorial romantics at the *Boston Globe*."

More recently, R. W. Apple of the *New York Times* reported in December 2003 that Kerry "and others blame what they see as negative coverage by *The Boston Globe*, as well as early organizational troubles" for the way his presidential campaign sputtered for so long in New Hampshire.

Yet the *Boston Globe* has consistently endorsed Kerry on its editorial pages. The newspaper's editorial board, which operates independently of its news department, endorsed Kerry in the general election for Senate in 1984, and it continued to endorse him for Senate in 1990, 1996, and 2002. Only in the Democratic primary for Senate in 1984 did the *Boston Globe* back Kerry's opponent.

When the newspaper endorsed Kerry in the New

Hampshire presidential primary in 2004, the editorial board summarized its impression of him over the years, declaring that he had "inspired, impressed, and sometimes infuriated us since he first became the top assistant in the Middlesex district attorney's office in 1977."

Journalists are accustomed to politicians' discontent with their coverage, particularly when the presidency is the prize they covet. Thus, irritation by operatives like one-time Kerry campaign manager Jim Jordan before publication of our series is understandable in the context of a heated contest. We recognize that the *Boston Globe* reported doggedly on the Kerry campaign, as we did on the other presidential candidates. We maintain that our coverage of Kerry and his opponents was also resolutely fair.

ABC's political unit, in its daily on-line newsletter, described our Kerry project as a "ground-breaking biographical series."

In expanding the series into a book, our reporters conducted even more research. In February, they requested more time with Kerry so that he could offer his perspective on additional information they had turned up. In rejecting our request, campaign manager Mary Beth Cahill calculated that the senator had already "set aside nearly ten hours of interview time and countless hours of preparation time for interviews" in connection with the newspaper series. She also said the campaign staff had spent "hundreds of hours in support of the *Boston Globe*'s efforts" and had made a "strong, best faith effort to answer all questions posed by the *Boston Globe* reporters, even in cases when information was presented on short notice." Cahill argued, too, that Kerry didn't have time in the middle of a national campaign, while battling attacks from Democratic rivals and the Bush White House, to sit for more interviews.

"Over the years," Cahill wrote, in rebuffing us, "the *Globe* has shown fairness and established a high standard of accuracy in its coverage of Senator Kerry, culminating [in] the groundbreaking series last year and the revelations contained there...." The tone of Cahill's letter certainly represented a change from the vituperative e-mails received last summer from her predecessor. In the end, though, the campaign gave us the heave-ho.

We would have welcomed the opportunity to sit down with Senator Kerry at greater length. Voters deserve to know well anyone who aspires to be president. We hope we have met our goal of assisting them, with a portrait that is complete, balanced, and authoritative.

Martin Baron
Editor, *The Boston Globe*
March 2003

INTRODUCTION

ON JANUARY 27, 2004, Senator John F. Kerry of Massachusetts accomplished one of the most spectacular turnarounds in modern American politics when he capped a surprise win in the Iowa caucus with a victory in the New Hampshire primary. Just weeks earlier, former Vermont governor Howard Dean was the apparent front-runner, and political insiders were taking bets on when Kerry—whose support landed him somewhere in the middle of a field of nine Democratic candidates—would drop out of the race. Kerry's presidential campaign, once expected to trump other challengers, had become riddled with internal strife; as a candidate, he was criticized as a stiff figure with a muddled message, particularly on the nation's most divisive issue, the war in Iraq.

But in the days following New Hampshire, the political pundit machinery went from writing off the Massachusetts senator as a disappointing has-been to embracing him as the ideal November match against Republican President George W. Bush. Conservative George Will extolled Kerry's "manliness" ("riding his Harley, gunning for Iowa pheasants, and playing hockey in New Hampshire"), while liberal Harold Meyerson declared him "the most effective politico since the fall of Bill Clinton."

"He is not the most affable of men, but somewhere in his gaunt frame is a rod of steely determination that enabled him to come off the mat and win the first two Democratic contests," declared liberal columnist Richard Cohen.

"He doesn't make many mistakes," asserted conservative columnist Robert Novak.

Who is the man likely to become the Democratic Party's nominee for president in 2004? And what kind of political leader is he? The outlines of John Kerry's life are familiar: A decorated Vietnam veteran who became an influential, if unlikely, antiwar protester. A lanky sixty-year-old who quenches his thirst for danger with high-speed kiteboarding, windsurfing, piloting, and motorcycling. As a senator, he stayed off the path of his more famous colleague, Senator Ted Kennedy—a lawmaker known for making laws—and instead developed a reputation as an investigator and foreign policy expert.

But beyond this broad picture, Kerry is something of a mystery to the public, largely because of a complex yet riveting personal and professional history, chronicled in this book. To his critics, Kerry is an aloof politician who lacks a core. His personal story has much to do with that image: Kerry is a man without geographic roots. He's not "from" a

Massachusetts neighborhood; rather, his youth stretched through a dozen towns across two continents with only a few years spent in the state he calls home. He enjoyed the cachet of illustrious family names but not always the nourishing bonds of a close family life. As a boy, he was shipped off for a seven-year odyssey at boarding schools in Switzerland and New England.

Kerry himself is wistful about his youth. "I was always moving on and saying good-bye," he said in a 2003 interview with the *Boston Globe*. "It steeled you. There wasn't a lot of permanence and roots." At a 2001 gathering of some 2,000 Bostonians honoring J. Joseph Moakley, a beloved congressman from South Boston who was dying from leukemia, William M. Bulger, the state senator from Southie, described the close-knit neighborhood and the nurturing effect it had on Moakley.

Then Kerry spoke. "I felt a pang as I listened to him talk about the lessons learned in that community," Kerry said. "Because one of my regrets is that I didn't share that kind of neighborhood. I didn't know that. My dad was in the foreign service. We moved around a lot."

More than to any one place, Kerry's ties were to a social milieu—that rarefied world of wealth and privilege where the French is fluent and the manners impeccable. As a young man, Bill Clinton was thrilled to get the chance to shake JFK's hand on a Boys Nation outing; by contrast, young John Kerry dated Jacqueline Kennedy's half-sister and once sailed Narragansett Bay with JFK at the helm.

But Kerry did not fully belong to this elite world, either. His father's government salary, combined with his own

struggles with money, left him planted further on the outskirts of New England's ruling class than many realized.
The boy who was educated at patrician prep schools grew
into a gentleman without significant means, part of a land-
less aristocracy that one might find in a Jane Austen novel.
He married wealthy wives whose net worth dwarfed his
own.

His political development was equally conflicted. Upon
graduation from Yale, he gave a class oration suggesting the
Vietnam War could mean "an excess of interventionism"
but enlisted as an officer, just as his friends were doing, just
as his hero JFK had done. He hoped to avoid combat, then
was thrown into the middle of it and earned the highest
honors for his bravery under fire. He left the war shaken by
the deaths of close friends—and by witnessing U.S. violence against Vietnamese civilians—and took up the man-
tle of antiwar activist at home. His words before Congress,
asking lawmakers, "How do you ask a man to be the last
man to die for a mistake?" provided powerful eloquence to
his cause. But he also accused American soldiers of committing atrocities; and Vietnam veterans, including some of
his former crewmates, saw betrayal in the crusade that was
transforming Kerry into a national figure.

"Vietnam is a lesson," Kerry told the *Boston Globe* in
2003. "It is history to me. It can guide me but it doesn't run
me. You have to move on and I moved on a long time ago.
But the lessons are valuable. I love the lessons. And I love
the friendships and the experience. Notwithstanding the
downside of it, it was a great extraordinary learning experience."

To Kerry, the war was "a great leadership lesson, a great human interpersonal lesson. Six guys on a boat, you know, helping to deliver a breech-birth child to a Vietnamese woman, and you are patching up a guy who was trying to shoot you three minutes earlier and put it back together. Those are experiences of a lifetime. Those are things that stay with you."

Kerry went to Vietnam as part of the "ask what you can do for your country" generation. Duty, honor, and standing up to communism, Kennedy-style. He returned, in the space of just twenty-four months, to a nation rocked by antiwar protests, by urban riots, by the assassinations of Robert F. Kennedy and Martin Luther King Jr., by the rise of a counterculture youth. Like his peers, he returned not to parades and confetti but to a bitterly divided nation. He returned, too, angry over the deaths of his friends, over an American military policy that condoned the shooting of civilians in the jungles of Vietnam, over government deceit and distortion.

As a senator, Kerry's Vietnam experience drove him to ferret out government misdeeds, though not always with success or political acuity. He was instrumental in moving the country toward normalized relations with Vietnam in the early 1990s. Ironically, in the course of that mission (his "last" Vietnam mission, he would say), he concluded that the government he once protested was not involved in lies and cover-ups; there were no mass prisons of American soldiers secretly being held in Indochina, as many families and conspiracy theorists insisted.

Vietnam left Kerry with conflicted views about war's

ultimate claim—on human life. He said he was not a pacifist. But the images of the horrors of combat, of American
GIs returning in body bags, haunted him and influenced
his positions on Central America in the 1980s and the Persian Gulf War in 1991. Yet he has also supported U.S. military intervention, particularly in Kosovo in 1999.

His critics accuse him of straddling positions on the two
biggest wars America has engaged in since Vietnam, both
against the same country—Iraq. In 1991, after Saddam
Hussein invaded Kuwait, Kerry voted against war, then
praised the quick defeat mounted by George H.W. Bush's
Pentagon. In 2002, he voted for war, then condemned the
invasion mounted by George W. Bush's Pentagon. "I mean,
I supported disarming Saddam Hussein, but I was critical
of the administration and how it did its diplomacy and so
forth," he explained.

There is a brashness about Kerry that can breed resentment. Whatever the setting, John F. Kerry leaves strong
opinions behind. As an antiwar activist, he was a target of
Richard Nixon, who characterized the twenty-seven-year-
old as "sort of a phony" but worried that he was "extremely
effective." But he was also a target of what was arguably
the leading antiestablishment voice of his generation,
Garry Trudeau's *Doonesbury*, which lampooned him as a
"gorgeous preppie." Among Vietnam veterans—those with
whom he served and those with whom he protested—he is
either revered, or reviled.

There is another side, rarely revealed, to the patrician
manner and diffident carriage that compose the public face

of John Kerry. Raymond L. Flynn, former mayor of Boston, has long since parted ways with Kerry since their political alliance of the 1980s. But in 1994, when Flynn was in Rome, serving as U.S. ambassador to the Vatican, Kerry visited Flynn's son Ray Jr. a number of times when he was hospitalized for treatment of a bipolar disorder. "He would stop by, with magazines, and talk sports and politics to Little Ray," the elder Flynn recalled.

Similarly, Toby Guzowski remembered how Kerry, in 1989, "spent many hours" at Beth Israel Hospital in Boston, at the bedside of his mother, Ann Guzowski, a longtime Kerry volunteer who was being treated for terminal breast cancer. Chris Greeley, a former aide and now a lobbyist, said he experienced that solicitous side of his boss in 1986 when his mother died. "His capacity to respond when you need it can be a little overwhelming," Greeley said.

In Massachusetts as a prosecutor and in Washington as a senator, Kerry often proved himself to be a crusading and articulate investigator and lawmaker willing to stand up to prevailing political winds. Yet he is trailed by a reputation for political opportunism, symbolized by his 1971 decision to protest the war by tossing medals and ribbons over a fence at the Capitol—and then to explain away the controversial deed by declaring the medals belonged to another veteran. By bold proclamations—such as his 1992 condemnation of affirmative action and the welfare system—that were dropped when they didn't yield political firepower. By his recent, sometimes tortured, explanation of why he voted in favor of military action in Iraq but now condemns the Bush White House for it. Later, Kerry voted against an $87 billion appropriation to fund the reconstruction and U.S. presence in Iraq.

Do these actions reflect the conflicts of a powerful intellect, of a man who appreciates nuance in policy and deeds but sometimes has trouble translating it to a mass audience? Do his statements and votes on military force reflect the natural caution of a man who was severely wounded in combat, who watched men under his command die, who lost five of his best friends in a war that ended in U.S. withdrawal? Kerry, a spokesman has said, is "proud of his independence and unashamed that his resistance to orthodoxy leaves him hard to pigeonhole."

But critics see him as an unabashed political operator. Unlike many who are driven to succeed in public life by a core belief system, the arc of Kerry's political career is defined by a restless search for the issues, individuals, and causes to fulfill a nearly lifelong ambition. John Forbes Kerry has had his eyes on the White House ever since he was a youth watching the war hero and Massachusetts Catholic bearing the same initials, John Fitzgerald Kennedy, take the oath of the Oval Office.

And yet it has taken him until now—at age sixty—to mount a campaign. His leadership of the Vietnam Veterans Against the War lasted five months. His first campaign for Congress, at age twenty-eight, left him defeated, a bit shaken, and forever marked as a carpetbagging opportunist in the clubby world of Massachusetts politics. His first Senate term, begun at age forty-one, was marred by divorce from a wife who suffered severe depression, by financial problems and no place to call home. His third Senate term began with a new life, and a new wife, Teresa Heinz, whose wealth was estimated at $675 million dollars. But in 2000, there were other, more seasoned presidential campaigners on the horizon.

The opponent that George W. Bush will face in the fall is combative, never more so than when he's falling behind. Kerry has proven an extraordinary ability to rebound from adversity; friends say he's at his best when he's under pressure or falling behind. He began the year 2003 with prostate cancer and ended it with nearly everyone in the political establishment predicting his demise.

He is also an experienced and effective money raiser. He proclaims that he limits the influence of special interest money by refusing money from political action committees. But he is a proficient bundler of donations, taking contributions from individuals who work at the same law firms, financial services and telecommunications firms, high-tech companies, and other sectors of the economy with business before Congress. Despite his protestations to the contrary, he has shown a willingness to tap personal wealth he accumulated largely as a result of his marriage to Teresa Heinz. (Heinz, originally a Republican, said she switched her party affiliation to Democrat in 2003.)

Kerry is known to push himself physically, often at high rates of speed, testing his athleticism, endurance, and ability to make quick decisions. Still, Kerry brings a certain gray-haired eminence to his first campaign for the presidency. At sixty, he is fourteen years older than Bill Clinton was when he launched his bid for the presidency, and six years older than George W. Bush was when he first ran for president in 2000.

John Kerry and George Bush are prep school graduates who attended Yale two years apart; they both belonged to the elite and secretive Skull and Bones society. But there the similarities end. In the November election, American voters will be choosing between two very different candidates, with two very different worldviews.

This is the story of one of them.

JOHN F. KERRY

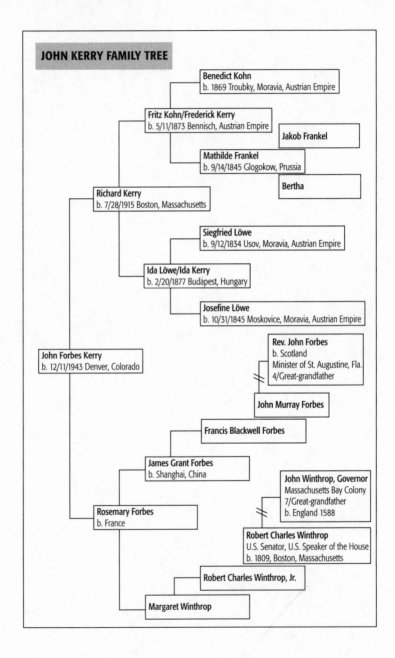

JOHN KERRY FAMILY TREE

Benedict Kohn
b. 1869 Troubky, Moravia, Austrian Empire

Fritz Kohn/Frederick Kerry
b. 5/11/1873 Bennisch, Austrian Empire

Jakob Frankel

Mathilde Frankel
b. 9/14/1845 Glogokow, Prussia

Bertha

Richard Kerry
b. 7/28/1915 Boston, Massachusetts

Siegfried Löwe
b. 9/12/1834 Usov, Moravia, Austrian Empire

Ida Löwe/Ida Kerry
b. 2/20/1877 Budapest, Hungary

Josefine Löwe
b. 10/31/1845 Moskovice, Moravia, Austrian Empire

Rev. John Forbes
b. Scotland
Minister of St. Augustine, Fla.
4/Great-grandfather

John Forbes Kerry
b. 12/11/1943 Denver, Colorado

John Murray Forbes

Francis Blackwell Forbes

James Grant Forbes
b. Shanghai, China

John Winthrop, Governor
Massachusetts Bay Colony
7/Great-grandfather
b. England 1588

Rosemary Forbes
b. France

Robert Charles Winthrop
U.S. Senator, U.S. Speaker of the House
b. 1809, Boston, Massachusetts

Robert Charles Winthrop, Jr.

Margaret Winthrop

Chapter 1

FAMILY TREE

TO HIS FRIENDS and neighbors, Frederick A. Kerry appeared to be the model of a successful businessman and family man. He lived with his wife, Ida, and their three children in the fashionable Boston suburb of Brookline, Massachusetts. They owned a rambling three-story stucco home a few blocks from the trolley line, counted their live-in servant, a German immigrant named Elise, as one of the family, and attended the local Roman Catholic church.

The nation of immigrants that Fred Kerry epitomized was prospering in 1921, while the Europe that he had left behind sixteen years earlier was coping with an assortment of crises, from the onset of communism to the gathering storm that would become known as Nazism. The grandfather of the future Senator John F. Kerry had earned—and had lost—two fortunes. Now he was working on his third.

Weighing nearly 200 pounds and towering an imposing six feet, two inches tall, Kerry cut a striking figure as a businessman. He had helped reorganize some of the nation's retail giants, including Sears, Roebuck and Co. Local papers described him as an important community leader, first in Chicago and then in Boston, where he had worked for seven years. Everything about Fred Kerry and his family bespoke success and an easy assimilation into the American way of life. In the nation's most Irish state, they fit in comfortably, and a newspaper article even suggested, incorrectly, that Fred Kerry's father came from Ireland.

But appearances could be misleading.

When the family responded to a U.S. immigration worker at Ellis Island or a census taker in Brookline, they did not hide their family background: Kerry and his family were Austrian, from an area then part of the Austrian Empire and later known as the Czech Republic. Austrian records tell the full story: Frederick Kerry was born a Jew with the name Fritz Kohn, to a family of brewers and shoemakers. This was a secret he apparently did not want his Brookline neighbors to know.

In fact, Fritz Kohn was born on May 11, 1873, in Bennisch in the Austrian Empire, now known as Horni Benesov in the Czech Republic, according to Austrian records. Fritz's father, Benedict Kohn, is described in Austrian records as a Jewish beer maker from Bennisch, and his mother, the former Mathilde Frankel, is described as the Jewish daughter of a royal dealer, someone licensed to trade throughout the empire. The tiny Silesian town of about 4,300 people had only a few dozen Jews, and in 1896, Fritz moved to a suburb of Vienna called Modling, where he managed a shoe factory owned by his uncle, Alfred Frankel.

Fritz Kohn married a Jewish woman from Budapest named Ida Löwe, and they had a son named Eric. Although the family appears to have been reasonably well off in Vienna, this was a time of rampant anti-Semitism in the city. The City Council was run by the Christian Social Party, which treated Jews harshly. Jews had legal rights, but it was difficult or impossible for them to attain high rank in business or the military, and they had little hope of becoming teachers, judges, or officers. In 1900, Kohn applied to change his name to Kerry.

> Fritz Kohn, factory manager in Modling, born and possessing legal domiciliary rights in Bennisch, Silesia, in the military reserves, seeks to change his name from Kohn to Kerry:
> 1) because of the frequency of the name, which is so typically Jewish; and 2) because he believes that the name will hinder his career in the military.

But why was the name Kerry chosen? According to family legend, Fritz and another family member opened an atlas at random and dropped a pencil on a map. It fell on County Kerry in Ireland, and thus a name was chosen. In fact, though there are many immigrants from County Kerry, it was not a common surname. The couple would heretofore be known as Frederick and Ida Kerry.

But the name change apparently was not enough. On October 9, 1901, Kohn and his wife and newborn son went to the St. Othmar Catholic parish in Modling and were jointly baptized as Catholics. They remained in the Vienna area for another four years. The name change was in effect by December 17, 1901, according to a notation in the Jewish marriage records of Vienna.

At this time, relatively few Jews from Vienna were immigrating to America; most came from Eastern European villages. But the newly christened Kerrys apparently felt that their opportunity lay across the ocean. They departed from an Italian port aboard the ship *Königen Luise* and arrived at Ellis Island on May 18, 1905. Fred Kerry and his wife, Ida, and their child, Eric, were listed in immigration documents as Austrian.

They soon moved to Chicago, where they prospered. Kerry ran an ad in a city directory that described "Fred A. Kerry & Staff" as business counselors, and Kerry himself was in the Chicago Blue Book, which listed city leaders.

By 1915, the Kerrys lived in Brookline with Eric and their two children born in the United States: Mildred, and a newborn, Richard, the father of the future Senator Kerry. By all accounts, they lived a prosperous life at 10 Downing Road. Inside, the walls were lined with elegant wood paneling, and the ceiling was spaced with finely carved wooden beams. The house, newly built when the Kerrys moved in, had a long porch in front, from which the family could see similar homes owned by the town's well-to-do. The family acquired a Cadillac and was able to travel to Europe.

But by 1920, the Kerrys appeared to have suffered a financial setback. They sold the house at 10 Downing Road and moved into a nearby apartment building. Still, the Kerrys could afford to go to Europe, and Ida and two of her children, Richard and Mildred, did so in the fall of 1921. The reason for the sea voyage is not known, but they returned to New York City on October 21, 1921, and then presumably went back to their home in Brookline, rejoining Fred. Perhaps something happened on their trip. Perhaps they learned bad news. Perhaps it was nothing more than a sentimental journey. But the timing seems extraordinary, given what happened next. On November 15, 1921, Kerry filed a will. He left everything "to my beloved wife, Ida Kerry, to her own use and behoof forever."

Eight days later, with rain clouds hanging low in the sky on a raw, cold day, Fred Kerry apparently stuck to his usual routine. He traveled from Brookline to his downtown office on Boylston Street, probably taking the trolley. Around 11:30 A.M., Kerry arrived at the venerable Copley Plaza Hotel, near his office. Opened in 1912 to rave reviews, the Plaza was designed by Henry Janeway Hardenbergh, as was its sister hotel on New York's Central Park. With its distinctive bow-shaped front, the Copley was known for its double-P insignia. The hotel's Oval Room, which at that time featured an angel painted by John Singer Sargent on the ceiling, was *the* place to be seen. Kerry, as a leading businessman in the city, was likely a frequent visitor.

But on the morning of November 23, Kerry was in despair. It was just before lunchtime, and the Copley was bound to be busy. He made his way to the washroom, pulled a handgun from his pocket, aimed it at his head, and pulled the trigger. The lunch crowd heard a sharp blast as he slumped to the floor.

Frederick Kerry was dead.

The story was front-page news in many Boston papers, including the *Boston Globe*, the *Telegram*, and the *Transcript*. The *Boston Globe* headline said, "Shot Himself in Copley Plaza—F. A. Kerry, Merchant, Died Very Soon," and later articles included speculation about the reason for the suicide. Some noted that Kerry suffered from severe asthma, and one suggested the possibility of financial difficulties. The death certificate states that Kerry was "suicidal during temporary insanity." A *Boston Herald* article said: "F. A. Kerry Ends Life in Hotel—Shoe Dealer Weakened and Depressed by Severe Illness—Reorganized Many Department Stores," and notes that he had left a note to his wife in his pocket, the words of which were not disclosed. The story included a quote from Kerry's attorney, who said Kerry "suffered severely from asthma and in consequence had become weakened and depressed from loss of sleep. This is the sole reason ascribed for his taking his own life."

But one of Kerry's granddaughters, Nancy Stockslager, said she was told the real reason: "He had made three fortunes and when he had lost the third fortune, he couldn't face it anymore."

The explanation makes sense. A probate court record said that Frederick Kerry left behind a Cadillac, some clothes, two stock shares worth $200 from the Boston Chamber of Commerce, $25 in cash, and "shares of stock in J.L. Walker Co. and Spencer Shoe Manufacturing Co.—worthless." A newspaper story said that Kerry's work involved Spencer, so he clearly was more than a simple stockholder. If this was his third fortune, as Stockslager was told, then the probate records leave little doubt he had lost it.

Kerry also left behind the family he treasured, including his younger son, six-year-old Richard, who would become a foreign service officer, and who one day would have a son of his own, John Forbes Kerry. John Kerry would not learn the details of his grandfather's Jewish ancestry or the circumstances of the suicide until 2003, when he was preparing to run for president of the United States. Indeed, even some of Kerry's closest associates and family members assumed the senator was Irish on his father's side and a Brahmin on his mother's side, which included the Forbes and Winthrop families. The combination was a potent mixture that was to prove useful in Massachusetts politics.

In 1763, the Reverend John Forbes, the great-great-great-great-grandfather of Senator John Forbes Kerry, was given an important job by the British Empire. The Scot was named minister at St. Augustine, an important post in the British control of East Florida. For the next twenty years, Forbes lived in Florida, serving on the Governor's Council and as chief justice. He married a wealthy Boston woman named Dorothy Murray, who preferred to remain at the family estate of Brush Hill in Milton, Massachusetts.

Then came calamity. When the American Revolution unfolded, Forbes remained loyal to the British Crown. A distraught John Forbes fled Florida in 1783 and returned to England, where he died within months. Such was the inauspicious beginning of this great Forbes family in America.

One of Forbes's three sons also returned to England—James Grant Forbes, the great-great-great-grandfather of Senator Kerry. The other two sons, John and Ralph, stayed behind in America and would play a crucial role in the transformation of Massachusetts. John was a Harvard classmate of future president John Quincy Adams, who later named him ambassador to Argentina. Ralph was a merchant whose own son, Thomas, helped establish the Boston-China trade in the early 1800s. In the course of just fifty years, the Forbes family had gone from being reviled loyalists to leaders of the American mercantile class.*

With the Forbes family prospering in the China trade, other family members were attracted to the business. Francis Forbes, the great-grandfather of Senator Kerry, lived for years in China and then in Europe. He was prosperous, excelled in business, promoted the Shanghai Country Club, and devoted many hours to his hobby of botany. But Francis's greatest legacy was that of his son, James Grant Forbes, who would outdo most of the family when it came to business. This man, Kerry's grandfather, would become perhaps the most successful member of the clan, working not only in the Boston-China trade but also in the establishment of post–World War II Europe.

Kerry's grandfather was born in Shanghai on October 22, 1879, educated at Harvard and graduated in the class of 1901, and went into banking in Boston. In a twenty-fifth

* All of the Forbes in this group are unrelated or only distantly related to another famous Forbes clan, which includes former presidential candidate and magazine mogul Steve Forbes.

anniversary book on the Class of 1901, the author noted that "the prize exhibit of the report goes to Jimmie Forbes. No one will dispute his claim to having the most fascinating family in the Class, after examining the proof he submits." The only regret, the author wrote, is that Forbes said little in his class report about the extraordinary woman he married: Margaret Winthrop of Boston.

If those in the Forbes family of Massachusetts were famous for their business acumen, the Winthrops of Massachusetts were their equal in politics. The marriage of James Grant Forbes to Margaret Winthrop had the air of a royal union, bringing together two of the Bay State's most famous families.

The Winthrop family history is the history of Massachusetts, starting with John Winthrop, the first governor of the Massachusetts Bay Colony. John Winthrop is the great-great-great-great-great-great-great-grandfather of Senator Kerry. The Winthrop Society, which is devoted to the family's genealogy, modestly says in its charter that "Governor John Winthrop and the Puritan colonists who came with him to plant the Massachusetts Bay Colony in 1630 were the most important and influential single group of Europeans ever to arrive in North America."

Winthrop, born in 1588 in England, believed that the Anglican Church should be "purified," calling for a removal of Catholic ritual and saying that the monarch should not head the church. Winthrop and about 1,000 other Puritans left England for Massachusetts, where he was selected as the first governor of the Massachusetts Bay Colony. Winthrop believed his mission was not just to settle in the New World but also to save the Old World. In a sermon during the sea voyage, he said: "We must consider that we shall be as a City upon a Hill, the eyes of all people are upon us."

On June 6, 1630, Winthrop and his followers arrived at Salem, Massachusetts, not far from where Kerry later would spend part of his youth. But many of the Puritans found the conditions difficult and deadly. Dozens died, and Winthrop sought to shore up morale by issuing a document titled "A Model of Christian Charity." "We must be knit together in this work as one man," Winthrop wrote. "We must delight in each other, make one another's condition our own, rejoice together, mourn together, labor and suffer together, having always before our eyes our Commission and Community in this work as members of the same body."

Winthrop believed that only those he considered "godly" should be allowed to hold office: only Puritan men (and no women) were allowed to hold office. Winthrop was elected twelve times as governor, but he used his power to isolate potential opponents. Most famously, he banished religious reformer Anne Hutchison from the colony on the grounds that she wanted to subvert moral law. Other dissenters, such as Roger Williams, left to establish a colony in neighboring Rhode Island, where there was separation of church and state, and Jewish traders were allowed to do business.

From this beginning, the Winthrops have played a major part in Massachusetts and U.S. politics for many years, setting the stage for the later arrival of John Kerry.

Kerry's great-great-grandfather, Robert Charles Winthrop, is one of the most notable figures. Born in Boston in 1809, he served as speaker of the Massachusetts House of Representatives. Then he was elected as a U.S. representative and served at the federal level as Speaker of the House from 1847 to 1849. He then was appointed to serve as U.S. senator from Massachusetts from 1850 to 1851, filling the term of his longtime friend Daniel Webster, who resigned to become secretary of state. Thus, John Kerry is the second U.S. senator from Massachusetts from his family.

Robert Winthrop was defeated in a bid for reelection, as well as in a subsequent race for governor of Massachusetts. He then refrained from running for public office, devoting himself instead to historical pursuits, including writing a history of his most famous ancestor, John Winthrop. He had a son he named Robert Charles Winthrop Jr., Kerry's great-grandfather, who in turn had a daughter named Margaret. This was the woman who would marry James Grant Forbes, merging these two great Massachusetts families and producing a daughter named Rosemary—the mother of Senator Kerry.

The much-celebrated marriage between Margaret Winthrop and James Grant Forbes on November 28, 1906, was graced by eleven children. Forbes, in keeping with his family's history and his roots in Shanghai, was drawn to foreign business, and he was soon working on railway ventures in Brazil, Argentina, and Paraguay. When World War I began in 1914, he was living in Paris, and he remained in

France working on U.S. relief projects and business ventures through the conflict.

There is a hint from the Forbes historical papers that James Forbes played some kind of role in U.S. intelligence or security matters. In his Harvard class history, he said that he had worked "with American security business and ... been on several interesting special missions, notably in 1922 to Moscow and Albania, and in 1924 to Persia. More recently, I have spent considerable time in Germany and Italy," he wrote in 1926.

Two years later, Forbes acquired a magnificent estate named Les Essarts in the Brittany resort town of Saint Briac, where he and his family spent many summers. During the 1920s and 1930s, Forbes played a major role in setting up the coal and steel business in Europe, as well as working in locations from the Balkans to Iran. Most notably, he worked closely with the famed Jean Monnet, who had played a role in the development of the failed League of Nations after World War I and tried to forge a union between Great Britain and France at the beginning of World War II. Failing in that venture, Monnet worked with U.S. officials on post–World War II recovery plans and on a scheme to unite Europe—an effort that eventually led to the creation of today's European Union.

The Forbes family says that Monnet and Forbes had a business relationship, although the details are unclear. One hint of their relationship comes from a letter that Forbes wrote to a relative on April 22, 1938, from Shanghai. Forbes was concerned about the effort by Communists to take over China.

"Monnet has been in Paris, but is now in New York," Forbes wrote to one of his relatives, W. Cameron Forbes in Boston. "We have been working on a plan which may be helpful to the Chinese, but it is a very long shot, and probably won't meet with the favor of Washington, so please don't say anything to anybody about it. The railway contract with the French, to connect the Indochina system with Nanning [China], has at least been signed after many postponements. I am planning to stay here all summer to relieve Mazot, Monnet's regular Shanghai representative ...." Forbes then expressed thanks for inviting his daughter, Rosemary, "to keep house for you."

Rosemary had just met a handsome young man named Richard Kerry, who was spending his summer at Saint Briac as an apprentice in a sculptor's studio. The two had fallen in love.

Kerry was a dashing, adventurous figure, the sort who one day sailed a ketch across the Atlantic and would serve as a U.S. foreign service officer in Berlin after World War II. It is not clear how much the Forbes family knew about Richard Kerry. He was not a Brahmin like them, but he certainly seemed to have all the right New England upper-crust credentials: He had graduated from Phillips Academy in Andover, Massachusetts, and Yale University, and now he was attending Harvard Law School, as James Grant Forbes himself had done. And he was from Boston, completing the fit with the Forbes and Winthrop families.

"My grandmother heard there was a young American in

the village and invited him to lunch," Diana Kerry, Senator Kerry's sister, said. Richard Kerry was immediately drawn to Rosemary: "My father did say he had eyes for none of the other sisters." Rosemary had planned to become a nurse. Richard was on the way to becoming a U.S. Army Air Corps pilot, but an ocean of distance separated them. Rosemary was in France, looking out over the waters from the Forbes family compound like some sea captain's wife. To the north loomed the English Channel. But to the east, the Nazis were preparing to attack.

Chapter 2

YOUTH

ROSEMARY FORBES fled the family compound at Saint Briac, just ahead of the invading German forces. She made her way to Paris, only to find the capital under siege as well. Twenty-six-year-old Rosemary stopped long enough to write a letter to her future husband, Richard Kerry, on July 14, 1940. She wished they were together again, like they had been on that lovely day they shared in Chartres a year earlier. But the world had changed.

> Dick Dearest,
>
> It is a shock to find a country that one has admired and loved crumbling away, eaten through to its very core by rottenness ... [U]ntil the station closed on June 11th we lived in pandemonium and panic; [the fleeing residents] were all so excitable and scared. If you had seen the station platforms—the men fighting for seats, leaving screaming women and children to fend for themselves. The streets all around the station

were crowded with people who spent the day and night on the pavements waiting for trains which never came to take them away to "safety."

In Paris, Rosemary absorbed the frightening scene. The refugees flooded across the Place de la Concorde, coming in "cars laden with every kind of house belongings, in hay-carts drawn by weary, perspiring horses, on foot with per-ambulators, handcarts, wheelbarrows, tricycles carrying invalids and babies dragging dogs, cats or birdcages. It was a terribly grim unforgettable sight. We never thought we would be joining them."

With her medical training, Rosemary wanted to stay and help the Red Cross. But within a day or so, she too fled on bicycle, leaving behind nearly everything except Richard Kerry's photo.

We left Thursday June 13 at 8:30 P.M. just after the gas and electricity had been shut off and explosions were going off where they were blowing up gasoline tanks.... At dawn the Germans entered Paris. Next day, we pushed on towards Orleans, missed being bombed ... [B]y taking a longer route though we saw the planes going on the mission of death and had to duck their machine guns.... I am so scared of coming to America but with you I know everything will be all right.

Cheri, je t'embrasse de tout mon coeur,

Rosy

Rosemary headed to unoccupied southern France, and finally made her way to Portugal, where she sailed to America. Richard Kerry, now training for the possibility of fighting in the war that Rosemary had left behind, awaited her at a military base in Alabama. Shortly after arriving in the United States, Rosemary learned that the Nazis had taken over the Forbes compound in Brittany and were using it as a lookout against a possible British invasion.

In this world in which every decision seemed affected by the war, Rosemary traveled to Alabama and accepted Richard's proposal of marriage. The couple was married in Alabama in January 1941, and their first child, Margaret, was born on November 11, 1941. Less than a month later, the Japanese struck Pearl Harbor, and there was every reason to believe that Richard Kerry would soon head off to war.

But first, the army needed Kerry for a special new assignment. An accomplished pilot, Kerry had been testing planes at a Dayton, Ohio, airfield, but the army had something bigger in mind. Just months before Pearl Harbor, it had acquired 86,000 acres of ranchland 150 miles north of Los Angeles for a facility that was then known as Camp Cooke, now called Vandenberg Air Force Base.

The army used Cooke to develop strategies that eventually would be used against the German blitzkrieg. The base was also used for high-altitude airplane tests, and Kerry was involved in that effort. But before he got a chance to spend much time in the skies over Cooke, he came down with a life-threatening case of tuberculosis. The contagious disease, spread through airborne droplets, starts with a cough, weight loss, and fever, and can quickly affect the lungs and many other parts of the body. If left untreated, it is deadly.

The army quickly moved Kerry and his family to a Denver facility built especially to treat tuberculosis patients. Doctors believed that the city's mile-high air helped clear the lungs, and Denver began promoting what some called "tuberculosis tourism," with the city's many sanitariums filling with patients. Luckily for Kerry, the army had just opened a state-of-the-art tuberculosis clinic at Fitzsimmons Hospital in 1941, and he received the best possible treatment. Kerry was just recovering from the illness when Rosemary, who was pregnant during her husband's illness, gave birth to their second child.

John Forbes Kerry was born in Denver on December 11, 1943. Richard Kerry, his military service over, now had a family of four and needed a home and a career. Four months after John's birth, the family left Denver and moved to a temporary home in Groton, Massachusetts. The Bay State felt like home: Richard Kerry had grown up in Brookline and graduated from Harvard Law School; his mother, Ida, still lived in the state; and several of Rosemary's siblings had moved to Massachusetts, which was populated with many relatives in the Forbes and Winthrop families.

Overseas, the D-day invasion was underway, and American forces would eventually liberate the Forbes compound on the Brittany coast, only to find that the Nazis had turned their tanks on the house and destroyed it. Back in Massachusetts, meanwhile, the Kerrys settled into a rather idyllic life. With some inheritance money apparently available, the family bought a large farmhouse in Millis with tall ceilings, fireplaces, a comfortable library, and six bedrooms.

Richard Kerry went to work for a Boston law firm, and Rosemary and their growing family spent the next six years in this semirural setting, enjoying the barn and the pond and the seemingly endless number of relatives who visited. (The Kerrys eventually had four children in addition to Margaret and John; Diana was born in 1947 and Cameron in 1950.)

When John Kerry was about four years old, the family took a trip to visit the Forbes family estate in Saint Briac. Little was left of the house except the chimney and a stairway. The family found a mine still planted on the property, with bunkers practically untouched since the Allies had ousted the Germans. The visit made such an impact on John Kerry that he says it remains one of his earliest memories.

"I remember ... the staircase in the sky, the glass under my feet and my mom was crying," Kerry recalled. The family was told that villagers had done what they could to save the property and that U.S. forces had eventually liberated it. The Forbes family decided to rebuild the home and turn it into a summer vacation playground for family members, enabling Kerry and many other descendants to enjoy the compound to this day. The Kerrys returned to Millis with a dramatic reminder of war and sacrifice, and it made a lasting impact on all of them.

Richard Kerry, having been unable to participate more directly in the war, began to envision ways to participate in the postwar effort. Thus, in 1950, Richard Kerry moved with his family to Washington, D.C., where he took a job in the Office of the General Counsel for the Navy. The family bought a house in Washington's Chevy Chase neighborhood.

Chevy Chase, like its sister village of the same name across the border in Maryland, was about as far from the rural atmosphere of Millis as John Kerry could get. It was populated with government officials, military leaders, lobbyists, diplomats, bureaucrats, and journalists, as well as scientists who flocked to the nearby government research centers. Chevy Chase was bisected by Connecticut Avenue, which was lined with elegant apartment houses and ran straight to the White House, about six miles away.

For the next four years, the Kerry household took on the classic qualities of a Washington home headed by a civil servant, with much of the dinner-table conversation revolving around politics and power and the place of the United States in the world. Richard Kerry moved up quickly, taking a job in 1951 in the Bureau of United Nations Affairs at the State Department, where he would work for the next three years.

As family members would later recall, there was an extra sense of excitement in moving from Massachusetts to Washington because of the emerging fame of a young congressman from the state: John Fitzgerald Kennedy. Kennedy, who had served on a navy patrol boat in World War II, was elected to the U.S. House in 1946 and to the U.S. Senate in 1952. During John Kerry's formative years, then, at a time when he was developing his political wits, he was living in Washington, where family discussions focused on the issues that both his father and Kennedy were dealing with.

Cameron Kerry said all of this had a deep effect on his older brother, John.

"It was all part of the dinner table conversation growing up in Washington—father in government service, paying close attention to presidential elections, and along came John F. Kennedy, a Catholic from Massachusetts with the same initials; all of those things resonated," Cameron Kerry said. "All of the excitement that represented for lots of people for our generation. I think that is really when John began to be actively interested in politics."

In 1954, when John Kerry was ten years old, his father made a dramatic announcement. Richard Kerry had accepted an important government post in the divided city of Berlin, where he would become the U.S. attorney for Berlin, advising U.S. officials about a variety of legal actions at the heart of the Iron Curtain that divided democracy from communism. Having missed combat in World War II, Kerry would now take his family to the center of the cold war. It would have a lasting impact on young John.

When the Kerrys moved to Berlin, much of the World War II rubble had been carted away, but the devastation remained. There was the added knowledge that the United States and its allies had inflicted much of the damage—that the cause was just and that freedom had a price that the city's residents would pay for many years.

"When my father was stationed in Europe, America was still [known as] the liberator," Cameron Kerry said. "This was the era of the Marshall Plan, when you saw the effects of that, when you walked into a hotel there would be a plaque that says 'This building was rebuilt with help from the Marshall Plan.' The memory of the GIs marching in and people pouring out of the streets to greet them was still there, still recent memories, and of course the scars of war were still there."

In few places was this juxtaposition more evident than in Berlin, where there were ever-present reminders of the war and the specter of communism. A West Berliner or an American who crossed that line into East Berlin could be shot or imprisoned.

All of these images had their impact on young John, but he was still a kid. One day, hoping to satisfy his curiosity about life across the line, he hopped on his bicycle and cycled into East Berlin. "I was twelve years old," Kerry said. "It was fun, it was an adventure. I remember [seeing] Hitler's bunker distinctly. My bike was sort of my great escape from parents and rules and all those things."

His parents were not pleased. If Kerry had been captured in East Berlin, it could have caused an international incident and deeply embarrassed his father, who was supposed to uphold laws, not condone a son who broke them. But Kerry still treasures the experience. "I got to ride through Brandenburg Gate and see things that other kids didn't get to see," he said.

The Kerrys apparently decided that the best thing for John was to send him off to boarding school. Richard Kerry was traveling around Europe constantly, attending meetings of the newly formed North Atlantic Treaty Organization, and it was decided that young John would be sent off to boarding school in Switzerland. It wasn't exactly abandonment, but it felt like it at the time, as John Kerry recalled.

The boarding school, called Montana, was set dramatically on a hill overlooking a lake in Zug, near Zurich.

Founded in 1926, the Institut Montana Zugerberg was housed in palatial buildings formerly occupied by the Grand Hotel Schonfels. Kerry was entranced by the Swiss countryside, but he was lonely. For the next seven years of his life, this would become routine: His parents would send him off to boarding school and he would adapt anew to a world of highly competitive boys from wealthy, privileged families. Kerry's father often was a distant figure. "My parents were fabulous and loving and caring and supportive, but they weren't always around," Kerry recalled.

Kerry experienced a distance from his father that was more than geographical; Richard Kerry retained a lingering bitterness over his father's suicide, as well as the death of his sister, Mildred, who suffered from polio and cancer. "My dad was sort of painfully remote and shut off and angry about the loss of his sister and the lack of a father," he added.

The remoteness became even greater in September 1956, when the Kerrys decided that they would remain in Europe while sending twelve-year-old John to boarding school in Massachusetts. The Kerrys chose the Fessenden School in Newton, Massachusetts, an all-boys school that featured the motto "Work conquers all." The students were required to wear a jacket and tie to class and conform to rigorous standards, but there was plenty of time for athletics as well. "I was always moving on and saying goodbye," Kerry recalled. "It kind of had an effect on you, it steeled you, there wasn't a lot of permanence and roots. For kids, not the greatest thing. I certainly didn't want that for my kids."

Summers were the best escape from the stilted, isolated world of the prep school, and Kerry spent most of his free time on the water, either off the shores of Cape Cod or in the fjords of Norway, where his father in 1957 became a political officer in the U.S. embassy in Oslo.

Separated from his family while at Fessenden, Kerry again established a routine of forming close friendships with like-minded boys. No relationship was more important than the bond Kerry formed with a boy named Richard Pershing. Like Kerry, the young Pershing had been educated in Switzerland and had been inculcated with the importance of America's role in the world. Pershing's grandfather was the famed World War I general, John Joseph "Black Jack" Pershing.

They were inseparable, Kerry and Dick Pershing, playing games and plotting a future that might include their own military careers. In 1957, when they left Fessenden and prepared to enter the prep school equivalent of high school, they stayed in close touch. Both traveled just an hour or so north to New Hampshire, with Pershing going to Phillips Exeter Academy and Kerry heading to St. Paul's School in Concord.

On the surface, it may have seemed that Kerry came from the higher income background, given his family's Forbes and Winthrop heritage, whereas Pershing's family had a much more modest background. But in fact, Warren Pershing was probably far wealthier than Kerry's father, who never went farther than a midlevel foreign service job. Warren Pershing was the senior partner in Pershing and Co., a stock brokerage on Wall Street.

Kerry, meanwhile, went to St. Paul's not on the finances of his father but on the generosity of his great-aunt Clara Winthrop, who had no children of her own. She owned an estate in Manchester-by-the-Sea, complete with a bowling alley inside a red barn. Winthrop offered to pay for much of John's prep school education, an expensive proposition far beyond the means of Kerry's parents. "It was a great and sweet and nice thing from an aunt who had no place to put [her money]," Kerry said. Such a gift today might be worth about $30,000 per year.

"We weren't rich," explained Kerry's sister Diana. "We certainly had some members of the family we thought of as rich. We were the [beneficiaries] of a great-aunt who had no children. My father was on salary from the State Department, and my mother had some family money, but not major."

Life in boarding schools in Switzerland and Massachusetts had prepared Kerry well for St. Paul's, but this was an even more elite world. Founded in 1856, St. Paul's was established on religious principles, relying on "the integration of the secular and the sacred," as a school history puts it. The school's motto, from the writings of St. Jerome, is: "Let us learn those things on earth the knowledge of which continues in heaven."

The school was Episcopalian, which meant that at the time of Kerry's arrival, a Catholic such as himself had to leave the school grounds and attend church in Concord if he wanted to go to Catholic services. (The school hired its first Catholic chaplain in 2002.) Indeed, Kerry was an odd man out in several ways, believing he was not of the same financial standing. In addition, he was a Kennedy fan on a campus dominated by Republicans.

But with his years of elite education, Kerry had no problem with the rigorous academics. He felt comfortable in the 2,000-acre campus, nestled amid white pines along the shores of Turkey Pond and dotted with a neo-Gothic architectural style that echoes Oxford. The students dressed in jacket and tie, and ate meals in an Elizabethan-style dining hall.

The school, boys-only at the time, was a study in structure. Breakfast began at dawn, followed by compulsory chapel at 8:10 A.M. Classes ran from 8:30 A.M. to 1:30 P.M., followed by afternoon athletics. Two more classes ran from 4:50 P.M. to 6:15 P.M., followed by dinner and then hours of homework. Kerry began at St. Paul's in the eighth grade and stayed for a total of five years, through graduation. "These days [it] would be called appallingly regimented," said Kerry's former English teacher, Herbert Church, who taught there for twenty-seven years.

Kerry entered St. Paul's as a short, pudgy boy, barely recognizable in early photos, focused on intellectual pursuits. Within a couple of years, however, he rocketed up in height and soon resembled the man he is today. He was one of the tallest boys on campus and, to his delight, became a sports standout, using his newfound height to advantage in hockey and soccer. One of his greatest pleasures was strapping on his ice skates and speeding down the glassy black ice of Turkey Pond, with the wind rippling across the exposed expanse.

Having spent years debating issues around the family

dinner table and at his earlier boarding schools, Kerry craved a forum for debate, and he founded the John Winant Society, an organization named after a former New Hampshire governor that still exists to discuss major issues of the day. Kerry recalled delivering an award-winning speech titled "The Plight of the Negro." St. Paul's officials could not find a copy of the speech but did unearth one Kerry gave for the Concordian Literary Society that won the top prize. It was titled "Resolved: that the growth of spectator sports in the western world in the last half century is an indication of the decline of western civilization."

Church, Kerry's English teacher, spent many hours outside of class with Kerry at the school's living quarters. Kerry lived in a large three-story building called Conover House, which had room for thirty boys.

"I can remember him sitting on my sofa in the evenings, talking a long, long time. I remember thinking the world of him, as I do still," Church said. "I thought this was a man who might go somewhere. I thought he might very well go into diplomacy. The thing that impressed me always was his very serious idealism. A lot of guys wanted to be head of Daddy's Wall Street firm, nothing wrong with that, but this young guy, you had a feeling he would do something for the world. He was a sincere idealist."

Aside from debate, politics, and athletics, Kerry found time for a favorite pursuit: rock and roll. He and six other boys formed a band called The Electras, which produced 500 copies of an LP that seemed mainly intended for their own amusement and the possibility that it might attract girls at the next Tea Dance mixer. The album, which featured songs such as "Guitar Boogie Shuffle" and "Summertime Blues," included liner notes that described Kerry as an electric bass player "from Oslo, Norway, and the producer of a pulsating rhythm that lends tremendous force to all the numbers." At the time, Kerry's father was a political aide at the U.S. embassy in Oslo, but Kerry lived most of the year at St. Paul's and with some relatives in Massachusetts.

The liner notes were written by one of Kerry's best friends, Peter Wyeth Johnson. One summer, Kerry and Johnson and some others had sailed on a boat owned by Kerry's father from Bermuda to the United States. It was such an innocent time, in retrospect, that it would be easy to romanticize the carefree lifestyle of Bermuda, boating, and the band. But this would turn out to be one in a series of memories that have a bitter ending for Kerry. Seven years after Johnson penned those liner notes in Kerry's junior year at high school, on February 13, 1968, First Lieutenant Johnson of the U.S. Army would die of hostile small arms fire in Binh Dinh in South Vietnam.

But that was in the future. At the time, St. Paul's seemed like such a safe, insular world, sealed off not only from war but also from poverty, racial tensions, and just about any other problem faced by most people in America. It was an all-male and nearly all-white community, but there was one exception. The Reverend John Walker had been hired as the school's African American teacher, and he became Kerry's mentor. Walker, who later became the bishop of the Episcopal Diocese of Washington, D.C., spent hours talking with Kerry about civil rights, racial problems, and many other matters foreign to the young student.

"Johnny Walker was my best mentor," Kerry said. "He was the closest teacher to me ... the first black ever to come to this school as a teacher. We would spend hours sitting in his apartment at night. It was quite different from [the rest of] St. Paul's."

The influence of Walker was one of several factors that reinforced Kerry's decision to become a lifelong Democrat. Undoubtedly, Kerry's father was a devout Democrat, and the family had long focused on the home-state senator, John F. Kennedy, as a role model. Then, in 1960, Kennedy ran for president, and the deal was sealed. Living at a school in which most others were supporting Richard M. Nixon only made Kerry more of a Kennedy zealot.

On November 7, 1960, Kerry traveled by passenger train from Concord to Boston's North Station in order to attend Kennedy's last speech before the election. More than 100,000 people lined the streets to greet the Massachusetts senator. Another 20,000 or so were inside the Boston Garden, including Kerry.

Kennedy was "surrounded on the dais by a covey of the puffy, pink-faced, predatory-lipped politicians who had so dominated Massachusetts politics before he had taken over," Theodore H. White wrote in *The Making of the President 1960*. For years, Kerry would say Kennedy's speech would have an everlasting impact, but the scene also surely made its mark. The *New York Times* reported: "It took Kennedy's motorcade 90 minutes to crawl two miles from his hotel to Boston Garden, where a shrieking, jam-packed audience of 20,000 had been waiting for hours."

Then, in his last televised address of the campaign,

Kennedy told a smaller crowd at Faneuil Hall that the contest was "not merely a race between two parties or two candidates, but a race between the comfortable and the concerned, a race between those who want to lie at anchor and those who want to go forward."

Kerry returned on the train to Concord filled with these thoughts, perhaps envisioning his own future. The next morning, he delivered his oration in favor of Kennedy's election to his St. Paul's classmates. Kerry's classmate John Shattuck, who would go on to Yale with Kerry, argued for Kennedy's election as well and still vividly recalls Kerry's speech.

> It was John and I who spoke for Kennedy. He was kind of out of step politically. He was a serious student, a well-rounded person, a good athlete; he had a close circle of friends. He was not a sort of typical prep school kid, he was serious and already captured by the political world, and particularly moved by the Kennedy candidacy and presidency.

Kerry never had a chance of winning over his mostly Republican friends, but he had convinced himself: He was a Democrat in the Kennedy mold.

If one could pinpoint the moment of Kerry's certainty about his political beliefs, then this was it, according to his sister Diana. "I've always felt it was really John Kennedy … that was the moment in John's life, when he was sixteen or so, he was already interested in debate, he was the head of the debate club."

It was during the summer of 1962, between high school and college, that Kerry solidified his Kennedy ties. He worked briefly for the U.S. Senate bid of Edward M. Kennedy, handing out leaflets. Although the two may have met, neither can recall anything about it. Kerry, meanwhile, read a book about President Kennedy's World War II experiences on a patrol boat, PT-109, which helped inspire Kerry to volunteer for duty on a navy patrol boat in Vietnam.

It so happened that one of Kerry's roommates, Lewis Rutherford, was dating a strikingly beautiful young woman named Janet Auchincloss, the half-sister of First Lady Jacqueline Kennedy. The eighteen-year-old Kerry also began to spend time with her in 1962. This caused a stir, as Kerry's friends had already become fascinated with the striking parallels between John Forbes Kerry and the American president, John Fitzgerald Kennedy. Aside from the identical initials, both lived at least part of their childhood in Massachusetts and shared a similar political philosophy. Kerry even sounded eerily like Kennedy, with the same deep Boston accent, even though Kerry had spent most of his life outside the state.

"[John] Kennedy was certainly a model for him," said Daniel Barbiero, Kerry's roommate at St. Paul's and Yale. "He admired the man greatly, admired the man's ability to speak and write."

Then, in August 1962, Janet Auchincloss invited Kerry to her family's palatial estate, Hammersmith Farm in Rhode Island, where John and Jacqueline had been married.

"We were friendly, sort of beginning to date, half-date, and she invited me in the summer of 1962," Kerry said. President Kennedy was visiting, and in a scene right out of *Forrest Gump*, the young Kerry had an extraordinary opportunity to visit with the president.

Arriving late for his date, Kerry was directed into the house and saw a man standing against a wall, his back turned. As Kerry approached, he realized it was his hero. "This guy is standing there, he turns around, and it is the president of the United States," Kerry recalled. "I remember distinctly saying, 'Hi, Mr. Kennedy,' and we chatted. He said, 'Oh, what are you doing?' I said, 'I just graduated from St. Paul's. I am about to go to Yale.'"

Kerry winced at his remark, recalling that Kennedy was a Harvard man. Just weeks earlier, Kennedy had taken great delight in gently jibing Yale when he received an honorary degree at New Haven, saying in the 1962 commencement address, "I am pleased to come to Yale, the daughter of Harvard. It might be said now that I have the best of both worlds, a Harvard education and a Yale degree." Now, with Kerry standing before him, Kennedy picked up on the discomfort, telling Kerry that with his honorary degree, "I'm a Yale man, too, now."

"He was incredibly warm, incredibly friendly, just relaxed," Kerry recalled. After a conversation about his brother's Massachusetts Senate race, the president took Kerry down to the dock, where they and some others went sailing on a Coast Guard yawl in Narragansett Bay. A White House photographer snapped the scene on the *Manitou:* There is Kennedy, at his most handsome in white pants, blue-as-the-bay shirt, and dark sunglasses; and there is Kerry, his white shirt-sleeves rolled up, leaning back, soaking up the sun and the presence of power.

A few weeks later Kerry once again met with Kennedy, this time at a September 1962 America's Cup race off the coast of Rhode Island. A photographer again captured the scene.

Kerry had lived half his life in boarding schools, had traveled extensively around Europe, and had gone sailing with his role model, John F. Kennedy. But he wouldn't follow Kennedy to Harvard—he wanted to get farther from his Massachusetts home and hoped to follow in his father's footsteps. This was his dream, to walk among the Gothic towers of Yale University.

One of the first things that Kerry did at Yale was write a letter to President Kennedy, apologizing for the way some Yale students had heckled him when the president delivered the commencement address earlier that year. There is no better insight into the mind of John Kerry as he was entering freshman year.

Dear Mr. President,

Having met you several times this summer at Hammersmith Farm, and having worked for your brother in Massachusetts during that same time, I am to say the least an ardent Kennedy supporter . . . I wish to apologize for the deplorable behavior of some of my fellow undergraduates at Yale. Your recent visit has left behind it much discussion—not on its political, but social aspects. Gradually the realization of the disrespect shown the office of the President of the United

States is sinking in to those who are the offenders. It does little good for a non-offender to write and apologize for the acts of others, but perhaps it will do something to say that people here are aware of the disgrace they brought on the University and themselves. It is possible that you personally were not bothered by what happened here, but the insult was made and there is no one here who is not now conscious of it.

May I also take this opportunity to thank you for a very unforgettable and exciting time the weekend of the America's Cup races.

With best wishes for the future ... Respectfully,

John F. Kerry.

In just a few short years, it would be Kerry himself leading hundreds of thousands of protesters against a different president, Richard M. Nixon. But first, Kerry had an education—in college, love, and war—ahead of him.

Chapter 3

YALE

IN THE DEPTH of the Great Depression, the overseers of Yale University embarked on a building project unlike anything in collegiate America. With visions of Cambridge and Oxford, the Yale brain trust decided to turn the campus into a Gothic wonderland, where libraries looked like cathedrals and dining halls and dormitories looked as if they were lifted out of the Elizabethan era. In 1932, construction began on one of a dozen "colleges"—elaborate dormitory campuses that housed about 400 students each. This first such dormitory—the word really fails to convey the grandeur involved—was called Jonathan Edwards College, named after a child prodigy. Jonathan Edwards, or JE, was a world unto itself, quite literally, ringed partially by a six-foot-deep moat and enclosed by elaborate gates. The main feature of the college might seem to be the dormitory rooms, but the college was most notable for its collection of grand common spaces: libraries, recital halls, and the granddaddy of them all, the Great Hall, with its cathedral ceiling, wooden beams, and paneled walls.

The architects intended to give students a feeling of extraordinary privilege, as if they all belonged to a remarkable club of fellowship, intellect, and well-being. The college was overseen by a housemaster, who would on a weekly basis use a special endowment for lectures or recitals or art exhibits. Little wonder that when a student graduated Yale, he (it was all undergraduate males at this time) was just as likely to identify himself as a graduate of Jonathan Edwards as Yale itself.

A JE man was reminded of his exalted status every morning as he woke up to the fireplace in a suite overlooking the well-tended English greensward. You did not just have roommates, you had "fellows"; you did not have just a hallway, you had the "Gold Coast." When you arrived at JE, you knew, in fact, that you had arrived in life and that many of the fellows you met here would be friends for life.

If that was not elite enough, the JE campus was adjacent to the most secret society on campus, Skull and Bones. Where JE was designed to delight the eye, enticing one to stroll through the gates and sample an architectural delight at every corner, Skull and Bones was designed to keep out nearly all—except the fifteen select ones. The two-story building had oblong slits on either side reminiscent of a prison. There was no sign of life here, only an ominous aura of "keep out."

John Kerry lived comfortably in both of these worlds. This was what he had dreamed of for much of his life: to follow in the footsteps of his father, Class of 1937, and walk among these towers of learning.

For some students, Yale was their first extended time away from home. But Kerry had been going to the equivalent of a small college from the time he was about twelve years old, and he barely lost a beat stepping into the Yale routine, comfortably fitting into the regimen of study and sports, debate and camaraderie, road trips and ski trips and journeys to New York City.

Kerry moved into the third-floor suite at Jonathan Edwards in 1963, his sophomore year. He had two roommates. The first was his buddy Daniel Barbiero, with whom he had roomed at St. Paul's School.

Barbiero marveled at Kerry's enthusiasm for the place, the way Kerry acted as if he had been waiting his whole life just for this moment. "In his mind it was just the place to go," Barbiero recalled. "I remember when we got there we were freshman together—it was our first week, in New Haven, he was just so excited about being at Yale, he had such a sense of history of the place. He is very sensitive to the history of things and knew a lot about the university."

The second roommate was Harvey Bundy, the nephew of the famed Bundy brothers of the Kennedy and Johnson administrations, William and McGeorge Bundy—two of the key architects of U.S. policy in the Vietnam War. William Bundy would eventually become a factor in Kerry's decision to go to Vietnam, and McGeorge Bundy would later become a focus of Kerry's anger about the war.

Kerry could burn out his roommates with his energy. He was often up until 5:00 in the morning, so they gave him his own bedroom, with Barbiero and Bundy sharing the other one. In addition to being on the soccer and hockey teams, Kerry would take ski trips to Stowe and Killington in Vermont. But his main interest was in politics, continuing the discussion that began around the dinner table when he was seven years old in Washington and that continued through Berlin and the St. Paul's debate society.

Almost from the start, Kerry was viewed as having political ambitions—indeed, presidential ambitions. Some turned this into a joke, playing a kazoo version of "Hail to the Chief" whenever Kerry appeared. But for every classmate who thought Kerry was too full of himself, there were plenty who believed he had the desire and intellect to become a senator or president.

"He certainly professed a desire to lead the country," said classmate Cary Koplin. "He had this early-on life plan that he wanted to be a leader."

Kerry fueled these beliefs by spending much of his time as a leader of the debate team and president of the famed Yale Political Union, a position that had previously been occupied by William F. Buckley Jr. and McGeorge Bundy. Founded in 1934 "to combat the insular and apathetic Yale political culture of the 1930s," the union was modeled on similar societies at Oxford and Cambridge. Kerry chose to represent what the union called the Liberal Party all four years. He was also treasurer of the Young Democrats; he said a Yale yearbook entry showing him changing his membership to the Young Republicans was a hoax.

The Political Union not only gave Kerry a chance to deliver speeches but also to listen to some of the leading political figures of the day. Much of Kerry's political and decisionmaking style stems from his membership in the union and the debate team. As a student and later as a senator, Kerry often internally debated an issue before making up his mind in a process that could take weeks. Senate aides would later say that Kerry's habit of walking onto the Senate floor without telling them how he would vote stems from his years of being asked to argue both sides of an issue.

By all accounts, Kerry was a champion debater on issues large and small. Kerry and his partner, William B. Stanberry, Jr., entered a debate challenge against a McGill University team in Montreal on the claim "[t]hat the age of chivalry is dead." The Yale duo won by a stunning vote from the Canadian audience of 250 to 1. Kerry and Stanberry went on win against a combined British Universities Team in a debate in which Kerry defended the purpose of the United Nations.

Kerry was also famous for engaging his classmates in debate on any topic. Kerry's friends learned that he was not apt to settle for discussion of sports or girls. He wanted a verbal boxing match.

There are conflicting reports about whether one such encounter took place with George W. Bush, who at Yale was the president of the Delta Kappa Epsilon fraternity. Kerry and Bush have both said they don't remember meeting at Yale, but Kerry's close friend David Thorne said he was with Kerry and Bush on that day and described the encounter in detail.

As Thorne tells the story, Bush, who was, two years younger than Kerry, was known around Yale as someone who tried to present himself at the ultimate Texan. Although Bush went to Phillips Academy in Andover,

Massachusetts, for prep school and spent some of his younger years in Connecticut, Massachusetts, and Maine, he had disdain for Eastern Establishment types. Kerry, of course, fit the Eastern Establishment Brahmin mold, as a progeny of the Winthrop and Forbes families, the son of a foreign service officer, and a graduate of St. Paul's School. At the time, Bush's father had lost a U.S. Senate bid and was launching a race for the U.S. House that would ultimately be successful, but the younger Bush expressed no interest in politics himself.

On this day, Bush met Kerry and the two had a discussion about busing, according to Thorne. Court cases involving school integration were in the news by 1965. Bush, whose father was running for Congress back in Texas, engaged Kerry, Thorne recalled. "I just remember fairly vividly, they were having a conversation about busing. John had been participating in busing stuff, but George was very conservatively placed and thought it was a crazy idea."

Political differences aside, young George W. Bush followed Kerry into Skull and Bones two years later, following in his own father's footsteps.

Kerry was intrigued by the Skull and Bones building next to the JE campus. Selection to Skull and Bones was supposed to set you up for life. Your fellow Bonesmen would help you in your career, in finding you the love of your life, helping financially if necessary. You could not apply to be a member. It worked like this: Each year, the fifteen members of Skull and Bones—all of whom were seniors—would pick fifteen members from the thousand in the junior class to replace them. The incoming fifteen often would not know each other, but they were expected to quickly become fast friends, and then lifelong friends. Everything discussed inside the Tomb was supposed to be secret.

Founded in 1832, the society was also known as the Brotherhood of Death. It was created by William H. Russell, whose family wealth came from the opium business, according to *Secrets of the Tomb,* an extensive history of the society by Alexandra Robbins. According to Robbins, Russell had a friend in Germany who led a secret society with a skull as a logo. "Russell soon became caught up in this group" and founded a similar one at Yale, Robbins wrote. "They worshipped the goddess Eulogia, celebrated pirates, and plotted an underground conspiracy to dominate the world."

Skull and Bones had changed much in the years since its founding, but Robbins contended that it is still a bastion for elites, dominated by a small group, including the Bush, Bundy, Harriman, and Taft families. "A rebel will not make Skull and Bones," she wrote. Some of the Bonesmen in the Class of 1966, familiar with the wild stories about their society, said many of them are either exaggerated or flatly untrue, including suggestions that members are automatically given cash gifts; they said the opposite is true because they are later asked to support the society financially. The suggestion by Robbins that the Bonesmen have a retreat with "a bevy of women at the members' disposal" evoked laughter.

But perception is everything, and the mythology surrounding Skull and Bones was part of its allure. For the Bonesmen of 1966, a major attraction was that the society provided an outlet for spending hours discussing the personal as well as the political. Most, if not all, of the fifteen members of the 1966 class have gone on to lead distinctive lives and careers.

It was not too surprising that Kerry would be among the Bonesmen. The debate champion, the soccer and hockey player, the descendant of the Winthrops and the Forbes—it was perceived as a done deal. Most of the Bonesmen had significant financial status: inheritances or trust funds or money expected upon graduation.

Although some may have thought Kerry had wealth, he was in fact not picked on the basis of money. In Kerry's case, he was recommended by several outgoing seniors, including John Shattuck, a St. Paul's alum who would later become assistant secretary of state for democracy, human rights, and labor in the Clinton administration. Kerry's selection was based not on his social standing, according to Shattuck, but instead was due to the widespread perception that Kerry would be a future political leader. "I remember pushing him as somebody who would be a very interesting person and had no doubt he would go into public life later," Shattuck said.

It was among the fourteen other members of Skull and Bones that Kerry counted his closest three friends at Yale: Fred Smith, who would stoke Kerry's interest in aviation; David Thorne, whose sister would become Kerry's fiancée; and Richard Pershing, who had known Kerry since they were thirteen years old and later helped convince him to go

to Vietnam. If Skull and Bones was the most ⸲
campus, then this quartet was the elite of the
there was another tie: Instead of trying to use con.
or deferments, they all went to Vietnam.

Smith and Kerry quickly formed a bond of the sk
resurrecting the Yale Flying Club. "I got him interested in
flying," Smith recalled. "During World War I, the Yale Flying Club became the backbone of naval aviation. They
taught themselves to fly and went down and got themselves hired. All of their alumni ended up running U.S.
naval aviation during World War II. We had resurrected the
Yale Flying Club." One of their inspirations was a professor
who reportedly flew a loop-de-loop around the Golden
Gate Bridge.

Kerry loved the thrill of flight, going far beyond what
most Yale aviators attempted. He learned aerobatics, practicing loop-de-loops and other dangerous maneuvers. "I
majored in flying my senior year at Yale," Kerry said. "I'm
serious. I cut classes, I didn't do much, I spent a lot of time
learning to fly."

Smith, meanwhile, was thinking of flying for another
reason. He wrote a term paper that envisioned "the fundamental automation of society, how automation of society
would have to have a completely different logistics system
to support it." The paper was given a barely passing grade,
but Smith was onto something. Using the principles he laid
out in that paper, he founded Federal Express, an air
freight business that today is one of the world's most successful companies.

The second close friend, Thorne, met Kerry during his

first year at Yale, and it nearly was a disaster. Within minutes of meeting, the two were discussing women. Kerry said he was dating Janet Auchincloss, the half-sister of First Lady Jacqueline Kennedy. Then Thorne said, "No, I'm dating Janet Auchincloss." As it turned out, her relationship didn't last with either Kerry or Thorne. (She wound up marrying Kerry's classmate from St. Paul's, Lewis Rutherford, and died of cancer in 1985 at a Boston hospital at the age of thirty-nine.)

The relationship between Kerry and Thorne, however, is a thread that has wound through Kerry's life ever since the two met forty years ago. Both of the young men had been partly raised in Europe; Kerry spoke French, German, and Italian, and Thorne spoke at least one foreign language. Thorne, who came from what he called a "rock-ribbed Republican family," and Kerry, whose family leaned Democratic, shared a common Continental viewpoint. They spent a leisurely summer together in Europe, traveling around the Continent in a used London cab. Aside from their world outlook, they also shared a love of soccer that they had learned abroad, enabling them both to make Yale's varsity soccer team. Eventually, Thorne would introduce Kerry to his winsome sister, Julia, who would become Kerry's wife.

The last member of the quartet was, by every account, the most outlandish and the most beloved. This was Richard Pershing, the grandson of the famed World War I general John "Black Jack" Pershing, a bon vivant whose star quality and outrageous behavior made him an unforgettable character.

Pershing could set the tone on some serious matters. "When a war comes along, you go," Pershing would tell the Bonesmen, in a leader-of-the-gang sort of way.

But there was much more to Pershing's appeal. If this were a movie, Pershing would be the dashing, heroic figure, the fun-loving troublemaker who always got the girl and never seemed to have a care. He was the opposite of Kerry in many ways, yet the two men were extraordinarily close, having met when they were thirteen and having shared the common experience of attending Fessenden School, living in Europe, and going to Yale.

Pershing was inevitably compared to Jay Gatsby, the fictional character whom F. Scott Fitzgerald described as having "some heightened sensitivity to the promises of life, as if he were related to one of those intricate machines that register earthquakes ten thousand miles away."

"Pershing was the closest competition that Gatsby had in the twentieth century," fellow Bonesman Alan Cross said, noting that both the fictional character and Pershing had lived "on the same neck of Long Island."

"Persh," as he was known to his Yale buddies, first got to know Kerry when the two went to Fessenden as seventh-graders. They parted for different New Hampshire prep schools: Kerry to St. Paul's and Pershing to Phillips Exeter. But they met at various prep school events in the Granite State, and rejoiced at meeting up again at Yale.

It was impossible to know Pershing without an appreciation of his grandfather's role in military history. Not only was General Pershing the general of the armies in the aftermath of World War I, but he was also a leader of the Tenth

Cavalry in 1895 in Montana, in charge of a group of black men known as the Buffalo Soldiers. Blacks were barred from serving with white troops at the time and until much later, but Pershing admired them and liked to lead them, thus earning the appellation "Black Jack."

His was an illustrious career, during which he earned the Silver Star at San Juan Hill in 1898, fought in the Philippines in the years up to 1912, and patrolled the Mexican border with the Buffalo Soldiers in 1914. While on patrol in Mexico, his wife and three children were staying at the Presidio in San Francisco in 1915 when fire broke out. Pershing's wife and two of his children were killed. Pershing would go on to fame as the leader of the American Expeditionary Force in World War I and was eventually named general of the armies. But the loss of his wife and two children provided a new reason for Pershing to be called "Black Jack," for the melancholy lasted the rest of his life. The only survivor of the fire was Pershing's son, Warren, who later had a son named Richard—the kid who became Kerry's buddy. Little wonder Dick Pershing wanted to live life to the fullest.

"We were just very, very close," Kerry said of Pershing. "We had some unbelievably raucous carefree times, good times."

Other Bonesmen noticed the bond as well.

"John was very serious, very interested in politics. Pershing was the opposite, he was the fun lover, get us all into trouble," said Dr. George Brown, a fellow Bonesman who was close to both Kerry and Pershing. "Pershing didn't take anything very seriously. The day before he left for Vietnam, he said, 'I don't have anyone to go drinking with. Let's go toast the town.' Pershing was the bon vivant.... He was our hero, because of his charismatic personality. He would run up these incredible bar tabs. He took me to restaurants in New York City where all the women knew him."

Smith recalled Pershing similarly, saying the general's grandson was "one of the most charming men I have ever met in my life. He had a personality that would remind me of a well-born American Michael Caine." It seems unsurprising, then, that Pershing would have a girlfriend from Smith College who caught everyone's eye: Kitty Hawks, the beautiful, smart daughter of the famed Howard Hawks, who directed films such as *The Big Sleep* and *Gentlemen Prefer Blondes*.

Indeed, in a 2003 interview, Kitty Hawks described her time with Pershing and Kerry and the other Bonesmen in cinematic terms: "To fall in love with one of them was to fall in love with all of them. It was an amazing time. There's not a day that goes by that I don't think about it."

So Pershing and Hawks and Kerry and Smith and some of the other Bonesmen would head to the bars of New Haven, or a hockey game, or anyplace where they could have a few drinks and laughs.

"There was just never a time that wasn't fun or filled with laughter and they weren't teasing one another," Hawks said. "They had enormous respect for one another. There was an element of sobriety to Johnny, and Dick didn't have that. All of us thought [Kerry] would be an important person in this country somehow. It didn't feel so much an ambition as destiny, that this was bound to happen to him in one way or another."

The tie to Skull and Bones played a crucial role, Hawks said. "I just know it was an extremely important part of the value system and bond between all of them," she said. "My sense of it was that it wasn't like a frat house, it wasn't 'Let's go get drunk and hang out.' There was something more to it. There is a point at which it stops being fun and games but life starts getting a little bit more serious, and that is one of the places where that happened. They start thinking of themselves as men instead of boys, and then you go to war, you become a man in no time."

By all appearances, Kerry fit in as one of the wealthy, privileged Bonesmen, or so his friends believed. One day, Brown recalled, he and Kerry and Pershing were part of a group that went sailing by Naushon Island, the compound near Cape Cod that is owned by Kerry's distant relatives on the Forbes side of his family.

"He said, 'My family kind of owns this island, guys,'" Brown recalled. "We couldn't believe it. He said, 'Nobody is allowed to go ashore but we can because my family sort of owns it.' Pershing razzed him about it, that John was taking us onto his blue-blooded island. We expected his childhood nanny to come give us a hug."

In fact, while Kerry was always a welcome visitor at Naushon, the Kerry family says it has never owned even a single share of the island, which they said is mostly owned by a branch of the Forbes family that consists of Kerry's fifth cousins. It was Pershing, whose father worked on Wall

Street, who was more likely to be living off inheritances or trust funds.

Late during a soccer match on the Yale campus on November 22, 1963, a ripple of noise went through the crowd, growing louder by the second. News was spreading: President Kennedy had been shot. It had been just fifteen months since Kerry had gone sailing with the president.

"We were all sort of numb," Kerry recalled. His hero, his role model, was dead. Kerry spent hours watching his small black-and-white television set in disbelief.

"It was a shock to him," recalled David Thorne, who was sitting on the bench next to Kerry during the soccer game. "It was his idol, his hero he had gotten as a young man. It was very deeply upsetting to him."

The memory of Kennedy's death was still seared into Kerry's psyche when one of Kennedy's "best and brightest," William Bundy, came visiting. Bundy, then assistant secretary of state for Far Eastern affairs, came to campus to speak in support of U.S. involvement in the Vietnam War, and he was greeted as a legacy of the slain president. After his speech, he visited his nephew's suite and talked with the roommates, including Kerry, into the wee hours of the morning.

"[We were] all drinking beer and sitting around and talking about, you know, Southeast Asia and domino [theories] and war," Kerry recalled. Bundy's overriding theme to the young men was this: "We need you. We need you to go into the officer program and to go to Vietnam." The visit nudged the students in the direction of Vietnam. "I don't know that he was the prime mover in us going," added Barbiero, "but he was certainly an influence. He was an assistant secretary of state."

As graduation approached, Kerry believed he had three choices: be drafted, seek a deferment for graduate school, or join up and position himself to become an officer. "I called [the draft board] because I was thinking one of the options was, maybe I'll go study aboard, which was a euphemism for screwing around a bit, but it was clear to me that I was going to be at risk. My draft board ... said, 'Look, the likelihood is you are probably going to be drafted.' I said, 'If I'm going to be drafted, I'd like to have responsibility and be an officer.'"

Military service had helped John Kennedy's career, of course, and Kerry clearly had political ambitions on the horizon. "John would clearly say, 'If I could make my dream come true, it would be running for president of the United States,'" recalled William Stanberry, Kerry's debate team partner for three years. "It was not a casual interest. It was a serious, stated interest. His lifetime ambition was to be in political office."

Why? What drove Kerry? "I don't think there was any one specific issue, such as 'I am going to spend my life working for racial integration or world peace.'" Stanberry said. "I don't think he had pet issues as much as he simply said, 'The life of a politician is the life I want. I want to speak out on issues. That is what I want to do for a job.'"

By senior year, Kerry was brooding about his future. He

would go flying constantly, then return to Yale, where he would spend hours inside the Skull and Bones headquarters. Women and sex and money were inevitably discussed at Bones, but what fellow Bonesmen most remember is how Kerry steered the talk toward Vietnam.

Kerry's friends could see his evolution in clear stages. Alan Cross, a fellow Bonesman, remembers that Kerry increasingly began to express doubts about Vietnam. "When [President Lyndon B.] Johnson had greatly increased the troops being sent into Vietnam, Kerry sort of made a spontaneous speech to the others of us in the audience decrying the implications of this political event and what this meant in terms of our engagement in Vietnam."

Cross remembers Kerry's talk because it was so unusual for a group of self-centered Bonesmen. "You had this group of the elite of the elite selected out of the Yale senior class who probably were most adept at gazing at their own navels and probably thought the world rotated around them," Cross said. But Kerry forced the group to focus on Vietnam. "I think he was alarmed by what we were doing. That doesn't mean we were opposed to what we were doing. He saw this growing quagmire we were heading into with good intention and certain results. My recollection of that talk is that it was not so much a statement of opposition but was really, a clarion, 'Hey guys, this is happening, this is going to define our generation, this is going to be critical.'"

In early 1966, Kerry had been chosen to deliver the class oration, a high honor. Kerry wrote a serviceable but forgettable speech, with vapid and airy phrases about the future.

"We need no ringing call to do great things but only a small stimulus to do that which will make a constructive contribution to society—if you will to make this a better world to live in," the oration, published in the class yearbook, said. "I would refrain also from trying to present any eternal truth which would enable us to leave this exercise as new men, directed and committed. At bare minimum, my purpose is to challenge and not to preach, to question and not to answer."

It was hardly high oratory.

For weeks, Kerry second-guessed himself. Should he talk about Vietnam? Should he question his country's direction? Kerry pondered these questions on a trip that turned out to be a final fling with his fellow Bonesmen, a vacation trip to Deer Island in the St. Lawrence Seaway. The forty-acre island was one of the perks of being a Bonesman. It was owned by Skull and Bones, and featured a variety of lodging, softball, and tennis courts, an amphitheater, and fifteen miles of walking paths, marked with the society's secret code number, "322."

Kerry and Pershing, as usual, were inseparable. But one day, they asked fellow Bonesman Michael Dalby to join them on a boat ride in the St. Lawrence. Dalby agreed to go along, only to realize too late that he was going on a trip with two men who seemed equally drawn to danger. "We were in the St. Lawrence, and it's a great big seaway, great big ships," Dalby recalled. "So Pershing, who was completely uncontrollable, got three of us in a small dinghy with a motor and started approaching this gigantic ship and I was completely terrified. I thought this was going to be it, and you know, it could have been. He was that crazy. So John seemed really nervous about this, figured out the last moment to turn back, and so the two played a complete ruse on me, I've never been so scared in my life. [Kerry] was very capable of that kind of switch back and forth between the humorous self and very solemn."

Indeed, Kerry had a solemn task during this island visit. He had decided to throw away his published class oration and deliver a much more controversial assessment of U.S. policy on the use of military force against Communist regimes.

Kerry had been thinking about the topic for years. He had lived in Berlin at the height of the cold war, and his father had left the foreign service partly because of his disenchantment with policymakers who preferred force over engagement. Although prowar sentiment was common at the time, Kerry may have taken his cue from Senator Robert F. Kennedy, who on January 31, 1966, questioned President Johnson's policy, commenting that Johnson's resumption of bombing in Vietnam "may become the first in a series of steps on a road from which there is no turning back—a road that leads to catastrophe for all mankind."

Kerry began writing a new oration, sending the pages to Dalby for suggestions.

"For some reason he got me working on the word-by-word level, so I remember we were having some arguments about grammar," Dalby recalled. "He said, 'You don't get it, I'm going to say it like this.' I remember being quite thrilled when he did it."

On June 12, 1966, Kerry delivered his new speech.

What was an excess of isolationism has become an excess of interventionism. And this Vietnam War has found our policy makers forcing Americans into a strange corner . . . that if victory escapes us, it would not be the fault of those who lead, but of the doubters who stabbed them in the back—notions all too typical of an America that had to find Americans to blame for the takeover in China by the Communists, and then for the takeover in Cuba.

Then, in a sentence that hearkened back to the Nazi aggression that his mother had fled, he said: "The United States must, I think, bring itself to understand that the policy of intervention that was right for Western Europe does not and cannot find the same application to the rest of the world."

And, in what may have been an allusion to his own plans to enlist, Kerry added: "We have not really lost the desire to serve. We question the very roots of what we are serving."

Kerry's critique of American policy stood out at a time when there were few protests, and most of the public assumed Vietnam would be a winnable war, producing a fresh crop of military heroes. The speech also reflected an evolution in Kerry's own thinking about the war.

Earlier in his college life, Kerry had been "gung-ho: had to show the flag," his father, Richard, a staunch critic of Vietnam policy, told the *Boston Globe* in 1996, four years before his death. By his senior year, Richard Kerry added, his son had "matured considerably."

Events were moving quickly. If Kerry glanced at the

New York Times on the day of his oration, he would have
seen an ominous pair of stories. One story quoted Secretary
of Defense Robert S. McNamara as saying that 18,000
more troops had been authorized for movement to Vietnam, bringing the total U.S. force to 285,000.

In what McNamara called an encouraging report—but
was essentially a body count—he said that the Vietcong
had lost 21,000 troops so far in 1966, while the United
States had lost 2,100 troops during the same six-month
period. But the second story, with a Providence dateline,
quoted John Kenneth Galbraith, the former ambassador to
India, as saying that the United States should reduce all
military actions in Vietnam, stop bombing, and pull out as
soon as possible. The State Department was "terribly mis-
informed" if it believed that U.S. policy was respected and
supported, Galbraith said at the commencement address at
Rhode Island College.

In retrospect, it is easy to wonder why Kerry would have
been so anxious to join the navy—even as an officer—if he
knew this might lead to service in a war he was already
beginning to question. When asked this question, Kerry
and many of his classmates respond by saying that 1966
marked the end of innocence at Yale. The Kennedy mantra
of "ask what you can do for your country" still rang loudly,
and the wide-scale protests and draft-card burning were
perhaps a year away.

"It was a lot less clear in '65, '66, what was going on,"
classmate Dalby said. "There was far less propensity to
assume the U.S. government was up to no good. On the
whole I can assure you that the atmosphere was much more

mixed, and it was against that background that what Kerry had to say was so bold."

As a class history primly noted: "The major reason for the sobriety and orderliness of protest and demonstration at Yale was the tradition of mature, responsible and free expression fostered by the University. The strident, narrow and objectionable character which the public associated with radical movements had always been scarce on the Yale campus."

Indeed, when a Yale assistant history professor named Staughton Lynd went on a peace mission to Hanoi in Kerry's senior year—and returned to give a January 1966 speech to 3,500 people at Yale—the university president castigated him as "offering aid and comfort to the enemy," which the class history noted came from the definition of treason in the U.S. Constitution.

This was the atmosphere in which Kerry lived during his senior year at Yale. He was no radical. He believed in the Kennedy credo—he had sailed with Kennedy and been asked by one of Kennedy's best and brightest, William Bundy, to serve as an officer.

Despite his doubts, Kerry was already signed up to attend the Officer Candidate School in Rhode Island, and he was heading off to war. It was as if he was questioning his own movements at a time when they were unstoppable. It was like that great ship in the St. Lawrence Seaway; Vietnam was looming ahead of him, and he was heading toward it, knowing a collision could be deadly. Something drew him to it nonetheless—a mixture of danger and duty and comradeship.

"I wanted to be there and be able to be part of it, make my contribution, have a sense of what it was all about. Like all young men who have a sense of adventure, who are testing themselves," Kerry said, he and his friends had "a sense of invincibility."

Persh was going, and so were Smith and Thorne—and Kerry was not about to be left behind.

Chapter 4

IN TRAINING

JOHN KERRY swerved his two-seater plane across San Francisco Bay, heading straight toward the Golden Gate. "Let's fly under the bridge!" Kerry shouted to his sole passenger and close friend, David Thorne, who tried not to panic as the tiny craft buzzed low over the swells.

Most students who had graduated from Yale with Kerry the previous year knew him as the ultimate Brahmin, the studious and serious class orator who seemed likely to run for president someday. But Thorne and other members of Skull and Bones knew another side of Kerry: He was a young man drawn to danger. Thorne also knew that Kerry had been fascinated with the legend of a Yale professor who once looped a bridge, pulling a 360 around the span.

It was a summer day in 1967, and Kerry, who had graduated from Yale in June the year before, had spent six months at Naval Officer Candidate School in Rhode Island. Now he was in the midst of a year of naval training in California. For several years he had been dating his friend's beautiful twin sister, Julia Thorne, who divided her time between the United States and Europe.

Kerry loved flying. But his father, Richard Kerry, a World War II test pilot, had warned his son that wartime piloting would diminish his fondness for flying. So Kerry enlisted as a sailor and flew for kicks, as he was on this day. The sky was clear as the Golden Gate Bridge came into view. Kerry clung to the controls of the rented T-34, a single-engine craft similar to those used for military training, and the two young naval officers headed toward the famous span.

Wham!

The plane jerked and veered. Out on the wing, the feet of an unfortunate seagull stuck out like a scene from a cartoon. Seconds later, the scene flipped from Looney Tunes to Alfred Hitchcock, as more birds appeared in front of them. If the bird had hit the windshield, Kerry's life might have ended right there: Yale aviator, dreamed of being president, killed on a joyride over the San Francisco Bay.

Instead, Kerry pulled up the nose of his small plane, ascending beyond the dangerous flock of birds.

"We were worried the wing would come off," Thorne recalled. Kerry steered the plane away from the bridge and toward a nearby airfield, leaving behind whatever stunts were lurking inside his twenty-three-year-old brain.

Kerry's relationship with David Thorne was one that would last a lifetime. After both discovered that they had been dating Janet Auchincloss, the sister-in-law of Jacqueline Kennedy, they moved on to relationships with other women and remained friends themselves. Then, one day as Kerry was preparing to enter his sophomore year at Yale, he visited the Thorne family's Long Island estate. As Kerry pulled up in a Volkswagen bus, Thorne's twin sister, Julia, was standing there in a bikini, loudly singing a song made famous by Peter, Paul, and Mary—"Five Hundred Miles."

"He just kind of stood there and looked," Julia told Alex Beam of the *Boston Globe* years later.

The attraction, apparently, was immediate. Both came from a long line of illustrious ancestors, both had lived in Europe. Julia's grandfather owned part of Hilton Head Island, which was later sold off for development. Her great uncle was Henry L. Stimson, FDR's secretary of war, and she was descended from William Bradford, who signed the Declaration of Independence and was the first U.S. attorney general. Her lineage was an ideal match for a man descended from the Forbes and Winthrop families. With their shared Continental outlook, their bilingual backgrounds, and their sense of privilege, the two hit it off. Kerry, for all his oratorical bluster and his imposing stature, was a shy person. Julia put him at ease.

Julia didn't go to college, in large part because her wealthy parents saw no need for it. "I was what you might call a high society jet-setter," she said. "I had been brought up in this rarefied world. My mother was very Edwardian in her value system. She had an idea of what was a decorous life for a young lady, and that didn't include going to colleges. It was more about knowing the right people in the right palaces. It was a waste of a good mind."

As their romance blossomed, Kerry became a kind of mentor to Julia, talking ceaselessly about his views on peace and politics and art and history. "I had a hunger for knowledge that John fed so wonderfully. He had so many things that he was thinking about—he began my education."

For months, Kerry and Julia dated, but she remained in Europe for most of the time that Kerry was at Yale. Then, when Kerry graduated, he had a commitment to keep with the U.S. Navy. In the fall of 1966, he walked up the steps of the Officer Candidate School in Rhode Island and, he later recalled, turned back, wondering whether he could really keep a six-year commitment to the U.S. Navy. Was it all a mistake? Some of his friends were off to graduate school. The war was becoming increasingly unpopular. His girlfriend was an ocean away, and this sailor was stuck stateside. Julia, meanwhile, dated other men in Europe. But she would periodically come to California, when her brother and Kerry were in training. And the romance with Kerry would heat up again.

By the beginning of 1967, Kerry had moved from Rhode Island to California for rounds of naval training, first at Treasure Island in San Francisco, and then in San Diego. The war in Vietnam was escalating rapidly. On January 1, 1966, when Kerry was in his senior year at Yale and had made his decision to enter the navy, the number of U.S. personnel killed in Vietnam was just 636. By the beginning of 1967, that number had multiplied tenfold to 6,644. By the end of 1967, it would more than double to 16,021. American military missions in Vietnam with names such as Operation Pershing—presumably named after Dick Pershing's grandfather—were conducted throughout the year.

On June 23, 1967, Kerry and David Thorne were both in Southern California when they heard that President Johnson was going to appear at a Los Angeles hotel. Thousands of protesters were expected to gather. Bursting with curiosity, the two changed into civilian clothes and went to the Century Plaza Hotel to watch.

As Johnson spoke to about 1,000 Democrats at a $500-a-plate fund-raising dinner, a column of about 15,000 protesters walked by the hotel, shouting, "Hey, Hey, LBJ, how many kids did you kill today?" When many of the protesters halted in front of the Century Plaza, a police force of 1,300 cracked down, arresting fifty-one people on grounds of unlawful assembly or refusal to disperse.

Kerry and Thorne soaked it all in. "We were on the outskirts listening and talking, a little worried," Kerry recalled. "It seemed like a perfectly peaceful thing," Thorne remembered, "and then the police got aggressive, started whacking people. The crowd dispersed, there was chaos, and I remember just being shocked, and John was shocked."

Another pair from Kerry's Skull and Bones class—Smith and Pershing—was on the ground in Vietnam several months later, by early 1968. The four Bonesmen were extraordinarily close, writing detailed letters and soliciting news about each other from mutual friends. Thorne and Kerry were always anxious for reports on how Smith and Pershing were faring.

Smith was in Vietnam serving with the U.S. Marines. Pershing, meanwhile, was trying to live up to his family's military history as a second lieutenant in the 101st Airborne Division. Pershing had terrible eyesight, which normally would have disqualified him for such service, but he managed to get a special waiver. So, in December 1967, he was off to war, following in the footsteps of his grandfather, and his father, Warren, who had served in World War II.

Shortly after Pershing's arrival, on January 31, 1968, the North Vietnamese Army launched the Tet Offensive, taking U.S. and South Vietnamese forces by surprise in a series of major attacks. Pershing was rushed with his troops into action—and the outcome was a bloody one. "There stood Dick Pershing," according to one account. "He was just standing there. He had just come from a mission ... he had lost half a platoon, maybe two-thirds. Now he had to arrange the tagging and the bagging of the dead, and the securing of their personal property for sending home. And the letter to the next of kin."

Despite the death toll, Pershing was determined to return to battle. A photo taken about this time shows a handsome, tanned, athletic-looking man in military garb and wearing thick glasses. His shirt is unbuttoned, exposing his chest; he wears a grenade at his waist and a rifle slung over his shoulder. In one hand, he clutches a Budweiser, and in the other, he holds a package and an airmail letter.

On February 17, 1968, just days after that photo was taken, Pershing and his men were in a rice paddy when the Vietcong launched a surprise rocket attack. At first, it seemed as if everyone had survived. Then Pershing noticed that one of his men was missing. As he walked through the paddy, looking for the soldier, a rocket-propelled grenade soared toward him.

Pershing was dead.

By extraordinary coincidence, Fred Smith was about three miles away from the scene of the battle. Smith, Pershing, and Kerry had so many rollicking times at Yale they could barely remember them all. Now Smith heard about Pershing's death. The deep connection of comradeship, of Yale, and Skull and Bones, drew him to the site of his friend's death.

> It was a typical area, rice paddies and dikes and villages, nothing remarkable about it. That is the ultimate tragedy. It was remarkable only to the extent that it was completely unremarkable—lives paid for basically nothing. We were trading American boys' lives for Vietnamese boys' lives.
>
> They would pick the time and place to fight and we would always take casualties in the first engagement. Dick and his platoon were out on patrol, got one or two kids injured or killed, he went out to try to get them, and was killed in the effort.

David Thorne was at sea aboard the USS *Maddox* when the ship's executive officer handed him a telegram with the news of Pershing's death. Thorne angrily cursed the ocean air.

Kerry, meanwhile, was aboard the USS *Gridley*, a guided-missile frigate, headed toward the Gulf of Tonkin. As the Gridley crossed the Pacific, an officer bearing a telegram tracked Kerry down on the deck. "Do you know a guy named Dick Pershing?" the officer asked. The officer handed him the paper, and Kerry feared the worst as he opened it. Pershing, the telegram said, had died due to "wounds received while on a combat mission when his unit came under hostile small-arms and rocket attack while searching for remains of a missing member of his unit."

For Kerry, the war was no longer an abstract policy issue. One of his best friends had died trying to find a fallen comrade. Kerry couldn't attend the funeral because he was so far out at sea. But he wrote anguished letters to Julia, to David, to Pershing's parents, and to his own mother and father.

Dearest Mama and Papa,

What can I say? I am empty, bitter, angry and desperately lost with nothing but war, violence and more war around me. I just don't believe it was meant to be this cruel and sense-less—that anyone could possibly get near to Persh to take his life. What a Goddamn total waste. Why? ... I have never felt so void of feeling before....

With the loss of Persh something has gone out of me—he was so much a part of my life at the irreplaceable, incomparable moments of love, concerns, anger and compassion exchanged in Bones that can never be replaced.

There was no way to turn back. Pershing was heading home in a casket, Kerry was heading to Vietnam. A war was waiting.

As Kerry continued across the Pacific, President Johnson and his war cabinet were facing a crisis. The Tet Offensive had cost the North Vietnamese 40,000 lives, compared to 1,100 American and 2,300 South Vietnamese losses. But the ability of the North Vietnamese to attack in so many places at once, and briefly occupy the U.S. embassy in Saigon, dealt a deep blow to U.S. morale. It was followed by a rapid succession of extraordinary events that shaped a generation of Americans.

U.S. and South Vietnamese forces took twenty-six bloody days to recapture Hue, the former capital of Vietnam, feeding doubts at home and spurring a new wave of antiwar activism. U.S. military commanders asked for an additional 206,000 soldiers. The top U.S. commander in Vietnam, William Westmoreland, and the U.S. secretary of defense, Robert McNamara, were both replaced.

During this same period, President Johnson, reeling from the turmoil over Vietnam, was nearly defeated by Minnesota's Senator Eugene McCarthy in the New Hampshire primary. CBS anchorman Walter Cronkite returned from Saigon and, in what later was considered a turning point, said that he was "more certain than ever that the bloody experience of Vietnam is to end in a stalemate."

Robert F. Kennedy announced his candidacy for the presidency. And on March 31, Johnson declared he would not run for reelection. Four days later, Martin Luther King Jr. was assassinated. Riots broke out, and some feared the war was moving to the home front.

Aboard the *Gridley*, Kerry received only sporadic news about these events. His tour aboard ship was, in some ways, surreal, strangely apart from the tensions both in Vietnam and America. He was floating on a frigate bristling with firepower, while traversing relatively tranquil seas from Hawaii to New Zealand. The ship stopped only briefly at a U.S. base in Vietnam, where he noticed bodies of Vietcong piled up like cordwood.

"I didn't have any real feel for what the heck was going on [in the war]," Kerry wrote years later in an essay published in a book called *The Vietnam Experience: A War Remembered*. "I went into Da Nang for eight hours one day and got to see the accoutrements of war, but most of the time we were just steaming around in circles behind aircraft carriers."

By early June 1968, Kerry and the USS *Gridley* were heading back to port in Long Beach, California. He was enthusiastic about the prospects of Robert F. Kennedy, who was participating in the California presidential primary on the very day Kerry was arriving off the coast.

As Kerry's ship prepared to dock, another shock wave from that tumultuous year hit. Bobby Kennedy had been shot at a Los Angeles hotel, just after winning the California primary. For Kerry, who idolized John F. Kennedy and looked to RFK to end the war, the death was another bewildering blow.

As the *Gridley* pulled into port, Kerry's best friend, David Thorne, was on the dock, waiting for him. When Thorne spotted Kerry from a distance, Thorne swung his fingers toward his head, in the motion of one pointing a gun at oneself. Kerry nodded, understanding that the hand signal was a reference to Bobby Kennedy's murder.

Julia was on the dock as well, waiting in the distance and wearing a turquoise dress. Her appearance was a surprise, and Julia would recall years later the sight of her husband-to-be doing a double take and tripping over a coil of rope. It was a joyous reunion for the Thorne twins and Kerry, but also a day of unspeakable sadness. The dream of another Kennedy presidency was gone. And so was the country Kerry had left just five months earlier. Antiwar protests abounded, a hippie counterculture was taking root, and in major cities, violence was in the air.

Kerry took a short leave to visit his parents at their home in Massachusetts, and on a summer day was lured to the Red Sox's Fenway Park—for politics, not for baseball. On July 25, 1968, Senator Eugene McCarthy, who was stridently antiwar and still making a long-shot bid for the Democratic nomination, drew an extraordinary throng of 45,000.

"It was the wildest night since the Red Sox won the pennant," *Boston Globe* reporter Robert L. Turner wrote. It was called the largest crowd in the ballpark's history, with all of the seats filled and some 5,000 people forced to stand outside. Just as Kerry had absorbed the protest scene in Los Angeles a year earlier, he was fascinated and disturbed by the antiwar candidate's speech. But he was still a sailor, still intending to go into combat. "I'm in the military, I'm on leave, I'm listening, I'm interested in politics," Kerry recalled.

By August, Kerry had returned to California, where he watched TV footage of antiwar protests roiling the Democratic National Convention in Chicago. But Kerry could not dwell for too long on the domestic political turmoil. Before he could leave again for Vietnam, he had to go to swift boat training school in San Diego, and then to his most grueling trial yet—survival camp in the wilderness outside San Diego.

In September 1968, Kerry headed off for Survival Evasion, Resistance and Escape training, in which sailors were treated as if they were prisoners of war. They were taunted, beaten, and psychologically harassed, all to prepare them for what to expect if they were captured. The survival camp was a reality check. Kerry was about to return to Vietnam, and this time the expectation was that he would come face-to-face with the enemy.

Before departing, Kerry had time for one last meeting with Julia. They both knew that Pershing had left behind a fiancée and never returned. Now, as Kerry and Julia parted, they made a decision about their future: When Kerry returned from Vietnam, they would marry. But the couple didn't want Julia to bear the burden of being a wartime fiancée, so they only told family and their closest friends.

In mid-November 1968, Kerry boarded a plane and headed back to Vietnam, this time for duty as the skipper of a six-man swift boat. Kerry left believing he would be relatively safe, patrolling off the coast of Vietnam. But in Saigon, the U.S. naval brass had other plans.

Chapter 5

SWIFT BOAT NO. 44

ON THE NIGHT of December 2, 1968, just two weeks after returning to Vietnam, Kerry set off on a covert mission. The operation was risky: He would leave the safe confines of the huge U.S. base at Cam Ranh Bay, climb aboard a small "skimmer" boat and go upriver in search of Vietcong guerrillas.

Kerry and two other sailors trolled the darkened waters. At one point, they turned a bend in the river and encountered two men in a sampan. This was a "free-fire" curfew zone, and naval regulations said anyone violating the curfew could be considered an enemy and shot. "Just by grace of God, they weren't blown away," Kerry said, recalling that the two Vietnamese men were taken prisoner and brought to a larger boat. Kerry's boat then had another encounter with two more men in a sampan, and captured them as well.

Several hours had passed when, Kerry said, "We got into

a firefight with six sampans or something" near a beach that was known as a crossing area for Vietcong contraband traffic. Kerry's crew lit a flare, and the men from the sampans ran along the shore. Kerry authorized firing to begin, his fellow sailors recalled, and in the ensuing minutes Kerry was wounded. "We came across the bay on to the beach and I got [hit] in the arm, got shrapnel in the arm," Kerry said in a 2003 interview.

Separately, Kerry told history professor Douglas Brinkley, author of the book *Tour of Duty*, that his M–16 had jammed, "and as I bent down into the boat to grab another gun, a stinging piece of heat socked into my arm and just seemed to burn like hell." Kerry said it was "a half-assed action that hardly qualified as combat, but it was my first and that made it very exciting." He added, "I never saw where the piece of shrapnel had come from."

Two men serving alongside him that night had similar memories of the incident that led to Kerry's first wartime injury. William Zaladonis, who was manning an M–60, and Patrick Runyon, operating the engine, said they spotted some people running from a sampan to a nearby shoreline. When they refused to obey a call to stop, Kerry's crew began shooting. "When John told me to open up, I opened up," Zaladonis recalled. Zaladonis and Runyon both said they were too busy to notice how Kerry was hit. "I assume they fired back," Zaladonis said. "If you can picture me holding an M–60 machine gun and firing it—what do I see? Nothing. If they were firing at us, it was hard for me to tell."

Runyon, too, said he assumed the suspected Vietcong fired back because Kerry was hit by a piece of shrapnel.

"When you have a lot of shooting going on, a lot of noise, you are scared, the adrenaline is up," Runyon said. "I can't say for sure that we got return fire or how [Kerry] got nicked. I couldn't say one way or the other. I know he did get nicked, a scrape on the arm."

Back at the base, Lieutenant Commander Grant Hibbard, who served as Kerry's commanding officer during this brief period at Cam Ranh Bay, said he observed Kerry's wound. Kerry told Hibbard he qualified for a Purple Heart, according to Hibbard.

Hibbard, however, said he was not impressed.

Hibbard recalled that he thought the wound was slight and he had questions about whether Kerry's boat had taken enemy fire at the time Kerry was hit. "Kerry said something about how he got wounded," Hibbard recalled in a 2004 interview.

"He had a little scratch in his forearm, and he was holding a piece of shrapnel. People in the office were saying, 'I don't think we got any fire,' and there is a guy holding a little piece of shrapnel in his palm." Hibbard said he couldn't be certain about whether or not Kerry did come under fire, and that is why he said he asked questions about the matter.

As for Kerry's wound, Hibbard said that thirty-six years later he can still remember it as resembling a scrape from a fingernail. "I've had thorns from a rose that were worse," Hibbard said.

The Purple Heart regulation in effect at that time said that a wound must "require treatment by a medical officer." The regulation does not state anything about the severity of the wound. Purple Hearts were widely given for many types of injuries, including minor ones. In addition, the regulation said that a qualifying wound is:

> (a) in any action against an enemy of the United States; (b) in any action with an opposing armed force of a foreign country in which the armed forces of the United States are or have been engaged; (c) while serving with friendly foreign forces engaged in an armed conflict against an opposing armed force in which the United States is not a belligerent party; (d) as the result of an act of any such enemy or opposing armed force; or (e) as the result of an act of any hostile foreign force.

Another person involved that day was William Schachte, who oversaw the mission and went on to become a rear admiral. In 2003, when asked about the nature of Kerry's wound, Schachte responded: "It was not a very serious wound at all." In a follow-up interview in 2004, Schachte declined to comment further.

Hibbard said that after he initially raised questions about the wound, Kerry persisted. To his own "chagrin," Hibbard recalled, he eventually dropped his questions. "I do remember some questions, some correspondence about it," Hibbard said. "I finally said, 'Okay, if that's what happened ... do whatever you want.' After that I don't know what happened. Obviously, he got it, I don't know how."

Kerry declined to be interviewed for this specific matter for this book, so it was not possible to say whether he remembers the conversation, and, if he does, whether he remembers it happening the way Hibbard recalled.

The Kerry campaign showed the *Boston Globe* a one-page document listing Kerry's medical treatment during some of his service time. The notation said: "3 DEC 1968 U.S. NAVAL SUPPORT FACILITY CAM RANH BAY RVN FPO Shrapnel in left arm above elbow. Shrapnel removed and appl. Bacitracin dressing. Ret to duty."

The Boston Globe asked the campaign whether Kerry is certain he received enemy fire and whether Kerry remembers the Purple Heart being questioned by a superior officer. The campaign did not respond to those specific questions, and instead provided a written statement about the fact that the Navy did find the action worthy of a Purple Heart.

Referring to the notation of the wound in Kerry's sick call list, the campaign press secretary, Michael Meehan, said in a statement that "the absence of any non-medical information in this document" is not unusual. "As the sick call sheet spells out, Naval medical personnel are to report details about the date of visit, nature of injury, and treatment and signature only."

A Purple Heart award is determined by a medical officer, and Meehan said in his statement, "We cite the Purple Heart memo and certificate as evidence that Kerry was awarded a Purple Heart for this shrapnel wound."

"Whatever slight differences that may exist in thirty-five year old recollections, Sen. Kerry and Messer. Zaladonis and Runyon firmly recall that they were engaging the enemy deep in enemy territory, surrounded by jungle and danger," Meehan said. "Sen. Kerry received the shrapnel wound early in the course of that combat engagement." Meehan added that after the operation was over, "Kerry immediately went to the infirmary" and that "The Navy determined according to its Purple Heart regulations that Sen. Kerry be awarded a Purple Heart."

The Navy Historical Center, which has the original cards recording Kerry's second and third Purple Hearts, said it could not locate a card for the first one, although it verified that Kerry did receive the first Purple Heart. Nor could the center locate an after-action report for the incident.

In any case, nearly three months after the incident, a document was sent to Kerry informing him that he would get a Purple Heart "for injuries received on 2 December 1968." The letter was stamped a by a naval staff officer named Donald A. Still, now deceased.

Whatever the circumstances, the night was a scary one for a young officer barely two weeks removed from San Diego. Kerry had been told to watch out for arms smugglers and snipers, and he was just learning the ways of the enemy. "We were all just scared to death," recalled Runyon who, like Kerry, had just experienced what he viewed as his first combat action. Kerry remembered it this way in the 2003 interview: "up most the night, flying by the seat of our pants, pretty improvised and pretty hairy."

In early December 1968, Kerry left Cam Ranh Bay and headed to An Thoi, an island town in the Gulf of Thailand that would become his base of operations for much of the next four months. An Thoi was the home of a large fleet of swift boats, which until just weeks earlier had mostly roamed the coast of Vietnam, a relatively safe mission. Kerry, who had loved to sail off Cape Cod, was drawn to the swifts, which typically had a skipper and five crewmates. The fifty-foot crafts were small enough for a young officer like Kerry to gain his first command post.

Kerry had written a memo to the chief of naval personnel in early 1968 requesting assignment to the swift boats. "Prior to joining the Navy I had extensive small boat experience which I believe would serve me well as an officer in charge of a 'swift' boat," Kerry wrote. After listing his qualifications, he added: "I consider the opportunity to serve in Vietnam an extremely important part of being in the armed forces and believe that my request is in the best interest of the Navy."

Allen W. Slifer, commanding officer of the USS *Gridley*, backed Kerry's request, writing, "Ensign Kerry is one of the brightest, most capable young officers I have ever had the pleasure of observing. Meticulous in attention to detail, he is a sound administrator and a natural, highly effective leader."

Kerry also believed a swift boat assignment would keep him away from the frontlines of combat. At the time, the boats "had very little to do with the war," Kerry wrote in his 1986 contribution to *The Vietnam Experience: A War Remembered*. "They were engaged in coastal patrolling and that's what I thought I was going to be doing. Although I wanted to see for myself what was going on, I didn't really want to get involved in the war."

But just as Kerry arrived in Vietnam, the swift boat mission changed—and Kerry went from having one of the safest assignments in the escalating conflict to one of the most dangerous.

Unbeknownst to Kerry, the navy brass was angling to expand the service's relatively small role in the war. While most of the other military services were engaged in direct combat, racking up large casualty counts, the navy was spending most of its time at sea in relative safety.

That changed dramatically with the arrival in September 1968 of Admiral Elmo "Bud" Zumwalt Jr. A former Eagle Scout, high school valedictorian, and Naval Academy graduate, Zumwalt had recently become the youngest naval officer ever promoted to rear admiral. At forty-seven years old, he was on his way toward becoming the youngest-ever four-star admiral and youngest-ever chief of naval operations.

Zumwalt was frustrated that U.S. coastal patrols had failed to stop the infiltration of Communist arms through the Mekong Delta waterways. Communist forces effectively controlled the river supply route because U.S. forces weren't supposed to cross the border into neutral Cambodia, and the delta's rivers were considered too dangerous for American boats. "We simply were not engaging the enemy," Captain Howard Kerr, Zumwalt's flag secretary, recalled in an oral history.

Shortly after Zumwalt arrived in Vietnam, General Creighton Abrams Jr., who was overseeing the U.S. military effort, told Zumwalt he wanted the navy to be more aggressive. "Abrams told me he was getting no help from the Navy in fighting the war," Zumwalt wrote in his autobiography. Zumwalt promised that would change.

Thus, in the fall of 1968, Zumwalt came up with one of

his famous "ZWIs," shorthand for "Zumwalt's Wild Ideas": Swift boats should leave their ocean patrols and run up Vietcong-infested rivers and canals, drawing enemy fire with their noisy engines. After using this method to pinpoint the enemy's location, the sailors would radio for air support to begin bombardments.

Sailors were also encouraged to be much more aggressive. The tone for this new assignment was set in October 1968, one month before Kerry's arrival. A daring swift boat skipper named Michael Bernique traveled up a canal near the Cambodian border, off-limits to U.S. forces due to concerns about violating Cambodia's neutrality. The Vietcong were stunned to see Bernique and his crew in the forbidden waterway and stood "openmouthed" as his crew opened fire, according to the documentary film *Swift Boats, Brave Sailors*. A vicious firefight ensued and five Vietcong were killed.

Upon returning to base, Bernique was called to Saigon to face a possible court-martial. But Zumwalt, impressed by the enemy casualties and Bernique's ability to maneuver through the dangerous canals, intervened. "I decided instead he should be awarded a medal, and we re-dubbed the canal 'Bernique's creek,'" Zumwalt said in recounting the incident on film.

Indeed, in an oral history, Zumwalt, who died in 2000, said that his own son, a swift boat sailor named Elmo Zumwalt III, went across the border into Cambodia, "in violation of the rules of engagement" and sank some sampans. "I had the problem of what to do about Elmo, so I turned that over to the chief of staff, who did a long analysis and decided that he should be court-martialed for violating the rules of engagement, and he should be given a medal for his discovery, and that, therefore, the one should cancel the other," Zumwalt recalled.

In an effort to protect the swift boat crews, Zumwalt in January 1969 approved a major increase in the spraying of Agent Orange, a chemical that killed the trees and foliage lining the riverbanks that had provided cover to Vietcong. Zumwalt calculated that without the aid of Agent Orange, a swift boat sailor stood a 70 to 75 percent chance of being killed or wounded over the course of a year.

"Swift boat hulls were made of aluminum only one-eighth of an inch thick," he wrote years later. "The enemy could hit them with B–40s, which are like old bazookas, automatic weapons and hand-held rockets. And under cover of the dense foliage that grew along the riverbanks, the enemy attacked the boats without being seen."*

By the second week of December 1968, Kerry took command of his first "Patrol Craft Fast," the official name for a swift boat. Kerry became skipper of PCF No. 44. Originally designed to ferry oil workers to ocean rigs, swift boats offered flimsy protection. Because bullets could easily penetrate the hull, sailors hung flak jackets over the sides. The boat's loud engine invited ambushes. The top speed of

---

* Zumwalt's reliance on the chemical defoliant had a sad twist. His son, Elmo Zumwalt III, died in 1988 from cancer that the Zumwalt family believes was caused by Agent Orange. But, in their joint autobiography, both men defended the spraying as necessary to save American lives. Kerry may also have been sprayed by Agent Orange. Although Kerry said his 2003 case of prostate cancer was likely genetic, he says he has "wondered" whether Agent Orange had any effect, given what happened to the younger Zumwalt.

twenty-five knots was its saving grace—but that wasn't always an option in narrow, heavily mined canals.

The swift boat crew typically consisted of a college-educated skipper, such as Kerry, and five blue-collar sailors averaging nineteen years old. The most vulnerable sailor sat in the "tub"—a squat nest that rose above the pilothouse—and operated a pair of .50-caliber machine guns. Another gunner was in the rear. Kerry's mission was to wait until hidden Vietcong guerrillas started shooting, then order his men to return fire.

To Kerry, the most questionable part of the strategy was the authority granted to American troops to fire on Vietnamese civilians violating U.S.-imposed curfews in so-called free-fire zones along key rivers and canals. The free-fire policy was launched in an effort to provide American sailors with protection against a common Vietcong tactic of posing as villagers and hiding among them. But the skippers had to be careful. A stinging naval report was written about an incident in which a Cobra gunship, acting in support of a swift boat, killed several civilians, prompting an officer to write that "the damage and loss of life caused by the U.S. unit involved was completely uncalled for" and arranging for compensation to be paid to villagers "to counteract the adverse psychological effect." Kerry's craft was not mentioned in the report, and Kerry said he was not involved in it. But the report highlighted the conflicting signals given to skippers. At the same time they were told to avoid killing innocent civilians, they were urged to be aggressive and were given wide latitude in shooting in free-fire zones. If a civilian was killed in a free-fire zone or was in the cross fire, such deaths were considered an understandable, if regrettable, part of being at war in a dangerous jungle where it often was hard to distinguish friend from foe.

Kerry initially kept some of his inner conflicts about the mission to himself. But with his patrician air, he attracted notice among sailors and his commanders. His habit of recording his observations—on paper, tape, and film—led some to believe that Kerry was obsessed with his destiny. Some sailors figured Kerry was following the path trod by John F. Kennedy. "We all knew he would run for president one day," said swift boat sailor Jerry Leeds, who went on joint missions with Kerry. "You figure you got the initials, JFK, you are from Massachusetts and you are on a gunboat. It wasn't hard to figure out."

Roy Hoffmann, the commander who oversaw all of the swift boats and pushed his skippers to be aggressive, had his problems with Kerry. "It was loud and clear he did not like anyone who had authority over him," Hoffmann said. "Whatever the task was, it was 'bungled' or a 'dumb damn' idea."

Although Kerry later expressed grave concerns about the swift boat strategy, Hoffmann said he never heard directly from him about such problems. What Hoffmann remembers is that he had to clamp down on Kerry and other skippers who didn't follow every order.

Kerry was, "a little bit, to put it gently, out of control, and it wasn't just him," Hoffmann recalled. "I did not single out Kerry, although Kerry was well in my mind as one of the problems." Asked to specify the problem, Hoffmann said, "He just was going off on excursions that were not part of the plan at the time." But Hoffmann said those problems were corrected and that he admired the gutsy way Kerry later went after the enemy.

Bernique, the model of the aggressive skipper, and one who shared much of Kerry's background as a highly educated New Englander, could see that Kerry turned off some naval people in Vietnam. "I liked the guy very much" in Vietnam, said Bernique, who later broke sharply with Kerry over his antiwar protests. "But I knew others thought he was cold, aloof." Whatever the qualms, Bernique had no doubt about Kerry's courage in Vietnam, having watched Kerry once walk through an area that was believed to be laced with mines.

"I said, 'Get the blankety-blank out of there.' John just shrugged his shoulders and left."

Bernique recalled, "John just was fearless."

On Christmas Eve of 1968, as Kerry's fifty-foot aluminum craft floated in the waters off Cambodia, he was about to get firsthand experience with the free-fire policy that he would come to despise.

The United States believed that the Vietcong would follow a Christmastime truce, and Kerry was expecting a quiet holiday observance. But the truce was only three minutes old when mortar fire suddenly exploded around Kerry and his five-man crew.

"Where is the enemy?" a crewmate shouted.

"Open fire; let's take 'em," Kerry ordered, according to his second-in-command, James Wasser of Illinois. In the distance, an elderly man in the cross fire was tending his water buffalo—and serving as human cover for a dozen

Vietcong manning a machine-gun nest. Wasser said he opened fire with his M–60, hitting the old man, who slumped into the water, presumably dead. With a clear path to the enemy, the fusillade from Kerry's navy boat, backed by a pair of other small vessels, silenced the machine-gun nest.

When it was over, the Vietcong were dead, wounded, or on the run. A civilian apparently was killed, and two South Vietnamese allies who had alerted Kerry's crew to the enemy were either wounded or killed.

On the same night, when some South Vietnamese allies launched several rounds into the river to celebrate the holiday, Kerry and his crew had come within a half-inch of being killed by "friendly fire."

To top it off, Kerry said later he had gone inside Cambodia, despite President Nixon's assurances to the American public that there was no combat action in this neutral territory. The young sailor began to develop a deep mistrust of U.S. government pronouncements, he later recalled.

Back at his base, a weary, disconsolate Kerry sat at his typewriter, as he often did, and poured out his grief. Kerry saw himself as a sailor but also as an observer, taking his inspiration from novels such as Joseph Conrad's *Heart of Darkness*.

Of all his "War Notes," as he called them, one of the most powerful recounts the events of Christmas Eve, when death was still new to him, and the unraveling of his rationale for serving in Vietnam had begun. The passage, written in second-person voice, reads like a novella—the peace and beauty of Vietnam drawing him in, and then the horror of gunfire jolting him out of his reverie.

"Today you move to the northern end of the area—towards Cambodia—and excitement tingles the nerves that appreciates the new and the unexplored," he begins. Kerry then recalls his enjoyment in starting the engine, hearing its "deep throb ... and the hums as the boat reaches for the step and shoots spray out on both sides as she moves up the river."

Kerry describes trees growing out of the water "and buffalo, dark black and strong, rub their backs against them and rid themselves of pesky itches. It is almost a crime that you should cause ripples to disturb this scene and you slow the boat to minimum revolutions—an act that causes you to almost drift with ghost like qualities through the morning mist."

As Kerry takes in the beauty, reflecting that "it is good to be alive," U.S. helicopters appear, "in formation, ugly and insect-like across the sky en route to some encounter with Charlie. They blot the sky and your mind and you think again of losing all that is in front of you.... "

He describes the local peasants, and the sampans drifting by. A "woman holds her baby tight against bare breast and nipple firm, gives life; my voice asks where she is going and unabashed she bares her breast to replace the youngster's fumbling, tiny lips...."

As Kerry's boat intrudes upon the peace of the local population, fishermen leave their nets and move away from the river. With curfew approaching, they risk being shot. "Fish nets dangling from teepee poles on the lush river bank are empty now," Kerry writes, "swaying to the gentle evening breeze. Waiting for high tide they will not fill tonight because it is nearing the hour for countrymen to go inside."

The young officer interjects a sardonic aside about the American presence in this faraway jungle: "Damn the fish and food; your property is mine. With the sun goes more than light. With it goes life and country for with the darkness comes the curfew and the silent stealth and steal of night ... "

Kerry's reverie is suddenly interrupted when his boat comes under fire.

"There is an explosion and a mortar lands on the bank near all these boats. You jump and grab binoculars and search the bank for activity but there is none and you wonder who sent it." As Kerry radios for backup, "another mortar round lands fifteen yards away in the water. The boats come alive" with return fire.

As the attackers retreat, two Vietnamese men run down the beach toward Kerry's boat, yelling for the sailors to come over. "You charge the engines with all their force," Kerry writes, "and not caring if there is sand or rock or no water at all the boat begins to charge the beach, jumping with excitement and with the power of a horse that has just been uncaged from the starting gate."

The men want to tell the Americans that Vietcong guerrillas have attacked their village and wounded a man. By Kerry's watch, the truce is only three minutes old. His crew moves to their battle stations, awaiting a new round of enemy fire.

"Suddenly, in a flash that is a moment of hell and blindness the reeds erupt and bullets walk out across the water at your boat and those around you," Kerry continues.

"Then screaming flashes of tracer, red and deadly, come at you with a terrifying suddenness that catches all by surprise and you watch for a moment as red streaks move at you in a three dimensional kaleidoscope out of the water."

Kerry and his crew return fire as they wheel the boat around and head back toward the main river.

"From somewhere reason calls and you grab the loud speaker and yell to your men to hold your fire until right on top of the spot and then there is thunder again and no hearing and only red streaks tearing towards the land."

Despite the danger, Kerry "cannot help but feel a throaty exhilaration because you have gone through and there are no scratches and you are still free." As Kerry's crew pauses in the river to rearm, nearby boats come under more sniper fire. "But it falls short of the boat," he notes, "and so you don't give a damn."

As Kerry and his crew head back to the base, the darkness of the night is broken by tracers "flying up out of a Vietnamese outpost that is celebrating Christmas. The bullets pass dangerously near your boat and you think of the stupidity of the whole thing and the ridiculous waste of being shot at by your own allies." Kerry angrily gets on the radio to ask "who the hell is shooting" and to warn them to stop before they risk return fire.

Back inside the safety of the base, Kerry recovers in the cool evening air, taking a Coke, peanut butter and jelly, and a tape-recorder to the cabin roof to reflect on the night's events "as flares float silently through the sky."

At one point, Kerry calls down to one of his men and asks him to draft a barbed message to Zumwalt, as well as the commander of "Market Time," as the swift boat operation is called. The message reads "Merry Christmas from the most inland Market Time unit," a reference to their incursion into Cambodia.

Kerry adds, bitterly and with a note of sarcasm: "You hope that they'll court martial you or something because that would make sense. But the night soothes everything and the people and things that are close to you dart through the mind and bring the only warmth and peace that there is. Visions of sugar plums really do dance through your head and you think of stockings and snow and roast chestnuts and fires with birch logs and all that is good and warm and real. It's Christmas Eve."

Despite the level of detail in his story, Kerry does not mention the old man killed near the water buffalo; he said he didn't know about the death until Wasser told him in 2003. But Wasser has never forgotten. "I don't even enjoy Christmas anymore," he said.

Most of the crewmates on No. 44, including Wasser and Zaladonis, spoke highly of Kerry's actions during his tenure as commander of that boat. "If you are ever in a tight situation, this is the guy you want to be with," Wasser said.

But crewmate Steven Michael Gardner, who manned the twin .50-caliber machine guns and was wounded by enemy fire a few nights later, criticized Kerry for being too cautious during those early weeks as a swift boat commander. During a firefight on December 28, 1968, Gardner looked down and saw blood in the gun tub, dripping over the boxes of bullets stored on the floor. After the momentary shock, he recalled, Gardner realized his injury was "no big deal" and kept on firing.

But Gardner said that when Kerry learned of Gardner's

wound, he ordered the boat turned around to get medical attention. Gardner argued that the retreat was unnecessary and worried that leaving the scene might endanger others on the mission. "I said, Lieutenant Kerry, I'm fine, nothing's wrong, I got a little flesh wound here. But [Kerry] was already backing out of the canal, getting ready to run for it," Gardner recalled. Crewmate Stephen Hatch said Kerry turned back with the injured Gardner because "we didn't know how hurt he was."

Gardner argued that Kerry retreated from firefights too quickly—a view at odds with descriptions by others of Kerry's aggression in later months. "He absolutely did not want to engage the enemy when I was with him," Gardner said. "He wouldn't go in there and search. That is why I have a negative viewpoint of John Kerry." He noted that he was comparing Kerry, whom he viewed as new to combat and still tentative, to three more experienced skippers he had served under.

Gardner said he and Kerry also clashed over an incident in swift boat No. 44 that left a deep mark on both men—the killing of a boy who appeared to be about twelve years old. Gardner recalled coming across a sampan violating curfew. He flashed a searchlight and ordered the craft to stop. Then, he said, he saw a figure rise up over the gunwale with a semiautomatic weapon.

Gardner said he laced the boat with bullets, and that others on Kerry's boat fired as well. Gardner recalled a man going overboard, presumably dead. After the shooting had stopped and Kerry had ordered a cease-fire, he said, the crew discovered a woman in the sampan who was alive. There was also the boy, dead in the bottom of the boat,

Gardner said. Gardner said there is no way to know which of the crewmates fired the shots that killed the boy, but he said Kerry was in the pilothouse and was not firing at the time.

Kerry recalled a similar incident, saying that he and his crew came upon a sampan and that someone started firing from his boat. Kerry said his crew rescued the mother, took her aboard the navy vessel for questioning, and left the dead boy.

Because of the dangerous location, and the possibility that the gunfire had drawn the notice of Vietcong, Kerry said he never had a chance to see whether the woman was hiding weaponry in the sunken boat and still doesn't know whether he and his crew faced a real threat. "It is one of those terrible things, and I'll never forget, ever, the sight of that child," Kerry said. "But there was nothing that anybody could have done about it. It was the only instance of that happening."

"It angered me," Kerry added. "But, look, the Viet Cong used women and children. Who knows if they had—under the rice—a satchel [containing an explosive], and if we had come along beside them they had thrown the satchel in [our] boat.... So it was a terrible thing, but I've never thought we were somehow at fault or guilty. There wasn't anybody in that area that didn't know you don't move at night, that you don't go out in a sampan on the rivers, and there's a curfew."

After Kerry's crew discovered the dead boy, Gardner said, "Kerry threatened me with a court martial, screaming at the top of his lungs, 'What the hell do you think you're doing? I ought to have you court martialed.' Thankfully

the whole crew was there in the middle of it ... they verified there were weapons being shot at us, that was the end
of it."

In March 2004, Gardner was quoted publicly for the first
time about his views of Kerry in the *Boston Globe* and *Time*
magazine's web site. Kerry declined to talk to the *Globe*
about Gardner. But in the *Time* article written by *Tour of
Duty* author Douglas Brinkley, Kerry was quoted as reacting
strongly to Gardner's criticism of him, saying that Gardner
had "made up" stories. Brinkley dismissed Gardner, a supporter of President Bush, as being motivated by "one word:
politics." Kerry said he couldn't remember the court-martial threat, and Wasser said that on the night Gardner was
wounded, their boat was already in the process of leaving a
canal and that the boat was not in a position to protect
other forces. Gardner denied politics had anything to do
with his comments, "Absolutely not," Gardner said, saying
that he has kept his feelings about Kerry to himself for
thirty-five years and only responded when a *Globe* reporter
tracked him down.

In any case, while Kerry said in a 2003 interview that he
wasn't sure when the boy in the sampan was killed, a navy
report says a similar sounding incident took place on January 20, 1969. The crew of No. 44 "took sampan under fire,
returned to capture 1 woman and small child, one enemy
KIA [Killed In Action]....believe four occupants fled to
beach or possible KIA." Kerry was the skipper of the No.
44 boat at the time. The Kerry campaign, sent a copy of the
report, did not respond to a request that Kerry review the
report to determine if it matched his memory of the night

the boy was killed.

Kerry was appalled that the navy's "free-fire zone" policy put civilians at such high risk. Two days after the incident cited in that report, he and other swift boat skippers traveled to Saigon for an extraordinary meeting with Zumwalt and the overall commander of the war, General Abrams.

The meeting was designed to be a pep rally, with Zumwalt and Abrams exhorting the officers to be aggressive and promising them a great naval future. But Kerry said he and other officers used the session to air criticism of the free-fire policy.

"We were fighting the [free-fire] policy very, very hard, to the point that many of the members were refusing to carry out orders on some of their missions, to the point where crews were starting to mutiny, [to] say, 'I would not go back in the rivers again,'" Kerry recalled during a 1971 television appearance on the *Dick Cavett Show*.

None of the swift boat sailors and officers who served with Kerry and were interviewed said they could recall a mutinous threat. Nor did Kerry's subsequent actions suggest he was gun-shy. Kerry not only went back into the rivers, he was about to make his reputation as one of the most aggressive skippers in the navy.

Chapter 6

THE DAYS OF HELL

NAVY SWIFT BOAT No. 94 was cruising down a canal in South Vietnam when rockets and automatic-weapons fire started raining down on the six-man craft. David Alston was a sitting duck as he manned two .50-caliber machine guns in the "tub" above the boat's cabin. Someone would later count ninety holes in the tub, but Alston, an African American who joined the navy because his family couldn't afford to send him to college, somehow survived. It was God's grace, he liked to say.

But the boat's skipper, Edward Peck, was hit hard, in the left arm, left side, and right ankle. A call went out for a replacement, and John Kerry—whose own crew on the No. 44 had dispersed under transfer orders—inherited Peck's gritty battle-tested quintet.

Peck, who wore his blue-collar roots proudly and didn't think Kerry was the right person to take over his crew, was disappointed that Kerry got the call. "I remember laying thinking, 'Put salt in the wounds.'" The new crew, meanwhile, readily adjusted to this Brahmin with the Kennedyesque accent.

The class barrier between Kerry and his crew was eased by Tommy Belodeau, a working-class guy from Chelmsford, Massachusetts, who went straight from high school to Vietnam and later became a state prison guard and electrician. Belodeau told his crewmates that Kerry was okay. Why? "He's from Massachusetts!" Belodeau replied.

For the next forty-eight days, this "band of brothers" would put their lives in each other's hands, living together on a fifty-foot boat, barely protected by a skin of aluminum and a few flak jackets. They were about to enter action so intense that Kerry would, in rapid succession, win the Silver Star, the Bronze Star, and two of his three Purple Hearts.

Alston, assigned to the barrel-shaped machine-gun nest, shared a love of the water with his crewmates. But he never imagined how dangerous his job would become. "The fear part was that at any point in time we could be fired upon," Alston recalled. "You are always uneasy. We would go into these rivers and we could not fire until fired upon. I had to think about a sniper who could take me out. I'm the one he wants to take out first."

Petty Officer Delbert Sandusky (who would, years later, star in a crucial Kerry campaign ad) piloted the boat. The Illinois native, nicknamed "Ski," said he could never consider himself off-duty, even for a second, while on board. When he met Kerry, he joked about the skipper's JFK initials. "Yeah, I'm from Boston, too," Kerry said, and that was it.

Eugene Thorson, a quiet Iowa farm boy, manned the engines. The fifth crewmate was the spark plug, the wiry Michael Medeiros of California, the quartermaster, rear gunner, and, in his spare time, unofficial photographer. The six young men jelled quickly, and none too soon. The days of hell, as the crew called them, were about to begin.

On February 20, 1969, six swift boats, including one skippered by Kerry, were cruising down the Dam Doi River in South Vietnam. Sailors aboard one or more of the swift boats—the naval report doesn't specify—started shooting at "targets of opportunity," meaning suspected Vietcong buildings and boats.

Suddenly, a crew member on Kerry's boat spotted three suspected Vietcong wearing traditional black garb on the port side. Kerry's crew came under intense automatic-weapon and rocket fire. Thorson was hit, suffering shrapnel wounds in the right arm. Kerry was also hit by shrapnel in his left thigh, an injury that would merit a second Purple Heart. He was treated on an offshore ship and returned to duty hours later.

Afterward, a navy report challenged the decision of unnamed skippers to fire at other "targets of opportunity" in the area and suggested that "psychological operations" to win the hearts and minds of villagers—a "psyop" in military parlance—might have been more effective.

"Area seemed extremely prosperous and open to psyops action, minimum number of defensive and no offensive bunkers detected," the report said. The naval official who wrote the report concluded: "Future missions in this area should be oriented toward psyops rather than destruction."

The destruction included forty sampans, ten hootches (a type of Vietnamese hut), three bunkers, and 5,000 pounds of rice. The crews had expended more than 14,000 rounds of .50-caliber ammunition. No enemy casualties were reported.

Kerry dismissed the report's questioning of firing at targets of opportunity. "The problem is ... three guys are ducking behind a bank, and you start taking arms fire," Kerry said. "At any place, at any time, anybody could turn around and kill you. That was the problem with the war."

Five days later, Kerry's boat was on patrol and under fire when a supporting helicopter ran out of ammunition. Even without air support, Kerry turned the craft directly toward hidden snipers, then beached it, ordering an assault party onshore.

With a second swift boat providing support, Medeiros and Kerry rushed ashore and found what they thought was a Vietcong guerrilla inside a bunker. Kerry called down into the darkness, trying to secure a surrender; hearing no reply, Medeiros threw a grenade inside. The two assumed an enemy had been killed, although Medeiros said he never saw the victim and wonders now whether it could have been an animal.

The next day, Kerry's swift boat detected five Vietcong in the river. Some of them appeared to be dead, but they were actually playing dead in an effort to stall the swift boat crews. It was a trap, and the swift boats came under rocket fire from the shore. The crews managed to capture the five guerrillas and sped away.

On the following day, February 27, Kerry's boat was nearly hit in a rocket attack. But the harrowing week was only beginning. The next day would be forever etched in the life story of John Kerry—Silver Star day.

From the shores of Bai Hap River, the 800 or so people in a small village near the Dong Cung Canal would watch and wait for the Vietcong attacks. The village was remote, and the residents lived in simple thatched huts, most of which lined the riverbank. They were religious people, practicing an indigenous faith called Cao Dai, which blends aspects of several religions, including Buddhism and Catholicism. There was one television in the village square, which drew in a single channel if the generator happened to be working.

But this village was a prime target for the Vietcong guerrillas terrorizing South Vietnam. The village didn't have access to roads, but it did have access to a river highway. It also held value as a psychological target because it was so far south, and presumably more protected by American forces. The Vietcong, who often came from other regions or observed different religions, were allied with the North Vietnamese Army that was trying to take over and unite Vietnam into a Communist nation.

Washington policymakers worried that the fall of even one village would lead to the fall of others, which would lead to the fall of South Vietnam, and then, like dominos, the fall of other Southeast Asian countries to communism.

The village already housed a U.S. Army advisory team of about six or seven men, who lived on the outskirts and provided a key listening post. Most of the days were languid and uneventful, but terror could arrive at any moment.

Earlier a group of ten or so Vietcong had tried to launch a surprise attack on a nearby hamlet. The guerrillas, some dressed as women, had pulled ashore in two sampans to attack the villagers as they gathered together, seeking the highest possible death toll. But a pair of lookout guards spied the ambushers and killed them, before redirecting their fire at the enemy's oncoming reinforcements.

One of the army advisers at the main village was Army First Lieutenant Doug Reese, who had developed an intimate knowledge of the South Vietnamese—and the challenges they faced daily—by living among them.

Thus, on February 28, 1969, Reese was pleased to see Kerry's crew and two swift boats pull to shore. The navy had come to flush out a suspected encampment of Vietcong just down the river. The navy, which was in the process of "Vietnamization" of the war, wanted to include more South Vietnamese in its actions, and this day was no exception. About seventy local South Vietnamese soldiers crowded aboard the three swift boats, according to a navy report, with Reese and two other army advisers joining them.

In addition to Kerry's swift boat No. 94, the flotilla included the No. 23, skippered by William Rood and the No. 43, skippered by Kerry's good friend Don Droz, whose wife, Judy, just weeks before had given birth to their daughter.

Leaving the wide Bai Hap River, the boats moved north on the Dong Cung Canal, about the width of a four-lane roadway. The water rippled between the banks, tossing the boats to and fro, as Kerry's crew scanned the shore for the enemy, fingers on the trigger.

Up in the No. 94 tub, a new man, Fred Short, had temporarily replaced David Alston, and he was as green as the Arkansas grass of his home. Short knew how to fire the noisy .50-caliber machine guns, but he would soon learn the limitations of the setup. For safety's sake, the tub was ringed with a railing that ensured that the guns couldn't accidentally be lowered enough to fire at someone on deck.

Belodeau, as always, was on the forward guns. Sandusky was at the wheel, Thorson was watching the engines, and Medeiros stood ready to back up Kerry. A few weeks earlier, Kerry and his crew had engaged in a heart-to-heart talk about the war. Kerry was frustrated that the swift boats were supposed to just race along the river, draw enemy fire, and speed away with guns blazing. Who knew if they shot the enemy? They usually couldn't even see the guerrillas.

Kerry insisted it would make more sense to beach the boat and chase down the enemy. It was questionable whether this tactic was allowed under navy policy, but Kerry, who had initially chosen swift boat duty as a route away from combat action, now wanted to storm right into battle.

Kerry complained "that we go up the rivers and try to shoot and suppress fire but we never know whether we are accomplishing anything," Medeiros recalled. "He said, 'If the opportunity presents itself and we can accomplish something, 'I'd like to go in and go after these people.' It was simply a frustration of always being shot at, always being sitting ducks. You are a big noisy target on a confined route, a river or a canal. They always know you are coming, they almost always get the first shot."

So Kerry proposed to his crew that they be prepared to beach the boat and, if necessary, run after the enemy. None of the sailors had been trained for this kind of mission; ground warfare was army work. The crew was attired in deck wear and didn't even own appropriate boots for walking through the jungle mud. "He asked the crew, and said, 'This is what I would like to do,'" Medeiros said. "And we said, 'We will do it.'"

On this night, Kerry was in tactical command of the mission, so he gave orders not just to his own craft but to all three, and the trio of skippers had agreed in advance to the beach-the-boat scenario. Just minutes after Kerry's boat set out along the Dong Cung Canal, he received word that Rood's swift boat was being ambushed.

The machine guns on the No. 23 boat were thundering in response to the attack as skipper Rood beached the boat. Reese, who believes in retrospect that this was the boat he was on, went ashore with other U.S. and South Vietnamese forces and promptly engaged in a firefight with Vietcong. As Rood later wrote in a naval report, the U.S.-led forces routed "more than 20 VC from their spider holes and entrenched positions, fleeing across open fields and heavy mangroves. Accurate ... gunfire cut down 3 VC and the chase which ensued netted Vietnamese militiamen, 6 VC dead and 6 weapons captured."

Kerry's craft, meanwhile, was just behind, and gunfire was erupting from Vietcong forces along the shoreline. Kerry's boat came under a B-40 rocket attack, which barely missed but suggested another rocket would be incoming within seconds. Rather than ordering his crew to hit the enemy and run, which was standard navy operating procedure, Kerry decided to chase down the Vietcong who were firing at his crew.

"Beach the boat!" he ordered, and Del Sandusky drove the craft right onto the shoreline. On the beach just a few feet away, a teenager in a loincloth popped out of a narrow spider hole, clutching a grenade launcher, a weapon capable of sinking the swift boat. He looked surprised that the navy swift boat had plowed into the riverbank instead of speeding away after coming under fire. Kerry's forward gunner, Tommy Belodeau, shot and clipped the young Vietcong fighter in the leg. Then Belodeau's gun jammed, according to other crewmates (Belodeau died in 1997). Medeiros tried to fire, but he couldn't get a shot off.

Fred Short—blocked by the tub's safety guardrail—realized that he could not maneuver his machine guns low enough take aim at the enemy. For a terrifying moment, Short recalled, the guerrilla looked straight at him with the rocket in his hands. Short believes the young man didn't fire because he was too close to avoid ricochet debris. Despite his leg wound, the Vietcong teen got up off the ground and started running. Kerry jumped off his boat and chased him. He recalled thinking, "We've got to get him, make sure he doesn't get behind the hut, and then we're in trouble."

Kerry, faced with the prospect that a deadly rocket grenade could come whizzing toward his crew, had made a split-second decision to leave his crew and pursue the Vietcong fighter. "This guy could have dispatched us in a second, but for … I'll never be able to explain, we were literally face to face, he with his B-40 rocket and us in our boat, and he didn't pull the trigger. I would not be here today talking to you if he had," Kerry said during an interview.

From the tub, Short tried to protect his skipper by firing with the twin .50-caliber guns. Around the boat, he said, "rounds were coming everywhere. We were getting fire from both sides of the river." As Short recalled, the guerrilla raced behind a hut.

Kerry followed and fired, killing the man. "I don't have a second's question about that, nor does anybody who was with me," Kerry recalled of his decision to shoot. "He was running away with a live B-40, and, I thought, poised to turn around and fire it." Asked whether that meant Kerry shot the guerrilla in the back, Kerry said, "No, absolutely not. He was hurt, other guys were shooting from back, side, back. There is not a scintilla of question in any person's mind who was there [that] this guy was dangerous. He was a combatant, he had an armed weapon."

The after-action report described Kerry's action this way: Kerry "chased VC inland behind hootch and shot him while he fled, capturing one B-40 rocket launcher with round in chamber."

The crewman with the best view of the action was Short, the man in the tub operating the twin guns, and he said there is "no doubt" Kerry did the right thing. "That was a him-or-us thing," said Short, whose first postwar conversation with Kerry was thirty-four years later, after a *Boston Globe* reporter contacted him. "That was a loaded weapon with a shape charge on it.... It could pierce a tank. I wouldn't have been here talking to you. I probably prayed more up that creek than a Southern Baptist church does in a month."

Charles Gibson, who served on Kerry's boat that day as part of a one-week indoctrination course, agreed that Kerry's action was dangerous but necessary. "Every day you wake up and say, 'How the hell did we get out of that alive?'" Gibson said. "Kerry was a good leader. He knew what he was doing."

The fighting had happened in a burst, and now it was over. Ten Vietcong had been killed and remnants of the Vietcong force had fled, according to after-action reports. U.S. forces and their South Vietnamese counterparts scoured the landscape and discovered an underground Vietcong encampment, complete with sewing machines to make uniforms.

When Kerry returned to his base, his commanding officer, George Elliott, raised a familiar issue with Kerry: the fine line between whether the action merited a medal or a court-martial. "When [Kerry] came back from the well-publicized action where he beached his boat in middle of ambush and chased a VC around a hootch and ended his life, when [Kerry] came back and I heard his debrief, I said, 'John, I don't know whether you should be court-martialed or given a medal, court-martialed for leaving your ship, your post,'" Elliott recalled in an interview. "But I ended up writing it up for a Silver Star, which is well deserved, and I have no regrets or second thoughts at all about that," Elliott said. A Silver Star commends distinctive gallantry in action.

Elliott said he raised the court-martial issue "half tongue-in-cheek, because there was never any question I wanted him to realize I didn't want him to leave his boat unattended. That was in context of big-ship Navy—my background—a C.O. [commanding officer] never leaves his ship in battle or anything else."

Kerry, Elliott added, was "pretty courageous to turn into an ambush" and stressed that he never questioned Kerry's decision to chase down and kill the Vietcong fighter. Indeed, the Silver Star citation makes clear that Kerry's performance on that day was both extraordinary and risky.

"With utter disregard for his own safety and the enemy rockets," the citation says, Kerry "again ordered a charge on the enemy, beached his boat only 10 feet from the Viet Cong rocket position and personally led a landing party ashore in pursuit of the enemy.... The extraordinary daring and personal courage of Lt. Kerry in attacking a numerically superior force in the face of intense fire were responsible for the highly successful mission."

Zumwalt, who had listened to Kerry's criticism just weeks earlier about the free-fire zone policy, now was thrilled with Kerry's action. "The devastating result ... in which PCF [Patrol Craft Fast] teamed with (regional forces) accounted for 10 KIA ... [is] considered outstanding," Zumwalt wrote in a memo that was widely distributed in the navy. Zumwalt decided to fly down to An Thoi to pin the Silver Star on Kerry's uniform himself.

*

James Rassmann, a twenty-one-year-old U.S. Army Special Forces lieutenant, had been in the best shape of his life when he left Ranger school, standing six feet tall and weighing 180 pounds. But months of duty in Vietnam had taken its toll. By the time he met Kerry, Rassmann weighed in at only 135 pounds. Only later would he realize that his weight loss would be a lifesaver.

During the rainy season, Rassmann rode on Everglades-style airboats over the marshes of Vietnam, taking Chinese mercenaries on patrol. But when the rains ended, Rassmann and his troops had free time on their hands, so he decided to head south and hook up with navy swift boat crews.

One day, he walked into a club and found Kerry sitting there, having a beer, and the two men quickly hit it off. For the next month, they hung out together and went on at least one mission together, during which Rassmann saw a fellow officer nearly lose his eye as a result of enemy fire.

At one point, Kerry and Rassmann threw grenades into a huge rice cache that had been captured from the Vietcong and was thus slated for destruction. After tossing the grenades, the two dove for cover. Rassmann escaped the ensuing explosion of rice, but Kerry was not as lucky— thousands of grains stuck to him. The result was hilarious, and the two men formed a bond.

On the morning of March 13, 1969, Rassmann was on a swift boat, following Kerry's craft, as they headed up the Bai Hap River. The horrors began early that day. A rocket attack killed a Chinese mercenary who was traveling with Rassmann. "He was literally blown to pieces," Rassmann recalled. "We bugged out of there with the remains under fire." But the action had only begun.

The flotilla of approximately five swift boats was cruising along a narrow canal, with Kerry's boat toward the front, when a mine detonated, throwing one of the crafts two feet into the air and knocking out its engine. In the swift boat behind it, Rassmann was eating a chocolate chip cookie in the pilothouse when his craft was also rocked by an explosion. Before he knew it, Rassmann was thrown into the water, a bobbing target as he dodged the bullets whizzing around him. He dove to the bottom of the canal and stayed under for as long as he could, but he was shot at each of the five times he returned to the surface.

Somehow, Rassmann avoided being hit, and someone yelled, "Man overboard!" As the swifts turned to rescue him, Rassmann swam toward Kerry's boat. He grabbed a netting at the boat's bow and tried to pull himself up. But he was too weak from being underwater for so long. Kerry, who had been hit in the arm and was bleeding, reached down with his good arm and pulled Rassmann to safety—a feat that might not have been possible if Rassmann had been at his normal weight.

Like others who went on missions with Kerry, Rassmann would later play a key role in Kerry's presidential campaign.

Kerry saved his life, Rassmann said, and "he deserved the Silver." As it turned out, Kerry received a Bronze, a lesser medal, but Zumwalt himself wrote a glowing citation: "Lt. Kerry's calmness, professionalism and great personal courage under fire were in keeping with the highest traditions of the US Naval Service."

Kerry's wound that day earned him his third Purple Heart and left him off-duty for a couple of days. (He had immediately returned to duty after the earlier two wounds.) It was not unusual for Purple Hearts to be granted for minor wounds. "There were an awful lot of Purple Hearts—from shrapnel, some of those might have been M-40 grenades," said Elliott, Kerry's commanding officer. "The Purple Hearts were coming down in boxes."

But Kerry thought he had seen enough. Navy policy, set forth in Bureau of Naval Personnel Instruction No. 1300.39, stated that any enlistee or officer who has been wounded three times "will not be ordered to service in Vietnam."

Under that directive, reassignment was requested for Kerry as "as a personal aide in Boston, New York, or Wash. D.C. area," according to a March 17, 1969, document filled out by Commodore Charles F. Horne, an administrative official in the coastal squadron in which Kerry served. Horne said the transfer was "above board and proper ... To get three Purple Hearts and not be killed is awesome."

Elliott, who was Kerry's commanding officer at the time, said Kerry could have stayed if he wanted to, and the naval policy permitted waivers for doing so. Cyril L. Kammeier, editor of *Purple Heart*, the official magazine of the Order of the Purple Heart, said that someone such as Kerry, an officer whose wounds did not require hospitalization, would not have been required to go home if he had wanted to stay.

Elliott's superior, Roy Hoffmann, said that he didn't know at the time why Kerry left. He remains upset that Kerry left more than six months ahead of schedule. "That just turned me off then and there, and as far as I was concerned, he bugged out," said Hoffmann, who was the commanding officer of the task force in which Kerry served. "He just simply bugged out, and any military man knows what I'm talking about."

Kerry's early departure meant that he was leaving behind a crew that had suffered through many bloody battles with him—but had survived. Worried that crew members would be killed in future missions, he arranged for them to receive safer assignments. When one crew member, Medeiros, tried to stay, Kerry "came and talked to me and said, 'I really would like you to go.... I'd like to know you are safe, or safer.'"

To his crew, Kerry was a success. "John performed well in getting us in and getting us all back out," said David Alston, who manned the twin .50-caliber machine guns. "We did not win the war in Vietnam, but John Kerry won his battle because he brought us all back."

While all of his crewmates survived their tour in Vietnam, at least five of Kerry's friends had died, including Yale classmate Richard Pershing and St. Paul's classmate Peter W. Johnson. Then, just days after Kerry left, another friend, Donald Droz—the fellow skipper who had provided support for Kerry on the day he won the Silver Star—died in a fiery ambush. Years later, the infant daughter that Droz left behind, Tracy Tragos, would make a documentary about the father she never knew, borrowing the title from the way Droz signed letters to his wife: "Be Good, Smile Pretty." Tracy would become one of 20,000 American children left without a father because of the war.

The mounting losses made no sense to Kerry. In Europe during World II, Americans had been liberators, as his grandparents in France could testify. But in Vietnam, many viewed the American force as an unwelcome foreign occupier. Kerry was unsettled by both his own role and the overall U.S. strategy. Too many friends, and too many innocent people, were getting maimed or killed.

"I thought it was time to tell the story of what was happening over there," he recalled. "I was angry about what happened over there. I had clearly concluded how wrong it was."

Chapter 7

WAR PROTESTER

APRIL 28, 1971, 4:33 P.M. President Richard M. Nixon took a call from his counsel, Charles W. Colson.

"This fellow Kerry that they had on last week," Colson told the president, referring to a television appearance by John F. Kerry, a leader of Vietnam Veterans Against the War (VVAW).

"Yeah," Nixon responded.

"He turns out to be really quite a phony," said Colson.

"Well, he is sort of a phony, isn't he?" said Nixon.

Yes, Colson said, alleging that Kerry had stayed at the home of a Georgetown socialite while other protesters camped on the Washington Mall.

"He was in Vietnam a total of four months," Colson scoffed, without mentioning that Kerry earned three Purple Hearts, a Silver Star, and a Bronze Star, and had also been on an earlier tour. "He's politically ambitious and just looking for an issue."

"Yeah."

"He came back a hawk and became a dove when he saw the political opportunities," said Colson.

"Sure," Nixon responded. "Well, anyway, keep the faith."

The tone was sneering. But the secretly recorded dialogue revealed just how seriously the Nixon White House viewed Kerry. Day after day, according to the tapes and memos, Nixon aides worried that Kerry was a unique, charismatic leader who could undermine public support for the war.

Other veteran protesters were choice targets, with their long hair, their displays of the Vietcong flag, and in some cases, their calls for overthrowing the U.S. government. Kerry, by contrast, was a neat, well-spoken, highly decorated veteran who seemed to be a clone of former President John F. Kennedy, right down to the military service on a patrol boat.

The White House feared him like no other protester.

The effort by Nixon and his aides to undermine Kerry went much deeper than even Kerry realized. Yet it is this chapter in his life, as much as any other, that helped turn the young combat veteran into a national political figure.

Kerry returned from Vietnam in late March 1969 and took on a cushy assignment as an aide to Admiral Walter F. Schlech Jr. in Brooklyn. The decorated veteran was confused, angry, and uncertain about his future. He had thought about running for public office long before the war.

But when he returned, he wasn't greeted as a hero, like the soldiers of John F. Kennedy's generation.

"I just came back really concerned about [the war] and upset about it and angry about it," Kerry said. "It took me a little while to decompress. I saw someone who said, 'What happened to you? Your eyes are sunk way back in your head.' The tension and the trauma in your life took its toll."

At the time, the country's troop strength in Vietnam was at its height—543,000, with 33,400 Americans dead. Protests were surging, but Kerry, still a naval officer, stayed on the sidelines—until his sister helped introduce him to the antiwar movement.

Peggy Kerry was working in the New York office of a Vietnam War protest group that was planning a multicity "moratorium" peace rally. One day in October 1969, one of the group's leaders, Adam Walinsky, a former speechwriter for Robert F. Kennedy, said he needed a pilot and plane so that he could deliver antiwar speeches around the state. Did anyone know a pilot?

Peggy Kerry volunteered her brother, and on October 15, Kerry was drafted into service, flying Walinsky around New York in a small private plane. He did not wear his uniform or speak at any events, but the experience drew him toward a desire to help lead the antiwar movement.

"He was still in the navy, still an aide to that admiral," Walinsky recalled. "I was sort of taken aback, a little surprised and impressed that he was doing this and I probably thought to myself, 'Wow, we must really be making more inroads and be more correct than we knew if this guy, who was a serious navy guy, cares enough to fly me around the state.'"

At the time, a sprinkling of Vietnam vets, and their families, were beginning to join the burgeoning antiwar protests. The star attraction at a Washington rally that November, which drew a crowd of 250,000, was Judy Droz, widow of Don Droz, who had skippered the swift boat that provided cover for Kerry on his Silver Star day. Droz had been killed in an attack two weeks after Kerry left Vietnam. Cradling their ten-month-old daughter in her arms, twenty-three-year-old Judy Droz led a procession in which she placed a placard bearing her husband's name on a coffin. "Too many families are suffering what I am suffering and too many children will have to suffer what my daughter will suffer," she told the crowd.

On January 3, 1970, Kerry formally asked Schlech to grant him an early discharge so that he could run for Congress on an antiwar platform. "I just said to the admiral: 'I've got to get out. I've got to go do what I came back here to do, which is, end this thing,'" Kerry recalled, referring to the war. The request was approved, and Kerry was honorably discharged, which he said shaved six months from his commitment.

For years, Kerry had dreamed of running for Congress. He had talked about it with his family and friends, some of whom debated whether it was better to run as a war hero or a hero-turned-opponent. Now he eyed a congressional race in Massachusetts.

In retrospect, Kerry's first run at office was doomed from the start. He had only lived in Massachusetts until he was seven years old, in addition to one year at Fessenden School in Newton and some summers at the house of a relative. Kerry was drawn to the race for representative from the Third Congressional District in part because he wanted to replace incumbent Philip J. Philbin of Clinton, a conservative seventy-one-year-old Democrat who was hawkish on Vietnam. At the time, Kerry held hard-left political views. He told the *Harvard Crimson* he wanted to "almost eliminate CIA activity" and wanted U.S. troops "dispersed through the world only at the directive of the United Nations." But a formidable candidate, the Reverend Robert F. Drinan, was already heavily favored by antiwar Democrats there. As a former law school dean and provost at Boston College, Drinan was well liked and respected in the district. Kerry was just getting to know the community.

On February 22, 1970, in the auditorium of Concord-Carlisle High School, seventeen miles outside of Boston, a "citizen's caucus" of 2,000—852 of whom were eligible to vote—met to endorse an antiwar Democrat to oppose Philbin in the primary. Kerry, fresh from his navy duties, "stunned the delegates with the power of his message and delivery," Jerome Grossman, Drinan's campaign chair recalled in his memoir. "Unlike Drinan, Kerry was tall, handsome, young, and smooth."

As the balloting proceeded, Kerry picked up support from other candidates as they were eliminated, Grossman recalled. "The speeches and balloting went from 9:00 o'clock in the morning until 6:30 at night," he wrote. "I could see some of my Drinan voters preparing to leave before the fourth ballot, and in my best Mayor Daley style I locked the doors to the high school and prevented anyone from leaving."

The tactic worked. Kerry withdrew before the fourth ballot and endorsed Drinan, preventing a potential caucus deadlock—and receiving a standing ovation. "I walked over to him, and I said 'I'll never forget what you have done,'" Grossman recalled, and he held to his word: He and many others involved in that caucus would help Kerry for years to come.

Three months later, in May 1970, Kerry married his girl-friend of six years, Julia Thorne, the sister of his best friend, David Thorne. Kerry, whose upper-class image was already well established due to his Forbes and Winthrop roots, starred in a glittering wedding.

The *New York Times* described it this way: "Miss Julia Stimson Thorne, whose ancestors helped to shape the American republic in its early days, and John Forbes Kerry, who wants to help steer it back from what he considers a wayward course, were married this afternoon at the 200-acre Thorne family estate" on Long Island.

The article noted that Miss Thorne's cream-colored dress had been worn by her ancestor Catherine Peartree-Smith, who married Elias Boudinot IV, who served as president of the Continental Congress under the Articles of Confederation. "Alexander Hamilton was best man at that wedding and among those present was George Washington," the story noted.

"Whether today's wedding becomes a similar footnote

to history may depend on the bridegroom, a graduate of Yale and a veteran of the Vietnam War, who is considering running for Congress from his native Massachusetts." (The article left unsaid that Kerry had just failed in that bid.) For his honeymoon, Kerry chose a telling location: the Pershing family's Jamaica home, where Dick Pershing had spent many happy days before being killed in a Vietnamese rice paddy. Julia was already transforming from a socialite into a social activist, and she supported Kerry's decision to become more active in the antiwar movement. Kerry had written what he called a "Letter to America" about what he saw in Vietnam, and he "shopped it" to various magazines, but it was never published.

During Labor Day weekend 1970, Kerry gave what was his first widely noticed antiwar speech outside Massachusetts, joining other members of a fledgling group called Vietnam Veterans Against the War at a rally at Valley Forge, Pennsylvania. One of the first to speak at Valley Forge that day was Jane Fonda, the actress and antiwar activist who at that time was raising money for a VVAW investigation into atrocities in Vietnam. One of the last to speak was Kerry, who foreshadowed his later Senate testimony when he said, "[I]t is not patriotism to ask Americans to die for a mistake."

Kerry's words deeply impressed Fonda. "I remember thinking, 'Wow, this is a real leader, a Lincolnesque kind of leader,'" Fonda recalled in a 2004 interview. She also liked his literary style of speaking and thought he was a moderating influence compared to some veterans who came across as radicals. But she doesn't recall talking with him or even shaking his hand at the time. Indeed, she said she didn't talk with him until he became a senator years later. But she would play an important role in his life, in any event.

Fonda had been speaking around the country, collecting $2,000 each for twenty-four speeches, and she gave all of the money to the VVAW for an investigation into U.S. war atrocities called the Winter Soldier hearings, which were held in Detroit for three days in January 1971. Kerry and Fonda were both there, but Fonda said she didn't recall seeing or talking to Kerry. Kerry, for his part, did not make a public statement but instead listened to the gruesome testimony of about 150 veterans.

Some of the most graphic testimony came from Sergeant Scott Camil, who described a horrific series of beheadings and other atrocities. "Two people had their heads cut off and put on stakes and stuck in the middle of the field," Camil testified.

"The way that we distinguished between civilians and VC, VC had weapons and civilians didn't and anybody that was dead was considered a VC," Camil asserted. "When we went through the villages and searched people, the women would have all their clothes taken off and the men would use their penises to probe them to make sure they didn't have anything hidden anywhere and this was raping but it was done as searching."

The event was quickly made into a film, *The Winter Soldier*, which briefly shows Kerry talking with some veterans before they described the alleged atrocities in grisly detail. Some critics would later question the veracity of some of the veterans and their statements, and the debate over the extent of atrocities continued for years afterward. Fonda said all of the veterans' credentials were verified. In any case, historian Stanley Karnow, author of *Vietnam: A History*, said that in retrospect, "atrocities were committed by both sides. This was a war."

Kerry not only believed his fellow veterans, but he based much of his subsequent Senate testimony on their statements.

"It really rocked him," Fonda said of the impact of the testimony on Kerry. But she said that there was "a tremendous amount of sadness" that the hearings did not receive more media coverage, and it was Kerry who suggested that the effort essentially be moved to Washington and brought before Congress. "That was when John sort of took over the leadership, in the sense that, 'what we have to do now is in Washington, do this in Congress.' We all knew the guy was a moderate, that he wanted everybody to clean up their act, he had friends in Congress, so this was the sort of what the VVAW needed."

"I was upset. These were very heartfelt stories," Kerry recalled. "I thought there was a legitimacy" to the testimony. So Kerry privately suggested to the organization's leaders that he organize a march on Washington. "That is when we basically decided to go to Washington because I felt Detroit wasn't the right venue ... [M]y sense was that [the issue] wasn't going to be heard unless we went to a place where the issue was joined. It was my idea to come to Washington; it was my idea to do the march."

While some members of the antiwar group viewed Kerry as an opportunist, others realized Kerry—erudite and clean-cut—was the ideal foil for those who viewed the group as hippie traitors or even Communists.

Still, when Kerry arrived in Washington the week of April 18, 1971, he was mostly an unknown. Indeed, the new issue of *Life* magazine featured a cover picture of Jane Fonda, with the title: "Busy Rebel, Jane Fonda, Pusher of Causes." This was before Fonda infamously visited Hanoi, and Fonda at the time was best known for her traveling road shows, in which she attacked U.S. policy in Vietnam. When she was denied entry to speak before troops at Fort Bragg, North Carolina, she went to "a local GI coffeehouse," as *Life* put it, and thereafter her shows played before "packed houses of cheering troops."

Nowhere in the *Life* story about the antiwar movement was Kerry's name mentioned. But he was about to become the face of the organization and a media sensation, eclipsing Fonda in the limelight at least for a while. One of his first tasks was to raise money to pay for buses to transport the veterans. He called his friend Walinsky, who had run unsuccessfully for New York attorney general and had excellent financial connections. Walinsky arranged a meeting of potential donors at the Seagram Building in New York City that included chief executive Edgar M. Bronfman Sr. and about twenty other New York businessmen who opposed the war. Kerry delivered a low-key speech about the importance of having veterans attend the protest. Then the businessmen were each asked to stand and declare how much they would contribute.

"We raised probably $50,000," Walinsky recalled. "It took an hour."

Not only did Kerry help raise the money, but he also learned a lesson about fund-raising that would serve him well as a politician for years to come: Call somebody influential who knows a lot of other influential people, get them together, and tell them their contributions could change America.

As Kerry prepared to come to Washington, one story in particular fueled the antiwar movement. On March 29, 1971, a jury convicted Lieutenant William Calley of killing twenty-two civilians in what became known as the My Lai massacre. Nixon had ordered Calley released pending his appeal. The news coverage of the case raised questions about how many more My Lais had been committed.

On April 18, 1971, in his biggest national media interview to date, Kerry appeared on NBC's *Meet the Press* to discuss the scope of American atrocities in Vietnam. Behind the scenes, the White House was trying to steer the questioning. A Colson memo noted that "[a] number of tough questions have ... been planted with the Vietnam Veterans Against the War questioners for 'Meet the Press.'"

On the show, Kerry was asked whether he had committed atrocities. In a thick Kennedy-like accent, Kerry bluntly admitted that he had—a statement that he would be asked about for years to come.

There are all kinds of atrocities, and I would have to say that, yes, yes, I committed the same kind of atrocities as thousands of other soldiers have committed in that I took part in shootings in free-fire zones. I conducted harassment and interdiction fire. I used .50 caliber machine guns, which we were granted and ordered to use, which were our only weapon against people.

I took part in search and destroy missions, in the burning of villages ... And I believe that the men who designed these, the men who designed the free-fire zone, the men who ordered us, the men who signed off on the air raid strike areas, I think these men, by the letter of the law, the same letter of the law that tried Lieutenant Calley, are war criminals.

Kerry's media star began to shine. A few days later, the *New York Times* ran a profile titled "Angry War Veteran: John Forbes Kerry." Kerry was quoted as saying he was "still a moderate. I'm not a radical in any sense of the word. I guess I'm just an angry young man."

Indeed, it was Kerry's appeal as a sober sailor, instead of being one of the "bearded weirdos" that Nixon privately disdained, that most concerned the White House. When Nixon officials learned that another veteran who had appeared on *Meet the Press* with Kerry misled viewers about his rank and experience, they tried to ascertain whether Kerry was also exaggerating his role in Vietnam.

One day after Kerry's TV appearance, Colson fired off a memo expressing exasperation that more wasn't being done to undermine Kerry and the other VVAW organizers. He ordered administration officials to show that Vietnam Veterans Against the War was "a fringe group, that it is financed from questionable sources, that it doesn't represent a veterans movement, and that the guys involved are a pretty shoddy bunch.... There just must be more that we can be doing."

The Nixon White House tried to prevent the veterans from camping on the Washington Mall. But the move back-fired when it brought the protesters the kind of media attention they could only dream about back in Detroit. Despite the White House efforts, the protesters were granted permits, and they set up their tents and banners. Senator Edward Kennedy of Massachusetts came down to meet with Kerry, drawing even more attention to the effort.

Although Kerry had worked briefly in Kennedy's 1962 campaign, this was the first extended meeting between the two. "I remember that very clearly, walking up to the tents, him taking me around, meeting some of the troops," Kennedy said. "I remember sitting down talking to them, that night there for ... a period of an hour or so."

With Kennedy in Kerry's corner, a meeting was arranged between eight VVAW leaders and some senators sympa-thetic to their cause. Kerry and Camil, who had delivered the grisly testimony in Detroit, and six other veterans met the senators at a fund-raiser at the home of Senator Philip A. Hart, a Michigan Democrat who was familiar with the Winter Soldier hearings and sympathetic to the cause. One of the guests that evening was Senator William Fulbright, the chairman of the Senate Foreign Relations Committee.

Camil remembered the event as a strange amalgam of scraggly veterans and polished politicians, with well-dressed waiters serving the famished protesters "little squares of bread." Kerry wore finely pressed clothes, looked clean, and had a patrician manner, Camil recalled, remembering that he and the other veterans wore rumpled gear and hadn't bathed for days while sleeping on the Mall.

The difference was obvious to the senators, too. When Camil harangued Fulbright about his support for the 1964 Gulf of Tonkin resolution, the official launch of the Vietnam War, the senator walked away. And when the senators discussed who should testify before the Senate Foreign Relations Committee, they readily settled on the more polished figure of Kerry. Kerry, who was there with his friend George Butler, then went to the Georgetown apartment of Butler's mother-in-law and stayed up all night writing the speech that would transform his life.

The hearing room of the Senate Foreign Relations Committee was jammed on April 22, 1971, as twenty-seven-year-old Kerry—dressed in green fatigues and wearing his Silver Star and Purple Heart ribbons—approached the witness table. Television cameras lined the walls, and veterans packed the seats. With a thatch of dark hair swept across his brow, Kerry sat at the witness table and delivered the most famous speech of his life.

"How do you ask a man to be the last man to die in Vietnam? How do you ask a man to be the last man to die for a mistake?" The Nixon administration, he said, "has done us the ultimate dishonor. They have attempted to disown us and the sacrifices we made for this country ... Someone has to die so President Nixon won't be, and these are his words, 'the first president to lose a war.'"

Where, Kerry wondered, were the architects of the war

such as Robert McNamara and—as he put it without providing a first name—"Bundy." Kerry had roomed at Yale with Harvey Bundy, whose uncles, William and McGeorge Bundy, were architects of the Vietnam conflict. It was William Bundy who had come to Yale when he was an assistant secretary of state and helped convince Kerry to become a naval officer.

Then Kerry looked up at the senators and asked: "Where are they now that we, the men whom they sent off to war, have returned? These are the commanders who deserted their troops, and there is no more serious crime in the law of war." (Kerry later said his speech reference to "Bundy" was aimed at McGeorge, who had been national security adviser to Kennedy and Johnson.)

For many observers, the most shocking part of Kerry's speech was a summation of what he had heard at the Winter Soldier hearings. He alleged that Vietnam veterans had "personally raped, cut off ears, cut off heads, taped wires from portable telephones to human genitals and turned up the power, cut off limbs, blown up bodies, randomly shot at civilians, razed villages in a fashion reminiscent of Genghis Khan, shot cattle and dogs for fun, poisoned food stocks, and generally ravaged the countryside of South Vietnam in addition to the normal ravage of war, and the normal and very particular ravaging which is done by the applied bombing power of this country."

To some veterans, including some of those who served alongside Kerry, this was too much. They thought they had served honorably, and they had seen Kerry as a gung-ho skipper who led and didn't voice such opposition on the battlefield. Kerry hadn't branded everyone a criminal, but he did tell the Senate about "the torture of prisoners, the killing of prisoners, all accepted policy by many units in South Vietnam." Such words were so strong and sweeping that they embitter some veterans to this day.

"I would go up a river with that man anytime. He was a great American fighting man," said Michael Bernique, a highly decorated veteran who served as a swift boat skipper alongside Kerry. But Bernique has objected to Kerry's assertion that atrocities were committed. "I think there was a point in time when John was making it up fast and quick. I think he was saying whatever he needed to say."

Edward Peck, whose boat was taken over by Kerry, said, "I thought it was sick. He looked ridiculous."

Many of Kerry's former crewmates were stunned, only coming to understand Kerry's position years later. "I felt betrayed," James Wasser said. Mike Medeiros remembered picking up a book about Kerry's antiwar activities and being stunned. "I was still kind of hawkish. I saw (Kerry's) picture in there ... and I thought, 'This is bad. That's not right.' But knowing what I know now, I would have totally agreed with him."

President Nixon watched television reports about Kerry with a mixture of anger and admiration. The "real star" of the hearing was Kerry, Nixon told chief of staff H. R. "Bob" Haldeman and national security adviser Henry Kissinger the day after Kerry testified, according to the secretly taped White House recordings.

"He did a hell of a great job," Haldeman said.

"He was extremely effective," Nixon agreed.

"He did a superb job on it at Foreign Relations Committee yesterday," Haldeman said. "A Kennedy-type guy, he looks like a Kennedy, and he, he talks exactly like a Kennedy."

"Where did he serve?" Nixon asked.

"He was a Navy lieutenant, j.g., on a gunboat, and he used to run his gunboat up and shoot at, shoot babies out of women's arms," Haldeman said. (A member of Kerry's crew had shot and killed a Vietnamese child in an episode that occurred in a "free-fire zone," according to Kerry, but it is not clear whether Haldeman knew about the matter or was trying to be jocular.)

"Oh, stop that," Nixon said. "People in the Navy don't do things [like that.]" With apparent sarcasm, Nixon turned to Kissinger, who assured him a naval officer would not shoot babies out of women's arms.

Nixon seemed particularly incredulous that Kerry had won so many medals. "Bob, the Navy didn't have any casualties in Vietnam except in the air," Nixon told Haldeman, apparently basing his knowledge of what had happened before the swift boats began patrolling the inland waterways.

Three days later, Haldeman arrived in the Oval Office and announced to the president: "We've got some interesting dope on Kerry."

Nixon was interested.

"Kerry, it turns out, some time ago wanted to get into politics," Haldeman said. "Well, he ran for, took a stab at the congressional thing. And he consulted with some of the folks in the Georgetown set here." Haldeman told the president that Kerry wanted to "get an issue ... a horse to ride," and then the tape abruptly ends.

Overnight, Kerry had emerged as one of the most recognized veterans in America. And he clearly understood the emphasis the media placed on imagery. So he put an exclamation mark on events by lining up with veterans to "return" their medals to the military on April 23. Kerry said he suggested that veterans place their medals and ribbons on a table and return them. But he said other members of the antiwar veterans group wanted to throw the medals and ribbons over a fence in front of the Capitol, and Kerry went along with the idea. Just days earlier, Kerry had been quoted in the *Washington Post* as expressing distaste over "medals for nothing."

Video footage of the scene shows hundreds of veterans angrily gathering in front of the Capitol, near a fenced-in bin that had a large sign saying "Trash."

One by one, the veterans, many of whom had long hair and wore combat jackets, threw their medals into the makeshift trash bin. Kerry threw medals and ribbons over the fence, declaring, "I'm not doing this for any violent reasons, but for peace and justice, and to try to make this country wake up once and for all." Initially, the impression was left that Kerry tossed his own medals, but Kerry said years later he threw only his ribbons, along with the medals of two other veterans.

Thomas Oliphant, who was reporting on the event that day for the *Boston Globe*, recalled that Kerry reached over the fence to place his own service ribbons as well as medals he had received from other veterans. "I never had any confusion about what he did," said Oliphant, now a *Boston Globe* columnist, "that he had kept his Silver Star, Purple Hearts and Bronze Star."

Kerry, asked in 2003 to clarify his actions, explained that he had met two veterans, one from the Vietnam War and another from World War II, who had asked him to return their medals. Kerry said he stuffed them into his jacket. As he prepared to throw his ribbons over the fence, he reached into his jacket and pulled out the medals from those two veterans. He said his own medals remained in safekeeping.

The week's events had an unquestionable impact. At the beginning of the week, a band of 800 or so Vietnam veterans gathered to protest the war, followed by Kerry's April 22 testimony, then the medal-tossing ceremony on April 23. By the following day, the publicity helped swell the crowd at a previously planned rally on the Mall to at least 250,000 people.

Kerry, wearing a blue button-down shirt under his combat jacket, addressed the rally from the Capitol steps. "We came here to undertake one last mission, to search out and destroy the last vestige of this barbaric war," Kerry told the cheering throng.

In one week, Kerry had gone from little-known former swift boat skipper to becoming the face of the protest movement. "The transformation was instant," said Kerry's friend George Butler, who sat behind Kerry during the Senate testimony. "Eight hundred people had turned into 250,000," said Kerry's then brother-in-law, David Thorne, who stood beside Kerry during the rally. "That is what made it so spectacular." (Later that year, this trio of lifelong friends—Kerry, Butler, and Thorne—would produce a book about the protesters titled *The New Soldier*, which featured veterans holding an American flag upside, the signal of distress—and an image that would cause political problems for Kerry.)

Inside the White House, Nixon was furious, and so was his secretary, Rose Mary Woods.

"Don't dare go around these people because I just want to hit at 'em," Woods told the president. "Umph!"

Responded Nixon: "These clever left-wingers who're, uh, the Communists, and basically a lot of this is Communist."

It was all the fault of those liberal senators like Teddy Kennedy, Nixon and Woods agreed. They were going to try to lose the war.

"Well, well, we're not gonna lose it," Nixon said. "I, that's the other thing. Ya see, these people want to get it over and let it go Communist. They really do."

WOODS: "They don't care what happens, and they, and then if, if, if everything goes Communist, and then if, eventually it's gonna react and ruin this country ... [Of] course they're tired of the war. Everyone's tired of war. No one could be more tired of it than you. No one!"

Then they focused on the problem of John Kerry.

NIXON: "[Of] course the real, one of the real problems, this goddamn press is so [unintelligible] unfair. They, they don't give our Republicans who are out tryin' to answer these people, and they put 'em on. Apparently the guy that's really good, the only good one of the damn veterans group, only good from a PR standpoint, is Kerry ... [the] news [is] all Kerry."

Four days later, Nixon and Woods met again, even more disgusted at the tens of thousands of protesters who had gathered on the Mall.

WOODS: "I think people are getting sick to death seeing nothing on their television but those bums."

NIXON: "Really? ... they ran, you know, that, that fellow Leary or—"

WOODS: "Kerry ... "

NIXON: "Kerry so much. He was very, very good, they say."

Then Nixon shared some gossip: Kerry hadn't even slept on the Mall, the president said. "He wasn't livin' down there with those guys."

WOODS: "No."

NIXON: "He's livin' out in a posh pad in Georgetown. That's where he was."

WOODS: "Oh, so, they ... yeah."

NIXON: "They're all a funny bunch, but, uh, well, I tell you, we're gonna stand firm against 'em. I got Henry [Kissinger] in here ... I said, 'Now look, just, they're not gonna rattle us one bit. We're gonna stay on our course. This country's not gonna be run by a bunch of goddamned rabble.' Don't you agree?"

WOODS: "I certainly do."

*

But Kerry's fame was only increasing.

A few weeks later, Kerry was featured in a lengthy segment on the CBS television program *60 Minutes*. Correspondent Morley Safer, in a segment titled "First Hurrah," portrayed Kerry as an eloquent man of turmoil with a Kennedyesque future ahead of him. The interview was taped in a cabin on the shores of New Hampshire's Squam Lake, where Kerry was visiting his friend George Butler.

"Do you want to be president of the United States?" Safer asked Kerry.

"No," Kerry replied. "That's such a crazy question when there are so many things to be done and I don't know whether I could do them."

But Kerry's image as a self-promoter soon became the subject of parody, none more on-target than a Doonesbury comic strip penned by fellow Yale alumnus Garry Trudeau. A character in the strip is heard urging that they all attend John Kerry's speech. "He speaks with a rare eloquence and astonishing conviction. If you see no one else this year, you must see John Kerry!" Two panels later, it turns out that the man advertising Kerry is Kerry himself. Another strip shows Kerry soaking up the adulation after a speech, smiling and thinking, "You're really clicking tonight, you gorgeous preppie."

At the White House, the plotting against Kerry continued.

"The concern about Kerry was that he had great credibility as a decorated Vietnam veteran," Colson recalled. So Colson and his staff tried repeatedly to dig up dirt on Kerry. The effort failed.

"I don't ever remember finding anything negative about Kerry or hearing anything negative about him," Colson said in a 2003 interview. "If we had found anything, I'm sure we would have used it to discredit him."

Vice President Spiro T. Agnew briefly led the White House charge against Kerry. Appearing in the Bahamas, Agnew echoed Oval Office gossip, saying that Kerry, "who drew rave notices in the media for his eloquent testimony before Congress, was later revealed to have been using material ghosted for him by a former Kennedy speechwriter, and to have spent most of his nights in posh surroundings in Georgetown rather than on the Mall with his buddies."

Both charges were contested. Walinsky, the former Kennedy speechwriter to whom Agnew referred, said, "While I might have suggested a touch here or there [in Kerry's senate testimony], the great bulk of that wasn't anything I wrote, it was his." As for sleeping on the Mall, Oliphant, the *Boston Globe* reporter on the scene, recalled seeing Kerry at 3 A.M. on two evenings on the Mall and seeing Kerry pulling the all-nighter finishing his speech at a Georgetown townhouse. That may explain where the sleeping-in-Georgetown rumors began.

Kerry began traveling around the country to carry the antiwar flag. During Memorial Day weekend, he joined a throng of antiwar protesters on the green in Lexington, Massachusetts, where he and hundreds of others were arrested. Kerry said the arrest, for which he paid a $5 fine and spent the night at the Lexington Public Works Garage, is the only arrest of his life. At the time, Kerry's wife, Julia, kept $100 under her pillow just in case she needed to bail out her husband on short notice.

The White House decided to find a better way to go after Kerry. Colson had seen a press conference featuring a young navy veteran named John O'Neill, who served in the same swift boat division as Kerry shortly after Kerry left Vietnam. O'Neill, like many swift boat veterans, was outraged at Kerry's claim of U.S. atrocities.

In short order, O'Neill became the centerpiece of the Nixon White House plot to undermine Kerry. O'Neill, later a trial lawyer in Texas, stressed that he did not receive any payment from the White House and was acting on his own because he thought Kerry's statements were unconscionable lies.

"I thought it would have been fair play to say the war was unwinnable, but the argument that there were large scale war crimes was a false charge," O'Neill said.

For weeks, Colson had been accusing Kerry of ducking a debate with O'Neill. On June 15, Colson, who grew up in Winthrop, Massachusetts, wrote to another White House aide: "I think we have Kerry on the run, he is beginning to take a tremendous beating in the press, but let's not let him up, let's destroy this young demagogue before he becomes another Ralph Nader. Let's try to move through as many sources as we can the fact that he has refused to meet in debate, even though he agreed to do so and announced to the press he would."

Nixon's aides wanted to buck up the young O'Neill for

what they believed would be a drawn-out fight with Kerry. So, in the ultimate gesture of White House power, O'Neill was invited for a personal meeting with Nixon. The two men bonded, and what was supposed to be a brief "grip and grin" session turned into an hour-long meeting.

Two weeks later, on June 30, the much anticipated debate took place. Kerry, who had been studying debate since he was about fourteen years old, appeared with O'Neill on *The Dick Cavett Show*. At six feet, four inches, Kerry towered over Cavett and O'Neill. With his thick dark hair, dark blue suit, and lean features, he cut a striking figure.

O'Neill came out swinging. Visibly angry from the start, wearing a light suit, short hair, and white socks, O'Neill used words seemingly intended to taunt his opponent.

> Mr. Kerry is the type of person who lives and survives only on war-weariness and fears of the American people. This is the same little man who on nationwide television in April spoke of, quote, "crimes committed on a day-to-day basis, with the full awareness of officers at all levels of command." Who was quoted in a prominent news magazine in May as saying, "War crimes in Vietnam are the rule, not the exception."

Where O'Neill was red-hot, Kerry sought to look calm and intellectual, toting a hefty briefing book. He said the veterans weren't trying to tear down the country but instead wanted to say to the country: "Here is where we went wrong, and we've got to change. What we say is, the killing can stop tomorrow."

On the question of war crimes, it is really only with the utmost consideration that we pose this question. I don't think that any man comes back to say that he raped, or to say that he burned a village, or to say that he wantonly destroyed crops or something for pleasure. I think he does it at the risk of certain kinds of punishment, at the risk of injuring his own character, which he has to live with, at the risk of the loss of family and friends as a result of it. But he does it because he believes intensely that people have got to be educated about the devastation of this war. We thought we were a moral country, yes, but we are now engaged in the most rampant bombing in the history of mankind.

Again and again, the question was asked: Did Kerry commit atrocities or see them committed by others? Kerry stuck to his script.

I personally didn't see personal atrocities in the sense I saw somebody cut a head off or something like that. However, I did take part in free-fire zones, I did take part in harassment and interdiction fire, I did take part in search-and-destroy missions in which the houses of noncombatants were burned to the ground. And all of these acts, I find out later on, are contrary to the Hague and Geneva conventions and to the laws of warfare. So in that sense, anybody who took part in those, if you carry out the application of the Nuremburg Principles, is in fact guilty. But we are not trying to find war criminals. That is not our purpose. It never has been.

The White House was thrilled. "Your boy, O'Neill, debated Kerry last night," Haldeman said afterward, according to the Oval Office transcripts. "I hear he did very well."

O'Neill became disillusioned with politics and government after the fall of Saigon in 1975. But he still harbors resentment at the way Kerry accused veterans of atrocities. "The primary reason I got involved was I thought the charges of war crimes were irresponsible and wrong," said O'Neill. "I thought they did a real disservice to all the people that were there. I thought they were immoral."

Asked whether he agrees with the view of some observers that Kerry was forever altered by the war, O'Neill responded: "The war didn't change [Kerry]. I think he was a guy driven tremendously by ambition. I think he was that way before he went and is that way today."

As quickly as Kerry's star had risen, it began to fade. When Kerry appeared with the family of some prisoners of war, they were heckled by four women whose husbands also were POWs. "You're stupid, Kerry is using you to run for office," one of the woman said, in an exchange recounted by columnist Mary McGrory in July 1971.

Moreover, Nixon had gotten the message, and he had launched an all-out effort to assure the American public that he was winding down the war. As Kerry traveled across the nation, he found that even some college audiences were not paying attention. An October 9, 1971, story in the *National Observer* said Kerry's college tour was "dogged by apathy." By December 1971, Kerry himself was quoted as saying that Nixon "has been very successful in quelling the emotions against the war in this country. He has convinced a lot of people that he is ending it."

Some Vietnam Veterans Against the War leaders viewed Kerry as a power-grabbing elitist, a source of internal friction within the antiwar movement. "There was no question but that the rift existed," said Butler, who was with Kerry at the time. "A wing of the VVAW were pushing so hard to the left that they were almost Maoist. Every time John did something useful like raise money or speak in front of the Foreign Relations Committee or give an interview, he was criticized for being a media whiz."

Camil, the veteran who worked closely with Kerry, said Kerry "was not as radical as some of the rest of us. He was a pretty straight shooter, and he came under criticism for things that weren't fair."

Still, Camil recalled that Kerry's patrician image was derided by others in the group, which was mostly composed of working-class veterans. Camil said a member had tried to reach Kerry by telephone and was told by someone, presumably a maid, that "Master Kerry is not at home." At the next meeting, someone hung a sign on Kerry's chair that said: "Free the Kerry Maid."

So, just five months after assuming a leadership role in VVAW, Kerry quit. He redirected his energy toward helping to organize a new group that focused on veterans' benefits, but he remained a vocal antiwar leader. Then, even before the explosion of the Watergate scandal, Kerry called for the impeachment of Nixon. That got the president's attention.

Some members of the antiwar movement began to suspect—with good cause—that their leadership had been infiltrated with spies planted by the Nixon administration. Kerry himself long suspected that a CIA or FBI "plant" was at work. And even though Kerry had left a leadership position in VVAW, he was still one of the most visible antiwar leaders.

For example, on April 22, 1972, a year after delivering his Senate testimony, Kerry appeared at a New York City rally with former Beatle John Lennon before a crowd of more than 20,000 people, including several dozen busloads from Boston. Like Kerry, Lennon had become a leading figure in the antiwar movement, returning his Order of the British Empire award in protest of Britain's support for U.S. policy in Vietnam, in much the same way U.S. antiwar veterans returned their war medals and ribbons. Lennon's recently released album, *Imagine*, was heavily influenced by the war, from its dreamy title cut to a gritty, painful song that included lyrics that reflected the pain and passion in the crowd he now addressed: "I don't want to be a soldier, Mama, I don't want to die."

Now Lennon, wearing his trademark round-lens glasses and cap, led the swaying crowd in Bryant Park in his signature antiwar theme, "All we are saying . . . is give peace a chance."

When it was Kerry's turn to address the crowd, he used the opportunity not only as a chance to call for a pullout from Vietnam but also to call for the removal of Nixon from the White House. Kerry's friend Butler snapped a picture of Lennon and Kerry, which the senator has long treasured as one of his favorite photos.

The event was one of several that set off a new round of paranoia at the White House. Nixon, who had established a "plumbers unit" to stop leaks such as the Pentagon Papers, was concerned that his Democratic opponent George McGovern was in cahoots with the Vietnam Veterans Against the War.

"Nobody was giving the benefit of the doubt to the Nixon White House," Colson recalled about the White House concerns about the protest movement. "That fed to the paranoia that spilled over and became Watergate."

On June 17, 1972, five men broke into the Watergate headquarters of the Democratic National Committee. The men were later revealed to have connections to the Nixon administration. There have been many explanations over the years for the break-in, which eventually led to Nixon's resignation, but one of the excuses given at the time was that the government was investigating whether the Democratic National Committee was working with the VVAW in some kind of plot to commit violence at the Republican National Convention. James McCord, one of the Watergate burglars, later testified: "I felt the Watergate operation might produce some leads in answering some of those questions, and I had been advised that the operation had the sanction of the White House."

That later led some to wonder whether the burglars were looking for material on Kerry, who had led the VVAW and was gearing up to run for Congress. (Bernard Barker, one of the Watergate burglars, said in February 2004 he had no memory of being told to look for material on John Kerry.)

Now that the antiwar movement had transformed him into a national figure, Kerry revived his desire to run for the U.S. House from Massachusetts. As a war protester, he had learned how to campaign, how to organize, how to raise money, how to attract the media, even how to debate on national TV.

He had battled the Vietcong, the Nixon White House, and the left wing of the antiwar movement. Now all he had to do was declare victory at the polls—by appealing to mostly working-class voters north of Boston.

Chapter 8

CARPETBAGGER

BY 1972, John Kerry was a national figure, but without roots in one place he could call home. His youth had stretched through a dozen towns across two continents. His family had left the Bay State before his seventh birthday, and, except for the year at Fessenden School, Kerry didn't return to live there until after his return from Vietnam. For a young man with political ambitions, his lack of roots was a handicap—one he would quickly compound.

The twenty-eight-year-old believed a seat in Congress was the logical extension of his activism to end the Vietnam War. He was ready to leave the streets to work within what some fellow protesters scorned as "the system." One friend urged him to run for an open state Senate seat in suburban Framingham, west of Boston, to "pay his dues for a couple of years."

But Kerry had national ambitions that were tempered only by political naïveté. He tried on congressional districts like suits off the rack. In less than two months in early 1972, the antiwar leader had accumulated mailing addresses in three different districts in Massachusetts. To this day he bears the brand of opportunist because of his brazen district-shopping. Kerry acknowledges this period as part of his "baggage" in his home state.

He began the year still living in Waltham, where he had explored a challenge two years earlier to aging Democratic hawk Philip Philbin, in what was then the Third Congressional District. Kerry's plans were derailed by the emergence of antiwar Jesuit priest Reverend Robert F. Drinan, who later won the seat. As Drinan's campaign took off that spring, Kerry told two journalists from the *Sun* in Lowell, the dominant newspaper in the Fifth Congressional District, that he was considering challenging F. Bradford Morse, a longtime Republican congressman who supported Nixon's position on Vietnam. Nothing ever came of it, however, and the 1970 election came and went with Kerry on the sidelines.

But by the next election cycle, Kerry was on the move, leaving Waltham for Worcester, about thirty miles away. On February 7, 1972, Julia put down $6,000 on a large $29,500 home at 690 Pleasant Street; the deed listed the house solely in her name. Her husband, meanwhile, briefly explored a challenge to Harold D. Donohue, an entrenched Democratic incumbent. He even hired a reporter from the *Worcester Telegram & Gazette* to begin laying the groundwork for a campaign.

But the young couple never moved into their new home. Instead, Kerry abruptly returned his attention to the

Fifth Congressional District after learning that Morse would be named under-secretary-general of the United Nations. Late in March, the couple packed up and rented an apartment in Lowell, a flat-on-its-back old mill city in the Merrimack Valley. Morse's impending departure promised to open up a congressional seat held by Republicans for generations.

Even Kerry's seat-searching had a Kennedy-like quality. In 1946, John F. Kennedy, also a war hero in search of a political career, plotted an inaugural campaign in the Massachusetts Eleventh Congressional District. "Here we have a candidate, a millionaire, and we ain't got an address for him," Patsy Mulkern, a Kennedy operative, recalled saying during a strategy meeting in the old Bellevue Hotel on Boston's Beacon Hill. Mulkern quoted Kennedy's grandfather, former Boston mayor John F. "Honey Fitz" Fitzgerald, suggesting: "What about upstairs?"

"So we got him a two-room apartment" at the hotel, "and that was the address that went into the book," Mulkern said.

Twenty-six years later, Kerry's quest was even more artless. After noting Kerry's political migrations, the *Boston Herald Traveler*, in an editorial headlined, "Multiple Listing for Congress," quipped: "If (Kerry) doesn't stop house hunting soon, he'll not only need a campaign manager, but a full-time real estate agent." Kerry's parents had lived in the area for the past ten years. But other than that, Kerry's ties to the Fifth were tenuous—and would prove to be a flimsy shield against the withering assaults to come.

His stock response to the carpetbagger question was, "I

learned to walk in the Fifth District." This referred to the fact that as a toddler, Kerry and his family lived for about a year in bucolic Groton, a town to the west of Lowell. There his father taught at Groton School, the exclusive boarding school that counts Franklin Delano Roosevelt among a long list of illustrious alumni. After a tour of diplomatic assignments for Richard Kerry, the family resettled in the leafy town around the time John went off to Yale in 1962. Groton was fifteen miles and a world away from Lowell, a city whose glory days existed only in history books. A revival, brought on by new high-technology companies and an urban national park, was several years away.

In 1972, the city was in another trough of its boom-and-bust history. Recessions always hit Lowell hard, and the economic downturn of the early 1970s drove unemployment to around 12 percent. All but a few vestiges remained of the vast textile industry that had made Lowell, the first planned industrial city in the United States, an economic wonder in the late nineteenth and early twentieth centuries.

The Yankee mill girls, the original workforce recruited from surrounding rural towns, had long since yielded to a horde of poor newcomers. The Irish, who helped dig the power canals, were followed by French Canadians, Greeks, Poles, Lithuanians, Portuguese, Armenians, and others.

Lawrence, the other tired mill city in the Fifth District, had its own distinctive neighborhoods. In 1912, the city had earned a place in American labor history, when more than 20,000 textile workers walked out of the city's mills to protest a wage cut. The Bread and Roses strikers spoke more than two dozen languages, and many of those could still be heard in 1972, in enclaves still influenced by Italian, Lebanese, and other Old World cultures. Like Lowell, Lawrence was pummeled by the economic times. Unemployment was 9 percent. In both cities, yeasty politics were infused with an often brutal ethnic survivalism. Careers were built one favor, one patronage job at a time in heavily Democratic, socially conservative, and mostly Catholic enclaves, each with its own ethnic social club. Lowell, in particular, was known for the blood sport of its political culture.

Into this world, the patrician John Forbes Kerry parachuted in early 1972. He was a Democrat and Catholic, but otherwise an alien political life form to most residents of the cities and their conservative suburbs. His pedigree would not be much of an asset here.

"I can understand people who were pissed at me," Kerry says today of that congressional run. "I came into the district, crash, 'Here I am.' There was a brashness to it ... If I had known what I know today about politics, I'm not sure I would have done it."

But there was another part of the Fifth District that could enable a candidate like Kerry to gain traction, particularly in a crowded field. While Lowell and Lawrence accounted for half of Democratic primary voters—with another 30 percent from the conservative towns ringing them—one-fifth of the contest's voters lived in affluent towns in the southern and western reaches of the district.

There, antiwar sentiment was strongest and the populace was a generation or more removed from the ancestral loyalties and rivalries of the cities. In these bedroom communities, with names like Concord and Lexington, Kerry was a fresh, exciting face, with a rock star's aura. The urban pols, by contrast, were viewed as parochial throwbacks, or worse.

Morse's departure had uncorked a generation's worth of local political ambition—all concentrated in the two mill towns. Jumping in beside Kerry were seven Democrats from the Lowell area, plus two from Lawrence. On the Republican side, Paul W. Cronin, a former state representative and one-time Morse aide from Andover, had three primary opponents. Roger P. Durkin, a conservative Lowell Democrat, complicated matters by running as an Independent in the November final.

Kerry waged an expensive, sophisticated campaign, driven by well-heeled contributors from outside the district and an army of young, idealistic volunteers who worked feverishly to identify Kerry supporters to be pulled to the polls on primary day. The Kerry volunteers also went beyond traditional organizing, deploying consumer education efforts to build goodwill for their candidate. The young activists distributed leaflets to the elderly, describing available government services and benefits; prepared a shopping guide that compared supermarket prices in the district's stores; and operated a "renter's hot-line" to handle complaints about landlords.

Filmmaker Otto Preminger, author George Plimpton, composer Leonard Bernstein (a Lawrence native), and other celebrities lined up behind the hero of the radical chic salons. Plimpton, an aristocratic New Yorker, showed up for a fund-raiser at Bishop's, a popular Lebanese restaurant in downtown Lawrence.

As September 19, primary day, approached, Kerry appeared to be leading his pack of rivals. He was well on his way toward spending his campaign total of $279,746, ensuring that the Fifth District race would be that year's most expensive congressional primary in the country. Then near disaster struck. Shortly before 2 A.M., the day before the election, a police officer on patrol spotted a break-in to the basement of a multifloor office building housing the headquarters of Kerry and another Democratic contender, state Representative Anthony R. DiFruscia of Lawrence.

When backup police arrived, they found Kerry's younger brother, Cameron, and campaign field director Thomas J. Vallely, both twenty-two, in an area near the trunk line for the building's phone systems. The pair was arrested on charges of breaking and entering with intent to commit larceny, and they were led away in handcuffs.

Later that day, the Lowell *Sun* blared a memorable double-deck headline: "Kerry Brother Arrested in Lowell 'Watergate.'" DiFruscia, getting some extra ink in the campaign's waning hours, had drawn the parallel to the break-in at Democratic headquarters in Washington three months earlier.

The Kerry camp declared the episode a setup, saying that the two young men had responded to an anonymous phone call, minutes earlier, threatening to cut the campaign's thirty-six phone lines on the day before its get-out-

the-vote effort. To this day, Kerry becomes animated talking about the episode, convinced it was part of a conspiracy against his insurgency. He said he does not know who
was behind it. He dismissed as ridiculous the charge that
DiFruscia was a target. "He didn't figure in the race," said
Kerry.

But some of Kerry's claims about the Lowell break-in
are wildly at odds with the facts. "That headline was held
open. That page was held open, according to *(Sun)* typeset-
ters, at 1 o'clock in the morning," Kerry said. "That doesn't
happen at a newspaper, you know that. And that headline
was out there on the streets the next morning, first thing."

The *Sun*, however, was an afternoon paper, and its first
deadline was eight or nine hours after the arrests, in plenty
of time to write the story for that day's editions. The *Eagle-
Tribune* of Lawrence, also an afternoon paper, reported the
arrests the same day. A smaller story ran in the *Eagle-Tribune*, under the headline "Shades of Watergate?"

Kerry's brother today declines to elaborate on the circumstances surrounding the arrests and charges, which
were dropped a year later. "It was an impulsive, rash thing
that we did and that John Kerry ended up having to deal
with," said Cam Kerry, now a partner at the Boston law firm
of Mintz Levin Cohn Ferris Glovsky and Popeo. "That's all
we're going to say on that one."

Vallely, a former marine who served in Vietnam and
later became a state representative in Boston, was more
forthcoming. "I kicked in the door" to the basement, he
recalled, and then police swarmed the area. His first worry
was not what voters would think but what his father would

say. "My father was a judge. I was afraid he'd disown me," Vallely recalled.

DiFruscia's office was of no interest, Vallely said; the Kerry phone lines were. There had been prior threats of sabotage, but in hindsight, he said: "We were probably overreacting to someone who was joking."

The arrests had little impact on the vote. The next day, Kerry carried eighteen of the district's twenty-two towns. In a ten-candidate field, he racked up astounding percentages in affluent communities such as Carlisle (82 percent), Concord (78 percent), and Lexington (72 percent), beating the entire field by margins of about 3 to 1. He fared far worse in the working-class cities, running fourth in Lowell and second in Lawrence. Overall, Kerry tallied 20,771 votes, 28 percent of the total. In second place, 5,130 votes behind and at 21 percent, was Paul J. Sheehy, a Lowell state representative. DiFruscia was third, with 12,222 votes, or 16 percent.

In the Republican primary, Cronin won easily, but Kerry had tremendous momentum on the Democratic side. He was an overwhelming favorite to win the general election seven weeks later. A poll conducted for the *Boston Globe* about two weeks after the primary showed Kerry leading Cronin, 51 to 24 percent, with Durkin at 7 percent.

But trouble was ahead. Between Kerry and victory stood Clement C. Costello, the eccentric, crusading editor of the *Sun*.

Costello was a piece of Lowell exotica. Maintaining an aura of incorruptibility, he shunned the close social structure of Lowell's upper class. A Francophile who wore fitted silk shirts with French cuffs over his hunched frame, he cut a strange figure, even in a *Sun* newsroom with more than its share of colorful characters. With long, flowing hair cascading from his beret to the top of the capes he was fond of wearing, Costello, then fifty-three, resided in the once-stately home of his parents on Andover Street, a grand boulevard through Lowell's upscale Belvidere neighborhood.

The house was filled with elegant furniture and expensive antiques, but Costello had let the Victorian manse lapse into a haunted look. Uncut grass grew to several feet. A gaping hole in the roof went unrepaired. One overnight guest, awakened in an upstairs bedroom by repeated thumping sounds, opened the door to find pigeons flying through the hallway.

Each day, after the city edition came off the presses, Costello would retire to the Foxtail Lounge, a nondescript watering hole near the *Sun*'s downtown plant in Kearney Square. He would mark up the paper from front to back, while sipping champagne and smoking French Gauloises cigarettes.

The image he cultivated stood in stark contrast to his brother, John H. Costello Sr., a straitlaced pillar of Lowell society. They had inherited the paper that their family had published since 1878. John, the publisher, ran the business side. Clemmy, as he was often called, presided over the news operation, which was very aggressive for a midsize daily. The Costellos invested heavily in the news product. The *Sun* had a full-time investigative reporter before it was fashionable and its own Washington correspondent, plus staff reporters at the State House in Boston and the court-house at the county seat in Cambridge.

The editorial page, however, was molded entirely in the image of Clem Costello, an ultraconservative who attacked government waste and abuse, and any local pols whom he considered hacks. He was not bound by convention: Later in the 1970s, Costello would urge the United States to annex Canada and invade Mexico as a solution to the oil crisis.

The anti-Kerry drumbeat in the *Sun* had been steady but restrained throughout the primary campaign. Costello had trained most of his editorial page firepower on the Middlesex County commissioners, a three-member panel that presided over a barony of patronage, cronyism, and ballooning cost overruns for a new high-rise courthouse in East Cambridge.

Costello had promoted a young, second-term Lowell city councillor named Paul E. Tsongas, who was leading a reform slate in the commissioner's contest. Tsongas's victory in the primary was tantamount to victory in the county, freeing Costello to turn his attention to the congressional race.

On the day before the primary, the *Sun* had endorsed Robert R. Kennedy, a Lowell city councillor (and no relation to the Massachusetts Kennedy clan that produced a president). The front-page endorsement appeared beneath the "Lowell 'Watergate'" screamer about the arrest of Kerry's brother.

Costello had actually set in type an editorial endorsing Sheehy. But Costello, at the last minute, changed the editorial, inserting Kennedy's name and photo instead. On the eve of the editorial, Kennedy had visited him, persuading Costello to switch his allegiance by displaying a poll that purported to show Kennedy with the best chance to beat Kerry. Kennedy finished a distant fifth in the primary field.

The early stages of the general election campaign were tame, and Kerry tried hard to douse some of the smoldering animosity, particularly in Lowell, where there was an electricity in the air. One powerful Massachusetts figure who came to his aid by attending rallies and fund-raisers in the mill towns was Senator Ted Kennedy.

Never a backslapper, Kerry one night bought the house a round of drinks and played pool at Mike Molloy's Pub, a shot-and-beer joint in Lowell's tough Acre section. Only a couple of regulars refused the free drinks. But other patrons gave Kerry credit for showing his face in a bar once owned by Sheehy, his chief foe in the primary.

Kerry was loved or loathed primarily because of his antiwar stand. But most of his campaign advertising tried to humanize the candidate, showing him talking to ordinary citizens and discussing economic issues. "He's not a politician. He listens," one slick brochure said. Kerry's platform called for activist, big government solutions to a host of problems. He advocated a national health insurance program and prescription drug discounts for the unemployed. He proposed a federal jobs program to clean the polluted Merrimack River and favored imposing rent control in Lawrence and Lowell.

In a district where opposition to abortion ran deep,

Kerry said he personally opposed abortion but as a public official would not interfere with a woman's right to have one. In an apparent jog to the center, he said late in the campaign that he would leave abortion decisions to the states. A few months later, the U.S. Supreme Court, in its landmark *Roe v. Wade* decision, overturned state statutes outlawing abortion.

Julia, shy by nature and awkward in political circles, nevertheless dutifully did her part, climbing stairs of three-deckers in the urban tenements. To prospective voters, or at events in certain neighborhoods in Lawrence and Methuen, she spoke to voters in fluent Italian, a product of her childhood in Rome, where her father was a diplomat and newspaper publisher. Her distinctive, upper-class accent earned her the title "La Professoressa" among residents.

From the outset, Kerry's campaign exhibited a tone-deafness to local culture. In insular Lowell, transplants like Kerry were routinely dismissed as "blow-ins," even decades after they had adopted the city as their home. Kerry nevertheless ran ads touting his endorsements by U.S. senators and congressmen from Oklahoma, Indiana, Michigan, and New York.

Cronin ran ads mocking Kerry's big-money, out-of-town sponsors. "What do Otto Preminger of Hollywood and Louis Biron of Lowell have in common?" one big newspaper ad said. "This year they're influencing a congressional race. Otto Preminger contributed $1,000 to John Forbes Kerry. Louis Biron gave $15 to Paul Cronin."

Durkin, the Independent, was even more aggressive. He placed newspaper ads with "CENSORED" splashed across them after he failed to win permission to reprint the cover of Kerry's 1971 book, *The New Soldier*. The cover featured a photo of Vietnam veterans with a U.S. flag flying upside down—a sign of distress.

Costello picked up on that theme and ran with it, among others, in a series of editorial-page broadsides against Kerry. The editor's attacks dovetailed with hard-hitting stories on the news pages about Kerry's district-hopping, his out-of-district money, and his antiwar activism.

As the 1972 congressional race wound to a close, Costello turned up the heat on John Kerry. In retrospect, the editorials are cultural artifacts, reflecting not merely the editor's parochial prejudices but also the cultural and political conflict of the era.

On October 18, three weeks before the votes would be cast, Costello fired his first volley, a scathing attack on *The New Soldier*, with its cover photo of, in Costello's words,

> three or four bearded youths of the hippy [*sic*] type carrying the American flag in a photo resembling remarkably the immortal photo by Associated Press photographer Joe Rosenthal of US Marines raising the flag on Iwo Jima after its capture from the Japanese in World War II.

> The big difference between the two pictures, however, is that the photo on John Kerry's book shows the flag being carried upside down in a gesture of contempt that has become synonymous with the attitude of youth groups protesting not only Vietnam but just about every-

thing else there is to protest in the United States ...
These people sit on the flag, they burn the flag, they carry
the flag upside down, they all but wipe their noses with it
in their efforts to show contempt for everything it stands
for.

Costello was merely warming up. After endorsing
Cronin's candidacy on October 29—ten days before the
election—Costello devoted his editorial page for the next
four days to a blistering assault on Kerry. The first blast,
titled "Kerry the New Soldier," arrived on October 30.

He put the good name that he had won for himself in
Vietnam on the line in defense of the radical peace agita-
tors. In fact, he led them ... Mr. Kerry's national reputation as a radical leftist war agitator which he himself
created in an immature judgment of America's role in
Vietnam will not inspire confidence or respect for Mr.
Kerry or the district ... in Washington.

On Halloween came "Kerry's travels."

For a long time Mr. Kerry has wanted to be a Congressman. Although he lists himself as an author and lecturer,
he has never held a job in commerce or industry. His eyes
have been fixed on a seat in Congress for a long time. It
didn't make much difference to him what district in the
state might best lend itself to his run for Representative
... it could have been the Third, the Fourth, the Fifth—
you name it ...

Mr. Kerry is more interested in what the Fifth can give him, namely, a seat in Congress, than what he can give the Fifth. He wants the national sounding board from which he can disseminate the radical ideas contained in his "books and lectures" and the welfare of the Fifth district and its people is secondary.

November 1 brought "Kerry's money."

The bulk of the big money that has financed Mr. Kerry's campaign to capture the Fifth's seat in Congress has come from ... New York. The next largest amount has come from ... Boston ... It is perfectly obvious that Mr. Kerry's intent is to buy this seat by drowning Mr. Cronin in a sea of money.

Will the loyalty and allegiance of Mr. Kerry go to the wealthy of New York's Park Avenue and Fifth Avenue and Scarsdale and Westchester County before it is offered to the people of the Fifth? Will the seat be used and re-used for all it's worth by the millionaires of New York ... ?

Costello wrapped up his attack on November 2, five days before the election, with "Kerry's Washington."

Can anybody think that Kerry's reception by the Nixon administration, from top to bottom, on all levels, in all Departments, would be anything less than one of frigid rejection?

The fact of the matter is that John Kerry, today, is cordially detested by the Nixon administration because of

Mr. Kerry's violent opposition to the administration ... If John Kerry's name is mud in Washington under President Nixon, we don't want to see that mud wind up in the face of the people of the Fifth district.

It was a press flogging that has been compared to the over-the-top exploits of the *Union Leader*, the archconservative daily in Manchester, New Hampshire, during the heyday of publisher William Loeb. "Maybe just a notch below that," said Kendall M. Wallace, who in 1972 was the *Sun*'s city editor and is now its publisher. "Without that kind of intense coverage, I think Kerry would have been the congressman."

Kerry said as much later in letters to contributors. "For two solid weeks, they called me un-American, New Left antiwar agitator, unpatriotic, and labeled me every other 'un-' and 'anti-' that they could find," Kerry wrote. "It's hard to believe that one newspaper could be so powerful, but they were."

The blitz took a toll. More than criticisms from his opponents, Kerry was hurt by "[t]he *Sun* and the whisperings," Cam Kerry recalled. "John Kerry was essentially sort of a cardboard cutout figure to people. When the attacks came, there weren't people there in the community who could vouch for him."

Julia was outraged. "The Lowell *Sun* ... (was) basically calling John a pinko Commie," she recalled. "It was unbelievable. I couldn't believe that anybody would stoop that low."

Four days before the election, Kerry's campaign suffered another blow: Roger Durkin, the Independent candidate and former conservative Democrat, abruptly dropped out of the race, endorsed Cronin, and decried Kerry's "dangerous radicalism." Durkin's pullout may have been the coup de grâce. A *Boston Globe* poll, conducted two weeks before the election, had Durkin third, with 13 percent of the vote. Kerry's lead over Cronin, once 27 points, was down to 10 by that time.

Despite the absence of persuasive evidence, Kerry remains convinced that Nixon political operatives were behind Durkin's decision. "Durkin's withdrawal was not spontaneous," Kerry said recently, reviving the notion that he was among the campaign targets of the Nixon dirty tricksters. Kerry said he was told by local supporters that "there were administration people up in Lowell."

Most of the conspiracy theories involve Charles W. Colson, the Nixon heavy who grew up in Winthrop, Massachusetts, and later was one of the Watergate conspirators to be imprisoned. In 1993 and again in a recent interview with the *Boston Globe*, Colson acknowledged trying to discredit Kerry's antiwar efforts but flatly denied any attempts to derail his congressional campaign.

Durkin, a businessman who moved to Boston, denied vigorously that he was a tool of the Republicans. Recently, he said he "fell on the grenade" only when he became certain his candidacy would ensure a Kerry triumph.

Kerry did become the target of at least one White House effort to defeat him. Ed Cox, President Nixon's son-in-law, went to Lowell and urged the election of Cronin. But Cox felt a bit odd about his effort because he was distantly related to Kerry's wife, Julia. Cox's sister, Mazie, was married to one of Julia's cousins. But Cox, who had gone to Harvard Law School and once served on the district attorney's staff as a student assistant in Lowell, gamely went ahead, arguing for both Nixon's reelection and a Cronin victory. Cox said he knows nothing about allegations that the Nixon White House was trying to undermine Kerry's campaign and has no recollection of Nixon discussing Kerry. But when Cronin defeated Kerry, Cox believed that it validated exactly what Nixon had been saying about support for his policies in Vietnam.

"This showed to me that there was a 'silent majority' even in Lowell, Massachusetts, in a blue-collar depressed area that supported the president and his policies," said Cox. If Kerry couldn't win on an antiwar platform in Lowell, Cox believed it showed there was widespread support for Nixon's policies. Kerry had failed to win a congressional seat at the height of the antiwar fervor, Cox noted, and when Kerry did finally win an election, the war would be long over.

On the final weekend of the campaign, Cam Kerry recalled, he sensed the election "slipping away" as he canvassed in Lawrence. "There was a lot of outright hostility," he said. The Vietnam War and abortion were polarizing issues.

In the end, it wasn't close. Cronin beat Kerry by 18,123 votes, almost 9 percent, of 207,623 cast. The Republican, who died in 1997, won Lowell, Lawrence, and nineteen of twenty-two towns. Kerry carried only Lexington, Wilmington, and Billerica.

To a packed house of stunned supporters at the campaign party in an Andover hotel, Kerry that night responded to Costello and those who had questioned his patriotism. "If I had it to do over again, I'd be in Washington with the veterans tomorrow," he said. "It was a huge loss, kind of like the crashing of the dream," recalled David Thorne, Kerry's old Yale friend and his manager for the 1972 race. "We lost, that wasn't supposed to happen."

In the clarity of more than thirty years of hindsight, Kerry acknowledges his shortcomings as a candidate of that era. "I did not have that network of roots, those personal connections of kids I grew up with, the high school I went to, the people who could say, 'I played football with him,'" he said. "Just relationships; I didn't have 'em. I came in cold ... It was an adventure based on an idea, which was ending the war."

His failure to respond directly to the *Sun*'s bludgeonings was a fatal blunder, Kerry now concedes. "We didn't know what we were doing," Kerry said. "We were kids. And we got our asses handed to us. It's a great lesson." And he learned never to repeat the mistake.

Chapter 9

DECADE IN EXILE

LOWELL HAD rejected him, but John Kerry did not immediately abandon his adopted hometown. Shortly before the election, Julia sold the Worcester house they had bought seven months earlier—at a $4,500 profit—and purchased, again in her name only, a handsome $51,000 home on Holyrood Avenue, in Belvidere, Lowell's most prestigious neighborhood.

But Kerry, the itinerant activist, had a campaign debt and no job. He had been defeated in his chosen field of politics and was unsure of his next step. Friends and acquaintances at the time have described him as devastated by the loss. Kerry's brother, Cameron, describes the period as the beginning of "the years in exile."

"He was shattered" and seemed aimless after the loss, said Frank Phillips, the Lowell *Sun* reporter who covered the campaign and later visited Kerry at his new home.

Phillips recalled Kerry telling him about plans to build a model helicopter to fly by remote control.

Moreover, Kerry was obsessed, Phillips said, with the conspiracy theories and rumors that were gaining credibility as the Watergate investigation was gathering steam and details of the Nixon White House's nationwide political sabotage operation were beginning to unfold. "The Watergate stuff was just exploding across the country, stories about dirty tricks," Phillips recalled.

In Lowell, Phillips pursued leads, checking local hotel registration and telephone records, in an effort to trace the activities of Republican operatives who had arrived in the area near the end of the campaign to help Paul Cronin, the GOP candidate in the congressional race.

"I came to the conclusion that it just wasn't there," Phillips said. "It wasn't the war or the dirty tricks that did John Kerry in, it was a class issue—class and resentment. There was a rage among local people that he created; an outsider, coming in and knocking off Paul Sheehy," the Lowell Democrat who was runner-up in the primary, Phillips said.

Kerry says the notion that he was crushed by the defeat is exaggerated. "I was disappointed; I mean it hurt," he recalled. "I wasn't devastated. I went to figure out what to do after that. But I remember feeling powerless about it ... I felt as if the thing had just compounded around me, and I didn't have the ability to fight back or control." In a 1974 interview, Kerry was more candid about the self-doubts he experienced as a result of his loss: "The defeat really put me down ... I even began to doubt my own ability to speak out on those issues I felt most strongly about, like Vietnam."

Even as Kerry was coping with his first political defeat, his old enemies in the White House were falling one by one. Indeed, some historians believe the June 1972 break-in at the Watergate office of the Democratic National Committee might have been motivated, in part, by an effort to get information on ties between the Democratic Party and the antiwar movement that Kerry had helped lead.

The Watergate break-in, while having little impact on the 1972 elections, began to unfold as a major story throughout 1973, the year when two of the president's top aides, John Ehrlichman and H. R. Haldeman, resigned in April. Vice President Spiro Agnew resigned in a separate scandal.

That same year, Kerry took several months off and then did a stint as a fund-raiser for CARE Inc., the international aid organization. Still, Congress beckoned, and Kerry again considered challenging Cronin.

In the late summer of 1973, Kerry even commissioned a poll to get the lay of the land. But Paul Tsongas, the new Middlesex County commissioner from Lowell, had decided to run and came to Kerry's home to learn Kerry's intentions. Soon after that meeting, Kerry decided against another campaign and turned over to Tsongas his "entire political operation—lists, bodies, contacts" for the 1974 campaign. Riding the post-Watergate tide that lifted Democrats, Tsongas knocked off Cronin to win the Fifth District seat.

Kerry, meanwhile, was settling on a career move that

would fit neatly with his ambitions for public office—law school. "I knew I didn't want to wind up in ten or fifteen years saying, 'A lot of time's gone by, and I don't have a profession,'" Kerry said. "And that's when I committed to go to law school." He also said he "wanted to learn the skill of advocacy and learn the law, understand the law well, know the whole lawmaking process in the context of public life."

Ten months after Kerry lost the congressional contest, his life opened a new chapter. On September 5, Julia gave birth to their first child, Alexandra. Days later, Kerry started classes at Boston College Law School, a Jesuit institution in well-to-do Newton, prominent for producing many of the state's political leaders. As her husband made the hourlong commute to law school, Julia—back at home in Lowell—was traumatized by the "negativity" and resentment that some local residents still harbored toward Kerry. "Just after Alexandra was born in the fall of 1973, a rock came through the window and landed right next to her bassinet, which was lying in the sun, in the middle of the living room, while I was at home alone," she recalled. "Can you imagine that?... You feel so helpless."

Notwithstanding Julia's family money, the couple's purchase of an expensive home and Kerry's attendance at law school produced financial struggles. "We couldn't make ends meet," recalled Julia, who subsequently took a job as assistant director of the Institute of Contemporary Art in Boston for about two years while an au pair cared for Alexandra.

At law school, Kerry stood out as a national figure, and a

man significantly older than most of the other students. "I remember looking up at my first-year class, and sitting there, big as life, was this guy I had seen on television, testifying before the Senate Foreign Relations Committee and running for Congress," recalled Thomas J. Carey Jr., one of Kerry's professors.

Even as a student, Kerry maintained a public profile. He moonlighted part-time as a radio talk-show host on WBZ-AM. And, from May to October 1974, he served as executive director of MassAction, a watchdog group that was then attacking state treasurer Robert Q. Crane's sloppy cash-management practices and cozy relationship with banks. It was a far cry from leading an antiwar movement, but it temporarily kept Kerry's name before the public.

In 1974, the White House finally released tapes revealing that Nixon had tried to cover up the Watergate break-in, and the president resigned on August 8. The scandal would leave behind a legacy of public distrust and suspicion about the nation's political leaders. Meanwhile, in Vietnam—the conflict that had provoked Kerry's own suspicions about government motives—U.S. troops were being withdrawn. A year later, South Vietnamese resistance would collapse and Saigon would fall.

Against these dramatic developments, John Kerry—war hero turned antiwar activist turned political candidate—was living a sedate life as husband, father, and law student. "Once a hot political property, student John Kerry just watches," a *Boston Globe* headline blurted in November. Kerry, once profiled in national newsmagazines as a surefire prospect for Congress, was now "just another second-year law student at Boston College Law School, struggling with the simultaneous challenge of coping and of constitutional law," wrote reporter Crocker Snow Jr.

But Kerry took great satisfaction in the changes he watched from afar that were underway in Washington, particularly Nixon's downfall. "Just think how much has changed, how much has happened in the last two years," Kerry told Snow. "When I was running for office, Nixon was still President, Agnew was still Vice President and our involvement in Vietnam was still a big issue. Now the whole context of things has changed."

In that same interview, the thirty-year-old Kerry reflected on his life as a young and inexperienced candidate for Congress two years earlier. "There was too much shouting, too much intensity, it was all too hyper," he said. "As a candidate you have too much temptation to talk and no time to think. So you say something stupid about something you don't know much about. And then later you're afraid to admit it for fear of looking more stupid. So you're stuck with a position you don't like and don't want to support."

In Kerry's third year at law school, Professor Carey interviewed him for a spot on Boston College's national moot court team. Even though Kerry was "a man with a lot of irons in the fire," he committed to make the team a priority, Carey recalled. "He worked long hours. He was an outstanding member of the team, preparing briefs and oral arguments for a Supreme Court–level case with very complex public policy questions."

In early 1976, with five months remaining in law school,

Kerry became a student prosecutor in the office of Middle-sex district attorney John J. Droney. And upon graduation on May 24, he accepted a full-time prosecutor job in the same office, a position that would chart a new course in Kerry's life—and later would produce a new set of contro-versies about the young man's ambitious nature.

Kerry's decision to become a prosecutor floored some of his liberal friends. "Most people would have told you then that it was a Nixonian-Agnew thing to become a prosecutor and law-and-order [advocate]," said Ronald F. Rosenblith, a former Kerry aide and longtime fund-raiser and adviser. "They couldn't understand why this great progressive shin-ing voice that could articulate things so well on our side would do that."

But Kerry said his father, a prosecutor before becoming a diplomat, inspired his move. He "told me it was a great way to learn how to do cases and try cases," Kerry recalled. "I wanted to be a trial lawyer. It was the best place in the world to get trial practice." Years later, the experience would also provide a convenient political weight against the dreaded "Massachusetts liberal" label.

Until he passed the bar at age thirty-two, Kerry said he handled minor cases before juries of six, winning all of the twenty-five to thirty cases he prosecuted. His first felony trial was a rape case in which the defendant was repre-sented by William Homans, a prominent Boston defense lawyer. Kerry secured a guilty verdict. "I'm glad to say I never lost a case in Middlesex," Kerry said.

*

Kerry was finally employed, though only on a government salary of $12,900 a year. Nevertheless, he and Julia bought a large $100,000 home on Chestnut Hill Road in Newton, moving from working-class Lowell to one of Greater Boston's most desirable neighborhoods—and one much closer to Kerry's East Cambridge office. On New Year's Eve in 1976, the couple's second daughter, Vanessa, was born.

Less than a month later, District Attorney Droney promoted Kerry to the position of first assistant, giving him free rein to overhaul the office—and stunning staff veterans. Many of Droney's assistants were resentful, a reaction that fit a recurring pattern in Kerry's life, as his thrusts to the forefront irked others who coveted his prominence. First it was members of Vietnam Veterans Against the War, then the Lowell and Lawrence politicians he had brushed aside in the 1972 primary. Now it was Droney loyalists.

Kerry had been out of law school less than a year. But he had star power and news media appeal. And Droney's attention was increasingly focused on his upcoming campaign for reelection in 1978. The promotion "shocked me, too," Kerry recalled. "I mean, I was surprised. John wanted to run for reelection [the next year], and he knew there were some issues in the office."

A wily pol, Droney was afflicted by Lou Gehrig's disease. Although his mind was sharp, his speech and mobility were impaired. In early 1978, Kerry was prepared to run for district attorney if Droney's illness forced him to bow out.

In the meantime, though, Kerry set about transforming a plodding hidebound operation into a modern, efficient DA office that would help Droney's reelection effort. "John

Kerry in effect became the legs and voice John Droney no longer had," recalled Peter W. Agnes Jr., then a young lawyer in the office and now a superior court judge. "He provided youth, vitality, and charisma."

With a $3.8-million infusion of federal funds he helped obtain, Kerry nearly tripled the staff, and many of the new hires were women. He launched initiatives that were innovative at the time: special units to prosecute white-collar and organized crime, programs to counsel rape victims and aid other crime victims and witnesses, and a system for fast-tracking priority cases to trial. "Some people didn't like the modernization process, didn't want it, and obviously felt they were more qualified [than me], and some were," Kerry said. "But we changed the office."

By late summer of 1977, Kerry was directing the investigation that led to the first conviction of Somerville's Howie Winter, one of the state's notorious gangsters. Winter was sentenced to two consecutive nine-year sentences in prison after being convicted in a scheme to force local businesses to install in their clubs pinball machines owned by a gang associate.

Kerry stepped out of his administrative duties and into the courtroom to try several cases, and he won convictions in a murder and a high-profile rape case. Robert Barton, the court-appointed defense lawyer in the murder case and who later became a trial judge, called Kerry "as good a trial lawyer as I ever saw." But Kerry's double duty as courtroom prosecutor and chief DA spokesman was sometimes hard to juggle. "The trial kept getting interfered with because John Kerry had to keep going outside and do television interviews on some other matters," Barton recalled. "You had to hang around for about forty-five minutes."

Kerry also won a rape conviction and an eighteen- to thirty-year prison sentence for George O. Edgerly, a former service manager at a Lowell auto dealership. Edgerly was later convicted of murder in another county in connection with the 1974 slaying of a General Motors executive investigating excessive warranty claims at the dealership.

Kerry's efforts—and the publicity they garnered—boosted Droney's record going into the 1978 race. The only complication was that Kerry had his eye on his boss's job. Two sources from the period—Barton, who had been a Droney assistant in the early 1960s, and a Droney friend who asked not to be identified—said Kerry approached them sometime in early 1978 and suggested Droney's ailment could cost him the election. Kerry asked them to talk to the DA about the possibility of bowing out and letting Kerry run, both sources said.

And even as Droney was on the verge of being reelected that fall, Kerry retained his interest in the post, according to one prominent state political figure. William F. Galvin, then a state representative, said Kerry told him that if Droney's ailment prevented him from serving out his term, Kerry hoped to secure an appointment from either of the two men running for governor.

Galvin, now secretary of state, recalled a conversation with Kerry shortly before the November election in which the young prosecutor mulled two possible scenarios: If Republican Francis W. Hatch Jr. won the governor's seat in the coming days, Kerry noted, his brother-in-law David

Thorne—who knew Hatch—could intercede on his behalf. Galvin responded that he doubted the partisan Republican would name a Democrat, especially one as young and promising as Kerry.

Kerry was crestfallen for a moment, Galvin recalled, but then brightened, telling Galvin he knew another influential political broker if the Democratic nominee prevailed. "'I'm very close to Johnny Zamparelli [then Middlesex South register of deeds], and he's very close to Ed King,'" Galvin quoted Kerry as saying. Edward J. King beat Hatch in a close race, but the point was moot. Droney had no intention of stepping down after being reelected.

"It was a joke," replied Kerry when told of Galvin's recollection. "I mean if he remembers it this long, more power to him. He may have seen it as some dark conspiracy, but I certainly wasn't thinking about it that way. I was loyal to the nth degree to help [Droney] get reelected. And indeed, had he not run, I did think about running if he didn't run. Absolutely, unabashedly."

Meanwhile, Kerry helped Droney's campaign, but twice almost landed in trouble for his efforts. After a Droney campaign advertisement violated a superior court judge's gag order in a murder case, Kerry appeared before the judge, Thomas R. Morse Jr., and took responsibility for the full-page newspaper ad that he helped design.

From the bench, Morse chastised the DA's office for "insensitivity" but stopped short of imposing sanctions and denied a defense lawyer's motion to dismiss the indictment of Anthony Jackson, the so-called hitchhike murderer, who was ultimately convicted. Jackson wasn't named in the ad—titled "The Inside Story on How John Droney Cracked Some of Massachusetts' Most Famous Crimes"—but it clearly referred to him and his prior convictions in a series of sex-related murders. "I don't recall that," Kerry recently said when asked about the incident. "If you tell me that's true, it's true, but I think it was inadvertent, and obviously, no one purposely steps over a court [order]."

In the weeks before the primary, a scandal involving the sale of county jobs hit the media through a gusher of news leaks quoting unnamed sources. The reports hinted at a wider conspiracy of government higher-ups and organized crime involvement. A defense lawyer for one of two suspects charged with selling low-level jobs accused Kerry directly of violating grand jury secrecy by leaking stories to the press. "We never leaked any grand jury information," Kerry said recently. "Not me, man.... We would call people in and try to find out where it was coming from, and I believe I know. I'm not going to say it on the record, here, now, but we had a considerable amount of concern, and you know, a few feathers were ruffled in the process of trying to find out who was leaking that." Reports about the investigation dropped out of the news after the election. No more suspects were charged, and of the two who were, neither went to prison. One paid a $5,000 fine.

In the closing days of the 1978 Democratic primary, Droney challenger L. Scott Harshbarger blasted the DA's office, saying it was timing indictments and investigations to influence votes. "Staged media events," he called them. Droney barely staved off the Harshbarger challenge in the primary, which was tantamount to victory with no Republican on the November ballot. Droney, because of his ailment, did not campaign and gave no interviews until the campaign's final days. Harshbarger, a former assistant attorney general, did not concede defeat until the paper-ballot returns, still being reported sixteen hours after the polls closed, showed Droney pulling ahead.

Harshbarger went to Droney's office after his concession. It was the first time the two had ever met. But after his reelection, Droney appeared reinvigorated, and by the spring of 1979, it was becoming clear that Kerry's days were numbered in an office he had remade. Droney instituted new office policies, some of them petty, and suspended Kerry's secretary and two of his protégés for relatively minor infractions. He also assumed more of the duties he had ceded to Kerry. "It became obvious in '79 that [Droney] was sort of feeling better . . . and he began to say, 'I don't want to do this, I don't want to do that,'" Kerry recalled. Certain his role in the office would be diminished, Kerry said he decided it was time to leave.

"I can't complain, and I'm not going to complain," Kerry said. "He gave me an unprecedented opportunity of a lifetime . . . and I like to think it worked for both of us, and the time came when it didn't. You know, that happens in life." Kerry said they remained friends until Droney's death in 1989. But many prosecutors in the office at that time believed Droney pushed Kerry out in part because his top aide was so obviously seeking to win the top job for himself.

After his reelection, Droney returned to an office bitterly divided in its loyalties. "There were Kerry people, and there were Droney people," said George E. Murphy, who served as an assistant DA in Middlesex for twenty years and now has his own practice. While many Droney loyalists resented Kerry, he also had strong supporters. "I won't say everybody loved [Kerry], but he was always there and probably the most natural trial lawyer on his feet I ever saw," said J. William Codinha, who succeeded Kerry as first assistant and remains a close friend. "There's no way John Droney would have been reelected without John Kerry."

Kerry certainly modernized the DA office, but he embellished his legacy in later years. For example, Kerry has, over the years, increasingly inflated his efforts in reducing the backlog of cases. Early in his campaign for the White House, Kerry often said he wiped out an inventory of 12,000 criminal cases. But a 1978 Droney election ad that Kerry helped write put the number at closer to 3,800 cases, and in a 1979 interview with the Lowell *Sun* he took credit for eliminating 2,772. But by 1982, a campaign biography had raised that number to 10,772. In fact, state records show that the entire superior court caseload, including backlog, never exceeded 7,265 during Kerry's tenure.

Kerry said he isn't sure where his figures came from but recalled a concerted effort to clean up a mess. "We adjudicated a number of them, we had to dismiss a whole bunch for lack of evidence, lack of witnesses, people had moved or didn't want to testify," he said. "We went through every case."

Another exaggerated claim involved the notorious Somerville pinball extortion case. A 1982 campaign announcement claimed Kerry prosecuted the case. Although Kerry did directly oversee the investigation, coaxed reluctant witnesses to testify, and introduced evidence to the grand jury, it was Codinha, an assistant DA—not Kerry—who tried the case. (The same announcement also described Winter as "the number two organized crime boss in New England," though Winter "was not even 'Number Two' in Greater Boston, much less in New England," the *Boston Globe* reported.)

After Droney's reelection as DA, followed by his crackdown on Kerry loyalists, Kerry realized his authority and role were diminishing. Whether he jumped or was pushed remains a matter of debate among former colleagues. Kerry says he decided to resign after realizing, "I'm not going to sit around on some kind of speculation about what his health was going to be. I went off and did my thing."

Kerry and Roanne Sragow, an assistant DA who was among those suspended by Droney, opened their own practice, setting up shop at a prestigious Boston address, a skyscraper at 60 State Street. Over the next two and a half years, the pair built a successful practice, specializing in litigation involving wrongful deaths, medical malpractice, corporate trade secrets, and what Kerry describes as "a string of relatively notorious hair implantation cases."

Kerry also developed a disparate set of sidelines, joining WCVB-TV (Channel 5), the ABC affiliate in Boston, as a regular public affairs commentator on the weekly program *Five on 5*. "It was really the vehicle whereby he maintained a certain level of visibility across the state," recalled Marjorie Arons-Barron, the producer of the roundtable-style program. "Because at that time, he was really nowhere politically." The program, she said, had a small but devoted viewership.

In late 1979, Kerry cofounded a cookie shop at Boston's Quincy Market with a friend, K. Dun Gifford, a Boston area socialite, restaurateur, and former aide to Senator Edward M. Kennedy. It's still there, Kilvert & Forbes Ltd. (named after their mothers' maiden names), though Kerry sold his interest in 1988.

Julia, meanwhile, fell into a bout of undiagnosed clinical depression—precipitated, she later said, by the February 1980 news of her father's terminal illness. But, she added, "my marriage wasn't in such great shape, either." During this period, Julia also suffered an inexplicable paralysis that forced her to use crutches. In February 1980, five months after her thirty-sixth birthday, "my mind ravaged by corroding voices, my body defeated by bone-rattling panics," Julia later recounted, "I sat on the edge of my bed minutes from taking my life. For weeks I had silently prepared my death. I believed I was a failure. I could no longer pretend I was of use to my husband or my children. I was too tired. I needed to lie down, curled up, never to wake again."

Her plan was interrupted by a phone call.

Julia's flirtation with suicide prompted her to seek treatment that would continue through the 1980s. Her husband was not unsympathetic, she said, but the illness remained her secret. "I functioned. I took the kids to school—never letting on that this was going on," Julia said. John was "at home as much as he humanly could be," she said.

Meanwhile, her husband's law practice was "doing very well." Kerry said that by late 1981, he had to decide whether to expand the two-lawyer firm. But as the 1982 election cycle approached, a political opportunity arose, though one less exalted than the congressional platform Kerry once sought.

Thomas P. O'Neill III, the son of U.S. House Speaker Tip O'Neill, was giving up the lieutenant governorship to run for governor. The number two post would be open on the Democratic ticket. It was an amorphous, do-little job, but certain to attract a large field. The law firm expansion was shelved. The old Potomac Fever yielded to a lower-grade Beacon Hill bug.

"I decided I was going to run for office," Kerry said.

Exile over. He was back in the game.

Chapter 10

LIEUTENANT GOVERNOR

AS HE BEGAN his return to politics in early 1982, John F. Kerry found a political landscape as changed as he was by events of the previous ten years. Gone was the rock star aura of the 1972 congressional candidate who had railed against the Vietnam War. In the more settled Reagan era, Kerry was now Mr. Mainstream, a downtown lawyer with a wife, two kids, and an expensive home in lovely Chestnut Hill.

Kerry's political goals had changed, too, at least for the short term. His sights once set on Congress and the hot-house of Washington politics, Kerry was entering the race for lieutenant governor, a post with few prescribed duties.

There were few other options that year: Incumbents occupied all of the Bay State's congressional seats, and five of the six statewide offices were held by incumbent Democrats. The only opening of any rank was lieutenant governor, a resting place for the near-great and often a graveyard for political ambition. Kerry could thank Thomas P. O'Neill III for the opportunity. The son of House Speaker Tip O'Neill was moving up or out, in what would prove to be a futile challenge to Democratic governor Edward J. King—and the man King had ousted four years earlier, Michael S. Dukakis.

There was even more traffic among Massachusetts Democrats for the second berth on the ticket. Joining Kerry on the primary ballot were Evelyn Murphy of Brookline, a former environmental secretary who served in the first Dukakis administration, and three Boston suburbanites with state legislative backgrounds—Senator Samuel Rotondi of Winchester, Representative Louis R. Nickinello of Natick, and former representative Lois G. Pines of Newton.

In a crowded Democratic primary contest that received scant public notice, Kerry tried to stand out, not only as a crime-fighting former prosecutor with progressive credentials but also as champion of a nuclear weapons freeze. For a candidate seeking a job with little influence over state policy, let alone global arms control policy, the posturing was quite a stretch.

But the Vietnam War, Kerry's signature issue in the past, had long since ended. His antiwar constituency's new rallying cry was opposition to President Reagan's arms buildup, and Kerry wanted them to know he was a staunch ally. That June, Kerry was among the speakers in New York's Central Park at a rally of hundreds of thousands of activists opposed to the U.S.-Soviet nuclear arms race. The freeze never caught on as an issue in the lieutenant governor's race. Instead, the campaign's core issues, as Kerry described them at the time, were "competency, experience, and vision." For a man who a decade earlier had debated the morality of a war, the thematic drop-off couldn't have been steeper.

The race, Kerry's first statewide contest, held out the prospect that he could reenter politics after a decade on the sidelines. It would also reveal Kerry's knack for deftly navigating the treacherous terrain of Democratic Party politics in Massachusetts, where blue-collar conservatives and trade unionists were expected to find common ground with staunchly liberal suburbanites, activists, and academics.

In 1982, the Democratic Party was split along conservative-liberal lines for the grudge rematch between King, the incumbent, and Dukakis, who had held the governor's office from 1975 to 1979. King's administration was plagued by high-profile investigations that resulted in the conviction of a cabinet secretary on corruption-related charges and the suicide of a top official in the state's tax department. The distinguishing feature of Dukakis's candidacy was a strident anticorruption, good-government platform.

But on May 22, at the endorsement convention in Springfield, the Kerry forces were ready for any outcome, offering delegates a choice of lapel buttons—"King/Kerry" or "Dukakis/Kerry." Beyond campaign buttons, the Kerry campaign tried to make policy appeals to both camps. To the King faction, they offered Kerry's law-and-order prosecutor's credentials and proposals for investment in public infrastructure, an issue in the cities. To the suburban Democrats, who were the core of Dukakis's constituency—

and a growing force in Massachusetts politics—Kerry laid out liberal positions on social issues and presented his strong support for the nuclear freeze.

Kerry was not a favorite of the party apparatchiks. His candidacy was hatched outside the tribal culture of party sachems and streetwise urban operatives who could turn out neighborhood votes. Most of the regulars were with Evelyn Murphy and Sam Rotondi.

During a seven-hour, five-ballot endorsement struggle at the Springfield convention, Kerry barely qualified for the September ballot by winning the required 15 percent of the delegate votes. But his floor troops artfully maneuvered delegates to help another candidate, Pines, reach that threshold on the second ballot.

That meant that Kerry would face a primary field of two activist women, Pines and Murphy, the convention's ultimate winner, and two male state legislators, Rotondi and Nickinello, the moderate and conservative, respectively, on the ballot. Pines and Murphy were both vying to become the first woman elected to statewide office in Massachusetts history.

Cameron Kerry, who managed his brother's 1982 campaign, was evasive years later when asked about tales of delegate trading on the convention floor to shape the field to his brother's advantage. "Whether that was done, people overestimate the control that campaigns have over delegates," he said. "I'm not going to confirm anything."

In the shadow of the Dukakis-King slugfest, the race for the second spot on the ticket became little more than a sideshow. "The oxygen was all with the King-Dukakis rematch," recalled Christopher Greeley, a Kerry campaign worker who often drove the candidate to events. "We spent an awful lot of time trying to figure out where we could find crowds to meet."

The race for the nomination was a grinding, low-key affair of kaffeeklatsches and forums before local Democratic and issue advocacy groups. "It was a different political era," Cam Kerry recalled. "People were not as excited about politics as they were in 1972. They'd moved on to other things." At one point, Kerry's team drove all the way across the state to an event that drew about twenty attendees. "And we thought it was a worthwhile trip," said Greeley, who would later join Kerry's staff.

Because of his controversial past and recent stint as a commentator on WCVB-TV, Kerry enjoyed wider name recognition than his opponents. It was a modest advantage. A poll conducted for the *Boston Globe* less than three weeks before the primary showed Kerry was the best known of the quintet, but even so, 65 percent didn't know enough about him to have an opinion.

Larry Carpman, the press secretary, recalled that the campaign tried anything to gain an edge, even issuing policy papers—"white papers"—on blue paper "so they would stand out." Media mentions were few and far between. There was one televised debate, in late August, on a UHF station in Boston, in which the five candidates politely made their points and avoided any conflict.

John Kerry's successful law practice became a major asset late in the campaign, enabling him to make $127,125 in personal loans to his campaign. Perhaps just as significant, he received a huge publicity boost shortly before the primary when he and his law partner, Roanne Sragow, won freedom for George A. Reissfelder, who was fifteen years into a life prison sentence for a murder he had always maintained he did not commit.

The low-key campaign was also noteworthy for the emergence in statewide politics of a young streetwise operative from Dorchester, Michael Whouley. After running Kerry's field operation, Whouley would go on to direct Kerry's impressive statewide organization in 1984, later becoming a prized operative in the presidential campaigns of Bill Clinton and Al Gore.

Kerry also picked up support from an up-and-coming Boston city councillor named Raymond L. Flynn. Like Kerry, Flynn was something of a solo act—but the alliance of these two very different men would later prove mutually beneficial. South Boston's Flynn, an opponent of school desegregation in the mid-1970s, was evolving into a rough-around-the-edges urban populist and aspiring racial healer. He was also preparing to run for mayor the following year against the political colossus incumbent, Kevin White.

In the closing days of the lieutenant governor's campaign, polls showed Kerry ahead in a field of mostly unknowns and a huge undecided component in the electorate. But late on primary day, as he crossed a pedestrian bridge over Boston's Central Artery, Kerry was downcast, recalled Joseph Baerlein, who crossed paths with the candidate at that moment. Baerlein, who was campaign manager for his leading opponent, Evelyn Murphy, said Kerry believed exit polls that showed him trailing Murphy, the former environmental secretary, in a very tight race. "I told him I thought it was going to be a long night," recalled Baerlein.

He was right. With 29 percent of the vote, Kerry edged Murphy by fewer than 40,000 votes out of more than 1.1 million cast. He carried Boston, Worcester, Lowell, and several other key cities and rolled up more than half his victory margin in the old Fifth Congressional District, which had snubbed him a decade earlier. That more than offset Murphy's strong showing in other areas.

"It was about 1:30 in the morning when the results in Worcester came in that I knew we had won," Cam Kerry remembers. Kerry, then leading by only 2 percent with returns still incomplete, waited until 3:30 A.M. to declare victory. Murphy called to congratulate Kerry but did not formally concede until seven hours later, shortly before a Democratic unity breakfast at a Boston hotel, attended by all the candidates. By then, the margin had doubled.

Meanwhile, Michael Dukakis, driven out of office by conservative Ed King in 1978—after breaking his "lead-pipe" guarantee not to raise taxes—regained his party's nomination, ousting King with promises to clean up the state government.

With the hotly contested Democratic primary behind them, Dukakis and Kerry faced a cakewalk against over-matched Republican candidates in the general election. The Dukakis team considered Kerry an asset and featured him in campaign advertising. One brochure showed them walking and talking, suit coats slung over their shoulders: "Mike Dukakis/John Kerry . . . Democrats for the Future."

With Kerry in the lower berth on the ticket, Dukakis crushed the GOP ticket of John W. Sears and Leon J. Lombardi, enjoying a victory margin of almost 23 percent.*

Kerry's election victory, however, came at a cost. Publicly, he was firing on all cylinders during the campaign, but it masked the turmoil of his private life. His marriage, troubled for some time, was in shambles. He and Julia had quietly separated that summer, though the split never became public during the campaign.

Struggling with depression since 1980, Kerry's wife felt abandoned. "Politics became my husband's life," Julia wrote in *A Change of Heart,* her 1996 book about divorce. "I tried to be happy for him, but after fourteen years as a political wife I associated politics with anger, fear, and loneliness."

In an interview in 2003, she declined to elaborate on this period, except to say: "The dissolution of the marriage was my doing, not John's. I wanted something else."

During a 1994 interview with the *Boston Globe,* Thorne was more reflective. "I had to be on my own," she said. "I had to force myself to be my own person, to call my own shots. My choice was not to do this within my marriage. It was very hurtful to John. But at that time I was not thinking rationally. I was all emotion."

Julia maintained appearances, though, posing for photo-

---

* One of Sears's opponents in the Republican primary had been a bright but obscure thirty-five-year-old state representative named Andrew H. Card Jr., now chief of staff to George W. Bush.

graphs with Michael Dukakis and his wife, Kitty, after John won the primary—and appearing again at the inauguration.

Kerry later became romantically involved with his former law partner, Sragow, for a few years, but Kerry said their relationship "had nothing to do with our marriage or breakup or anything." Sragow, now a state district court judge, declined to be interviewed.

As lieutenant governor, Kerry threw himself into his work and the excitement of returning to public life. When he took the oath in January, he stepped into a job with few responsibilities, except to serve as acting chief executive in the absence of the governor and to chair meetings of the Executive Council, a vestige of colonial government primarily charged with confirming or rejecting judicial nominations.

But Dukakis delegated other tasks to Kerry, who seized the opportunity. Not only would Kerry's office be the liaison to the federal government, a role O'Neill had assumed, but also quarterback the administration's anticrime agenda. Kerry was pleased. "Frankly, the governor doesn't have to give me anything to do," Kerry told reporters.

But as he tried to make a mark, Kerry maintained a breakneck pace, squeezing in fatherly time with his two daughters, Alexandra and Vanessa, now living apart from him with their mother. His own experience, with long absences from his parents while at boarding school, helped him become "a better father ... [and] make sure I was there" for his daughters, Kerry said.

But he acknowledged that the "juggling act" of public

life took its toll. Family time had to be shoehorned into his hectic schedule. For some events, Kerry's staff attended to details, including instructions in his daily schedule, such as this entry for December 11, 1983, a Sunday:

!!!HAPPY BIRTHDAY!!! [Kerry turned 40 that day.]

2:30 P.M. Arrive Cabot Theater (in Beverly). Go to the box office and pick up the tickets (6). Note: There are no reserved seats. It's first come first serve—This show is sold out.

3 P.M. The Magic Show begins. After the show, you and the kids are to meet your mother at Friendly's Restaurant for a snack.

Kerry's public schedule was a blur of activity—travel to conferences, endless political and ceremonial appearances, fund-raisers, and meetings. But it provided Kerry with an opportunity to establish a statewide presence, to create the political infrastructure he had lacked, and he took advantage of it. And his office's federal relations duties—monitoring budget, grant applications, and regulatory issues—gave Kerry a direct line to Washington, his first choice for political office.

When the governor had placed his criminal justice agenda in Kerry's portfolio, he also threw his deputy a curve. In February 1983, when Dukakis assembled his Anti-Crime Council, he named himself chair, relegating Kerry to vice chair. Nevertheless, Kerry played an important role, taking the lead crafting a computer crimes bill and pushing for a state racketeering law and victim-witness assistance program.

When the state legislature took up a bill in April 1983 to repeal a death penalty statute that had been approved by voters the previous fall and signed into law by King before he left office, Dukakis sent Kerry to testify against capital punishment. "We do not believe government should be in the business of killing people," Kerry told a legislative committee. "It cheapens life and demeans us all." About eighteen months later, the state's highest court struck down the law. Massachusetts today is one of twelve states without a death penalty law on its books.

The Dukakis team considered Kerry a loyal team player. A university professor today, Dukakis calls himself "a fan" of Kerry. "We had a great working relationship," he said. Dukakis, who won the 1988 Democratic presidential nomination but lost in a landslide to then vice president George H.W. Bush, supports Kerry's presidential bid.

John Sasso, who was Dukakis's chief of staff, said he "never had to worry that [Kerry] was trying to upstage Mike. He couldn't have been more loyal." Sasso has informally advised Kerry's 2004 presidential campaign.

For a lieutenant governor, loyalty usually meant a spot in the background. There was a mind-numbing quality to the job. The office was inundated with requests for small favors and Kerry's presence—at bar mitzvahs, Boy Scout installations, youth sports banquets. Most invitations were politely declined.

Kerry's office files, now at the Massachusetts Archives, are filled with the back-and-forth correspondence that reflects the everyday life of a politician—including a Kerry note to the registrar of motor vehicles requesting a four-digit license plate number for a constituent; a letter checking the status of a student's law school application; and an offer to Kerry for free passes to the Foxboro Raceway, a harness-racing track. (Kerry politely declined on ethical grounds.)

A lawyer in South Hadley wrote in August 1983 to thank Kerry and his staff for help "in clearing up the liquor license transfer to allow our client to open as scheduled." That prompted a playful note from Kerry's chief aide, James R. Gomes, to everyone in the office, regarding "Facilitating the Sale of Intoxicating Beverages"

Gomes headed a staff that would form the core of Kerry's future political team, including Whouley, Mary Anne Marsh, Bonnie Cronin, Patricia Foley, Ron Rosenblith, Christopher Greeley, Larry Carpman, Joseph Newman, Timothy Barnicle, and Jonathan Winer. Many now work as consultants, lobbyists, fund-raisers, or lawyers.

Despite a sometimes mundane schedule, Kerry managed in 1983 to emerge as a national figure in the fight against acid rain, the industrial pollutant that was killing off lakes and streams, weakening forests, pockmarking monuments and buildings, and causing respiratory ailments in people. During Kerry's first year as lieutenant governor, his schedules show at least twenty-three trips out of state on official business, eleven of them related to acid rain.

"John had a natural inclination to pursue environmental issues, and we hammered away on acid rain," recalled James S. Hoyte, Dukakis's environmental secretary at the time. "He threw his energy into it in a big way and gained a lot of visibility for the issue."

Kerry's efforts culminated in a February 1984 resolution of the National Governors Association calling for cuts in sulfur dioxide emissions that were polluting waterways in the Northeast. The resolution was a public relations coup and later would prove an important step toward enactment of the federal 1990 Clean Air Act amendments. But it avoided the nettlesome issue of cost, which would have been borne mostly by the industrial Midwest.

On January 12, 1984, one year into his four-year term as lieutenant governor, Kerry was in Germany's Black Forest on an acid rain fact-finding trip when he received the stunning news of an announcement that would be made later that day back in Boston: Illness was forcing forty-two-year-old Paul E. Tsongas to retire from his U.S. Senate seat after just one term.

"I was woken up at 3 in the morning and told Paul Tsongas was not running," Kerry recalled. An incredible opportunity was at hand. "But it was tricky," he added.

As a candidate, Kerry had assured Massachusetts voters that he was not seeking the lieutenant governor's job as a political stepping-stone. "I was concerned that it would be viewed as not having learned the lessons [of 1972] and that it was premature," he said. "One year into the lieutenant governor's office, to stand up and say, 'Hey, I think I should be senator.' You know, it was ballsy."

But, Kerry added, "it was the right place for me in terms of the things that were my passions. The issue of war and peace was on the table again."

Two weeks later, Kerry jumped into the race. He had plenty of company.

Chapter 11

LITMUS-TEST LIBERALS

LIEUTENANT GOVERNOR John Kerry entered the 1984 Senate race with the advantage of a statewide presence. What he lacked was Washington experience. U.S. representatives James M. Shannon and Edward J. Markey, his chief rivals for the nomination early in the race, had plenty of that. Both, in fact, were on leadership tracks in the House. They also had a fund-raising advantage—access to Washington's cash cow, political action committee (PAC) money from big labor and other national interests.

Kerry upended the money edge early with a declaration that he would disavow political action committee money—and a challenge to his opponents to follow suit. Kerry had taken some local PAC money during his lieutenant governor race. But the 1984 declaration introduced a line of attack that Kerry would deploy against virtually every opponent in the years to come.

During his long political career, Kerry would raise special interest money, bundles of it. But he would use the no-PAC shield to great symbolic advantage. "There is a clear pattern between political action committee contributions and congressional votes," Kerry argued during an early debate in 1984. "I don't believe our government should be up for the highest bidder."

Kerry's pledge was intended to distinguish himself in a competitive field. But it also served as a way to partially disarm his opponents. Markey, a liberal young member of Congress, was the first to blink. On April 16, his campaign said he would renounce PAC money and refund $7,250 in contributions.

Shannon, stung by a *Boston Globe* editorial cartoon that lampooned him as being in the pockets of special interests, followed two weeks later, returning $51,400 in PAC donations. In hindsight, Shannon said it was the "right thing to do." But returning all that money, he said, left him "cash-strapped the whole campaign."

On May 1, four months before the primary, Markey got cold feet and dropped out of the Senate race, opting instead to seek reelection in his Seventh Congressional District, just north of Boston, thereby preserving his position in Congress as a leader of the burgeoning nuclear freeze movement.

That left Shannon as Kerry's major rival for the Democratic nomination. Both men were firmly planted on the political left. Two lesser rivals in that year's Senate race offered nicknames for the Shannon-Kerry pairing: Secretary of State Michael J. Connolly dubbed them "the liberal twins." Former Massachusetts House speaker David M. Bartley called them "litmus-test liberals."

Nine years younger than Kerry, Shannon had educational credentials to match his rival. A graduate of prestigious Phillips Academy in Andover, he had earned his bachelor's degree a year ahead of schedule at Johns Hopkins University in Baltimore and picked up a law degree from George Washington University. In 1978, at age twenty-six, this son of a Lawrence physician won a hard-fought Democratic primary before going on to capture the Fifth Congressional District seat that Kerry had once sought. Six years later, he maintained a rock-solid base in that district, with a strong record on issues dear to organized labor and the party's socially progressive wing.

Shannon had been on a fast track almost from the day he arrived in Washington. House Speaker Thomas P. O'Neill Jr. warmed to him immediately, helping to install the freshman on the Ways and Means Committee. Shannon used that clout to channel federal money into his district, becoming an advocate of lunch-bucket delivery of services.

In personality, Shannon and Kerry were a study in contrasts. Kerry was considered by many to be aloof and patrician. Shannon was from Tip O'Neill's arm-around-the-shoulder, all-politics-is-local school. But Shannon was a virtual unknown in much of the state. His challenge was to raise his profile—and fast. He and Kerry quickly began to battle for the approval of the state's liberal interest groups, which enjoyed heightened influence in Democratic primaries.

First and foremost among those groups was the nuclear freeze movement. By the early 1980s, supporters of a freeze on developing nuclear weapons systems had transformed into a vibrant national movement—fed by wide-spread public fears about the global presence of 50,000 nuclear warheads and loose talk by officials from Ronald Reagan's administration about the possibility—and "man-ageability"—of nuclear war.

In 1984, with Reagan up for reelection, the nuclear freeze was a signature issue for liberal Democrats eager to advertise their opposition to the president's military buildup, particularly nuclear weapons such as the MX missile. (This year would prove the peak of the freeze movement's power: After 1983, Republican polling revealed Reagan's reelection vulnerability on the issue and the president's rhetoric and approach toward the Soviets shifted, easing public concern over the threat of nuclear war.)

In the liberal strongholds of Massachusetts, freeze activists were particularly well organized and, in a Democratic primary, they wielded both power and resources. Both Kerry and Shannon planned to ardently court this key bloc of liberal activists. After the exit of nuclear freeze leader Ed Markey from the race, Shannon thought he had an opening to win the blessing of these activists. But that opening would close quickly. In spring, with the September 18 primary date months away, candidates seeking an endorsement were asked about their positions. On a crucial test, the Freeze Voter '84 questionnaire submitted to both candidates, Shannon outscored Kerry by 100 to 94.

Then a strange thing happened. Paul F. Walker, Shannon's most prominent backer on the group's executive committee, graded the answers and laid out for Kerry campaign manager Paul L. Rosenberg both the flaws in Kerry's responses and what the "correct" answers should be. "Walker was confused about your answer" on funding the Trident submarine, Rosenberg wrote in an internal memo to Kerry, who had originally hedged in his opposition to funding new subs. "It is critically important that we get a 100 percent rating," Rosenberg added, in a memo that was first made public last year by the *Boston Globe*.

"You should explain how your position was misinterpreted so that he will correct the rating before it is distributed to the board tomorrow evening ... [Walker] is favorably disposed to change the grading because he knows of your strong support for the freeze and knows this is what you must have meant,'" Rosenberg concluded.

Kerry revised his answers, tied Shannon with a perfect score, and at the activists' meeting in late June, denied Shannon the 60 percent majority he needed to secure the endorsement for himself. Instead, Shannon and Kerry shared the group's stamp of approval in the primary field.

Kerry today says he does not recall the amendments to his Freeze Voter '84 questionnaire. When they were publicized at the time, Kerry said he mistakenly believed new Tridents would be needed as replacements for older submarines. "I wasn't trying to be on both sides of it," Kerry said.

Rosenberg did not respond to a request to be interviewed. But Walker, who said he later served as an informal adviser to Kerry, asserted that fairness, not politics, was behind his role. "We wanted to provide Kerry, and all candidates for that matter, an opportunity to clarify their positions," wrote Walker, who became an administrator with the Washington-based environmental advocacy group Global Green USA, in an e-mail. Shannon, however, was stunned to learn of his erstwhile ally's back-channel role. "I can guarantee you this is all news to me. I never knew that," Shannon, now president of the National Fire Protection Association, said in 2003. The stalemate for the Freeze Voter '84 endorsement was an important tactical victory for Kerry then, but it has proven to be a handicap in his presidential campaign.

In his zeal to keep pace with Shannon's leftward drift on disarmament, Kerry supported cancellation of a host of weapons systems that have become the basis of U.S. military might—the high-tech munitions and delivery systems on display to the world as they leveled the Iraqi regime of Saddam Hussein in a matter of weeks in 2003. These weapons became conversation topics at American dinner tables during the Iraq war, but candidate Kerry in 1984 said he would have voted to cancel many of them—the B-1 bomber; B-2 stealth bomber; AH-64 Apache helicopter; Patriot missile; the F-15, F-14A, and F-14D jets; the AV-8B Harrier jet; the Aegis air-defense cruiser; and the Trident missile system. During the campaign, he also advocated reductions in many other systems, such as the M-1 Abrams tank, the Bradley Fighting Vehicle, the Tomahawk cruise missile, and the F-16 jet.

In retrospect, Kerry said some of his positions in those days were "ill-advised, and I think some of them are stupid in the context of the world we find ourselves in right now and the things that I've learned since then." But he defended his opposition at the time to the MX missile, the

"Star Wars" strategic defense initiative, and some other programs.

"Some of this stuff was ahead of its time. Some was not as well thought out as it might be," Kerry said of his campaign posture then. "I'm not ashamed of that. I was [forty] years old, running for the United States Senate for the first time ... and I'm sure that some of it was driven at the time by the nature of the beast I was fighting politically." "I mean, you learn as you go in life," said Kerry. He characterized as "pretty responsible" his subsequent Senate voting record on defense.

The Massachusetts Democratic Party convention is an early organizational test of a statewide candidate's appeal to core party activists. But endorsements from the party faithful are unreliable predictors of primary results, since Independents are allowed to vote in those elections.

At the convention in June, Shannon spent much of his campaign war chest and edged out Kerry for the endorsement of the party activists. The Lawrence politician received no bump in the polls, however, and limped through the summer, short of cash. "Everybody told me I had to win that convention to raise my statewide recognition, and, if I won, it would catapult me," Shannon said. In hindsight, the all-out effort was an error. "I came out of it broke and not having moved the needle a bit," Shannon said. Snubbed again by the state party faithful, Kerry nevertheless turned defeat into an asset, portraying himself in the ensuing campaign as an "outsider" to Shannon's "insider."

After the convention, Kerry's campaign focused on shoring up support with different constituency groups. A key endorsement loomed—Boston's Black Political Task Force, an important barometer for the state's African Americans, who composed about 3 percent of adults.

On June 19, Kerry staffer Michal Regunberg wrote a memo to top campaign officials rating the candidate's standing among black voters. One problem, the memo noted, was that Kerry had alienated some of Boston's black leaders in 1983 when he endorsed Ray Flynn in the city's mayoral race. Kerry was returning the favor of Flynn's support for his lieutenant governor campaign. But Flynn's opponent was Melvin H. King, a former state representative and the first African American ever to qualify for the two-person runoff in a Boston mayor's race.

This and other Kerry negatives were surmountable, Regunberg believed. But the Kerry campaign should also exploit a Shannon vulnerability: "In five and a half years in Congress, he has not hired one single minority on his Congressional staff," she wrote. In contrast, Kerry's office manager in the lieutenant governor's office, Jeanette Boone, was an African American. Shannon's hiring record surfaced briefly in the campaign. And Kerry clearly overcame whatever doubts existed about his record on race: The task force endorsed him.

Through the spring and into summer of 1984, campaigns nationally were kicking into gear. Former vice president Walter Mondale, standard-bearer of old-style Democratic liberalism, beat back challenges from "new ideas" candidate Gary Hart and "rainbow coalition" leader

Jesse Jackson to emerge as the Democrats' presidential nominee.

In Massachusetts, the so-called liberal twins plowed through an exhausting thirty-eight candidate forums before various advocacy groups and party activists. "We were vying for the same pool of votes," Shannon recalled. "We kept outbidding each other ... appealing to the margins. In the end, many people never saw much difference between us on the issues."

What Shannon didn't know at the time was that looming in his opponent's not-too-distant past were two potentially damaging episodes. But news of these financial transactions, which could have hurt Kerry, did not surface until years later.

In the first case, Kerry as lieutenant governor made use of cars provided by a Lynn, Massachusetts, auto dealer over the course of sixteen months without making lease payments. In the second, revealed in 2003 by the *Boston Globe*, Kerry became involved in an exotic offshore investment scheme that he said he aborted because he feared political embarrassment.

In April 1984, as Kerry's race for the Senate was taking off, Frank Phillips, then a *Boston Herald* reporter, made inquiries into reports that the lieutenant governor was driving a car that he wasn't paying for. But Phillips—faced with confusing documentation and statements by Kerry's aides that the incident was a staff-generated billing mix-up—did not write the story.

Shortly after the reporter's inquiries, state records show, Kerry's lieutenant governor campaign committee paid the

auto dealer $2,000. Kerry later said he also made payments
with his own funds that totaled $13,600, including interest
of 18 percent.

Kerry's relationship with the Lynn car dealer, Bob Brest,
was disclosed eight years later, when his lease surfaced
during the federal investigation of U.S. Representative
Nicholas Mavroules of Peabody. In 1993, Mavroules
pleaded guilty to the free use of Brest cars and fourteen
other corruption-related charges and was sentenced to fifteen months in federal prison. Brest, who went out of business in 1991, routinely provided free or cut-rate deals on
cars to other North Shore political figures. By then, the
Kerry lease had long since been paid in full, and the U.S.
attorney said there was no basis for any action against
Kerry. Kerry says he knew Brest "slightly." His calendars
show he had visited Brest's dealership at least four times in
1983.

He attributed his temporary free use of the car to "lousy
bookkeeping" and said he repeatedly told his aide Christopher Greeley to clear up the problem. Said Greeley: "It
was my responsibility to take care of it, and I didn't do it."

The other questionable financial transaction can be
traced directly to Kerry. In 1983, Kerry received $225,105
from his former law practice with Roanne Sragow, a sum
that represented his share of proceeds from cases the firm
had handled. That income was subject to a punishing mar-
ginal tax rate of 50 percent. Like many well-to-do Americans from the period, Kerry went looking for a tax shelter.
Acting on the advice of one of his fund-raisers, he invested
in a scheme using offshore corporations.

In December 1983, a little over a month before Paul Tsongas announced he was giving up his Senate seat, Kerry, by his own estimate, invested between $25,000 and $30,000. It was a scheme known as a "straddle" that involved forward contracts to buy and sell certain commodities through companies in the Cayman Islands. The shelter, mostly involving only paper transactions, was supposed to create long-term capital income gains, which were taxed at a much lower rate than regular income, and would be offset by short-term losses in income, the other side of the straddle.

Early in his Senate campaign, probably in March or April, Kerry said, he canceled the deal after his accountant questioned its legitimacy. He explained, "I did not want to file an income tax return as a public person that I thought could have been subject to question," adding that he forfeited his investment and never claimed any tax benefit from the loss. "I thought it was a way to try to minimize tax consequences," said Kerry, who could not recall many details of the transaction. "It wasn't, and I learned a hard lesson."

Kerry and aides who reviewed his dealings said he met all public disclosure requirements, both as a Massachusetts elected official and a Senate candidate. But records obtained by the *Boston Globe* revealed that much went undisclosed about the complex scheme.

On December 13, 1983, Kerry pledged 2,470 shares he held in a company called Peabody Commodities Trading Corporation as collateral for a $238,527.40 promissory note signed the same day to Sytel Traders, Ltd. Both companies were registered in the Caymans, where strict secrecy rules conceal corporate ownership interests.

Kerry has never disclosed a stake in Peabody Commodities or an indebtedness to Sytel Traders. He did not dispute the authenticity of the documents produced by the *Boston Globe*, but dismissed them as meaningless "paperwork" that did not reflect real assets, actual debt, or liabilities arising from the transactions. "There was no collateral that I was involved in; none whatsoever," Kerry said. "It was paperwork. That's why my accountant said it sucked."

Kerry said he was unaware that the companies involved were based offshore in the Caymans and that he "would have opposed it" if he had known. However, the pledge agreement, bearing Kerry's signature, states in the first line that Sytel Traders was organized "under the laws of the Cayman Islands." Within two years of Kerry's actions, the Internal Revenue Service began cracking down on tax shelter abuses, including some involving Sytel and its subsidiaries. Some Sytel investors paid steep penalties.

In the spring of 1984, weeks after he quietly pulled the plug on his own tax shelter, candidate Kerry inveighed against an unfair system. "You need a major overhaul of the tax structure," Kerry told a panel of reporters on a Boston television station on May 6. "You need to close those crazy loopholes that are nonproductive."

As the September 18 primary approached, Shannon racked up the bulk of endorsements by labor unions, newspapers, and public officials.

Kerry, meanwhile, won backing from some key mayors, including Carlton Viveiros in Fall River and Brian Lawler in New Bedford. But his most important ally was the mayor of his new hometown and the state's biggest city—Boston's Ray Flynn. Kerry had moved into the city's posh Back Bay neighborhood in 1983, after his separation from Julia. But he was not well known in the tribal world of Democratic politics in the city. So Flynn, the son of a longshoreman and champion of organized labor, became an invaluable ally. "I always admired him because of his Vietnam record, the war part of it," Flynn said. "He was a wealthy kid going into the military. Usually, it's poor kids who fight these wars."

Flynn, who later served as U.S. ambassador to the Vatican, took plenty of heat for supporting Kerry. "All my buddies were with Shannon, and they were all over me for supporting Kerry," he recalled. Some warned that the Kerry alliance would hurt Flynn in future elections. "It was that intense," Flynn recalled. "Tip [O'Neill] calls me, all upset with me for not supporting Jimmy Shannon. [U.S. representative] Joe Moakley, same thing," Flynn recalled of his South Boston neighbor. "Organized labor and all the important politicians, it seemed, didn't like John Kerry."

But Flynn returned the favor of Kerry's earlier support by opening critical Boston doors for the Senate candidate. On Labor Day, fifteen days before the primary, Flynn introduced Kerry to union leaders at their annual breakfast at the Boston Park Plaza Hotel. He brought Kerry to various union halls and accompanied him to some of the city's famous saloons—the Eire Pub in Adams Village, J. J. Foley's in the South End—as well as many Irish bars along the four-mile length of Dorchester Avenue, which runs through the city's most populous working-class neighbor-hood.

"Getting into the Eire Pub at 4 o'clock on a Friday afternoon, when people stop off to have one, the word got around that Kerry was trying to meet people where they actually gather," Flynn said. Perhaps more significant, Flynn's large political organization became a proxy army for Kerry in Boston, where field operatives still move votes. Among those helping Kerry was Raymond C. Dooley, Flynn's chief administrative aide and political guru. It would not be the last Kerry campaign in which Dooley would play a role.

Kerry was leading the race in virtually every poll—until the final days, when Shannon began to close in. Eleven days before the primary, the *Boston Globe* enthusiastically endorsed Shannon, noting, however, that the candidate was "far superior to his current campaign, which has been con-ducted in a sloppy, unfocused fashion."

The editorial praised Kerry's courage in war and in the protest that followed and included a backhanded compli-ment. "Of [Kerry's] eloquence there can be little doubt," wrote Martin F. Nolan, the editorial page editor. "Effective representation in the Senate requires more than oratory, where an ambitious speechmaker is often ineffective. An ability to understand other points of view and to grasp the details of legislation is also required."

In late tracking polls, Shannon was surging slightly ahead. Then, Vietnam came to Kerry's aid. Up until now, the chief emphasis of Kerry's "War and Peace"–themed campaign had been peace—freezing nuclear weapons and cutting military spending. Now the "war" side of that equation would become Kerry's trump card against his liberal twin.

Smarting from Kerry's taunts that the congressman had reversed himself—voting first for and later against the MX missile system—Shannon tried to turn the tables. During a televised debate a week before primary day, Shannon contrasted his own U-turn on the MX to Kerry's change of heart on the Vietnam War.

"If you felt that strongly about the war, you would not have gone," Shannon said. "I was very proud that you changed your mind."

Kerry's counterstrike came two nights later, in another debate. He recast Shannon's remarks as an insult to those veterans who served in Vietnam. "You impugn the service of veterans in that war by saying they are somehow dopes or wrong for going," he said.

Shannon refused to yield. "John, you know that dog won't hunt," he said. "I don't owe anybody an apology."

With Shannon appearing critical of military service, a band of Vietnam vets, all Kerry men, then wheeled into action. "There was a kind of raw, gut instinct, and the campaign acted on it the way you wouldn't today," said longtime Kerry strategist John Marttila. What he meant was there was no polling data as a guide. They were flying blind.

Vietnam veterans began shadowing Shannon in the primary campaign's final days, traveling around the state, "looking for ways to pick fights," Marttila said. "This was not fake stuff. John's bona fides had been called into question, and these guys had gone to Vietnam. It was powerful material." With help from the vets, who called themselves "the dog hunters," Kerry stopped Shannon cold. His athletic stamina and what one campaign staffer called "laser-like focus" also became major assets in those frenzied final days.

The September 18 finish was memorable. Kerry's field organization pulled him over the top. He lost Lowell and Middlesex County, the state's most populous, by big margins. But Kerry beat Shannon in Boston by 7,244 votes, and in Worcester, Fall River, New Bedford, and most other major cities. In a four-way race, Kerry won with 41 percent of the vote. His statewide margin over Shannon was paper thin, only 24,529 votes, or 3 percent, out of 790,000 cast.

The general election was less than two months away. But Kerry's camp expected light opposition from Raymond Shamie, a self-made millionaire who in the GOP primary had upset Elliot L. Richardson, the résumé-rich icon of the flagging Brahmin wing of the Massachusetts Republican Party. Democrats outnumbered Republicans nearly 4 to 1 in Massachusetts, and Shamie, an entrepreneur, represented a conservative wing out of step with most Massachusetts voters. Kerry did to Shamie what Kerry's tormentors had done to him in the 1972 congressional race, when they painted the upstart as a radical leftist. In the Senate race, Kerry's campaign portrayed the avuncular businessman as a right-wing extremist who had flirted with the John Birch Society years earlier.

Kerry also puffed up his Democratic Party credentials, exaggerating both his campaign work for John F. Kennedy in prep school and his involvement as a Yale student in the Freedom Summer of 1964, when white volunteers headed to the South to help blacks push for voting rights. A campaign flyer, titled "A Message from John Kerry," began: "Ever since I worked as a young volunteer in John Kennedy's presidential campaign, I have been deeply committed to participation in politics and political issues. . . . Back then, I joined the struggle for voting rights in the South."

But Kerry's involvement with JFK's 1960 campaign was minimal, at best. Today, he acknowledges he may only have participated in a single literature drop in Concord, New Hampshire, while boarding at St. Paul's School. Moreover, Kerry's role in the struggle to register black voters in Mississippi was confined to the Yale campus in New Haven. Kerry's accounts over the years of his involvement have sometimes left the impression—and resulted in press reports—that the young Yalie was actually down South, with the freedom riders. He wasn't.

"I remember we saw the buses off and helped raise money for the buses and were supportive of it, but I did not personally go down there on a freedom ride," Kerry said. Not long thereafter, he did visit the South, he said, "to see what was going on, which was an eye-opener for me. I had never seen a sign that said, 'No colored, whites only.'"

In the 1984 general election, however, the main thrust of Kerry's candidacy was an attack on Reagan's economic, foreign, and military policies. He was particularly scornful of the Grenada invasion, launched by Reagan the previous October to evacuate U.S. medical students after a Marxist-backed military coup on the Caribbean island.

At one point he likened the military action to "Boston College playing football against the Sisters of Mercy." He told the *Cape Codder* newspaper that the Grenada invasion represented "the Reagan policy of substituting public relations for diplomatic relations ... no substantial threat to U.S. interests existed and American lives were not endangered ... The invasion represented a bully's show of force against a weak Third World nation. The invasion only served to heighten world tensions and further strain brittle U.S.-Soviet and North-South relations."

Twenty years later, in his campaign for president, Kerry would rewrite history by listing Grenada among the U.S. military incursions he had supported. "I was dismissive of the majesty of the invasion of Grenada," Kerry says now. "But I basically was supportive. I never publicly opposed it."

On November 6, Election Day, Ronald Reagan routed Walter Mondale, winning forty-nine states, all but the Democrat's home state of Minnesota. In Congress, Republicans lost two seats in the Senate and gained fifteen in the House. And in Massachusetts, Democrat John Kerry soundly beat Republican Ray Shamie, with a comfortable ten-point margin.

More than thirteen years after he rocketed onto the national stage with his antiwar speech, Kerry was returning to the Senate. Now, he would be a member of the club.

Chapter 12

GIVE PEACE A CHANCE

AT FIRST, a trip to Nicaragua seemed like a stroke of media genius for two freshmen senators eager to regain the national prominence they had enjoyed more than a dozen years earlier as Vietnam veterans opposing the war. By early 1985, Kerry was a member of the same Senate committee he had testified before fourteen years earlier, asking lawmakers, and the nation: "How do you ask a man to be the last man to die for a mistake?" His friend and colleague, Tom Harkin of Iowa, a navy pilot who tested planes after they were repaired during Vietnam, was returning as a senator fifteen years after he had been lauded by the antiwar movement for exposing South Vietnam's tiger-cage torture chambers.

More than most, this pair of senators was attuned to the dangers of government lies and wartime atrocities. Kerry's swift boat was making incursions into Cambodia at a time when the Nixon White House was denying any military operations there. Kerry returned from the war sickened by the sight of U.S. soldiers killing civilians. As a congressional aide on a fact-finding trip, Harkin discovered underground cells where hundreds of men, women, and children were crammed into cages like animals and tortured with caustic lime by South Vietnamese guards. Resisting efforts to suppress evidence of atrocities by a U.S. ally, Harkin went public with photos and, in doing so, energized antiwar activists.

Now Kerry and Harkin intended to stop government lies and wartime atrocities—on a closer continent. Two years after the fall of the Nicaraguan dictatorship in 1979, the U.S. government had secretly begun using the CIA to finance and train an army of guerrillas known as "contras" to overthrow the country's Marxist Sandinista government. Congress ordered the Reagan White House to cut off contra support when it found out that the CIA had directed the mining of Nicaragua's harbors. But Reagan wasn't giving up.

In January 1985, the same month Kerry and Harkin were sworn in as U.S. senators, President Reagan gave a State of the Union speech portraying the contras—and other "freedom fighters" like them around the world—as heroic warriors against communism. America, Reagan said, "must not break faith with those who are risking their lives on every continent, from Afghanistan to Nicaragua, to defy Soviet-supported aggression." He intended to ask Congress to approve military and humanitarian aid to the contras.

To Kerry, the contras were not freedom fighters but a CIA-funded "mercenary army, which has been guilty of atrocities against civilians and has resorted to terrorist methods in attempting to undermine the Sandinista government," as he told Senate colleagues at the time. "The American people are being misled on a systematic basis about what we are doing, and by what means, in that region."

Nicaragua was Vietnam all over again, Kerry and Harkin were certain. And these two combat-veterans-turned-anti-war-activists planned to lead the charge to stop Reagan's secret war. If the strategy unfolded as planned, the freshmen senators would be applauded by anyone who cared about an American foreign policy conducted peaceably and with honor. They would emerge as heroic foes against a warmongering Reagan White House.

But Kerry's game plan had a hitch. And that hitch had a Marxist face—Nicaraguan president Daniel Ortega.

On Thursday, April 18, 1985, Kerry and Harkin boarded a plane to Managua, Nicaragua's capital city. Just three months in office, Kerry was already on a roll. He had secured Paul Tsongas's old seat on the prominent Senate Foreign Relations Committee and was hurriedly carving out a reputation as a vocal opponent of Reagan's foreign and military policies. He had just completed a six-day fact-finding mission to the Philippines, where he was determined to see the beginning of the end of U.S. aid to dictator Ferdinand Marcos.

The Senate, led by the independent-minded majority leader Bob Dole, was in the hands of Republicans. Nevertheless, the chamber offered plenty of high-profile running room for those Democrats (and there were at least half a dozen on that side of the Capitol) considering a run for the Oval Office. Kerry, who turned forty-one a month after his election, had arrived in Washington as the second-youngest in a class of seven new senators; only thirty-six-year-old Al Gore of Tennessee was younger, and he had the advantage of eight years' experience in the House.

If Kerry was new to the intricacies of Washington, he was an old hand at attracting media attention. One month into his tenure, the *Washington Post* published a lengthy profile on this soon-to-be bachelor, a handsome figure "gushed over" at parties, with medals for wartime bravery and a thirst for athletic extremes. West Virginia senator Robert C. Byrd, a man highly attuned to the niceties of Senate protocol, inserted the article into the *Congressional Record*, noting that "in the short time [Kerry] has been with us he has shown the promise of becoming an outstanding contributing member of this body."

The *Washington Post* article hinted at a national future for the junior senator from Massachusetts. But, in a pattern that was becoming familiar to Kerry, it also cited the JFK initials monogrammed on his white shirts, the surgery to correct his jaw that "coincidentally made him more attractive to the cameras," and the colleagues who considered him a "cocky smooth operator." The jaw surgery was the result of a chronic ailment: an abnormality in the way his teeth aligned that caused a clicking in his jaw. Evidently, the clicking was exacerbated when he slammed into a goal post while playing hockey.

"I think I got something of a rap ten years ago which I brought on myself, partly because of my impatience and

partly through my total focus, my absolute, total commitment to ending the war," Kerry told writer Lois Romano
when asked about his reputation for political opportunism.
"I think there was an element of brashness ... I admit that
now ... Why do people dwell on that so?"

Kerry's reputation had followed him to Washington like
a mangy stray dog. He told another reporter at the time that
"the perception of me as a showboat has persisted by virtue
of the strong image people have of 1971 and 1972, which
has proven indelible." Even Kerry's mother acknowledged
her son's image problem that year: "He's a very warm, caring person, despite possibly an outer appearance of being
self-centered and ambitious."

Kerry was flirting with those same labels again as he and
Harkin jetted toward Managua, reporters in tow, to meet
with top Sandinista officials. A congressional vote on Reagan's request for aid to the contras was just five days away.
And the pair of senators hoped that their efforts could
jump-start stalled peace negotiations between the U.S. and
the Sandinistas, bringing an eventual end to the contras'
guerrilla war against the Nicaraguan government. "My generation, a lot of us, grew up with the phrase 'give peace a
chance,' as part of a song that captured a lot of people's
imagination," Kerry would soon tell his Senate colleagues.
"I hope that the president of the United States will give
peace a chance."

"Look at it," Kerry told a reporter sitting next to him as
their plane touched down in Managua. "It reminds me so
much of Vietnam. The same lushness. The tree lines."
More than physical geography, and Third World poverty,

Kerry saw in the U.S.-Nicaragua situation a direct parallel to Vietnam: The U.S. government was deceiving its own people about its role in escalating the killing in a guerrilla war.

The contras, mostly national guardsmen from the former dictatorship of Anastasio Somoza, were becoming notorious for atrocities committed against Nicaragua's civilian population. But the Sandinista officials on the senators' itinerary carried their own baggage: The Marxist government had imported Soviet and Cuban military advisers. It had censored the media, confiscated property, jailed dissidents. It stood accused, like the contras, of violence against civilians.

Kerry acknowledged the Sandinistas' failings and planned to press officials for assurances that needed changes were on the horizon. After dinner at the foreign minister's residence the night they arrived, Kerry told a reporter accompanying him on the trip: "We asked for a statement of their response on a number of issues that ranged from the status of the contras to individual liberties to the issue of Soviet bases in Nicaragua."

During their two-day stay, the two senators talked to Nicaraguans on both sides of the conflict—a businessman who denounced the Sandinista government's repression, a political leader who described the government as a "Marxist regime" uninterested in fair elections, a priest who had watched the contras massacre thirty-five civilians, and a mother who described how her daughter and three teachers had been ambushed and killed by the U.S.-backed guerrillas. "It didn't have to be," Kerry said after meeting with the mother. "There was another way, a way without violence; she was a victim and I'm tired of looking at victims."

The visit culminated Friday night in a five-hour dinner meeting, joined by Nicaraguan president Daniel Ortega, that centered on ways to restart peace talks with the United States. As the senators were leaving early Saturday morning, they were handed a two-and-a-half page offer from Ortega to the U.S. government: The Sandinista government would agree to a cease-fire and would restore civil liberties if the U.S. government ended its support to the contras. "If the United States is serious about peace, this is a great opportunity," said Kerry.

Kerry and Harkin arrived back in Washington Saturday afternoon and took their places center stage in the brewing debate over Reagan's request for contra aid. The trip to Nicaragua had already been a media boon for Kerry. "Time and again, reporters and television crews focused on the more telegenic Kerry, leaving him, embarrassed at times, speaking for both of them as Harkin stood in the background," noted a reporter on the trip.

Back at home, Kerry was on the network news within hours of landing, saying he was delivering a proposal to the White House to "stop the killing." On Sunday, when Senate leaders met with President Reagan at the White House to discuss aid to the contras, Kerry—who won the only spot available to the two freshman by flipping a coin—was in attendance.

On Sunday morning, the same day as the White House meeting, Kerry squeezed in an appearance on CBS's *Face the Nation*. It was the tenth anniversary of the fall of Saigon,

the nightmarish ending to the Vietnam War when terror-
ized people stormed planes and helicopters, hoping to flee
the conquering Vietcong. Before Kerry's appearance, CBS
viewers watched a film clip of Reagan calling Vietnam "a
noble cause," while former secretary of state Henry
Kissinger appeared in person to argue that Nixon had
achieved "an honorable peace."

Then Kerry described his own lessons from Vietnam:
"We have to learn how to define our interests, define
achievable goals ... bring the American people into the
process, and do it honestly." On the subject of Nicaragua,
Kerry rejected the assertion that Ortega's offer was an
eleventh-hour PR campaign designed to derail the aid-to-
the-contras vote. "This is an offer which I believe is a substantive one," he said.

Just three months on the job, and Kerry was the man of
the moment in the most contentious policy debate in
Washington. He was on network TV offering lessons from
Vietnam. He had met with the Nicaraguan president. Now
he was meeting with the U.S. president and Senate leaders.
He was carrying a peace offer with the potential to derail
Reagan's cherished request for aid to the contras, on which
the House was scheduled to vote on Tuesday.

Then things started turning sour.

That afternoon, the White House denounced the
Ortega peace offer as a slick "propaganda initiative" and
suggested the naive senators had been used by a Marxist
government intent on affecting the upcoming Tuesday
vote. "I'm sure it's quite a problem for us when senators
run around and start dealing with the Communists them-

selves," said Secretary of State George P. Shultz. Arizona senator Barry Goldwater accused the freshmen senators of breaking a 1799 federal statute prohibiting private citizens from negotiating with foreign governments.

The Reagan administration, eager to overthrow the Sandinistas, had plenty of ideological reason to denounce the Kerry-Harkin mission. But some of the fine print of the administration rebuttal suggested the senators might have created some problems of their own making. In the document Kerry delivered, Ortega reaffirmed the "non-aligned nature" of the Nicaraguan revolution, despite the country's ties to the Soviet Union and Cuba. And, in response to promises that civil liberties would be restored, the State Department said Ortega had extended for six months the government's repressive state of emergency—the day after meeting with Harkin and Kerry.

Kerry said he was not naive about the Sandinistas' repressive behavior. A Kerry adviser on the trip recalled that Kerry was "disgusted" by the foreign minister's lavish home, which had been confiscated, even while purportedly leading a "people's revolution" in the poverty-plagued country. Nevertheless, Kerry told his Senate colleagues on Tuesday, the day of the House vote on a $14-million contra aid package, that it was time to end "the bloodshed, the suffering, the terrorism." He stated, "I am willing ... to take the risk in the effort to put to test the good faith of the Sandinistas."

That day, the Sandinistas collected an important victory when the House rejected Reagan's request for aid to their enemy, the contras. A day later, Daniel Ortega, who had promised to force Soviet and Cuban advisers out of his country if contra aid ended, boarded an Aeroflot jet to Moscow to collect a $200-million loan. Reagan's speechwriters couldn't have scripted a better I-told-you-so ending.

Ortega's trip to Moscow—which at least one account, by a columnist sympathetic to Kerry and Harkin, said the senators were informed about during their meetings in Managua—left Democrats red-faced. "He's embarrassed us, to be perfectly truthful," Kerry's powerful Massachusetts colleague, House Speaker Tip O'Neill, said of Ortega. (Although Connecticut senator Chris J. Dodd wondered aloud why his Democratic colleagues were so stunned: "Where did my colleagues think he was going to go? Disney World? The man is a Marxist.")

Kerry issued his own response to the Ortega trip. "I'm as mad as anyone that [Ortega] is in the Soviet Union," he said. "But the fact is, if we're not willing to talk, the question has to be asked: Where else is he going to turn for help?"

Ortega's Moscow trip also produced an opening for the White House to renew its crusade for contra aid. Six weeks later, the Democratic-led House dramatically reversed itself and approved $27 million in nonmilitary funding for the contras. The Senate also approved aid; and a Kerry amendment requiring the money be disbursed in compliance with international law passed only after being watered down to allow activities authorized under U.S. law.

In this highly charged ideological environment, Kerry was caught off guard by the attacks suggesting he had been cavorting with, and used by, the Communists. "He was perplexed and surprised at the response," recalled his chief counsel, Jonathan Winer. "He hadn't done anything wrong. But he hadn't experienced the Washington press corps."

The Nicaragua episode played into the hands of conservatives eager to portray Kerry as soft on communism. Columnist Robert Novak accused Kerry of "playing kissy face with Ortega" and others began accusing him of being committed to a "radical leftist agenda." In early 1986, when a senior administration official suggested Kerry and Harkin had acted as Ortega apologists, Kerry responded with this statement: "The White House is saying that if you're not with their policy, then you're with the other guys. No one on the Hill I know of has ever apologized for the Sandinistas. Nor should they. But the Sandinistas' failings should not be an excuse for ignoring opportunities for peace."

In fact, Kerry's views had been consistent throughout 1985 since his return from Nicaragua: The White House should engage the Sandinistas, whatever their failings, in peace talks rather than fund a covert war that would destabilize the region and push Nicaragua further into the arms of the Soviets. Reagan was threatening America's reputation in the region, and within the international community, by its promotion of a CIA-backed contra army.

Never far from Kerry's mind was Vietnam, and the prospect of American soldiers arriving back from the Central American jungles in body bags. On this and related issues, Kerry's relentless drive came largely from "Vietnam veteran syndrome," said former aide and investigator Jack Blum, describing the disillusionment that returning soldiers often felt as a result of that divisive war. "You come home and discover that people who are running the war are just interested in covering their ass; meanwhile, real people are dying real deaths.... This was a very searing business."

On the floor of the Senate, Kerry told colleagues his "experience of sixteen years ago has taught me that where you have the opportunity to pursue a chance of talking before you shoot you owe it to the next generation of Americans, as well as the present, to do so."

Kerry had built an experienced staff of experts. But one of his most eager advisers on foreign policy was his own father. "My brother used to laugh about getting faxes from my father," said Kerry's sister Diana. "He was really upset when they were capitalized. My father had a political opinion, which he was happy to express to John."

Richard Kerry, a veteran diplomat, held opinions that, in the political environment of 2004, would fit neatly with Democratic primary voters or European commentators angry about the American invasion of Iraq. In a 1990 book, he decried an American attitude that "other people ought to share our view of world order," that "only American democracy currently embodies the virtue essential to maintain that order and peace."

Although it is unclear whether Richard Kerry advised his son on Central America, it was certainly a subject of keen interest to him. In his book, he singled out Nicaragua in the 1980s as an example of the Reagan-era insistence on "viewing the cold war in stark black-and-white terms that divide the world into the communist Soviet and democratic American camps." It is an "illusion that the Sandinistas are the obstacle to democracy when they are little more than a symptom of the conditions which prevail in Nicaragua," the former diplomat wrote.

The Ortega episode, combined with his voting record, planted Kerry firmly at the left end of the Senate political spectrum. In his first year in office, he compiled one of the most liberal voting records in Congress—achieving a rating of 85 out of 100 from the left-leaning Americans for Democratic Action. According to *Congressional Quarterly*, he voted against President Reagan 73 percent of the time.

Many of those votes were cast against the president's favorite weapons systems—which were the same ones that Kerry concluded were "extremely expensive, destabilizing, and didn't work," said counsel Jonathan Winer. Kerry gave his maiden speech asking the Senate not to move forward on deploying the MX missile, which the Reagan White House wanted in part as leverage for upcoming arms control talks with the Soviets.

In May, the Senate rejected a Kerry proposal to continue a ban on anti-satellite weapons testing. In June, he unsuccessfully tried to freeze funding for the Strategic Defense Initiative (commonly known as Star Wars), which he called "fundamentally incompatible" with U.S.-Soviet arms control agreements. In September, at a nuclear freeze conference in Geneva, he proposed recasting arms control efforts to establish a verification process that would eliminate the need for the United States and the Soviet Union to trust each other.

Kerry made the argument that "national security in a

nuclear environment entails three fundamental elements: A strong national defense, the pursuit of true arms control and arms reduction agreements, and the maintenance of our twenty-year strategic doctrine of mutual deterrence."

But if Kerry was a staunch opponent of the GOP's defense and foreign policies, he would surprise his allies by supporting conservatives on fiscal policy. In the fall of 1985, he became one of the first Senate Democrats to sign on as a co-sponsor to the Gramm-Rudman-Hollings deficit reduction measure.

"I remember it clearly because I was a bit taken aback," recalled then senator Warren Rudman, Republican of New Hampshire. "I didn't know Senator Kerry and at that time, in the fall of '85, there was a lot of reflexive opposition from Democrats who ended up supporting it. I remember John wanting to talk about this. He was concerned—as we were concerned—about the escalating deficit."

"All the bill really did was set limits on how much the government could borrow," Rudman noted. "You could cut programs or raise taxes, but you couldn't borrow more money. That wasn't understood. Kerry understood it clearly." At the time, the federal government was running $200-billion budget deficits and the national debt had doubled to $2 trillion.

Kerry's position stunned many of his liberal staffers, who—like many Democratic lawmakers—worried that the law would result in social spending cuts. "We would go back and forth, back and forth, with extraordinarily lengthy debates," recalled one aide.

"It was not particularly comfortable for him vis-à-vis

other Northeastern Democrats," recalled Winer. "It created as many political problems as it solved. He agonized over the decision—[noting] Teddy's going to be unhappy, Chris is going to be unhappy...." In fact, many liberal Democrats were unhappy—at first.

But a number of them, including Kennedy and Dodd, ended up supporting the measure, in part to "impose real sacrifice" on Reagan's military "spending spree," as Kennedy put it. "John Kerry took an impressive leadership role on the issue," Kennedy noted at the time. (Gramm-Rudman passed Congress by a wide bipartisan margin and was signed into law by Reagan. But it later was substantially revised after the original law's automatic spending cuts were declared unconstitutional.)

Nearly a year later, on a summer day in 1986, members of the Senate Foreign Relations Committee gathered behind closed doors off the chamber floor to hear a sales pitch from Kerry, who had spent the spring conducting a freelance investigation into reports that the Reagan administration was illegally providing aid to the Nicaraguan contras. At this closed session, he planned to urge the committee to launch an official probe.

To Kerry's critics—and they were especially fierce toward a Massachusetts liberal at the height of President Reagan's popularity—the action seemed like another case of Kerry grandstanding. Several committee members were wary of Kerry's reputation for self-promotion; one griped aloud that the senator's staff was already leaking to the press.

The Republican senators who controlled the committee owed their majority status to Reagan's popularity. Privately, they were feeling increasing pressure from a shadowy figure at the White House, a Marine lieutenant colonel named Oliver North, who was orchestrating support for the contras.

But behind the scenes, Kerry had forged an alliance with Senator Jesse Helms, the hidebound conservative from North Carolina. As a senior Republican on the committee, Helms was the key to Kerry's hopes. And the key to Helms was the drug war. In the course of their investigation, Kerry and his staff had found evidence that some contras had ties to drug smuggling. If there was one class of villain that Helms deplored as much as the Communists, it was drug traffickers.

On matters of political philosophy, Kerry and Helms were opposites. Yet each was something of a maverick, contemptuous of the capital's courtiers and willing to rock the clubby Senate. "I spent time with Jesse," Kerry recalled. "I talked to him. Talked his language. Jesse didn't believe the same things I did in many cases, but he was a gentleman. He was a man of his word."

As Kerry finished his presentation, the senior members turned to Helms, taking his temperature on the issue. "Jesse? What do you think about this?" asked Senator Joseph Biden of Delaware, the ranking Democrat on the panel, according to a transcript of the then-secret session. "I know you are a contra supporter."

"I will tell you what I do not support, and John Kerry and I have talked about this: anybody sending drugs into this country," Helms told his colleagues. "I do not care whose side they are on." Helms was on board. The committee reached a consensus: It would investigate the contras and the contra-drug connection.

As the Iran-contra scandal unfolded, John Kerry would find an outlet for his prosecutorial skills, his thirst for media attention, and his still-simmering outrage over "seeing the government lie, and realizing the consequences" in Vietnam, as he later put it.

John Kerry and Oliver North were just three months apart in age. Both had served in Vietnam. Both were renowned for their daring and both had won Silver and Bronze Stars. Kerry had three Purple Hearts; North had two. Whereas Kerry returned from the war speaking against needless deaths and government lies, North believed that Vietnam was an honorable stand against Communist tyranny. North blamed antiwar protesters for forcing the United States to prematurely bring its troops home. The Iran-contra probe would pit these two determined figures against each other.

Congressional investigations are a set piece, an American ritual: John and Robert Kennedy taking on Teamsters boss Jimmy Hoffa; Richard Nixon chasing Alger Hiss over allegations of Communist influence at the State Department; the televised Watergate hearings that led to Nixon's resignation. The format suited Kerry. He was a restless former prosecutor with a taste for televised acclaim, an ambitious politician consigned to the shadow of a law-passing, back-slapping seatmate, Edward Kennedy. "He is, by nature, an investigative figure," said Kennedy, summing up Kerry's primary role in the Senate. "You can investigate and then legislate. He's investigated."

At the time, North was an obscure White House aide, a man with a ramrod-straight disposition, short-cropped hair, patriotic zeal, and unflagging allegiance to Reagan. North had secretly begun to organize a complex scheme to raise money from wealthy conservatives, foreign nations, and eventually from the proceeds of secret arms sales to circumvent the law and keep the contras in the field.

Word that something was afoot began to seep into Kerry's Capitol Hill office, which had become a magnet for tips from left-leaning journalists, activists, and conspiracy theorists drawn to the senator's antiwar history and his criticisms of Reagan's Central America policy. "A central part of my campaign had been the notion that I would bring to the Senate the experience of the Vietnam period, which cautioned me against the kind of illegal activities we were hearing about, and the things that were going on," Kerry recalled. "Literally, I did do an ad hoc investigation."

The Vietnam skipper who once beached his boat to kill an enemy guerrilla assembled a combative and single-minded crew inside the Russell Senate Office Building. Kerry's scrappy staff had minimal Washington experience and, like Kerry, little desire to fit in with the normally genteel style of the U.S. Senate. In his choice of aides, as with the senators he sought out as partners, Kerry was eclectic. "John formed nonconventional alliances," said former chief of staff Frances Zwenig. "You can't pigeonhole him. He likes feisty people who are fighters like him." Another for-

John Kerry Christmas photo from 1947 in Millis, Massachusetts: Diana, John, and Margaret Kerry.

John Kerry's father, Richard J. Kerry, lived in Manchester-by-the-Sea, Massachusetts. He died at the age of eighty-five on July 29, 2000, of complications from prostate cancer. He was a former Foreign Service officer as well as an author and attorney.

John Kerry (number 18, front row) in a 1962 hockey team photo. Seated next to him and wearing number 12 is future FBI director Robert Mueller.

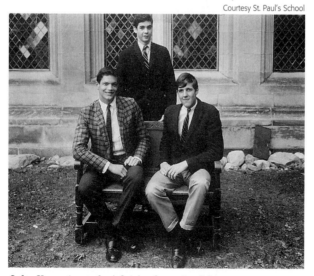

John Kerry (seated, right) in the 1962 debate team photo in the St. Paul's yearbook.

John Kerry in Yale debate team photograph.

*President John F. Kennedy on vacation at Hammersmith
Farm. Mrs. Hugh D. Auchincloss, John Forbes Kerry, and
Janet Auchincloss (at the wheel) were among those joining
the President on board the USCG yacht* Manitou *in Nar-
ragansatt Bay, Rhode Island.*

*Richard Pershing days
before he died in Vietnam.*

*Sailors stand together in An Thoi, Vietnam, on February 28, 1969,
after a medal presentation for Silver Star action. From left: Del
Sandusky, John Kerry, Gene Thorson, Thomas Belodeau. Kneeling
from left, Mike Medeiros, Fred Short.*

David Thorne, John Kerry, and Fred Smith on small plane.

Kerry watches President Richard Nixon announce an agreement on a Vietnam cease-fire on television, January 23, 1973. Kerry said, "My initial reaction is thank God that the prisoners are coming home and that we at least have stopped American participation in the war."

DOONESBURY   by **Garry Trudeau**

At left: *Cameron Kerry, John's brother, in 1972. On the eve of the primary, Cameron and campaign field director Thomas J. Vallely, both then twenty-two, were arrested in the basement of a Lowell building that housed the headquarters of Kerry and another Democratic contender, state Representative Anthony R. DiFruscia of Lawrence.* Right: *Lt. Governor Nominee John Kerry and his wife Julia Thorne display and wear Dukakis–Kerry buttons as he thanks workers upon his victory.*

Boston College law student John Kerry sits among BC Law graduates in 1976.

Kerry, his mother, Senator Edward M. Kennedy, and Boston Mayor Ray Flynn at Christopher Columbus Park in Boston on September 24, 1984.

Kerry celebrates his 1990 re-election victory at the Copley Plaza.

Shortly after taking office in 1985, Kerry and Senator Tom Harkin of Iowa went on a fact finding trip to Nicaragua where they met with Daniel Ortega (right) and other Sandinistas. The trip was criticized when the Sandinistas cemented ties with Moscow.

*Images from the 2004 Democratic Primary campaign. John F. Kerry and his wife, Teresa Heinz during a campaign stop (*top, left*), the morning after winning the Iowa caucuses (*top, right*), and at a victory party at George Mason University (*bottom*).*

mer chief of staff, Ronald Rosenblith, offered a telling description of his own personality: "I annoy people. All I know how to do is tell the truth."

In late 1985, an intriguing report came to Kerry's staff from John Mattes, a public defender in Miami whose sister was a Massachusetts peace advocate. Mattes had a client who claimed to know all about the contras' secret supply network. Kerry's staff interviewed Mattes and his client and traveled to Costa Rica to quiz other young men who had allegedly been working in a U.S.-sanctioned contra supply network.

"It was like a detective story at that point," recalled Winer, Kerry's counsel at the time. The clues pointed to "violations of U.S. law by the Reagan administration, including this guy Ollie North, who I didn't know anything about." On hearing some of the wilder allegations brought to him by his staff—tales of mercenaries and smugglers and assassination plots—Kerry recalled he would grimace and complain: "This is cockamamie. It cannot be true."

But he gave his people plenty of running room. Kerry enjoyed the trust of Senator Richard Lugar, the respected Republican who chaired the Senate Foreign Relations Committee, with whom he had worked during a trip to monitor the 1986 Philippine elections.

"He understood that I was ambitious and serious about the work that we were doing, an enormous agenda, and in fairness, he regularly participated," Lugar recalled. "He was not one of the dissident types. I did not see in him someone who was out there going after President Reagan, out after a Republican president."

But North, who declined equests for an interview, did see Kerry as a threat to Reagan. His notebooks, later obtained by Congress, were peppered with notations of concern about Kerry, his staff, and their freelance investigation. On April 18, 1986, North wrote: "Sen. Kerry trying to get evidence linking RR [Ronald Reagan] to La Penca," the location of an assassination attempt against a contra leader by hard-liners in the movement.

Before long, Kerry encountered resistance. Congressional investigators would later detail how the government intimidated Kerry's witnesses, including a mysterious figure named Jack Terrell, who claimed to have been a contra adviser operating under the nom de guerre "Colonel Flaco."

Terrell told Kerry and a handful of investigative reporters that North's supply network had been used to smuggle arms and drugs. Kerry's staff interviewed Terrell in New Orleans, brought him to Washington, installed him in a safe house, and obtained funding from a liberal think tank, the International Center for Development Policy. In a memo to Reagan, later obtained by the Iran-contra committee, North warned that "Terrell's accusations are at the center of Senator Kerry's investigation." North labeled Terrell a possible Nicaraguan spy, potential presidential assassin, and "terrorist threat."

The Secret Service was alerted, and the FBI placed Terrell under surveillance. Agents tailed him, combed his telephone records, searched his garbage, and pressured him into taking a polygraph test. They ultimately determined he was no threat to the president, but his eagerness waned and he never testified.

Elsewhere, Republican staffers on the Foreign Relations Committee leaked details of Kerry's probe to the administration. The conservative-leaning *Washington Times* published stories containing allegations that Kerry's office was inducing witnesses to commit perjury. At North's insistence, the FBI began to compile information on the Kerry investigation.

Despite Kerry's work, and that of House investigators, North's covert enterprise thrived. But on October 5, 1986, a C-123 aircraft was shot down in Nicaragua. Documents found in the wreckage connected the plane to a CIA proprietary airline, Southern Air Transport. A surviving crew member, Eugene Hasenfus, said he was involved in an effort to arm the contras.

To Kerry's investigators, the operation smelled like a covert CIA plot. Suspicions about North's involvement intensified. By now the full committee, at Kerry's urging, had launched its investigation, and Kerry used an October 10, 1986, hearing to interrogate Assistant Secretary of State Elliott Abrams about whether the Reagan administration had involved foreign governments in arming the contras.

ABRAMS: "I can say that while I have been assistant secretary, which is about 15 months, we have not received a dime from a foreign government, not a dime, from any foreign government."

KERRY: "'We' being who?"

ABRAMS: "The United States."

KERRY: "How about the contras?"

ABRAMS: "I don't know. But not that I am aware of and not through us. The thing is, I think I would know about it because if they went to a foreign government, a foreign government would want credit for helping the contras and they would come to us to say you want us to do this, do you, and I would know about that."

This testimony, and similar statements to a House committee, would later result in Abrams pleading guilty to charges of withholding information from Congress. (He was pardoned by President George H.W. Bush in 1992 and now serves in the White House under George W. Bush.)

On October 15, five days after the Senate Foreign Relations Committee hearing, North again fretted about Kerry's work. "John Kerry—has 8 votes," he wrote in his notebook. Kerry's name was underlined.

Then, in early November 1986, a Lebanese newspaper broke the news of U.S. arms sales to Iran. A few weeks later, the White House disclosed that funds from the sale had been diverted to supply the contras.

Suddenly, Kerry's theories didn't seem so far-fetched. He hoped this would be his moment to help lead the investigation into this extraordinary episode. The Iran-contra scandal was the top story in town, and there was worried talk in the halls of Congress that the United States might suffer another failed presidency.

But when congressional leaders chose the members of the elite Iran-contra committee, Kerry was left out. Those selected were consensus politicians, not bomb throwers. The disappointed Kerry and his staff felt that the committee members were chosen to put a lid on things. "He was told early on they were not going to put him on it," Winer recalled. "He was too junior and too controversial.... They were concerned about the survival of the republic." Even some Democrats "thought John was a little hotter than they would like," said Rosenblith.

As a consolation prize, the Democratic leadership gave Kerry chairmanship of the Subcommittee on Terrorism, Narcotics, and International Operations and a charter to dig into the contra-drug connection. Although disappointed, Kerry stuck with his investigation, and the subcommittee published a report in 1989 that concluded the CIA and other U.S. agencies had turned a blind eye to drug trafficking occurring on the fringes of the contra network. In many cases, traffickers were using the same airplanes, airfields, and other resources that the contras were using.

To the disappointment of the conspiracy theorists, Kerry and his team found no evidence that the United States ran or sanctioned a contra drug ring.

During the investigation, an Oregon businessman claiming CIA ties, Richard Brenneke, whose testimony was taken by Kerry's committee, made the sensational and undocumented charge that Vice President George Bush's office had sanctioned a contra-drug smuggling operation. Bush challenged Kerry to "show some evidence and stop leaking out information that is not fair or true." Kerry denied he was the source of the leak, and the committee dropped the Brenneke angle.

Republican senators were suspicious of Kerry's motives. The Kerry investigation—conducted in the midst of the 1988 presidential campaign pitting Bush against Massachusetts governor Michael Dukakis—was "being conducted as if it were a division of the Dukakis campaign," recalled Senator Mitch McConnell of Kentucky, who served as ranking Republican on the subcommittee. The probe "deteriorated into a biased partisan agenda" that, to McConnell, was primarily aimed at cooking up allegations to tarnish Bush's reputation and presidential hopes.

Ultimately, the subcommittee's findings on the scope of the contra-drug connection were validated by two subsequent federal investigations. Inspectors general at the CIA and the Justice Department found that these agencies had done little or nothing in response to hundreds of allegations that elements of the contras and their supply networks were involved with drugs.

By the late 1980s, Kerry was running his senatorial staff the way he helped run the Middlesex district attorney's office a decade earlier: concentrating on investigations, depositions, and testimony. But now, instead of local crooks and criminals, he had aides probing the global netherworld of drugs, spies, and money laundering.

In an offshoot of the contra-drug investigation, Kerry examined reports that Panamanian dictator Manuel Noriega was involved in drug trafficking. The probe led to information that Noriega was shipping money out of Panama with the help of a bank called BCCI—which prompted yet another Kerry investigation.

The Bank of Credit and Commerce International was an

institution of Middle East origins whose employees asked few questions of their wealthy and powerful customers, making it a favorite of arms merchants, drug dealers, despots such as Noriega, and intelligence agencies. At the CIA, which sometimes used the bank to launder its own activities, it was known as the "Bank of Crooks and Criminals."

Kerry's investigation, launched in 1988, helped to close the bank three years later, but not without upsetting some in Washington's Democratic establishment. Prominent BCCI friends included former defense secretary Clark Clifford, former president Jimmy Carter, and his budget director, Bert Lance. When news broke that Clifford's Washington bank was a shell for BCCI—and that the silver-haired Democrat had handsomely profited in the scheme—some of Kerry's Senate colleagues grew icy.

"What are you doing to my friend Clark Clifford?" more than one Democratic senator asked Kerry. Kerry's aides recalled how Jacqueline Kennedy Onassis and Pamela Harriman, a prominent party fund-raiser who had hosted an event for Kerry at her Georgetown home, called on the senator, urging him not to pursue Clifford.

Kerry and his staff were under intense pressure, and Foreign Relations Committee chairman Claiborne Pell, the Democrat from Rhode Island, began to request that Kerry's investigation end. Blum brought the evidence against BCCI to the Justice Department but was rebuffed. With Kerry's blessing, he left the staff and took the case to New York district attorney Robert Morgenthau, who filed the indictments leading to the bank's collapse in the summer of 1991.

When he finally got the eighty-four-year-old Clifford to the witness table during a Senate hearing that fall, Kerry seemed conflicted, pulling his punches and allowing the elderly statesman to claim a loss of memory. During a recess, his aides urged him on. "He's an old man. He couldn't remember. I'm not going to humiliate an old man," Kerry barked, in an exchange recalled by David McKean, a cousin of Kerry and member of his staff, who later wrote a book on Clifford.

Years later, Kerry said he was "shocked ... surprised" but "resigned that you had to go in and let the chips fall where they may" when he discovered that Clifford and other prominent Democrats had become involved with BCCI.

He defends his decision to treat Clifford with deference: "There was a balance of what I thought was decency. I am one of those kids who grew up watching Joseph Welch respond to Joe McCarthy and I remember his line about decency."*

"I thought we had proven the points we needed," Kerry said of the Clifford inquiry. "We had got the testimony that was essential. And I didn't see any reason to cross the line of what I considered to be necessary."

---

* In 1954, Welch, an attorney for the army, replied to Senator Joseph McCarthy's latest Red-baiting accusations with the words: "Have you no sense of decency, sir, at long last? Have you left no sense of decency?"

Chapter 13

GYPSY YEARS

BY EARLY 1987, with just two Senate years behind him, John Kerry had become a favorite scourge of the political right. Already on conservative hit lists for his antiwar activities, particularly the ribbon toss, Kerry's Ortega trip, and his votes against the Reagan weapon systems made him a ripe target for the Right's increasingly vocal activists and commentators.

And with the Iran-contra scandal threatening to derail Republican hopes to retain the White House in 1988, Kerry's role as an investigator unplugged even more conservative venom. In early 1987, the *Washington Times* accused him of covering up evidence of Sandinista drug smuggling. *Conservative Digest*'s publisher accused him of taking a "pro-Sandinista, pro-Communist" position, just as he had done years earlier as a "disaffected veteran making excuses for the Vietcong." In March, the *Wall Street Journal* noted that Kerry appeared to be replacing Ted Kennedy and Tip O'Neill as the Right's favorite bogeyman.

"I'm really tired of having my patriotism impugned by this crowd," said Kerry, who repeatedly noted his support for a Central America free from Soviet or Cuban military presence. "I have fought and bled for this country. I voted for a $300 billion defense budget last year."

But among his Senate colleagues, the lawmaker who entered the Capitol two years earlier with a reputation for showboating was earning respect as a careful politician. "When he took to the floor to speak, it was always a well thought-out point of view," recalled former Republican senator Warren Rudman of New Hampshire. "He wasn't engaging in loose rhetoric. He presented the case like the prosecutor he was, building up a factual basis."

Kerry began the year with a key post inside the Democratic Party, as chairman of the Democratic Senatorial Campaign Committee (DSCC), a role that would boost his standing among Democrats and enhance his ties to a wealthy and glamorous world of party supporters. In 1986, under the leadership of Senator George Mitchell, the committee had been credited with helping the Democrats win back control of the Senate. Now Kerry—one of just three senators who had spurned political action committee money for his own race—intended to expand that margin by raising millions from PACs and wealthy donors.

"John started off behind the eight ball because he didn't take PAC money and PACs are big givers," noted Robert A. Farmer, a Kerry fund-raiser who was on his way to becoming a legendary money-raiser for Dukakis's presidential bid. "People were skeptical of him because of the PAC thing and because he was a liberal from Massachusetts. But he impressed people with his pragmatic approach." And his vigorous fund-raising.

On February 26, with Farmer orchestrating, Dukakis and Kerry hosted the largest political fund-raising event up to that point in Massachusetts history, selling $10,000 tickets to wealthy donors for a total take of more than $475,000. At Boston's Meridien Hotel, well-heeled donors shared caviar and filet mignon with half a dozen Democratic senators and three governors.

The events continued in such wealthy Democratic strongholds as Miami and Hollywood. And by June, Kerry's DSCC had raised nearly $2.7 million for Democratic candidates, nearly 50 percent more than for the comparable period in 1985. About one-third of those donations came from PACs.

At the time, Kerry told a reporter he continued to hold his position "personally on PAC giving" but would consider taking PAC money for his own campaigns "if the mix" with other contributions "were different." After winning in 1984 without benefit of PAC money, Kerry sent supporters a letter asking, "Should I continue to refuse PAC money?" The letter added, "I'm frequently told by cynics in Washington that refusing PAC money is naive ... Do you agree that it is naive to turn down special interests and their PAC money?" An aide later assured reporters that Kerry was not wavering on the issue and would continue to push for public financing of campaigns.

But even as he collected millions for the Democrats, Kerry's personal finances were in shambles. Later, his sec-

ond wife, Teresa Heinz, super wealthy heir to the condi-
ment company fortune, would call the late 1980s Kerry's
"gypsy period," because for months at a time he had no
fixed address.

When Kerry first moved to Washington in 1985, he
bought a $175,000 townhouse on Capitol Hill with a
$473,313 mortgage that he used mostly to pay off campaign
debts. Kerry described it as a way to consolidate all his
debts, but it was a convoluted transaction that required
Kerry to put $50,000 into an escrow fund and purchase a
large life insurance policy as additional collateral. It also
allowed Kerry to repay himself $156,000 that he had loaned
the Senate campaign in personal funds. But buying the
house was "a huge mistake," he later said, because he
found himself returning to Boston most weekends to be
with eight-year-old Vanessa and eleven-year-old Alexandra.

Back in Boston, Kerry was a man without a real home.
He was relying on friends and family. He was now a U.S.
senator but living like a transient in his hometown. He had
given up the apartment at 216 Beacon Street because, at
$1,500 a month, the rent was too expensive. So around the
time he went to Washington in early 1985, he began to
bounce around when he came back to Massachusetts.

For several months that year, he stayed in Boston's
South End at a condo unit owned by Wesley E. Finch, his
chief fund-raiser. Kerry paid rent on a per diem basis only
for the nights he was in Boston. The nature of that arrangement would become public—and an issue—years later in a
Senate campaign.

Many weekends, Kerry said, he was with his daughters

at the Brookline home of his wife, Julia, when she was away. They had separated more than two years earlier, and Julia, like Kerry, was dating someone else at that time. He also had a key to the Back Bay home of David Thorne, his old friend and brother-in-law, and stayed in "a bedroom upstairs on the attic floor" for much of 1986. At other times, he bunked at his brother Cam's house in Brookline or spent weekends with Roanne Sragow, his former law partner and girlfriend at the time.

From late 1987 through the following summer, Kerry entered into another per diem housing arrangement, this time with Edward Callan, a real estate developer and Kerry supporter.

In a three-and-a-half year period, Kerry would call home at least six different addresses in and around Boston. "Let me paint a picture of my life," Kerry said. "I was newly elected. At that time I was retiring my debt for the campaign so I was traveling around the country on many weekends," said Kerry, who would late in 1985 tell a Senate committee he spent half his time raising campaign money. "When I wasn't traveling around the country, I was with my children on the weekend."

"I spent a lot of time and energy with my kids from 1985, post campaign, to the present," Kerry recalled in a 1996 interview. "It was a period where they needed focus. And my wife spent a lot of time with them, and we worked very hard together on that." Despite the separation, Kerry said he stored personal effects in the basement and garage of Julia's home in Brookline.

Julia was continuing to fight depression, and in 1985

checked herself into a psychiatric hospital because she was "having a love affair with suicide" and needed to feel safe, as she later recounted. For Julia, that move was a personal turning point—and she would finally find the help she needed to declare herself better five years later.

The Kerrys' divorce was finalized in 1988, and throughout this period, the senator was strapped for cash, straining to meet child-support payments, campaign debts, and tuition costs. "He was broke," said Jack Blum, a former aide. "He was up against a wall financially, politically, and emotionally. He wanted to be in this business, and he took the risk to be in it. But it is tough. What seemed like a simplistic route to political glory ... he began to understand there was more to it."

Other friends at that time said that they would pick up the check when they went out for dinner or drinks with Kerry. Some describe him as restless and unhappy during this period, despite all the outward signs of being a successful, high-powered Washington politician.

Many of his social contacts in the late 1980s were with political associates, among them Boston-based fund-raisers Robert Crowe and John Manning. There was also a guardedness about him, a wariness brought on by a recurring pattern: His name would surface in the local gossip columns after being seen at dinner with certain companions. Early in their relationship, one longtime friend recalled, Kerry basically conducted an interview, as if to ascertain what this friend was looking to gain from their relationship.

Among Kerry's haunts was Locke-Ober, the clubby old-money restaurant with a grand dining room, located off an alley in downtown Boston. For decades, it was a bastion of the old Brahmin aristocracy and a power-lunch mecca for the city's business, social, and political elite.

Kerry was also a semi-regular at Yvonne's, the private club within Locke-Ober that thrived in the late 1980s and early 1990s. One habitué called it "a yuppie/*Bonfire of the Vanities* club" for young, affluent, and usually single Bostonians, "the Boston version of the Town and Country set."

The senator's unsettled personal life did not seem to affect his political performance. By the end of his first year in the Senate, Kerry was winning high marks for his attention to local issues—seeking federal funding for Massachusetts projects that involved job retraining, research, and public works construction. He and his staff paid close attention to mayors and other local officials.

But his globe-trotting on foreign policy matters was also drawing some snide commentary on the home front. At a testimonial in March 1986 for retiring U.S. House Speaker Tip O'Neill, Senate president William M. Bulger, Massachusetts's reigning political quipster, hailed Kerry. "Just back from the Philippines," Bulger said, calling Kerry "senator of the world." Two weeks later, at his St. Patrick's Day breakfast, Bulger tweaked Kerry for "having come all this way from the far end of his district, Nicaragua."

When Kerry wasn't on foreign fact-finding missions, he was often on the road, making speeches. To make ends meet during his first term, Kerry collected speaking fees, averaging about $1,400 per appearance, for a total of $26,000 a year during his first five years in the Senate. Most of the honoraria were from think tanks and schools; some were paid by trade associations such as the Massachusetts Bankers Association or corporations such as Goldman Sachs and Chevron, which had legislative interests before Congress.

Kerry has acknowledged that money "was tight" for him in those days. "I was spending all I had; I was not in a situation where I was flush," he said. Regarding honoraria, which Congress banned in 1991, Kerry said: "I did not take honoraria from anyone who had anything in front of my committee." In addition to the Foreign Relations Committee, Kerry by 1990 had seats on three committees at the nexus of competing financial interests and their relations with government—Banking, Housing, and Urban Affairs; Commerce, Science, and Transportation; and Small Business.

In 1986, Kerry pocketed another $21,000 in a low-risk real estate deal, arranged by his campaign treasurer, developer, and recent landlord, Wes Finch. In a business brochure the next year, Finch boasted about his relationship with Kerry, stating he "works closely with the senator and his colleagues on tax and economic issues that come to the floor of the United States Senate." At the time, Kerry spokesman Chris Greeley defended Finch's use of ties to Kerry to promote his company, "He has a right to put his public service record in his brochure. I don't think there is any problem with a conflict of interest."

Finch had cut in his friends—Kerry and his then Senate aide, Ronald Rosenblith—on an investment in condominium units in two Massachusetts communities, Salem and Clinton. One of the units was already under a purchase-and-sales agreement by the time Finch brought in Kerry and Rosenblith as partners, although all three said Finch never informed them of that. The *Boston Globe* calculated their profit at 31 percent in about six months.

Kerry has long maintained he never used his influence on Finch's behalf, but he did acknowledge he was stung by the press reports about the deal and soured on investments after that. "I thought it was legitimate," Kerry said of the deal. But "I found that the inquiries made me profoundly uncomfortable, and I never invested again in the eleven and a half years after that.... I have never since invested one penny in anything" as exotic.

He said the flap over the Finch condo deal also convinced him to sell his interest in the cookie shop he opened in Boston before he entered public office. "I didn't want people asking questions alleging ... a sweetheart deal in Faneuil Hall," Kerry said during a 1996 interview with the *Boston Globe*. "I sold it. I got out." It was that same self-preservation instinct, the fear of the potential for embarrassment, that Kerry would acknowledge years later when the *Boston Globe* found documentation of his aborted tax shelter investment through Cayman Islands companies in 1983, more than two years before the condo deal.

Kerry's finances took a temporary turn for the better in 1988 when he sold the Capitol Hill townhouse in a red-hot Washington market. Fellow senator (and 2004 presidential candidate) Robert Graham of Florida paid him $420,000. Even after taking into account the expensive renovations done by Kerry, it was a huge profit after only three years of ownership.

He used the profits from that sale to make a $275,000 down payment on a $575,000 condominium unit on Boston's elegant Commonwealth Avenue. But he later said he "lost his shirt" on it when he sold the Back Bay condo. Amid the collapse of the Massachusetts real estate market in the late 1980s and early 1990s, Kerry sold the unit for $445,000 in June 1991.

That gave Kerry a fixed address in Boston for the first time in years. But now he was homeless in the capital. Again, he turned to friends for help. One was Bob Farmer, who had made millions in educational publishing, had built the Dukakis presidential money machine, and had become one of the nation's premier Democratic fund-raisers. But he had since left Boston and moved to Washington, taking a position as an executive at Cassidy & Associates, a top-tier lobbying firm.

In February, March, and possibly part of April 1989, Kerry had the use of a bedroom at Farmer's $8,000-a-month apartment at the chic Washington Harbour complex, overlooking the Potomac River. By Kerry's estimate, he stayed there a total of twelve to fourteen nights. Farmer didn't ask for rent, and Kerry didn't offer to pay any. This arrangement would also become a campaign issue when it became public years later.

Despite the financial pressures, Kerry was developing a reputation as the Senate's bon vivant. He was handsome, daring, fluent in French, and, with his 1988 divorce, available. Gossip columnists linked him to actress Morgan

Fairchild and Catherine Oxenberg, daughter of a Yugoslav princess and star of the TV series *Dynasty*. The *Boston Globe* reported that Kerry skied with Oxenberg in Colorado and accompanied her to Ethel Kennedy's New Year's Eve party in Aspen. But Kerry said his relationship, like that with other women publicly linked to him, was a friendship misinterpreted. "He said he merely dined with her and talked about St. Paul's School in New Hampshire where they both were students," the *Boston Globe* reported at the time.

Kerry complained about all the speculation swirling around his personal life. "I don't really want to be linked publicly with anyone until I'm committed and want that relationship known," he said. "I'd just like to fall in love. I'd rather have a relationship than not."

In more recent years, Kerry has dismissed inquiries about his private life during this period. "If George Bush can run around and say 'When I was young and irresponsible, I was young and irresponsible,'" he said, "I can say when I was young and single, I was young and single."

While Kerry kept the shades down over his romances, there was no doubt that he enjoyed a glitzy lifestyle, skiing in Aspen, vacationing on the Forbes family's Naushon Island off Cape Cod, hanging out with the likes of his longtime friend Peter Yarrow of the song trio Peter, Paul, and Mary. And even during his time of financial distress, Kerry maintained his zeal for expensive hobbies, including high-speed boats, motorcycles, and stunt flying. (On a 1986 fact-finding trip to Israel, he took over the controls of an Israeli military training jet and did a favorite maneuver. "This is an appropriate view [of the Middle East], upside down," he said in a reference to the region's complex political dynamics.)

He kept a 1986 Sea Craft speedboat, worth an estimated $20,000-plus, in Falmouth, where it bore the registration 1-JK and was powered by twin 200-horsepower Yamaha engines. In 1993, he paid $8,600 for a high-powered Italian motorcycle, a handmade Ducati Paso 907 IE, according to state motor vehicle records. The machine, said an expert, qualified as "the Ferrari of motorcycles." The senator's fondness for this high-performance touring bike would later seem to be an expensive self-indulgence when it became an issue in one of Kerry's campaigns.

As the Reagan era moved toward a close in 1988, Kerry's former ticket-mate, the cool and cerebral Massachusetts governor Michael Dukakis, emerged as the Democratic nominee for president. In July, after the Democratic convention, Dukakis was leading his Republican rival, Vice President George Bush, by up to 17 percentage points in some polls. Dukakis played up his roots as a son of Greek immigrants. Running on a platform of "competence, not ideology," he promised a federal government that efficiently addressed the problems facing everyday Americans. He advertised his tenure as governor during the vaunted "Massachusetts miracle" of economic growth.

The Iran-contra controversy and insider trading scandals in the business community had weakened the president's public standing. Still, Reagan held a job approval rating of about 50 percent through that summer. The coun-

try was at peace, and Reagan, defying critics, had backed
the Soviets into an arms control agreement. The economy
had survived the October 1987 stock market crash and was
humming along in the longest peacetime expansion in history.

Still, a Bush victory depended on keeping Reagan's
unlikely coalition of supporters together. So campaign
adviser Lee Atwater embarked on a strategy to broaden
Bush's appeal. To moderate suburban independents, Bush
offered a "kinder, gentler" agenda of strengthening the
Clean Air Act, questioning Dukakis's commitment to clean
up Boston Harbor and supporting the "full funding" of
popular social programs such as Head Start. To retain more
working-class Reagan Democrats—economic moderates
but social conservatives—Atwater intended to run a race
centering on cultural values rather than issues.

To accomplish that, the Bush campaign planned to
define Dukakis as an out-of-touch Massachusetts liberal.
The Republican attack dossier included Dukakis's veto of
a bill to make the Pledge of Allegiance mandatory in public
school, his membership in the American Civil Liberties
Union, and his support of gun control. But there was
another matter that would inflict far more damage: his prisoner furlough policy.

At the time, states commonly agreed to release prisoners for small amounts of time, as a reward for good behavior
and to prepare them for life outside. But Massachusetts
went further, granting furlough privileges even to prisoners
serving life-without-parole (the stiffest sentence available
because Massachusetts had no death penalty). In 1987, a

local paper, the Lawrence *Eagle-Tribune*, launched a Pulitzer Prize–winning crusade against the furlough program, focusing on a murderer named Willie Horton, who had raped and brutalized a woman after fleeing the state while on one such furlough. It was one of many furloughs Horton had enjoyed under a policy that Dukakis had repeatedly defended. After a burst of outrage among voters and legislators, Dukakis in early 1988 signed a bill to tighten the state's furlough policy.

Nevertheless, Al Gore raised the issue in an April 12 Democratic primary debate. And that summer, Bush made the Dukakis furlough policy a centerpiece of his speeches and campaign commercials. Dukakis's double-digit lead in the polls began to melt away.

Kerry, who had overseen Massachusetts crime policy during his two-year tenure as Dukakis's lieutenant governor, came to his defense. On July 6, knowing that Pennsylvania Republican senator Arlen Specter was heading to Massachusetts to publicly attack the Democratic presidential candidate on furloughs, Kerry boarded the same plane out of Washington. When Specter arrived at the sun-baked steps of the State House in Boston, expecting to conduct a press conference, he was instead greeted by a band of state officials—and Senator Kerry. A phalanx of uniformed police chiefs stood by to attest to the Dukakis record of building a bipartisan assault on crime. Specter, looking surprised and harried by the ambush, gamely tried to deliver his message that the furlough policy was "indefensible." Making clear he was speaking on behalf of Bush, Specter added: "I believe it raises a question as to [Dukakis's] overall judgment."

As TV cameras rolled and confused tourists stopped to take in the scene, Kerry stepped up to the microphone to change the subject: "It's no accident that we're here listening to criticisms of Michael Dukakis at the very moment that it's most necessary to hide the reality of what the Justice Department under Ronald Reagan and George Bush has not done" to combat the drug trade. "This nation," Kerry proclaimed, "does not need a silent leader on the war on drugs or the fight against crime." Kerry then defended the Massachusetts furlough program, noting that the policy had been tightened and saying its eligibility standards were stricter than many state programs and the federal prison system.

The Dukakis decline in the polls, fed by the furlough issue and other factors that fall, continued. On election day, Bush won forty states, while Dukakis carried only ten. In the congressional races, meanwhile, Kerry's efforts at the DSCC helped the Democrats gain one seat in the Senate. Two years later, despite his success in raising money for those efforts, Kerry would plead with Senate colleagues to combat "the broadly held and extremely negative perception that money controls and grossly distorts the political process" by adopting campaign finance reform.

The plan Kerry forwarded in 1990 would enable voters to check off a contribution box for general election campaigns for Congress, a system similar to the funding mechanism for presidential elections. Kerry's proposal, offered as an amendment to a campaign finance bill, was defeated on a 60–38 vote.

*

By 1990, the landscape of Massachusetts politics was in turmoil. A riptide of a recession had pulled down the state's economy faster and harder than it had in other parts of the country. The real estate market collapsed, taking with it many banks. Whole sectors of the Massachusetts economy were stalled or crippled, and the state budget was awash in red ink.

For a politician, the atmosphere was almost toxic, and Dukakis, governor for twelve of the previous sixteen years, was a lame duck facing public scorn. "The economy fell apart, the state budget collapsed and Dukakis's popularity sank lower than General Manuel Noriega's," the drug-running Panamanian strongman who was under indictment in the United States, noted *Boston Globe* financial writer Charles Stein. "Today, as the decade comes to an end, the feeling of doom and gloom is so strong you might think we were finishing up the 1930s."

Into this climate strode John Kerry, candidate for reelection. Early in the campaign, his personal history caught attention when, in response to a *Boston Globe* survey of politicians, Kerry acknowledged that he had smoked marijuana after returning from Vietnam. "About twenty years ago, I tried marijuana. I didn't like it. I have never used or tried any drug since," he said through a spokesman in his Boston campaign office.

That issue settled, the incumbent senator moved into his easiest campaign to date. Kerry didn't know it, but he caught a break when William F. Weld, a Republican and former federal prosecutor, decided not to challenge him. "In early 1989 . . . I had thought about challenging Senator

Kerry," Weld said recently. A former U.S. attorney in Boston, Weld had gone on to head the Justice Department's criminal division. Now his sights were set on Massachusetts's open governor's seat, leaving Kerry to face a lesser Republican foe, businessman James W. Rappaport.

Rappaport had followed his controversial father, Jerome Lyle Rappaport, into the real estate development business. Jerry Rappaport, a real estate lawyer who had been an aide to Boston mayor John B. Hynes until 1953, initially won the urban renewal rights in 1957 to redevelop Boston's West End. The project razed a forty-eight-acre neighborhood and replaced it with a high-rise, luxury housing complex called Charles River Park.

The younger Rappaport poured more than $4 million of his own money into the campaign. After the September primary, a poll showed the Republican within striking distance of the incumbent. That fall, Rappaport issued a Reagan-like assault on big government. But his hardest shots at Kerry involved the senator's relationship with David Paul, who had emerged as a principal figure in the savings and loan scandals of the time and who had ties to BCCI.

Paul's CenTrust Savings Bank of Miami failed in 1990 and cost taxpayers an estimated $2 billion, according to a report prepared by the Republican staff of the Senate Judiciary Committee. The investigation found that Paul "spent millions of dollars of insured deposits on such lavish personal perquisites as an art collection, the leasing of an airplane frequently used for personal and political purposes, operating expenses of a $7 million yacht ... the purchase of a sailboat, Persian rugs, Baccarat crystal, foreign linens, and other expensive furnishings."

Kerry was among those politicians who flew on Paul's jet, and the Democratic Senatorial Campaign Committee, which Kerry chaired, leased Paul's yacht for fund-raisers. As DSCC chairman, Kerry had appointed Paul to a fund-raising position. When their relationship became known, Kerry acknowledged that Paul in 1989 had asked for special consideration to help CenTrust by weakening a portion of the savings and loan bailout bill. Kerry wrote Paul a friendly letter, inviting him to Washington "so that we can sit down and perhaps follow up." But, the senator said, he ultimately opposed Paul's request, which failed to win support in Congress. Jack Blum, the former Kerry aide, says the senator "came to understand he was being compromised." Blum stressed that Kerry in the end "got out of there."

Rappaport, however, kept the issue alive during the campaign. He endorsed a Republican effort to have President Bush name a special prosecutor for the overall savings and loan scandal and said Paul put off "the day of reckoning ... costing the taxpayers hundreds of millions of extra dollars" by cultivating the favor of Kerry and other politicians. Kerry, however, had never accepted any contributions for his own campaign from Paul, and, in a Senate committee meeting, voted to shut down his S&L.

Rappaport also tried to wrap the unpopular Dukakis around Kerry's neck. In a memorable TV ad called "Metamorphosis," Rappaport's campaign tried to link the pair, showing an unflattering photo of Dukakis morphing into an

equally unappealing image of his former lieutenant governor.

Kerry's campaign responded with devastating and
clever negative television ads, produced by his media consultant, Dan Payne of Boston. One ad, called "Hot Heir,"
featured Rappaport in a balloon image, drifting over ren-
derings of family businesses that had benefited from federal funding. "They outgunned us with commercials that
showed how you could kill a guy with humor," said Jack
Quinlan, Rappaport's campaign director. "They got a picture of Jim speaking to a Republican convention, one of
those god-awful winks, and they kept running commercials
about outlandish things that would flash to Jim winking."
Dubbed the "wink" spots, each closed with a narrator saying: "Do you trust this man to look after our interests?"

In November, Republican Weld won the governor's
seat. John Kerry, the foe Weld had considered challenging
that year, rode into another six-year term, thumping Rappaport by a 57-43 percent margin.

The Kerry-Weld matchup would have to wait.

Chapter 14

GHOSTS OF VIETNAM

ON AUGUST 1, 1990, as the Boston Red Sox tied for first place and John Kerry managed a healthy lead in his Senate reelection campaign, Iraqi dictator Saddam Hussein rolled his army across a desert border and into the tiny but oil-rich emirate of Kuwait. Hussein, who had been openly lusting after his next-door neighbor, now declared Kuwait his country's nineteenth province, thus threatening neighboring Saudi Arabia—and Western oil supplies.

Hussein was fresh from an eight-year war with Iran, a massive bloodletting provoked by his earlier invasion of that country. His ruthlessness was well established; two years earlier he had murdered as many as 7,000 Kurds in northern Iraq by dropping canisters of poisonous gas on a city of 50,000. Hussein's willingness to use weapons of mass destruction against his own people, and his naked ambition to expand Iraq's borders, made him a clear threat to an already unstable region.

The international community responded swiftly to the

Kuwait invasion, imposing an embargo on Iraq until Hussein agreed to withdraw. President George H.W. Bush, meanwhile, ordered a massive buildup of U.S. military force in the region—and began the arduous work of stitching together one of the most diverse international coalitions in history. In November, he convinced the United Nations Security Council to adopt a resolution authorizing the use of "all means necessary" to oust the invading forces if Iraq didn't remove its forces by January 15, 1991.

Then the president asked Congress to sanction a military strike if Hussein refused to meet that deadline. To John Kerry, this would become "the most important vote" of his Senate career. He would be one of twenty Vietnam veterans in Congress debating whether to send hundreds of thousands of U.S. men and women into battle against the world's fourth-largest army—one possessing chemical, biological, and possibly nuclear weapons.

During the 1980s, Kerry had feared that Central America would become a quagmire that, like Vietnam, needlessly produced waves of American soldiers coming home in body bags. But it didn't. The region's people fought and suffered as proxies in the cold war between the Soviet Union and the West. CIA agents and American military advisers flocked to Central America, and the United States liberated the small Caribbean island of Grenada. But for the most part American troops stayed off stage. The Persian Gulf crisis, with the prospect of a major military intervention, now spurred fresh comparisons to Vietnam, locus of an unpopular war that had claimed the lives of more than 58,000 American men and women.

From the outset, Kerry argued for a diplomatic solution.

Three weeks after Iraq invaded Kuwait, Kerry said he supported President Bush's swift deployment of troops to the region and the administration's insistence that Hussein pull out. But he said Hussein should be given more diplomatic wiggle room for withdrawal. "My greatest fear is this issue is too much box and not enough capacity to move out," Kerry told editors and reporters at the *Boston Globe* on August 27, 1990. "That line is pointing in a very dangerous direction."

Instead, Kerry said, the White House should use back channels to Baghdad to signal a willingness to see Iraq's claim on specific Kuwaiti territory adjudicated in an international forum. He added that the Bush administration should also indicate possible support for new initiatives to settle the Arab-Israeli stalemate over the occupied West Bank. These options, Kerry said, could produce a diplomatic opening for Hussein's withdrawal. He was worried about "saber rattling" from Washington, but he insisted that Iraq's nuclear program must be dismantled "by diplomatic, covert, or overt measures."

A week later, Kerry and a congressional delegation left for the Middle East and meetings with King Fahd of Saudia Arabia and President Hosni Mubarak of Egypt. Upon his return, Kerry said that Mubarak had expressed anger and accused Hussein of committing acts of treachery and betrayal that pitted Arab against Arab. Saudi Arabia and other nations were poised to cut off $250 million in annual aid to the Palestine Liberation Organization because the PLO supported Iraq's invasion, Kerry reported.

Despite the economic sanctions, Hussein stayed put in

Kuwait that fall. With the U.N. ultimatum and threat of force now in place, President Bush declared in November: "This will not be another Vietnam.... If one American soldier has to go into battle, that soldier will have enough force behind him to win ... I will never, ever agree to a halfway effort."

In early December, Secretary of State James Baker appeared before Kerry and other members of the Senate Foreign Relations Committee. For months, Baker had counseled patience, hoping the American military buildup and economic sanctions would force Hussein's hand. Now the secretary of state said the administration was ratcheting up its response. "We have to face the fact that, four months into this conflict, none of our efforts have yet produced any sign of change in Saddam Hussein," he said. If Iraq refused to withdraw, Baker told the senators, the United States was prepared to hit the country "suddenly, massively, and decisively." Kerry responded, "I'm disturbed because you seem to have given up on sanctions" and have accepted war as inevitable.

There was still some hope that war could be avoided: Hussein had agreed to President Bush's offer for high-level talks. But as the January 15 deadline approached, Kuwait remained in his hands.

A cloud of solemnity and gravity settled over the capital in mid-January as members of Congress gathered to debate the president's request for authority to send American

troops into war against Iraq. In the House, Speaker
Thomas Foley, Democrat from Washington, prayed, "may
God bless us and guide us and help us in the fateful days
that lie ahead." In the Senate, protesters interrupted from
the gallery with cries of, "No blood for oil! No war for
Bush!" Other antiwar demonstrators lay on the snow outside the Capitol in mock body bags.

Polls showed a majority of the public favored going to
war to force Iraq out of Kuwait—but not if it meant heavy
casualties. Computer models at the Pentagon raised the
prospect of American deaths in the tens of thousands. A
factory in Philadelphia had interrupted its normal routine
of producing infants' bedsheets to fill a rush order from the
Defense Department for 16,099 body bags.

In the Senate, many Democrats who worried about war
but wanted to stand tough against Hussein took their cues
from Sam Nunn of Georgia, chairman of the Armed Services Committee. The hawkish Nunn stood for a strong
and well-funded military. No one could accuse Sam Nunn
of being a fuzzy-headed peacenik—and Nunn wasn't ready
to go to war in the Persian Gulf. His reluctance gave cover
to other Democrats who worried about the price of a war.
Along with George Mitchell, Democrat from Maine, Nunn
put forward a resolution calling for sanctions to be given
more time to work. John Kerry was among those supporting
the Nunn-Mitchell alternative.

Four days before the January 15 deadline, the junior
senator from Massachusetts rose on the Senate floor to
argue against war. Kerry would later say that he wanted to
contain Hussein, but in his speech that day, he dwelled on

the horrors of war, which he had witnessed firsthand in Vietnam, and not on the transgressions of a brutal Iraqi dictator.

"I had hoped after my reelection, and given the economic problems that we face in Massachusetts, to be able to return here and to talk about ... economic priorities, about education, and the crime in our streets, and about the plain and simple anxiety that thousands of our citizens feel today just about survival at home," Kerry began. Instead, "we are talking about war, about countless of our families torn apart by duty and commitment to our country, of countless lives put on hold."

"We have a way of quietly saying 'war is hell' or 'war is horrible' and then we move on," Kerry said, "lost again in the words which describe the passions and the politics...." Then he reminded his fellow senators of the human costs still being born by Vietnam veterans, the lingering injuries and illness, the alcoholism and drug abuse. "Are we ready for the changes this war will bring—changes in sons and daughters who return from combat never the same ... Are we ready?

"Are we ready," he asked his colleagues, "for another generation of amputees, paraplegics, burn victims" and the enduring traumas faced by those who have fought in combat?

Despite his leadership of an antiwar movement two decades earlier, John Kerry had, during his six years as a senator, made it clear he was "not a pacifist." As he said in 1989, "I believe the military is an arm of the tool of foreign policy and, at the most appropriate moments, it may be legitimate to be used." But the failures of Vietnam had never been far from his thoughts, and now, with a war looming in the Persian Gulf, that war's sad legacy clearly shaped his views. (It also happened to shape some public opinion: While one prewar poll showed that 59 percent of Americans favored military action, among opponents of the Vietnam War, support was in the mid 20s.)

Since Vietnam, Kerry said, the American public had been "reaching for a set of ruling principles about when we go to war," with the consensus arriving that "we should go to war when our vital interests are at stake in a way that the majority of Americans have identified and are agreed upon, and when we have exhausted all peaceful alternatives."

That was not the case in the Persian Gulf, Kerry argued. "There is a rush to war here. [Because we think our military force can overwhelm Iraq], we are willing to act ... with more bravado than patience."

Pressure on Congress to rally around the president was wrongheaded, Kerry said, as it had been years earlier when "it cost us thousands of lives" in Vietnam. "It looks to me like backing up the President's decision has become the new vital interest, not the immediate liberation of Kuwait ... It sounds like we are risking war for pride, not vital interests!" He also rejected the argument that supporting Bush's resolution would give the administration leverage to force Hussein out of Kuwait. But eleven years later, Kerry would say that was precisely his intent when he voted in favor of a resolution that resulted in a second war against Iraq.

"That thinking is dangerous ... and flawed," Kerry said.

"This is not a vote about sending a message. It is a vote about war."

In his lengthy speech (and Kerry's speeches usually were), he repeatedly criticized Bush and his "unilateral" rush to war. "We are in this position today because the president of the United States made a series of decisions that have put us in this position." With economic sanctions tightening their grip on Iraq, "there is no one who suggests that Saddam Hussein is winning anything today," Kerry said.

In contrast to Kerry's detailed condemnation of Bush, his references to the dangers posed by Hussein were brief and dismissive. Kerry acceded he was "well aware of the long-term danger of his arsenal—of nuclear, chemical, biological weapons." But, he said, if the United States killed Hussein, another despot would take his place—unless the United States were to pursue "real peacemaking in the region."

Kerry condemned "our impatience with sanctions and diplomacy," noting that the country was not ready for the horrors of war, "for what it will witness and bear if we go to war."

The combat veteran who had begun his speech on the horrors of war ended his remarks on the same note, quoting Dalton Trumbo's *Johnny Got His Gun*, about a young soldier who lost his arms, legs, sight, hearing, smell, and speech in World War I and lay in a hospital for years. "He would be an educational exhibit," Trumbo wrote. "People wouldn't learn much about anatomy from him but they would learn all there was to learn about war."

On January 12, three days before the U.N. deadline, a Congress controlled by Democrats voted to give the Republican president the authority to go to war against Iraq. In the House, the vote was a wide margin of 250 to 183. But in the Senate, where the final tally was 52 to 47, three votes could have altered the outcome. Supporters included two Democratic presidential prospects: Albert Gore Jr. of Tennessee and Joseph Lieberman of Connecticut.

Among Vietnam veterans, fourteen House and Senate members voted with the president. One of those was Republican John McCain of Arizona, who argued that "if we fail to act there will be inevitably a succession of dictators, of Saddam Husseins ... [who] will see a green light for aggression."

The six Vietnam vets who opposed the resolution included Kerry, Tom Harkin of Iowa, Bob Kerrey of Nebraska, and three House members.

Another vocal opponent of the war was John Kerry's ex-wife, Julia, who marched down Boylston Street and into the Boston Common chanting, "No blood for oil!" "We must not repeat the mistakes of the Vietnam era," she wrote at the time under the name Julia Stimson Thorne. For more than a year during that war, she had lived with fear and confusion while her fiancé and two brothers served simultaneously in Vietnam. She did not want others to suffer what she and many of her generation had.

As the January 15 deadline passed, President Bush gathered his national security advisers while Hussein called his ambassador back to Baghdad. It was clear there would be no backing down: Hussein beefed up his half-million troops in and around Kuwait and dared the United States to attack. If American soldiers expected to perform "acrobatics like Rambo movies," the Iraqi dictator warned, they are going to be sorely surprised and sorry.

By then, the U.S. military force in the region had swelled to 425,000 troops, with soldiers joining from twenty-eight other nations, including five Arab countries. Antiwar vigils continued around the capital. Members of Congress were warned to take personal security measures against possible terrorist attacks. Public tours of the White House were suspended. Appearing on CBS's *This Morning*, Kerry said, "I'm convinced we're doing this the wrong way." Nevertheless, he added, "I'm going to back the president if a shot is fired."

For all the comparisons to Vietnam, the Persian Gulf War ultimately was a dramatically different conflict that produced very different public attitudes toward the soldiers who served. Operation Desert Storm opened on the evening of January 16, as the Baghdad sky lit up with flashes and antiaircraft fire. Massive air strikes continued for six weeks, featuring star performances by America's latest high-tech weapons.

The accuracy and effectiveness of U.S. cruise missiles, stealth fighters, and laser-guided bombs renewed military prestige at a time when the public was wary of bloated Pentagon spending. "The decisive character of our victory in the Gulf War is attributable in large measure of the extraordinary effectiveness of air power," Defense Secretary Dick Cheney wrote in a report on the war, a conflict he would manage again more than a decade later.

After the successful launch of Operation Desert Storm, Kerry's position became so nuanced that his office at one point mistakenly mailed letters to constituents that positioned him on both sides in the debate. On January 22, 1991, Kerry's office sent a letter to one man, thanking him for expressing opposition to the deployment of additional U.S. troops in Saudi Arabia and the Persian Gulf. "I share your concerns," Kerry wrote, noting that on January 11, he had voted against a resolution giving the president immediate authority to go to war.

On January 31, the same constituent received a letter stating, "From the outset of the invasion, I have strongly and unequivocally supported President Bush's response to the crisis and the policy goals he has established with our military deployment in the Persian Gulf." Kerry blamed the mix-up on a computer error and subsequently wrote in defense of his position on the Gulf War: "The debate in the Senate was not about whether we should or should not have used force, but when force should be used."

On February 24, 1991, U.S. ground troops joined the invasion, crossing hundreds of miles of desert and routing the Iraqi army in just 100 hours.

On February 27, facing the prospect of significant American casualties if U.S. troops pursued the retreating Iraqi military back to Baghdad, President Bush ordered a cease-fire, leaving Saddam Hussein and much of his Republican Guard alive to fight another day.

During the course of the six-week war, a total of 148 U.S. troops were killed in combat, including 35 hit by friendly fire, and 467 were wounded. Of the nation's ten major wars up until that point, military historian Rick Atkinson has noted, "this one was the cheapest in blood and treasure."

Two decades earlier, when Kerry and his friend David Thorne returned from Vietnam, "no one thanked, them, no one congratulated them," recalled Julia Thorne. "They, in turn, were not sure they wanted to be congratulated or thanked ... They brought home a sense of shame and doubt about the war they had put their lives on the line for."

By contrast, the Persian Gulf veterans returned to parades and confetti and yellow ribbons. In Hollywood, an estimated 1 million spectators turned out to watch a grand procession that ended with a replica of a Patriot missile poking out of a launcher. In Chicago, people shrieked as soldiers marched by buildings draped with flags and ribbons. Washington was home to a $12-million gala, and the war's commander, General H. Norman Schwarzkopf, was treated like a folk hero in the halls of Congress, where he was interrupted by applause and standing ovations a dozen times.

In March, Kerry joined other senators to visit U.S. troops still massed on the Iraq border. "It's unbelievable," he said, as he congratulated the soldiers. "A lot of those of us who served in Vietnam found a new breath of air in your courage and optimism." Gone were the references to the crippled, scarred Johnny of Dalton Trumbo's book. Kerry now proclaimed he was "delighted by the outcome" of the war.

But the Bush administration's abrupt cease-fire had not only left Hussein in power, it also left rebels inside Iraq at the mercy of the dictator's wrath. Kurds and Shiites took Bush at his word and believed he would support them when he encouraged them to "rise up" against Hussein. Instead, the president stayed on the sidelines, saying he didn't want to get "sucked in" (Vietnam-style) to a messy civil war. "I do not want one single soldier or airman shoved into a civil war in Iraq that's been going on for ages," Bush said. The dictator, meanwhile, launched a brutal crackdown on his detractors.

Bush refused to shoot down Iraqi helicopters attacking the rebels, a decision that Kerry at the time condemned as "a backhanded intervention in support of Saddam Hussein." In the Senate that spring, Kerry helped lead a Democratic effort to publicly castigate the administration for failing to stop Hussein's slaughter of the rebels. "Bush has had a standstill, misguided policy, not unlike the lack of leadership seen prior to the war," Kerry said.

Watching the newfound hawkishness of their counterparts, Republicans chided Kerry and other Democrats who had opposed the war. "I must say I am amused at some of the criticism from the same people who objected to the use of any force whatsoever suddenly saying we should shoot down their helicopters," said Rhode Island senator John Chafee.

Three months after hostilities ceased, John Kerry attended a meeting of local Democrats in Gloucester, Massachusetts, and conceded. "I'm not convinced," he said, "given the nature of Saddam Hussein," that a peaceful resolution to the Kuwait invasion had been possible. Then he attacked Bush for leaving Hussein in power:

"This administration, having likened Saddam Hussein to Hitler, having committed troops in the war against him, actually sided with Hussein in the aftermath of the war. That is a disgraceful chapter."

By the time John F. Kerry had begun his second term as U.S. senator in 1991, his nickname among Massachusetts political insiders was "Live Shot," a reference to his relentless courting of reporters, especially those with TV cameras in tow. (He now says now his media visibility was part of a deliberate political strategy to counter Rappaport's negative ad campaign.) Despite his success as an investigator, Kerry was sometimes seen as an impatient new breed in the Senate, where seniority and decorum still matter. His seatmate, Ted Kennedy, had built a reputation, even among Republicans, as a master legislator. Kerry, by contrast, was known for being more interested in generating headlines than mastering the sometimes tedious process of lawmaking.

Among those who harbored a simmering distrust of Kerry was John McCain, who had been tortured as a prisoner of war in Hanoi. The Arizonan had campaigned for Ray Shamie, Kerry's Republican opponent in 1984, denouncing the Democrat for joining the veterans who tossed medals and ribbons over the Capitol barricade in 1971. The North Vietnamese had taunted the American POWs with accounts of that antiwar rally.

In the spring of 1991, McCain found himself seated across from Kerry inside a cramped military jet on a fact-finding mission to the Middle East. In the Senate, the two men had circled each other warily. But now, strapped into uncomfortable seats with an interminable flight before them and only a flimsy table between them, they had no place to go. They made small talk about airplanes and baseball with Senator John Glenn, the Democrat from Ohio, until Glenn fell asleep.

From there, "it kind of segued into John and I talking about Vietnam," McCain recalled. Deep into the night, as the plane droned over the Atlantic, Kerry and McCain revisited the defining experience of their lives. Said Kerry, "I asked a lot of questions about him, and he of me, and we talked about how he felt about his war, and my war."

In the ensuing weeks and months, McCain and Kerry individually, and then together, concluded that the unresolved divisions of the Vietnam War were causing too much national anguish and that it was time to put the war to rest. Over the course of the next four years, as the pair worked toward reestablishing relations with Vietnam, thus closing out a painful chapter in American history, Kerry earned the "unbounded respect and admiration" of McCain. "You get to know people and you make decisions about them," McCain says now. "I found him to be the genuine article."

In terms of politics, "there weren't going to be any winners" in resolving the Vietnam issue, noted Ted Kennedy. "It was deeply a part of [Kerry's] soul: rooted in his own service over there." Before there could be any rapprochement with Vietnam, Kerry and McCain had to tackle the thorny, and explosive, issues of military personnel still listed as missing in action in Indochina. In the two decades that followed the U.S. withdrawal from Vietnam, the lives of more than 2,000 U.S. troops were unaccounted for. And Americans had been haunted by unsubstantiated reports that U.S. prisoners of war were still being held captive in Vietnam, Cambodia, and Laos.

The story was irresistible to Hollywood, which had produced the *Rambo* movies and other fantasies; to a relatively small but energetic cast of businesses and nonprofit groups that cashed in on the rumors and the hopes of missing in action (MIA) families; and to the American media, which published or broadcast unverified photographs and stories of POW "sightings."

In the summer of 1991, *Newsweek* magazine and other mainstream news organizations published a photograph that later became known as the "three amigos" picture, purportedly showing three U.S. pilots alive and in captivity in Southeast Asia. The photo, it turned out, was a crude scam; the three men were Russian farmers, whose photo had been published in a magazine. But for weeks that summer, the POW-MIA myth gained renewed vigor.

Kerry's advisers told him to stay away from the controversy, that it was a no-win cause, a "tar baby." But Kerry persisted, assuming the chairmanship of the newly formed Senate Select Committee on POW-MIA Affairs, which was granted a one-year lease on life to investigate and determine the truth.

Kerry originally wanted his newfound friend McCain to serve as Republican co-chair. But McCain was a hot potato in a POW-MIA community wedded to the theory that hundreds, if not thousands, of Americans were still trapped inside Southeast Asia prisons. Extremists in the movement branded McCain a brainwashed "Manchurian candidate" because of his refusal to adopt their theories. "Things were said about him that I find ... beyond cruel," said Kerry. At hearings where McCain's anger at his critics flared, Kerry would reach over and place his hand on McCain's arm to calm him down. "I remain grateful to him for doing that," McCain said.

Kerry's Republican co-chair was, instead, a navy veteran allied with MIA-POW activists, Robert Smith of New Hampshire. Smith worried aloud that Kerry's hearings might turn out to be "more show than substance. It's a lousy way to get to the heart of things."

In August, Kerry left on his first fact-finding mission to Southeast Asia, telling reporters at a press conference that he considered this voyage a final step in his military service, a "last mission. This is a responsibility as a former soldier and somebody that served in Vietnam." As he departed the country, the circulation of the "three amigos" photo was still reverberating among families of missing American soldiers: Five families had come forward to make the case the men in the photo were their relatives.

On this and future trips to the region, Kerry brought with him a powerful incentive for Vietnamese officials to cooperate: The possibility of renewed trade and diplomatic relations with the United States. Already, Kerry was lobbying the Bush administration to lift the trade embargo against the country.

"If you want to quickly begin to provide yourself better access to information, by God the best thing you can do is get everyone you can into that country and be able to have an exchange not only in goods but in information," he said during a press conference in Bangkok, before heading on to Hanoi.

During his weeklong trip, Kerry secured a commitment from Vietnamese official to allow U.S. investigative teams to use their own helicopters and to visit remote sites on short notice. The vice chairman of the People's Committee of Ho Chi Minh City held Kerry's hand, in a gesture of friendship, and pleaded that the economic embargo made no sense.

Upon his return, Kerry expressed doubts that any Americans were being held in government prisons. "I think the likelihood that a government is formally holding somebody is obviously tiny," he said. "But is it possible that somebody fell into the hands of bandits or uncontrolled entities in jungle areas that are out of reach of the government? That's possible."

Over the course of the next year, Kerry and his committee pursued leads in the United States and overseas, and ordered key government officials to testify. In February 1992, Smith and Kerry flew to Moscow, where authorities handed over documents purporting to clarify the fate of hundreds of MIAs and the country's vice president promised his help in urging Vietnam and Laos to cooperate.

Kerry's committee, together with the Pentagon and the media, began exposing hoaxes, including direct mail operations using fraudulent photos and other phony evidence to raise millions from hopeful MIA families. Although Kerry doubted that American servicemen remained in Southeast

Asia, he did suspect that the Nixon administration had—in its haste to pull out of Vietnam in March 1973—left behind U.S. prisoners of war.

"To say that all prisoners of war had returned, as the president announced ... was wrong. You knew it was wrong," Kerry told a former Pentagon official during a June 1992 hearing before his select committee. Kerry was joined in his denunciation by four Republicans, including Iowa's Charles Grassley, who accused the Nixon administration of ignoring evidence that 100 prisoners had not been repatriated. "People are incensed because of the deception around this issue," Grassley said.

Among those who asserted that prisoners were left behind were former defense secretaries Melvin Laird and James Schlesinger. But at a stormy hearing before Kerry's committee in September, Henry Kissinger, who was Nixon's national security adviser at the time, called those accusations "a flat-out lie."

Kerry and McCain continued to come under fire from MIA-POW activists during their investigation. Nevertheless, the select committee was clearly moving closer to the truth. At the prodding of the lawmakers, Vietnam had begun to provide unprecedented access to its files, prisons, and military bases.

In November 1992, Kerry again traveled to Vietnam, this time bearing a letter from President Bush promising improved relations in return for increased cooperation on the issue. Hoping to mend ties with the United States, authorities handed over to Kerry—there along with South Dakota Democrat Tom Daschle and Colorado Republican

Hank Brown—a treasure trove of relics, including photos and flight suits from American GIs.

At one point, the Massachusetts senator asked officials point blank if any American servicemen were still alive in Vietnam. He was told no. The country's president offered to allow visits by doubtful American families.

By December 1992, Kerry's select committee was moving toward its conclusion that "there is no compelling evidence that proves that any American remains alive in captivity in Southeast Asia." A key witness that month was retired rear admiral James Stockdale, who had won the Medal of Honor as a POW, and whose wife helped found a league of POW-MIA families. Stockdale, who also served as Ross Perot's running mate that year, offered a harsh dose of reality to MIA families still pursuing their loved ones. "We've become a litigious society, where we believe that somebody owes us an explanation and an apology and a payback if something is not quite right," Stockdale said. And then he noted: "When you lose a war, you don't get to go in and account for your people."

When the panel released its report, Kerry—who had spent much of his political career fighting government lies—was now positioned to argue that "we have not had people willfully trying to hide something." His committee's report asked the question: "Is there anyone left alive?"

And then came this answer: "As much as we would hope that no American has had to endure twenty years of captivity ... there is nothing the Members of the Committee would have liked more than to be able to prove this fact

... Unfortunately, our hopes have not been realized." The committee said this conclusion was not "a failure of investigation" but rather a "confrontation with reality."

The panel concluded that about 100 Americans who had been expected to return with the U.S. pullout did not return. Some were known to be captives or known to have survived battle incidents. But the committee said they weren't "knowingly abandoned"—because the government didn't have information on their whereabouts—but rather were "shunted aside" by officials' failure to search for them.

The panel's work launched a long and difficult effort to locate the remains of more than 2,000 MIAs. As time passed and U.S. businesses began to push Washington to renew trade with the Vietnamese, Kerry and McCain said the cooperation of these countries merited a lifting of the trade embargo against Vietnam; Robert Smith, Kerry's co-chair, argued that this would be an insult to Vietnam veterans. Congress ultimately agreed with Kerry.

As someone who dodged military service in the Vietnam era, President Bill Clinton was never out front on the issue of normalization. He needed the kind of political cover that only genuine war heroes could provide.

Kerry and McCain were willing to conduct the painstaking work of building a consensus, first in the Senate, and then in the White House, bringing a close to a painful chapter in American history. Said Kennedy: "The work John Kerry and John McCain did is truly one of the most extraordinary events we have had in the last fifty years."

On a summer day in 1995, Kerry and McCain stood beside President Clinton in the East Room of the White House as he announced that the United States would normalize diplomatic relations with Vietnam. For a president who most famously had not served in their war, the two combat veterans served as wingmen.

Chapter 15

NEW ERA

JOHN KERRY had a habit of keeping his staff guessing. Aides describe freewheeling bull sessions in which he often reveled in playing devil's advocate, suggesting he might (or, might not) switch his position on an important issue. This one-time prosecutor and alumnus of the Yale Political Union excelled in the art of debate—and he liked to draw staffers into his Socratic dialogues. "It was very frustrating," recalled his counsel, Jonathan Winer. "But he has to feel it's right in his gut, even when the staff preferred a shorthand [guide to his views]. No one was going to tell him what to do."

And in the spring of 1992, no one was going to convince John Kerry to rethink his plan to launch a broadside against affirmative action, the program that offers preferences to women and minorities in employment and education as a corrective for past discrimination. "It wasn't us," Winer said of Kerry's decision. "You think anyone on the staff was going to encourage him to criticize affirmative action?"

This was the season of the New Democrat. Party centrists were calling into question the old-style liberalism that had contributed to the resounding defeats of Walter Mondale in 1984 and Michael Dukakis in 1988. Lawmakers and thinkers at organizations such as the Democratic Leadership Council were asking uncomfortable questions: Were liberal sacred cows such as welfare and affirmative action dividing the country and hurting those they were supposed to help?

Leading Democrats offered tough-love prescriptions for American cities reeling from crime and a crack cocaine epidemic. Democratic senator Bill Bradley of New Jersey asserted that "silence or distortion has shaped the issue of race and urban America.... The result is that another generation has been lost... It is time for candor." And Bill Clinton, the emerging front-runner for the Democratic presidential nomination, declared that America must "provide more opportunity" but also "insist on more responsibility."

In his Capitol Hill office, Kerry began scribbling his own thoughts on a legal pad. The speech that took shape over the course of several months would become a fifty-minute discourse entitled "Race, Politics, and the Urban Agenda." In it, Kerry labeled affirmative action an "inherently limited and divisive program."

The result was a political firestorm.

In hindsight, the danger signs were evident: John Kerry, descendant of the Winthrop and Forbes families, product of St. Paul's and Yale, intended to criticize a program that—whatever its failings—was expressly designed to allow outsiders in. Clinton, Arkansas white and the stepson of an alcoholic, chose an alternate appeal to middle-class frustrations, focusing his calls for reform on a welfare system that was leaving generations of single mothers and their children trapped in poverty. "We should insist that people move off welfare rolls and onto work rolls," Clinton told voters that year.

The venue for Kerry's March 30, 1992, speech was another problem. In a few months, Clinton would make his famed campaign-year pitch to the center by stepping to the podium at Reverend Jesse Jackson's Rainbow Coalition convention to condemn rapper Sister Souljah for lauding the Los Angeles riots as rightful revenge against white oppression. Kerry came to the elite and august halls of Yale and spoke to 100 Ivy League students.

And there was one more thing: Clinton never had to face the awesome wrath of the liberal Massachusetts political establishment.

"For the next few minutes," Kerry began, "I ask you to consider a different part of the reality of America today; a violent, drug-ridden, rat-infested reality; a reality in which the institutions of civilized social life have broken down; of disintegrated families; boarded-up storefronts; schools that have become armed camps and crack houses replacing community centers as the focus of neighborhood life.

"I ask you to consider a reality where more than 80 percent of babies are born to single mothers; where young men die violently at a rate exceeding that of any American war; where only one child in three finishes high school and even then, too often, can barely read; where the spread of AIDS and homelessness rips so visibly at the fabric of community; where far too many families are on welfare for far too long; and where far too many children carry guns instead of lunch boxes to school ...."

It would be simple, Kerry told members of the Yale Political Union, the debating society he once presided over, "to blame all this on racism, and there is no doubt that white racism persists in our society, that it is ugly and insidious ... But the issues and the reasons for our dilemma go deeper and are more complex than that. They have their roots in the changing nature of the movement for civil rights, in the turbulent history of race relations and the persistence of racial stereotypes."

And here, Kerry began to slip into a political danger zone. Clinton and others had tried to take race out of the equation of crime and poverty—arguing that everyone, regardless of race, should be held to the same standards of accountability and responsibility. Kerry, by contrast, injected race into the conversation by linking problems such as urban crime to a program that mostly offered a leg up to minority students and job seekers.

Later, he would explain that he was trying to make the case that the nation was focusing on affirmative action as a panacea to the problems plaguing ethnic minorities and that complementary programs rooted in traditional values were needed. But that's not the message much of his audience heard.

"The truth is that affirmative action has kept America thinking in racial terms," Kerry said. Insisting that he still supported affirmative action, Kerry outlined its costs, particularly the white resentment that racial preferences had fostered. "We cannot lecture our citizens about fairness and then disregard legitimate questions about the actual fairness of federal regulation and law," Kerry said.

Aides recall that the Kerry speech was inspired in part by what he was hearing from blue-collar voters. In some Boston neighborhoods in particular, there remained lingering resentment over court-imposed busing in the mid-1970s and contemporaneous consent decrees ordering the city's police and fire departments to hire more minorities.

But the ugly racial clashes that had ensued from those court attempts to redress decades-old patterns of discrimination also left the state's white liberals embarrassed. An air of political correctness settled in over the state's dominant political and media culture. U.S. representative Barney Frank, the outspoken Massachusetts Democrat, quipped about lists of "nosapostas"—truths that liberals are "not supposed to" talk about. On matters of race, especially, there could be no backsliding, even if it meant young, white ethnics with perfect exam scores might not become cops or firefighters in Boston.

With his Yale speech, Kerry had issued a direct challenge to that liberal orthodoxy. "He has always chafed under the stigma of being labeled just another Massachusetts Democrat, in the long shadow of Ted Kennedy," his pollster, Thomas Kiley, said at the time. "He's working to publicly assert what those who know him already know, that he is independent minded on issues.

The public flogging that followed Kerry's Yale speech was swift—and fierce. Longtime friends and supporters publicly accused him of race baiting. Bill Owens, state senator and chairman of the Massachusetts legislature's Black Caucus, made a biting comparison to the nation's most famous racist: "David Duke could have made the point that the white majority doesn't like affirmative action."

One Boston city council member praised Kerry for not wanting to be "a liberal dinosaur." And Ted Kennedy described his colleague's speech as a "thoughtful and constructive contribution to an important national debate on race discrimination and the most effective means of eliminating it." But the media, especially the *Boston Globe*, brimmed with commentary attacking Kerry.

At Kerry's office in Boston, dozens of angry calls poured in, prompting his spokeswoman to concede that "there does have to be some smoothing of ruffled feathers." Kerry delivered his speech on a Monday. By Friday, he was ensconced in a series of damage-control meetings with local leaders. "I was pointing out the problems of growing resentment" toward affirmative action, Kerry insisted that week. "I'm not moving away from a sound affirmative action program."

Under fire during a local TV roundtable the following Sunday, Kerry again tried to clarify his remarks, saying it was not just a speech about affirmative action. "It's a speech about why we can't move America to deal with what is happening in our cities. I say this, and I don't back away: if the entire resolution of what is happening in our cities is to rest upon a program that only scratches the surface, then we're in trouble."

Months later, Kerry would confess that he should have vetted the speech with friends and supporters. But he still stood by his central premise. "We have to get rid of the perception that we need to do things for people and create the perception that we are willing to help people help themselves," he said. When Kerry delivered the Yale speech, he promised a series of talks to come on race and urban America. In the firestorm that followed, he dropped that plan.

Laced through the attacks in the days and weeks that followed Kerry's speech was an assumption that he was motivated by personal ambition, running for the vice president's slot on a ticket headed by Clinton, who by then was the front-runner for the Democratic nomination. Kerry had endorsed and lent staff to Clinton's opponent and his Senate predecessor, Paul Tsongas.

But by the end of March, Tsongas had suspended his campaign, Clinton had the nomination nearly sewn up, and Kerry critics insisted he was pandering to the front-runner. Kerry had even borrowed a Clintonism in his remarks, transforming the Arkansas governor's call for a "new covenant of social and personal responsibility" into his own call for a "social contract, a covenant wherein every right is matched with a responsibility."

Following the speech at Yale that early spring night, he was asked if he was interested in the VP spot. He demurred by saying, "It's pie in the sky." When he was asked on a Sunday TV panel whether he wanted to be president, he answered: "Not right now. Would I think of it in the future? Possibly."

Later that spring, vice-presidential headhunters

stopped by Kerry's office. But despite the hopeful public musings of his supporters, the Massachusetts senator didn't make the short list. Clinton ultimately tapped Al Gore, who had entered the Senate the same year as Kerry.

At a late May luncheon that year in Los Angeles, Kerry yielded his place on the program to the presumptive Democratic nominee. When Clinton rose to speak, he joked: "I never thought I'd get ahead of John Kerry in anything." Kerry, though, played the loyal soldier that election year, defending Clinton against attacks over his lack of military service. In September, he led a contingent of congressional war veterans defending Clinton against Republican questions about his Vietnam record.

The 1992 presidential campaign was a three-way race among George H.W. Bush, Bill Clinton, and Independent candidate Ross Perot. Clinton won with less than half the vote. In January 1993, when he started work in the Oval Office, his administration was already under strain. The new president's decision to fulfill a little-noticed campaign promise by drafting an executive order to repeal a ban on gays in the armed forces was provoking a huge uproar. Even his own military advisers fought him.

Rising to the administration's defense, Kerry called the ban "fundamentally wrong. There is nothing inherent in homosexuality that makes a gay incapable of serving." In May, Kerry appeared as a witness before the Senate Armed Services Committee and engaged in a sparring match over sexual practices with two supporters of the ban, Democrat

Sam Nunn of Georgia and Republican Strom Thurmond of South Carolina.

Thurmond declared that only homosexuals perform sodomy. "Heterosexuals don't practice sodomy," he shouted, prompting laughter from the audience.

Kerry pointed out that there were gays working in Congress, none of whom had been arrested for sexual practices.

"You want them arrested for that," Thurmond said.

"Do you, sir?" Kerry replied.

"Sodomy is against the law," Thurmond responded. "Why shouldn't they be arrested?"

Proponents of the ban argued that the military's disciplined and tight-knit culture would be disrupted by openly gay members. Kerry and others argued that attitudes would shift if the ban were lifted. "Change is hard to accept," Kerry said at the time.

President Clinton ultimately split the difference by adopting a policy of "don't ask, don't tell," permitting gays to serve as long as they didn't reveal their sexual orientation. Seven years later, Kerry would revise his stance slightly, saying he favored giving commanders of small, specialized forces the authority to remove a gay person if his or her conduct disrupted the unit. The flexibility to remove a troublesome individual—whether that person was gay, homophobic, or bigoted—could help prevent violence within a unit, he added.

In June 1993, Kerry came to the administration's rescue as a supporter of Clinton's $500-billion deficit reduction measure, a bill that combined spending cuts with tax hikes. Not a single Republican in either the House or the Senate was going to support the bill, so the vote was going to be a close one. Kerry, saying he wanted more spending cuts, considered opposing the measure but ultimately sided with the president in a tie vote that Vice President Al Gore was forced to break.

Two months later, Kerry wrote a commentary proposing that Congress adopt a requirement that the president send a monthly list of suggested spending cuts to Congress. At a time when the government was routinely running huge deficits, many lawmakers had their favorite example of ridiculous pork programs. Kerry's was the wool and mohair subsidy, a throwback to a wartime economy when soldiers' uniforms were needed. (In 1993, Kerry and Kennedy were finally able to eliminate those subsidies.)

Kerry helped the Clinton administration on another initiative: the crime bill. In 1993, high urban crime rates—symbolized by the random murders of tourists and others—were capturing headlines. As part of his campaign platform, Clinton had promised to deploy federal funds to put another 100,000 police on the street. But with budget deficits swelling, the initiative faced internal resistance, and the administration was planning to cut its cop-on-the-beat commitment by half.

That fall, Kerry called Bruce Reed, Clinton's domestic policy adviser, to his office. "He thought the administration was making a mistake by not doing 100,000," Reed recalled. "He showed me charts of how federal assistance to local law enforcement had declined. He talked about his years as a prosecutor. I was ecstatic to have an ally. I had been making similar arguments within the administration."

It "certainly strengthened my hand within the administration," Reed recalled, "to have a Democratic senator of some stature leaning on us to get it done." Led by Senator Joseph Biden, Democrat of Delaware, the Senate passed a crime bill that included the 100,000 new cops at a cost of $13.5 billion, as well as an assault weapons ban and an expanded federal death penalty. On amendments, Kerry voted against expanding capital punishment, but he voted in favor of the final omnibus crime bill that included it. A similar version later passed Congress, but only after House Democrats almost destroyed the effort by loading up the legislation with extraneous social spending.

In the new era of the New Democrat, Kerry moved toward the center. In the fall of 1993, he provided a crucial vote for Clinton on another centrist issue, supporting the North American Free Trade Agreement. The treaty, initiated by George H.W. Bush, Clinton's Republican predecessor, lifted most trade barriers among the United States, Mexico, and Canada. But opponents, led by the AFL-CIO, feared that it would cost American jobs as U.S. companies moved their operations across the border to take advantage of lower wages in Mexico.

Kerry argued that American job losses in some sectors would be more than offset by expanding markets in others. "Job loss is taking place without NAFTA," he told reporters in November 1993. "The hard reality is that as a nation we can't put our heads in the sand like ostriches."

Congress passed NAFTA shortly before Thanksgiving, but going into the vote, the House was too close to call, and in the Senate, Kerry was considered a critical vote for a president who, for political reasons, needed a majority of

Democrats behind him. "In what was the most difficult battle for the soul of the Democratic Party, every vote counted a lot," said Reed. The measure passed the House, 234-200, and the Senate went 61-38, with Ted Kennedy joining Kerry to support Clinton.

Kerry's NAFTA stance paralleled his position on China, in which he broke party ranks to support most-favored-nation trading status for the Communist regime in 1991, just two years after Beijing's deadly crackdown on dissidents connected with the Tiananmen Square demonstrations. In the fall of 1994, Kerry led a delegation of executives from Massachusetts companies to China, saying he hoped they could tap into the country's huge and potentially lucrative consumer market. That same year, he sponsored an amendment to urge Clinton to ease U.S. restrictions on travel to Cuba.

Budget deficits remained a concern for Kerry, who had been one of the earliest Democratic backers of the 1985 Gramm-Rudman spending control law. In early 1994, he aired his internal wrestling over whether to support a proposed amendment to the U.S. Constitution to require a balanced budget. In February, he was one of ten undecided senators; by March, he had decided to oppose it. "It is not what our Founding Fathers intended," he said. The amendment failed.

Kerry was less clear about his position on the Clinton health care plan, a wide-ranging proposal—involving unprecedented government intervention in the health markets—to dramatically expand insurance coverage. When Clinton introduced the initiative in September 1993, Kerry praised the president for framing "the issue with a good tone that invites sensible debate." Kerry, who had once suffered his own bout with skyrocketing health costs when he was forced to pay $500 out of pocket for an abscessed tooth, said a crucial question to be considered was: "Does it reduce cost?"

Four months later, Kerry appeared on CNN's *Crossfire* to defend Clinton's plan from attacks by conservative commentator Pat Buchanan and Republican senator Phil Gramm of Texas. Both conservatives had adopted the GOP mantra that Clinton's plan would lead to "socialized medicine."

"You guys keep throwing these terms, and you love it." Kerry complained. "This is the way politics is played here, throw out socialist threats, and Phil comes in and says, 'You want choice.' ... This is a program of choice ...."

"Let me get in one point here," Buchanan responded. "I think what most Americans are saying is, 'Look, if there's people that want health insurance and don't have it, let's find a way for them to get it—'"

"Correct." Kerry interjected.

"But [they are saying] 'I've got a fine program, don't take over my program. Don't socialize it. I mean, don't change my program—'"

"But you see," Kerry responded, "you're saying socialize. This is a competitive system. I don't happen to agree with all of the system, and the system the President's put together is at least the opening gambit of the first discus-

sion of a major problem this country faces, which you and
your folks and your President avoided for years."

By the fall of 1994, insurgent Republicans led by House
Minority Whip Newt Gingrich were engaged in a full-
frontal assault on Clinton. The president who began his
term with the uproar over gays in the military was now suffering from the controversial health care proposal that
Hillary Clinton and senior aides had crafted behind closed
doors. Aided by an industry ad campaign, the conservative
label "socialized medicine" began to stick. Religious
activists from groups such as the Christian Coalition and
free-marketers such as Americans for Tax Reform stood
poised to provide troops and money to Republican candidates for the House and Senate.

On Election Day, Republicans took control of both
houses of Congress for the first time in forty years. The
earthquake reverberated beyond Washington: Republicans
gained eleven governorships and 472 state legislative seats.
The Republicans who took control of Congress were a
combative and righteous new breed, eager to wage war on
Clinton and his Democratic allies.

Kerry mostly had marched in lockstep with the Clinton
White House. But with the Republican sweep, he went
into full maverick mode, blaming the victory on "screw-
ups" by Clinton and saying he "was delighted by the
shakeup." "I'm a Democrat," he said, "and there are reasons I'm a Democrat. But I have to be honest in acknowl-
edging that mistakes were made and that the agenda was

not as focused as it should have been. To not acknowledge that is to court further disaster."

But Kerry's comments courted political disaster at home. The powerful Representative J. Joseph Moakley, a Democrat from South Boston and chairman of the House Rules Committee, publicly accused Kerry of political opportunism. "A lot of guys want to go off and do their own thing until election time," said Moakley, who died in 2001. "Then they want to rally around the flag. That's not the way I play."

The winds were changing in Washington. They were also changing in John Kerry's personal life as he entered into his first serious relationship since the painful breakup of his marriage. Teresa Heinz was the earthy, auburn-haired widow of another tall Yale alumnus, a U.S. senator from Pennsylvania described as "intense and aloof": H. John Heinz III, heir to his family's food fortune. Heinz was killed in an April 1991 helicopter-plane collision. There was speculation that Teresa, active in a range of causes, would seek his Senate seat, but she decided instead to devote her energies to philanthropy and her three sons. Like her late husband, she was a Republican, though far too liberal for Gingrich & Co.

Maria Teresa Thierstein Simoes-Ferreira Heinz was born and raised in Mozambique, then a Portuguese colony. Her childhood was spent at a seaside home that was lost to Marxists, along with family savings, when they took over the country in 1975. Her Portuguese father, was an oncologist who had practiced at the renowned Mayo Clinic; her mother, of mixed European descent, grew up in Mozambique.

Teresa studied literature at a South African university, where she participated in marches against apartheid. She became fluent in five languages and attended the interpreters' school at the University of Geneva before working as a consultant to the United Nations in New York.

At age fifty-five, Teresa was five years older than John Kerry. She still spoke with a soft Portuguese accent. She loved roses and gardens that instilled "an indigenous sense of spirit and wildness." In Pittsburgh, she had a reputation for giving generously, for speaking her mind, and for displaying a Mediterranean-style volatility.

Teresa Heinz, whose personal inheritance has been estimated by *Forbes* magazine to be in the neighborhood of $760 million, lived in the grand style of the superrich. She traveled by private jet. Her residences included the Rosemont Farm, a ninety-acre estate outside Pittsburgh, and a $2.2-million Georgetown residence with one of the most revered private collections of seventeenth- and eighteenth-century Dutch still lifes. Her Sun Valley, Idaho, getaway was built out of timber imported from a fifteenth-century barn. In 1984, she and Heinz built a seaside "cottage" in Nantucket.

In addition to running the Heinz Family Philanthropies, she sat on the boards of the Carnegie Foundation, the Brookings Institution, the Yale Art Gallery, Georgetown University, the National Council of Families and Television, and the National Gallery of Art. She had served as chairwoman of the Campaign for Public Safety, a group pushing for an assault weapons ban in Pennsylvania. In 1993, she began offering an annual $250,000 award, in remembrance of John Heinz, to honor achievers whose work defies "our cynical age ... who are masters of the art of the possible."

Teresa Heinz shared with John Kerry a passion for environmental causes. One of Kerry's first acts as a new senator was to introduce acid rain legislation, an issue he continued to champion. He also pressed for giving states more authority over offshore oil drilling, for higher automotive fuel efficiency standards, for stricter controls over nuclear energy facilities, for global limits on fishing.

Heinz, inspired by the rain forests and savannas of her African youth, was vice chair of the Environmental Defense Fund and was involved in a variety of related groups. In a 1993 interview with the Pittsburgh *Post-Gazette*, she said she favored moving beyond the eras of conservation and government intervention and toward "sustainable development and eco-efficiency ... finding low-cost ways [for economies] to grow that don't pollute or deplete natural resources."

"Our highest priority should be redesign—redesign of our commerce and our products where the goal is to be inspired by and to imitate nature," she said in a speech to the U.S. Chamber of Commerce in Japan. To a Pennsylvania audience she offered her "cradle to cradle" theory: "True consumer goods should be literally consumable without persistent toxic effects. They should be able to be returned to the soil, water, and air without danger of any kind." Part of the EDF's strategy was to lobby large companies such as McDonald's to use more recycled and chemical-free products.

Heinz and Kerry knew each other casually through her late husband. But when they both attended the United Nations "Earth Summit" in Rio de Janeiro in 1992, the pair became reacquainted. They began dating in early 1994 when they attended the same Washington dinner party and Kerry drove her home, stopping for a stroll through the Vietnam Veterans Memorial on the way. They became engaged that November, just as the Republicans were taking over Congress.

On May 26, 1995, at an evening ceremony underneath a canopy, Kerry exchanged gold rings with his bride. Social and political glitterati gathered at Heinz's home on Nantucket Harbor. Peter Yarrow of the folk group Peter, Paul, and Mary performed at the wedding.

Both Kerry and Heinz were Catholic. But they parted ways with the Catholic Church on social issues. As a senator, Kerry staunchly resisted restrictions on abortions, including a ban on the procedure abortion opponents have labeled "partial birth abortion." Teresa, while describing herself as "not 100-percent pro-choice," said she believed the church must come to terms with overpopulation.

In a 2003 interview, Kerry said he and his second wife regularly attended Mass. But, he said, "I believe in the separation [of church and state]. I believe in not wearing it on my sleeve....I have my obvious, clear differences with respect to some of the liturgy." He added, "there are other parts that are quite stirring and meaningful."

Kerry's differences with the Catholic Church extended to its prohibition against priests getting married. "I think that if you look back historically at the church, that was something that was put into effect in the second millennium," he noted, "and it was put into effect mostly as an economic measure because the church was not able to afford the families as part of the effort ... But celibacy was not anywhere in the teachings of the Bible, so I have no problem with [the] idea," of priests marrying.

In 1996, John Kerry again parted with the church when he voted against the Defense of Marriage Act, which created a federal definition of marriage as the union between a man and a woman and prohibited the extending of federal marital benefits, such as Social Security, for same-sex partners. The measure, forwarded by lawmakers who feared that a Hawaii court ruling in favor of same-sex marriage would extend to other states, authorized states to refuse to honor these unions. Most Democrats, including Clinton, supported the law.

Calling the Defense of Marriage Act "fundamentally ugly, fundamentally political, and fundamentally flawed," Kerry joined a small minority of fourteen senators voting against it. During that same congressional session, Kerry co-sponsored legislation to prohibit hiring discrimination based on sexual orientation.

On another marriage issue, the Kerry-Heinz union reflected strict Catholic tradition. In the fall of 1996, Kerry's ex-wife, Julia, received a letter from the Catholic

Church informing her that her former husband of eighteen years, with whom she had two daughters, requested "an ecclesiastical declaration of nullity for our marriage"—in other words, an annulment.

The Roman Catholic Church considers marriage a sacred bond that cannot be broken by civil divorce. Therefore, a grant of annulment—a finding that a true marriage never existed—is necessary before a couple can remarry in the church. Otherwise, a divorced Catholic who remarries can't participate in sacraments, including receiving communion. Teresa Heinz told *New Yorker* writer Joe Klein that her second husband "had never been married"; friends dismissed this as a reflection of her Catholicism.

When Thorne received the church letter requesting her to participate in an annulment investigation, she crafted a pointed reply. "I regard your ecclesiastical investigation as hypocritical, anti-family and dishonest," wrote Thorne. "I cannot look my children in the eyes or stand before them with integrity and know in my heart that I have contributed in any way to a process that invalidates and nullifies the union from which they were created."

"History cannot be changed," she added. "Because I believe truth is sacred, I wish to set an example for my children of courage, honesty, forgiveness, and compassion by taking responsibility for my actions and history." Thorne told the *Boston Globe*'s Frank Phillips that she wouldn't contest the annulment proceeding because she didn't recognize its validity.

"I loved John when I married him and there will always be a marriage," she told Phillips. "I support his career and I really know he is happy with Teresa and they both deserve the right to pursue their faith."

At the time Kerry requested his annulment, the issue was in the news because of the publication of a book by Sheila Rauch Kennedy, ex-wife of Representative Joseph P. Kennedy II, attacking church policy. Kerry himself initially released a terse statement in response to his own ex-wife's comments. But later, on Don Imus's radio talk show, he took a more lighthearted approach toward the controversy over annulments: "It's one of those special Catholic things. It's like confession or feeling guilty about things you haven't even thought of doing."

Kerry told Imus and his listeners that he was "very sympathetic" to concerns about annulment. "The fact is, it doesn't affect the status of the child at all," he said. "It's just in the eyes of the church ... they view that there was or wasn't a marriage according to the faith, which is different from whether or not there was a marriage according to the state."

With his second marriage, Kerry would have by his side a woman accustomed to getting her way. After the couple bought a $2-million mansion on Boston's Louisburg Square, she made news by complaining about a neighbor's trellis that didn't match and also by altering the design of a utility grate on her sidewalk. After racking up many tickets for illegal parking, she also paid to move a fire hydrant from the front of the manse, which had once been a convent.

Teresa Heinz, who kept her name and political party affiliation after the wedding ceremony, was also accustomed to saying what was on her mind. In front of reporters, she referred to her late husband John Heinz as "my husband" and her current spouse as "John Kerry." Describing the courtship by her second husband to Joe Klein, Heinz said Kerry reminded her of a "pet wolf who comes in and you say, 'Yeah, cute.'" In October 1998, as she accompanied Kerry on his first full day of testing-the-waters style campaigning in New Hampshire, Heinz was asked by a reporter what she thought of talk about a Kerry presidential run in 2000. "It's ridiculous, isn't it?" she answered.

But she also praised her second husband for his "elegant mind. His thinking is not brutish. He really likes to take his time, talk things through, to deliberate."

Friends saw an immediate change in Kerry after his marriage to Teresa. There was now a sense of permanence as he settled down. He seemed, said one, more comfortable in his skin. His personal life no longer unsettled, Kerry's comfortable political career, however, was about to be upset.

Stirring in his State House office, about 500 yards from the elegant new Heinz-Kerry home on Beacon Hill, was Governor William F. Weld. The Republican was now an extremely popular political figure in Massachusetts, but he seemed disengaged, bored with his job. He was also ambitious and, like Kerry, considered himself presidential material. Weld was looking for the next challenge. By midsummer 1995, the governor's advisers were whispering that Weld was seriously considering a challenge to Senator Kerry, the Democratic incumbent. The only thing holding him back was his role as national finance chairman in the presidential campaign of California governor Pete Wilson. When Wilson abruptly dropped out of contention on September 29, Weld was free to explore a Senate campaign. He didn't waste much time. Weld concluded that Kerry's record on domestic issues left him vulnerable. Late that November, Weld announced he would run.

Chapter 16

BATTLE OF THE TITANS

WITH MASSACHUSETTS governor Bill Weld now his challenger, it was clear that 1996 would be nothing like Kerry's first two campaigns for the Senate. In those races, he had walked over fairly light Republican opposition—the millionaire businessmen Ray Shamie in 1984 and Jim Rappaport in 1990.

After more than a decade in the exclusive club of senators, Kerry would finally be tested as a candidate. But this time, he could not brush off his opponent by painting him as an extremist, as he did Shamie, or as a member of the robber baron class, as he had done with Rappaport.

Weld was Kerry's equal or better in lineage, education, and résumé. And he'd proven a Republican could win— and win big—in a Democratic state. In 1994, Weld had crushed Mark Roosevelt, a Democratic state legislator, to win a second term as governor. It was a rout of historic proportions. In heavily Democratic Massachusetts, Weld bagged 71 percent of the vote.

There was a counterintuitive element to Weld's decision to challenge Kerry. In essence, he was asking voters to remove two popular figures, himself and Kerry, from their current jobs and install Lieutenant Governor A. Paul Cellucci in the governor's office. In the event of a Weld victory, Republican Cellucci, who was not as well known, would automatically become governor. But the Weld challenge was a jolt to Kerry, who had become comfortable in the Washington bubble of perks and coat holders. And now, after marrying Teresa, he had the added luxury of access to the Heinz Gulfstream jet and five fine homes.

As he became more accustomed to the title of senator, Kerry had started to lose touch with his Massachusetts political infrastructure. This was an unpardonable sin in a state where politics is serious business and the spawning ground for more than its share of presidential candidacies. Even Senator Edward M. Kennedy, a towering presence in Massachusetts, had to reintroduce himself to the Bay State's political culture two years earlier, when he turned back a stout reelection challenge by telegenic Republican upstart Willard Mitt Romney.

Kerry and his advisers have long maintained that the out-of-touch accusation was a bad rap. For years, Kerry returned to the state most weekends, barnstormed for a week or two every summer, and made time for the requisite glad-handing, they said. But the buzz was growing.

Early in the spring of 1996, Kerry showed up one Sunday at the Irish American Association in Malden, a blue-collar suburb north of Boston, to attend a political fund-raising event for one of the local politicians. It was "a time," in the regional vernacular, one of an endless schedule of mostly Democratic gatherings where the denizens of the political subculture convene to exchange gossip and slaps on the back. For Kerry, it was a chance to be seen, to begin solidifying his base within the party.

As he mingled with some of the local officials, Kerry was approached by a man who shook his hand and introduced himself as "Butchy Cataldo," a former state representative from nearby Revere. Kerry "reacted with gusto, slapping him on the back and telling 'Butchy' how good it was to see him again." But "Butchy" was actually William Reinstein, a state representative and former mayor of Revere. Had Kerry known his true identity, he might have been less enthusiastic. After three decades in politics, Reinstein was best known for surviving three trials before his acquittal in 1982 on charges he conspired to accept kickbacks on a high school construction project.

The prank resonated among political insiders as a symbol of Kerry's distance from rank-and-file party officials. Many had no relationship with him; others saw him as an opportunist who courted them and moved on. These were local satraps, but also the underpinning of the dominant Democratic Party. They provided workers and kind words, the foundation of strong statewide candidacies.

Weld, with control of the state's purse strings and patronage, was already making inroads, as he had against Roosevelt, romancing Democrats at the local level. Even some senior Democratic figures were sitting out the race. A few, like former state secretary Michael Connolly, a Kerry opponent in the 1984 Senate primary, went over the partisan wall to help Weld. If there was ever any doubt that Weld was a serious threat to Kerry, there was none now.

Like Kerry, William Floyd Weld was descended from one of America's founding families. And as Kerry had, he took an unconventional route to political prominence in his adopted home state. "It is said that the Welds arrived in 1630 with only the shirts on their back and 2,000 pounds of gold," Weld would joke of his ancestors. The Welds had settled near Boston, but Weld was raised on a 600-acre farm in Smithtown, Long Island. He was named for a forebear, William Floyd, a New York signatory of the Declaration of Independence.

Weld had glittering educational credentials: exclusive Middlesex School in Concord, Harvard College (a summa cum laude classics major), Oxford University fellowship, and law degree from Harvard Law School. Married to Susan Roosevelt, a great-granddaughter of Theodore Roosevelt, Weld launched his political career in 1978, challenging Attorney General Francis X. Bellotti, a warhorse in Massachusetts politics. Weld lost 349 of 351 cities and towns but established his Republican bona fides in the process. In July 1981, President Reagan appointed him U.S. attorney in Boston.

Attacking political corruption became his hallmark, and his office scored a string of convictions in Somerville and Boston, where Weld's team of aggressive prosecutors ran a dragnet through Kevin White's City Hall. Weld was on the map and, in 1986, on his way to Washington as chief of the Justice Department's criminal division. Eighteen months later, with his superior, Attorney General Edwin S. Meese III, compromised by multiple ethics investigations, Weld abruptly resigned.

In early 1989, he briefly considered challenging Kerry, who was up for reelection the following year. Then practicing law at Hale and Dorr, a white-shoe firm in Boston, Weld ruled it out, but the ambition was still burning. With Michael Dukakis a lame duck, Weld instead declared he would run for governor the following year.

In 1990, the Republican Party was a lowly underdog in Massachusetts politics. With only 13 percent of registered voters, Republicans held one of thirteen seats in Congress, one-fifth of the seats in the state legislature, and none of the six statewide constitutional offices. But the sagging economy, following the implosion of Dukakis's presidential campaign, had weakened the Democrats. Pent-up voter anger produced a record flood of Independents in the primaries of both parties, helping Weld overtake his conservative foe, Steven D. Pierce, the House minority leader.

Weld's slogan that year was "Tough on taxes, tough on crime." He was cool and collected. By contrast, his Democratic opponent, John R. Silber, the fiery Boston University president, was a modern-day fury, a white-hot embodiment of the public's demand for change. He ran as a cultural moderate with New Deal sensibilities. But Silber's caustic, imperious style produced a series of "Silber shockers," as the *Boston Herald* dubbed them—wildly impolitic remarks that, over time, cost him support. In the November election, Weld nosed past Silber in one of the closest elections in modern state history.

During his campaign, the former prosecutor had likened

cleaning up state government to "riding into Dodge City." After his victory, he was about to become sheriff, surrounded by Democrats whose party had held the governor's office for sixteen years. Weld was a fiscal conservative with a libertarian streak. His liberal social policies, his critics said, evolved less out of conviction than a sense of good politics. For two years, Weld and the legislature battled over spending cuts and his efforts to scale back government. Eventually, the deficit was brought under control and a series of bipartisan tax cuts were enacted.

Weld's popularity soared. He disarmed opponents with a self-effacing manner and suffered his partisan scolds without complaint. His amiable nature was a huge asset, a buffer against critics who said his policies hurt the poor. Weld made no secret of his fondness for Jack Daniel's Old No. 7 sour mash whiskey, took time from work to play squash, and traveled the world on official "trade missions" that detractors dismissed as junkets. Lou DiNatale, a long-time Boston political analyst, called Weld "the first media-savvy [baby] boomer" to become governor. It's ironic that Weld almost never watched television.

In his 1994 reelection campaign, the incumbent rented the loyalty of many Democrats, some of whom would find their way onto the state payroll at good wages. In his challenge to Kerry, Weld wooed even more. After steamrolling Mark Roosevelt (a second cousin of Weld's wife), Weld apparently got drunk at his second inaugural ball, and local radio talk-show hosts had a field day, replaying his slurred remarks.

At the outset of his second term, he began thinking

about national office, even president. By October 1995, it became clear that Weld saw a path to the White House running through the seat of the junior senator from Massachusetts. On November 29, he declared his candidacy, slamming Kerry's support for tax increases and opposition to the death penalty and welfare reform.

In Washington, Kerry fired back, noting that Weld had declared himself an "ideological soulmate" of Newt Gingrich, the ultraconservative Speaker of the U.S. House of Representatives.

Daily shots rang back and forth between Boston and Washington, prompting *Boston Globe* columnist Mike Barnicle to write: "Already, Weld and Kerry make the Serbs and Muslims look like they're playing kissy-face in Bosnia. They came out scratching like a couple of fishwives, throwing a month's worth of ashcans in only five days."

It was the beginning of a political death joust. For nearly a year, these sons of Yale and Harvard would grapple, almost without pause, in the marquee Senate race in the country. This was a crucible from which only one would emerge as a national figure.

"Beyond the bare-knuckles battle between two tall Brahmins, beyond the 'blood on the floor' predicted by both camps ... John Forbes Kerry and William Floyd Weld can give Massachusetts a campaign for the ages," wrote Robert L. Turner in the *Boston Globe Sunday Magazine* in January, as the election year began. Kerry and Weld, Turner wrote, "represent strong new strains within their parties, strains that move away from the stereotypes of liberal, tax-and-spend Democrats and moralizing, country-club Republicans that each party has long used to portray the other." Expectations for the campaign were high from the outset. Weld and Kerry would exceed them.

They would each turn in polished performances in eight televised debates. Neither combatant gave an inch of ground, as they prodded and probed for any weakness that could yield advantage. Rarely would there be consensus about who had won or lost any of the encounters.

Early in the contest, Weld exploited one of his major advantages. With a large State House press corps situated one floor above his office, the governor made news almost daily. Kerry, meanwhile, most days was trapped in Washington, preoccupied with an ongoing partisan stalemate over the budget. Sound bite opportunities were few and far between. Every step and misstep was recorded, amplified, and dissected by the news media. Even their ability to tell jokes became grist for the mill.

In heavily Irish Massachusetts, there is a long tradition of political roasts and gibe fests around St. Patrick's Day. In March 1996, they took on added significance as an early test for the Senate combatants. At one breakfast in Worcester, Weld "stole the show, brimming with self-confidence, self-deprecating humor and a theatrical flair," a *Boston Globe* reporter at the event noted. Kerry, by contrast, "seemed distant, even distracted at times." He did not engage Weld.

At the main event in South Boston a week later, Kerry was much better prepared. He received a big assist from his wife, whose white Jeep Cherokee had recently been featured in a newspaper photo illegally blocking a fire hydrant in front of their trophy home on Louisburg Square. As Kerry rose to speak, Teresa arrived, carrying a plastic hydrant. "I was out finding parking, and I couldn't find one, so I made one," she said to loud applause. (A year later, the Kerrys would pay to have the hydrant moved from the front of their home.)

In past years at this Southie event, Kerry was perennially skewered by the roastmaster, state Senate president William M. Bulger. But in 1996, reciting a long satiric poem, Kerry got some digs in at Weld. At one point, Kerry chided the governor for leaving town on a political trip the prior year rather than visiting a western Massachusetts town that had been ripped apart by a killer tornado.

It seemed a minor victory at the time, but Chris Greeley, Kerry's campaign manager, said it gave the candidate and the campaign a needed boost. "It was a big moment," Greeley recalled. The campaign had been foundering, Weld was making inroads in working-class South Boston, and Kerry "really drilled him, and Weld knew it," he said. "It's a milieu where the cards were always stacked against John, politically and culturally, but that was a very important day in the campaign," Greeley said.

Less than a week later, Weld gave Kerry his first real opening, climbing off the fence to voice his opposition to an increase in the federal minimum wage, saying it would kill jobs and harm small businesses. A day earlier, Kerry had announced he would push for the increase. Weld, who had earlier vetoed a bill to increase the state minimum wage, did reap some benefit. National restaurant chains opposed to an increase poured at least $23,000 into his campaign coffers through their political action committees.

In his formal announcement on March 27, Weld made four stops around the state, signing a pledge at each to oppose any tax increases in Washington. Adding welfare reform and a tough-on-crime component to his speech, Weld laid out what would be the basic themes of his senatorial campaign. They were the same issues that had propelled him to the governor's office and landslide reelection.

The following week brought Kerry's formal campaign launch. He framed the race in broader, starkly partisan terms—a "fierce clash" of Democratic defenders of government programs and the "extreme agenda" of Republicans, embodied by Gingrich, who in 1994 led the GOP to take control of the House for the first time in forty years. On the crime issue, Kerry emphasized his role in providing federal funds to hire 100,000 new police officers. Kerry didn't have to wait long for a platform to use the issues against Weld. Their first debate, on April 8, in Boston's historic Faneuil Hall, gave him an opening.

The freewheeling debate set the themes and contours of the entire campaign. Each candidate began to unload magazines of ammunition accumulated by his opposition research team. Besides the minimum wage, Kerry touted his support for Medicare and equity in the tax code. Weld positioned himself as the candidate who would reform welfare and cut taxes.

In a moment of high drama, Weld, a death penalty proponent, pointed toward the mother of a police officer slain in the line of duty. "Tell her why the life of the man who murdered her son is worth more than the life of a police officer," Weld said to Kerry. "It's not worth more," Kerry replied. "It's not worth anything. It's scum that ought to be thrown in jail for the rest of its life."

But, Kerry added, "the fact is, yes, I've been opposed to the death penalty. I know something about killing," Kerry said, without having to mention Vietnam. "I don't like killing. I don't think a state honors life by turning around and sanctioning killing." Eight years later, Weld acknowledges that the line "I know something about killing" had an effect. For Kerry, who had killed a man in combat, the death penalty was more than an abstract concept.

But Weld kept up the attacks, condemning Kerry's 1994 vote against mandatory minimum sentences for anyone convicted of selling drugs to a minor. (Kerry has defended this vote with the argument that mandatory sentencing procedures lock judges into rigid, and sometimes unfair, penalties.)

Weld then slammed Kerry's Senate votes on a number of issues, including his support for a 4.3 cent per gallon hike in the federal gas tax, part of President Clinton's 1993 deficit reduction package. (Kerry later advocated, then dropped his support for a 50 cent increase.) Weld also attacked Kerry's past opposition to tough welfare reform measures and a balanced budget amendment to the U.S. Constitution. "I hope everybody will study Senator Kerry's record," Weld said. His campaign was ready to assist and later published a 182-page compendium of Kerry quotes and votes.

In the early going, Weld's was by far the nimbler campaign. In late May, the campaign rented the billboard on a wall outside Kerry's headquarters in Boston. For the rest of the campaign, Kerry staffers could look out their windows and see Weld's rotating messages.

Their second debate, on June 3, was equally furious and left Kerry on the defensive for several days. At one point Weld jabbed Kerry for his meager charitable giving over the years. "It's perhaps easier for some to spend other people's money than their own," Weld said. The previous year, Kerry claimed zero deductions for charitable donations, according to his tax return. Weld and his wife listed $24,010 to thirty-six charities, 22 percent of their adjusted gross income. A few weeks earlier, *Boston Globe* columnist Jeff Jacoby had reported that over the prior six years, the Welds had donated an average of 15 percent of their income to charity. Kerry, by contrast, had given away less than 1 percent.

Kerry bristled at the unwelcome attention, calling the subject "off limits" and "making a mountain out of a molehill." He said the expense of maintaining homes in Washington and Boston, plus private-school tuition costs for his children, left little for charity. But ten days later, the *Boston Herald* weighed in with its own tabloid take on the matter: In 1993, a year in which Kerry donated $175 to charity, he paid $8,600 for a handmade Ducati Italian motorcycle.

That day, Kerry appeared on the Don Imus radio program, *Imus in the Morning,* and pledged "to do more" charitable giving. In less than two weeks, he would make good on that promise, but it was not just an act of personal generosity. When *Boston Globe* reporters Stephen Kurkjian and

Frank Phillips informed Kerry that years earlier, he had raised $7,000 in contributions from two Miami business- men later accused of running a money laundering operation for a Colombian drug cartel, Kerry's campaign immediately gave $1,000 to a drug rehabilitation center in Dorchester.

"This is the first time I have heard their names," Kerry said of the donors, Duvan Arboleda and Harry A. Falk. Arboleda had contributed $1,000 to Kerry's campaign in 1989, and in 1987 and 1988 he and Falk gave $6,000 to the Democratic Senatorial Campaign Committee, which Kerry was chairing at the time. Kerry said he knew nothing about them. The two were associated with MetalBanc, which bought and sold precious metals and in 1987 had paid Kerry a $1,000 speaking fee.

As Kerry limped out of June, an internal Weld poll showed the governor, for the first time, edging ahead of Kerry, albeit by a single percentage point. For most of the early going, Kerry had led in polls by as many as 13 points.

There was no summer letup in the slugfest. While vot- ers were off to the beach or the lakes, the debates contin- ued, the air war of television ads began, and both candidates played significant roles—albeit radically differ- ent—at their parties' national conventions. The tension caused by the race was also beginning to produce a specta- cle. The election was still four months away, but when the combatants met for their third debate on July 2, thousands of boisterous supporters milled outside the Emerson Majestic Theater in downtown Boston.

Kerry's campaign polls had continually shown that his menu of issues—education, environment, and health care—were uppermost in the minds of most voters. The Weld mantra of welfare, taxes, and crime rated lower. Weld, however, was convinced that a continued assault in those areas would soften up Kerry. His campaign would pound away to the very end.

In late July, Weld's campaign hit an unforeseen bump when the *Boston Globe* reported that Lieutenant Governor Cellucci's personal debts on heavily mortgaged assets totaled about $750,000, including $70,000 in credit card debt. Weld stood by his lieutenant governor, saying he was "managing his personal finances perfectly well." But because Cellucci would succeed Weld if he won, it became a new side issue.

A few days later, Kerry would all but wipe from the board one of Weld's best game pieces. On August 1, Kerry voted in favor of a sweeping bill to overhaul and place new limits on the country's welfare system. The legislation had become a priority for President Clinton, who, in his January 1996 State of the Union speech, declared "the era of big government is over."

Clinton and other centrist Democrats promoted welfare reform in part to reduce what they described as a culture of dependency that also contributed to a rise in poverty-stricken single-parent households. Kerry, as far back as his 1972 congressional campaign, had been critical of the welfare system, calling it then "an instrument of enforced poverty which limits rather than encourages the desire to work for those who are able."

During his years in the Senate, Kerry had opposed many Republican amendments he considered too harsh or punitive, such as one in 1992 to allow states to withhold payments to parents of students who failed to attend school regularly. But Kerry invariably voted for the final version of the reform measures. Indeed, before casting his vote in favor of the 1996 reform, he opposed a tougher earlier version that would have removed federal guarantees of health insurance for children in welfare families.

Splitting with his Bay State seatmate, Senator Edward M. Kennedy, Kerry said the final welfare reform bill had flaws but would be "an important change." With substantial Democratic support, the bill passed, 78-21. Human service activists back home in Massachusetts were outraged, saying Kerry had sold out under political pressure. "He is turning Clintonesque," said Jane Collins of the Massachusetts Human Services Coalition. Weld's campaign said it was an act of political expediency. But Kerry had defused one of Weld's hot-button issues. Weld today acknowledges that Kerry's vote "definitely helped him."

Until Kerry's vote, Weld had considered welfare his best weapon, an issue that resonated with voters. It was one Weld always rode hard, and to this day he still quotes almost verbatim from a 1994 *Boston Globe* story about a four-generation welfare family—about 100 people, virtually all of whom had never worked—as justification for a tough work component for public assistance recipients. The story, by reporter Charles M. Sennott, concluded with a remark by one of the family members who was asked by Sennott what she would say to taxpayers. "Just tell them to keep paying," she said.

For months, Weld's campaign, worried about Kerry's

access to Teresa's fortune, had pursued Kerry to agree to a spending cap. The two candidates met at Kerry's house, and on August 7, the campaigns issued a joint statement that each agreed to limit overall spending to $6.9 million, with no more than $5 million going to paid advertising and a cap of $500,000 on personal funds they could expend.

Initially, Kerry had a big fund-raising edge, but by summer, Weld had $1 million more cash on hand than Kerry. Weld promptly spent about $800,000 on unanswered television ads.

The Weld campaign made a second splash on the day of the spending-cap deal. At a signing ceremony for a bill designed to protect the state's rivers, he dove into the Charles River, fully clothed. A spontaneous event, Weld insisted. But it was not without a moment of premeditation. Before taking the plunge, Weld turned to his official photographer, Rose Marston, and said: "Rose, are you ready?" The jovial redheaded Weld was on a bit of a roll.

And he had something to show for it, too. On August 12, for the first time in a public poll, Weld was leading. The *Boston Herald* survey showed Weld up, 46–38 percent, with a commanding lead among men. By emphasizing welfare, crime, and taxes, Weld was locked in the hardware department of politics. Even in this trough of his popularity, Kerry enjoyed a healthy lead among women voters, the poll found.

That day, Weld's campaign tried to press the advantage, striking hard with a harsh ad strafing Kerry on Weld's core issues and charging "flip-flops" on welfare. It was the first negative ad of the campaign. It would not be the last.

By the time the ad hit the airwaves, Weld was already in

San Diego for the Republican National Convention. He was 3,000 miles from home, but his three-day California itinerary was carefully scripted for consumption back in Massachusetts and to position him as an outsider within an increasingly conservative GOP.

Weld and other abortion rights advocates said they were muzzled during the official proceedings, but each day the Massachusetts governor held one or more events to attack the party plank that called for a constitutional amendment to ban abortion. Kerry's campaign airlifted its deputy press secretary to San Diego for a belated effort at counterspin and to accuse the Republican of grandstanding. But Weld had made his point. He did not stay for the convention's conclusion. He had another date with Kerry on August 19.

During the fourth debate, a panel of journalists tried to steer the conversation to the candidates' personal qualities. At one point, Kerry all but acknowledged he was losing a popularity contest to the more affable Weld. "I don't sort of wear every part of me on my sleeve as easily as some people do, and I know that," Kerry said. "On the other hand, what I do know about myself is that when you have a fight, I am a good person to be in a foxhole with."

A week later, Kerry was off to Chicago for the Democratic National Convention. His strategy was the opposite of Weld's San Diego gambit. Kerry dove right into the proceedings, enjoying an official but minor speaking role in which he attacked Republican education policies. On his return to Boston, Kerry declared: "I'm going to be going whole hog, hell-bent for leather, town for town, community for community," he said.

His campaign seemed to be rounding into form, too. In August, Ray Dooley came aboard to manage communications strategy. Kerry's campaigns had always had a balky decisionmaking structure—what one veteran called "the college of cardinals." Dooley's was one more voice, and his painfully deliberate ruminations were later derided by some critics as "Ray delays."

But Kerry campaign adviser John Marttila considered him "a political intellectual," and Dooley was no stranger to Kerry. He had been an informal adviser until then and had helped out in 1984, for Kerry's first Senate race. Moreover, Dooley had demonstrated a steady hand in steering Ray Flynn to the Boston mayoralty years earlier. Now, he was taking a leave as the chief aide in the Boston office of U.S. representative Joseph P. Kennedy II. It would not be the last time a Kennedy loaned political talent to help a Kerry campaign in trouble.

The final piece fell into place a few weeks later when Robert Shrum came aboard as media adviser, replacing Dan Payne, who had been at odds with Kerry for months over the advertising strategy. Knives were in the air, and the Kerry campaign needed a slasher to counter Stuart Stevens, Weld's ace media man. Stevens-crafted TV ad attacks were starting to hit Kerry in waves. Enter Shrum. He changed the tone almost immediately. Weld today says Shrum's arrival was a turning point: "Bob Shrum sharpened and toughened Senator Kerry's message and ads from the day he joined the campaign."

A few days later, on September 16, Weld and Kerry locked in their most ferocious debate yet at grand Mechanics Hall in Worcester. In a clever move, Weld's campaign had already cut a new negative ad to reinforce a new line of attack Weld planned to introduce during the debate. This time, Weld accused Kerry of supporting welfare payments for drug addicts and alcoholics under the Supplemental Security Income program. "You are looking at the issue, as usual, from the point of view of the drug addict and criminal," Weld said in the debate.

Kerry offered a tepid response, replying that many of those recipients were Vietnam veterans. Only later would he accuse Weld of a "duplicitous and brazen distortion" of a complex issue. A year earlier, Republicans in Congress had pushed to eliminate the program, which had been reformed after years of abuse. Kerry twice tried unsuccessfully to salvage the reformed program.

When Weld criticized Kerry for opposing the death penalty for terrorists, a vote the senator had cast three times since 1989, Kerry shot back that many nations would not extradite anyone who could face the death penalty. "Your policy would amount to a terrorist protection policy," said Kerry. "Mine would put them in jail." Kerry would change his mind about that policy five years later.

Kerry also slammed Weld's television ads, calling them "a disgrace." In response to a charge that his ads distorted Kerry's record, Weld retorted, "I couldn't possibly make it any worse than it is." By the time the debate ended, Weld's new attack ad about payments to drug addicts was on the air.

"Sleazy," Marttila, the Kerry adviser, said the next day of Weld's new ad. "If they want a tough campaign, they will get one," Shrum responded, designing ads that attacked Weld on education and the environment, tying him to Gingrich and Bob Dole, the Republican presidential nominee, who was running far behind President Clinton in Massachusetts polls.

The Kerry candidacy was starting to benefit from the gravitational pull of Clinton's presence at the top of the ticket. Weld may also have been hurt slightly by another factor: Conservative third-party candidate Susan Gallagher was also on the Senate ballot.

On September 24, Kerry received some local help when the Boston Police Patrolmen's Association endorsed him. Symbolically, at least, that took some of the sting out of Weld's relentless assault on the crime issue. The union had severely undercut Michael Dukakis's presidential campaign in 1988 when it endorsed Vice President George H.W. Bush.

Clinton appeared at a major Kerry fund-raiser in Boston on September 28, the first of two campaign visits on behalf of Kerry. Vice President Al Gore would also drop into the state late in the campaign. With a Massachusetts Democratic safely in the presidential contest, they were trying to save a precious Senate seat for the party. Around this time, Kerry was struggling to keep pace with Weld's surging— and PAC-heavy—fund-raising. During a visit to Beverly Hills in September, Kerry received $10,000 in contributions arranged by an obscure California businessman, Johnny Chung. The significance would not become apparent until the following year when Chung was linked to a cash-for-access investigation involving the Clinton reelection campaign and the Democratic National Committee.

The donations to Kerry, the *Los Angeles Times* later revealed, occurred shortly after the senator's office facilitated a meeting between Chung and his Chinese business associates and officials at the Securities and Exchange Commission. Chung would disclose that a portion of the more than $300,000 he gave the DNC and other political figures had been funneled through him by Chinese nationals. And he would plead guilty to fund-raising charges, including using straw donors for donations to Kerry and Clinton. Kerry by then had long since returned the contributions, which he did not know were tainted, and said his office never made any "public policy decision" on behalf of Chung or his associates.

The timing of the revelations spared Kerry embarrassment during his campaign, but he was about to face a series of tests.

Midway through his reelection campaign, Kerry had—with much fanfare—announced he had submitted a bill to provide health care to the nation's millions of uninsured children. When Kerry on October 1 did actually file the children's health insurance bill he had announced three months earlier, Weld's campaign pounced, noting that Kerry in June had said he had already "introduced" the bill. Kerry, who said the bill was being drafted at the time, dismissed the episode as a semantic slipup. Weld nevertheless accused Kerry of a "falsehood," a statesmanlike synonym for a lie.

In fact, Kerry's ownership claims on the child health insurance bill had been the product of Ted Kennedy's eagerness to assist his seatmate in this close race. Kennedy's staff, renowned for its legislative expertise, had helped craft the bill and gave it to Kerry to introduce a month before the election. The junior senator used the issue in his TV ads and speeches, attacking Weld for vetoing a similar measure as governor.

After the election, though, it was Kennedy who did all the heavy lifting to move the bill along: finding a Republican cosponsor in Utah senator Orrin Hatch; raising money to run ads to battle the tobacco lobby; and going to war with Republican Senate leaders and the Clinton White House, when necessary, to win passage of a $24 billion health-care program for uninsured children.

To his critics, this was all vintage Kerry. "Mostly Kerry is more interested in the titles of his bills than the actual guts of the legislation," says Rob Gray, who was Weld's campaign spokesman and is now a GOP consultant. "He worked on bills that sounded good in press releases and gave him good media, and then moved on to the next thing."

On October 18, the campaign took a dramatic turn when the *Boston Globe* broke a story stating that Kerry had received free or reduced-price housing in the late 1980s. In Boston, two real estate developers provided the lodging, rented on a per diem basis, over a period of more than a year. One of the developers, fund-raiser Wesley E. Finch, would later cut Kerry in on a low-risk and highly profitable condominium sale. In 1989, for two or three months in Washington, Kerry had the free, intermittent, and undisclosed use of an $8,000-a-month apartment of his fundraiser and friend, Bob Farmer, who at that time was a registered lobbyist with business before Congress. There was no evidence that Kerry had taken any official actions specifically to help these short-term landlords.

Kerry replied that the arrangements were within legal and ethical guidelines. He said he did not disclose the Farmer accommodation because it fell under a "personal hospitality" exemption in Senate disclosure requirements. But the story changed the tone of the campaign in the final weeks. Weld tried to capitalize, calling for a federal investigation. Within three days, his campaign aired a tough new television ad, raising the question of Kerry's ethics.

Two days after that, the subject dominated their seventh debate, in Springfield, with Weld thrusting at every opportunity. The governor lumped in for good measure the old story about Kerry's leased vehicle when he was lieutenant governor, neglecting to mention that Kerry had belatedly paid for the car.

The other major theme of the debate was the ballyhooed but fast unraveling campaign spending cap they had agreed upon in August. Kerry had mortgaged his Beacon Hill home and dumped the first $900,000 of what would be $1.7 million in personal funds into his campaign kitty.

Kerry's camp asserted he could break their spending agreement, which was a signed contract, because Weld's media consultants were charging less than Kerry's, leaving Weld more money to buy commercial airtime. The contract, however, made no mention of discounted fees, and Weld's campaign said Kerry came up with a canard to dig deep into his own money because his campaign fund was running dry.

"Weld was stunned," Gray, his campaign spokesman recalled years later. "He thought they had an agreement and that Kerry would never break it."

On Sunday, October 27, nine days before the election, *Boston Globe* columnist David Warsh suggested the possibility of a darker version of events twenty-seven years earlier when Kerry had earned a Silver Star in Vietnam. Warsh quoted a crewmate on Kerry's swift boat who said he had wounded a rocket launcher–carrying enemy soldier before Kerry chased the soldier and killed him behind a hut.

"What's the ugliest possibility?" Warsh wrote. "That behind the hootch Kerry administered a coup de grâce to the Vietnamese soldier—a practice not uncommon in those days, but a war crime nevertheless."

Kerry reacted with outrage that day. Flanked by crewmates and a retired admiral, Kerry ripped the column as "absolutely inappropriate, out of order, conjecture, and malicious." He said it impugned not only his honor but "the honor of those of us who served." With him at the Charlestown Navy Yard was retired admiral Elmo R. Zumwalt Jr., commander of U.S. Navy forces during the Vietnam War. Zumwalt said the column "was such a terrible insult, such an absolutely outrageous interpretation of the facts, that I felt it was important to be here." Once again, in the last days of a campaign, an insult to Kerry's service in Vietnam became a rallying cry.

The next night, the epic series of eight debates, stretching across more than six months, concluded where it began, in Boston's august Faneuil Hall—the "Cradle of Liberty," where more than two centuries earlier, colonists had met to protest British tax laws. Outside, the autumn night was electric. Thousands gathered. Many were labor union members loyal to Kerry. Signs, catcalls, and chants filled the air.

"It's the battle of the titans, the best race in the country," Weld's ad man, Stuart Stevens, said at the debate. In eight days, voters would decide the race, which polls showed was extremely tight.

Weld and Kerry were both on their games. The zings went both ways, at breakneck pace, reprising the themes developed early in the contest. Their moment of truth was approaching. After the votes were counted, a place was assured on the national stage for only one. It was a stirring and fitting finale.

In the final week, Weld continued his barrage of tough ads, running three bruising spots in rotation. Polls, however, indicated the negative campaign was starting to hurt his candidacy.

President Clinton, riding high in state and national polls, appeared in Springfield with Kerry two days before the November 5 election, thanking him for his efforts on behalf of campaign finance reform and funding for 100,000 new police officers in the 1994 crime bill.

Two days later, Kerry survived. Winning big in most of the lopsidedly Democratic cities, he defeated Weld by 191,508 votes, or 7.5 percent of the 2.56 million cast. At the same time, Clinton beat Dole in Massachusetts by 853,656 votes, a victory margin of more than 33 percent.

To this day, Weld believes his fortunes sank as the race

became "nationalized" in the waning days. The effect of the Clinton coattails is still debated. Rob Gray of Weld's campaign said Weld's late ten-point lead in the Springfield TV market vanished after the president's visit.

Election night, on the ballroom stage at the Boston Sheraton Hotel, Kerry vowed to be "a much better senator" in the next six years. "I think it is fair to say I learned more in this campaign about you, about politics, and about myself than I have learned in any run I have ever made," he said.

The battle over, the weary gladiators praised each other. Kerry called Weld "obviously an extraordinarily capable, extraordinarily tough competitor." Six blocks away at the Boston Park Plaza Hotel, Weld said Kerry "[deserves] a great deal of political and personal credit ... He has prevailed in a fair and equal fight if ever there was one." Two nights later, Kerry and Weld met at McGann's Pub near North Station, hoisted beers, and toasted each other.

"This is exactly how it should finish," Weld said.

Chapter 17

NATION AT WAR

ON MONDAY NIGHT, September 10, 2001, the World
Affairs Council honored John Kerry and John McCain for
their work on behalf of normalizing relations between the
United States and Vietnam. "I don't want to exaggerate in
any way what happened between me and John Kerry,"
McCain said in a joint interview at the time. "In some
ways, I think it is symbolic of what is happening in our
country. There's been a healing and a reconciliation and a
friendship amongst people who were divided on the issue
of the Vietnam War."

What McCain didn't know, and couldn't know, was that
even as he spoke those words, America stood on the brink
of another major war, one that would unite, more than
divide, the nation—for a while.

On Tuesday morning, Kerry was entering his Capitol
Hill office, planning a quick stop before heading off for a
9:00 A.M. meeting of the Senate Democratic leadership,

when an aide broke the news. "John," said Tricia Ferrone, "a plane has crashed into the World Trade Center." Kerry rushed to a television set and stared at the gaping hole in the side of the 110-story building on the Manhattan skyline. "This is no accident," he said. There was no way, he told Ferrone, that a pilot could accidentally hit that building in clear flying conditions.

At 9:03 A.M., Kerry was at the leadership meeting, televisions on, when a second jet slammed into the Trade Center towers. Forty minutes later, the senators heard a loud "boom" in the distance. It was a third jet, crashing into the Pentagon, two miles away across the Potomac River.

The United States was under attack. Seventeen minutes later, the extent of the destruction was becoming apparent to the world as the south tower of the World Trade Center began to crumble.

The phone rang in the Capitol room where the senators had gathered: The White House was being evacuated. Another plane was still in the air, the lawmakers were told, and Washington was the presumed target. Kerry returned to his office across the street in the Russell Office Building to tell his staff to leave and to contact his family.

His shock turning to anger, Kerry continued to watch the news unfold alongside his aide David Wade. About an hour after the World Trade Center attacks, a fourth jetliner plunged into the countryside eighty miles southeast of Pittsburgh. Frantic calls from those aboard indicated that this airplane, too, had been hijacked by terrorists. At 10:28 A.M., Kerry and Wade watched footage of the World Trade Center's north tower crumbling. Seventeen minutes later, all federal buildings in Washington were evacuated.

That evening, President Bush addressed a shaken and bewildered nation. "These acts of mass murder were intended to frighten our nation into chaos and retreat. But they have failed," he said. "Terrorist acts can shake the foundations of our biggest buildings, but they cannot touch the foundation of America." The president added that he had "directed the full resources for our intelligence and law enforcement communities to find those responsible and bring them to justice. We will make no distinction between the terrorists who committed these acts and those who harbor them."

Later that night on CNN's *Larry King Live*, Kerry called the attacks "an act of war" by a "stealth enemy." He said he was "heartened" by the president's resolve to pursue the sponsors and protectors of terrorists. The United States, Kerry said, must respond "boldly and bravely—not recklessly—but boldly."

"We must be prepared, absolutely, to move unilaterally, if we need to, to protect the honor and civility that we stand for," Kerry said. "And I think everybody in this country would support that based on the proper response with the proper information."

For Kerry, the day's events had been a national tragedy, and a personal one. His friend Sonia Mercedes Morales Puopolo, a philanthropist and Democratic activist, had been aboard United Flight 175, the second plane to hit the World Trade Center.

That week, Kerry and Kennedy used Teresa Heinz's private jet to fly to Boston, the departure city for two of the hijacked planes. The senators met with acting governor Jane Swift and called for federal control over passenger and baggage checks. "We must ask the federal government to assume the burden of airport security," Kerry said.

Three days after the terrorist attacks, Kerry joined a 98–0 Senate vote to give Bush broad powers in the use of American force against nations, organizations, or persons who were involved or who harbored those involved in the attacks three days earlier. "People were concerned that it not be blanket approval for any kind of action, for any event, for any interpretation," Kerry said.

Even then, Kerry had Iraq in mind. In an interview with National Public Radio, broadcast on September 14, he said the resolution prohibited the president from using "this as an excuse to invade a country that had nothing to do with the events of September 11th. A very clear example: For instance, if Iraq had nothing to do with what happened, you can't use this as a pretext to suddenly attack Iraq, as much as you don't like Saddam Hussein."

The terrorist attacks came at a time when Kerry's attention, like the nation's, was focused on more peaceful pursuits. In the Senate that year, Democrats were enjoying a brief window of majority control after Senator James M. Jeffords of Vermont decided to drop his GOP affiliation and become an independent. Kerry had intended to make the most of the Democrats' newfound power. That fall, he was planning hearings on raising fuel efficiency standards and was orchestrating a strategy to block Bush's plan to drill for oil on federal lands in the Arctic National Wildlife Refuge.

On the campaign trail, the Massachusetts senator was

already looking beyond his 2002 reelection race, where he faced no serious opposition, to a 2004 bid for the presidency. He had interrupted an August recess of sailing and windsurfing off Nantucket to attend fund-raisers for local officials in New Hampshire (where, it was safe to say, he—and not the mayor of Manchester or the state legislator being feted—was the reason for the presence of CNN cameras). Two days later, Kerry threw open the doors of his Louisburg Square mansion to host a fund-raiser for Thomas J. Vilsack, governor of Iowa, the official kickoff state in the 2004 nomination process.

Asked about his budding presidential race in the summer of 2001, Kerry would say only that he was not 100 percent certain that he would run. "I am more comfortable saying that ... I would like to be in a position to make a judgment about whether or not it makes sense," he said.

Kerry's serious test of presidential waters dated back to 1998, when he delivered a school reform speech that his aides billed as a foundation for a possible 2000 presidential campaign. In that speech, Kerry positioned himself as a centrist at odds with teachers' unions, traditionally staunch Democratic backers. Kerry proposed to gut tenure systems that protected bad teachers and to dismantle certification programs that prevented professionals in other fields from teaching.

"The fact is, the resistance to accountability and creativity is too evident all across the nation," Kerry told an audience at Northeastern University in Boston. Kerry later co-sponsored a bill with Oregon Republican Gordon J. Smith to give state and local educators more authority over their schools (though it called for federal matching funds of $25 billion to help pay for an array of new programs.)

And in September of 1999, he broadened his education critique to include Republican governor George W. Bush of Texas. The Texas governor, already considered a candidate for the Republican presidential nomination, advocated taking federal funds away from poorly performing public schools and giving the money to parents to spend on tutors or private schools.

But Kerry's school reform campaign had about the same shelf life as his 2000 presidential campaign. At one point in early 1999, he and his friend John McCain, who did run in 2000, mused that the impeachment trial of President Clinton was making it difficult to launch a presidential campaign. Every week that the candidates tried to avoid looking "political" during this sensitive period, they were falling behind in raising the double-digit millions they needed. "Free the Senate!" Kerry quipped after the Senate acquitted Clinton. "I am ready to quote Martin Luther King and say, 'Thank God Almighty, I am free at last!'"

Two weeks after the Senate vote, Kerry decided not to run in 2000. By the end of that year, he had stopped making headline-grabbing speeches about school reform.

In 2001, all signs finally pointed toward a Kerry presidential run, a path that would be reflected in his own positions on the war on terrorism. In the days immediately following the 9/11 attacks, when estimates of the lives lost in the United States were careening toward 10,000 (the final tally would be just shy of 3,000) and jittery citizens hunkered inside their homes, members of Congress stood squarely behind President Bush.

Like Bush, Kerry responded to the 9/11 attacks with a combination of tough talk toward terrorists and denunciations of the ensuing violence against America's Islamic and Arab citizens. Calling Islam "a religion of peace," Kerry told a gathering of about 100 Muslim student and community leaders at Tufts University outside Boston that "we will not deter terrorists or stop terrorism by becoming like them. No person can claim to call themselves a patriot or even a full American if they defy the principles on which this country was based."

In the same speech, delivered one week after the attacks, Kerry also warned that the next act of terrorism would most likely be a bioterrorism attack on another area of vulnerability. "What about water supplies? What about food?" he asked.

As a leading member of both the Senate Foreign Relations Committee and the Senate Intelligence Committee, Kerry knew something about the threat of terrorism. In 1997, he wrote a book, *The New War*, that focused on a growing web of international crime but also rang alarms about "the globalization of terror."

"The terrorists of tomorrow will be better armed and organized," Kerry wrote. "It will take only one mega-terrorist even in any of the great cities of the world to change the world in a single day ... ." Kerry warned that terrorists might use chemical or biological weapons against American targets. But he was particularly worried about unsecured nuclear stocks in the former Soviet Union. "What most encourages and emboldens terrorists now are the unprecedented opportunities inherent in the new world of porous borders, instant communications, and access to weapons of mass destruction," he wrote.

Kerry's book did not mention the name Osama bin Laden, but a year later it would become evident that this Saudi Arabian millionaire, the mastermind behind 9/11, was a growing menace. In August 1998, his Al Qaeda terrorist network bombed U.S. embassies in Tanzania and Kenya, killing 257 people, including twelve Americans. American officials warned that more attacks were in the offing.

When President Clinton decided to retaliate, a number of Republicans accused him of hankering to start a war to divert the nation's attention from investigations into his extramarital affair with White House intern Monica Lewinsky. Kerry vigorously backed President Clinton's decision in August to launch simultaneous long-range cruise missile attacks against terrorist strongholds in Afghanistan and Sudan that were linked to bin Laden.

"Those who strike out against us with terror have to understand we will pursue them and do everything in our power to protect American citizens and interests," Kerry said. Several months after those strikes, Kerry, by then a member of the Senate Intelligence Committee, said that American bombs "came within yards, literally, of taking out bin Laden himself. He got away by luck." Intelligence officials at the time said they feared a retaliatory attack from bin Laden.

Kerry also defended Clinton's decision, on the eve of the House vote to impeach the president for lying under oath about the Lewinsky affair, to launch air strikes against Iraq. The American attack was prompted by Saddam Hussein's decision to expel U.N. inspectors searching for weapons of mass destruction. "The president does not control the schedule of UNSCOM," Kerry said in a reference to the U.N. inspections team. "The president did not withdraw the UNSCOM inspectors. And the president did not, obviously, cut a deal with Saddam Hussein to do this at this moment."

In the weeks following 9/11, American flags were plastered on buildings and cars and hanging outside homes. Communities held candlelight vigils for the victims. So many volunteers showed up to blood drives that many had to be turned away. Kerry picked up on Bush's economic call to arms as well, imploring citizens to return to air travel and to spend their consumer dollars. Terrorists, he said, could claim further victory if the nation's economy faltered. "People, if you want to do an act of patriotism, if you were going to buy a car, go out and buy that car," he said on CBS's *Face the Nation* two weeks after the attacks. "If you were going to do some trip, go do that trip. It is safer to fly today in the United States than it has been in a long time, and it will get safer by the day because of the things that we are doing. People need to have confidence in this country."

Questions were aired about the quality of the nation's intelligence gathering: How could such a large-scale terrorist plan, one that included prospective hijackers attending American flight schools, go unnoticed? Kerry told *Face the Nation* viewers that although intelligence gathering is "the single most important weapon for the United States of America" in the war on terrorism, we are "weakest, frankly, in that particular area. So it's going to take us time to be able to build up here to do this properly."

But Kerry's critics asserted that he was one of those lawmakers responsible for the decline of intelligence gathering. As a member of the Senate Intelligence Committee, Kerry had previously called for spending cuts in the nation's intelligence apparatus, proposals he would later call attempts to "change the culture of our intelligence gathering." In September 1995, Kerry had proposed $90 billion in budget cuts in numerous agencies, mostly to eliminate what he called "pork." The bill included cuts of $1.5 billion over five years in intelligence but went nowhere. The Senate that day, however, on a bipartisan voice vote, did call for cuts in the National Reconnaissance Office, which was under fire for mismanagement and hoarding $1 billion.

In May 1997, Kerry worried that the country's vast intelligence apparatus, built for the cold war, continued to grow exponentially. "Now that that struggle is over," he asked Senate colleagues, "why is it that our vast intelligence apparatus continues to grow even as government resources for new and essential priorities fall far short of what is necessary? Why is it that our vast intelligence apparatus continues to roll on even as every other government bureaucracy is subject to scrutiny and, indeed, to reinvention?" Kerry added that the scope and secrecy of the system made it difficult to judge its effectiveness.

Kerry's cautious support of President Bush's war on terror initiatives continued through the fall of 2001. When it became clear that Al Qaeda was responsible, and that Afghanistan's Islamic fundamentalist Taliban regime was providing safe harbor for the terrorists, Bush demanded that bin Laden be turned over. When the Taliban refused, Bush launched a military strike, fulfilling his promise that the United States would "pursue nations that provide aid or safe haven to terrorism."

In early October, Kerry voted to support U.S. military action in Afghanistan, though he stressed the need for enhanced diplomacy with the Muslim world. "The administration needs to be exceedingly careful and thoughtful and sensitive as they go down the road pursuing that," Kerry said.

Kerry's position on the use of ground troops shifted. In an October 8 interview with the *Boston Globe*, he said that a large-scale invasion by U.S. ground forces probably wasn't needed, noting that air strikes would reduce the capabilities of the ruling Taliban militia. (He also raised questions about "some players" in the Bush administration but said he was "comfortable with the experience" that Secretary of State Colin Powell, Defense Secretary Donald Rumsfeld, and Vice President Dick Cheney "bring to the president.")

But in early November, he told the *Los Angeles Times:* "I think some ground forces are going to be necessary. No doubt about it. And I think we have to do whatever is necessary to win."

The military action against Afghanistan began with relentless air strikes—as many as 100 sorties a day—against the Taliban's radar, air support, and command-and-control systems, as well as Al Qaeda training camps. Ground support included U.S. and British special operations forces allied with 15,000 troops from the Afghan Northern Alliance. Later, when it was clear the Taliban was falling, thousands of Pashtun soldiers in southern Afghanistan came to the aid of the U.S.-led coalition.

That fall, vocal commentators on the political Left blamed the 9/11 attacks on an insensitive U.S. foreign policy that, among other sins, punished the Iraqi people with economic sanctions and supported a heavily armed and aggressive Israel against Palestinians seeking to establish their own state. They condemned American military action in Afghanistan for killing innocent people—and for exacerbating anti-American sentiment in the Arab and Islamic world.

Kerry picked up some strands of this antiwar sentiment, repeatedly worrying that the Afghanistan bombing would antagonize the broader Muslim world. He said he urged Defense Secretary Rumsfeld to limit the bombing campaign inside Afghanistan to military sites. "I am not for a prolonged bombing campaign," Kerry said. "This is not a campaign against civilians. There are only so many military targets in Afghanistan. We cannot lose our values in prosecution of this war."

With this same argument, he distanced himself from the

Republican president he was preparing to challenge, even as he expressed support for Bush's war. "If all you do is create a lot of innocent victims and wind up with a more radical Islamic state in Pakistan with nuclear weapons, are you safer? We have an obligation to ask those questions." And then he added a phrase that would become a signature of his presidential campaign: "Patriotism isn't blind."

On October 20, while praising President Bush's handling of the war against terrorism, Kerry nevertheless said the United States needed to reevaluate its foreign policy to deal with the root causes that fostered bin Laden's "farm system of terrorism." Terrorism is "being allowed to fester in the world because all of us are not doing enough to face those questions about poverty and opportunity and governance and development," he said.

But Kerry rejected the leftist argument that America brought the 9/11 attacks on itself, that the suicide hijackings constituted a "crime" but not an act of "war," and that U.S. action against an impoverished Afghanistan was comparable to its aggression in Vietnam. "This is as clear-cut as it gets," said Kerry, who also described bin Laden as "evil."

Going into the Afghan war, the president prepared the public for large-scale casualties, saying, "This war will not be like the war against Iraq a decade ago, with a decisive liberation of territory and a swift conclusion." Five days after Bush cautioned Congress, Defense Secretary Donald Rumsfeld told reporters: "It will not be an antiseptic war, I regret to say. It will be difficult. It will be dangerous. The likelihood is that more people may be lost."

When Western forces suffered early setbacks, those

words seemed accurate. But in November, the tide began
to turn. Taliban fighters fled as their leader broadcast a
demand that his troops "stop behaving like chickens." On
November 13, the capital city of Kabul fell, and three days
later the Taliban controlled only about one-third of the
country.

"There's no question that we're closer to getting [bin
Laden]," Kerry said in mid-October. "The Taliban is in
very tight straits. The effort is to keep the pressure on, and
that pressure is intense right now. There's a lot more going
on than meets the eye. I have confidence that those harboring bin Laden, such as the Taliban and the Qaeda network,
are going to be under the most extraordinary and intense
pressure and manhunt ever mounted. We will succeed."

In fact, although U.S.-led forces succeeded in ousting
the deadly and repressive Taliban regime and destroying
much of the Al Qaeda network at a cost of twenty-three
combat deaths, they did not capture bin Laden. Kerry later
called the Tora Bora raid a "failed military operation"
because bin Laden escaped capture in the mountainous
region.

At midnight on October 11, 2001, one month after the terrorist attacks, the Senate adopted legislation to give law
enforcement agencies sweeping new domestic surveillance
powers, including the expanded use of wiretaps. "At this
time, more so than at any time in the past forty years, the
American people are standing firmly behind the federal
government and they trust government to do the right

thing," Kerry told his colleagues. "The American people support the idea that we must provide the FBI and the Department of Justice with the tools necessary to punish the perpetrators of the terrorist attacks and to prevent future attacks."

Kerry noted that there was broad agreement on some elements of the package, such as the need to update anti-terrorism laws to account for new technologies such as cell phones and "to ensure that counter-terrorism investigators wield the same powers that apply to drug trafficking and organized crime." But, he added, "agreement was more difficult to reach on other issues, like detaining foreign nationals, and I am pleased that we are in a position to move forward on the legislation."

Kerry had reservations about the effect on civil liberties of some sections. But he stressed the importance of quick passage. "Just today the FBI issued a statement warning of terrorist attacks and put law enforcement on the highest alert. I believe these serious threats to our security justify our passing this legislation swiftly," Kerry said. After prolonged debate, the Senate, in a 96–1 vote, approved its version of the law to provide appropriate tools required to intercept and obstruct terrorism—the U.S. Patriot Act.

The only senator opposing the bill was Democrat Russ Feingold of Wisconsin. Feingold tried unsuccessfully to limit the amount of time that law enforcement could monitor suspicious activity without a court order. Kerry voted to table Feingold's amendment measure "because I strongly believe that we must move forward with this anti-terrorism legislation." But the Senate bill did include a provision, sponsored by Kerry, to give law enforcement agencies more tools to crack down on money-laundering havens, some of which are used to support terrorists.

That same day, the Senate passed an aviation security bill that would make baggage screeners federal employees, place more air marshals on planes, and increase airline anti-terrorist training. Later, Kerry sharply criticized House Republicans for resisting plans to federalize airport security.

"We don't contract out the security of the president, or allow the Army, Navy or Air Force to be subject to the whims of market forces," he wrote in an op-ed for the *Boston Herald*. "With lives on the line, Americans wouldn't want the chaos of hundreds of different, unaccountable private security firms patrolling our ports and waterways."

Kerry was among those lawmakers who helped broker the partisan impasse over the issue. On November 19, 2001, President Bush, appearing at Ronald Reagan National Airport, signed into law legislation that, for the first time ever, made airport security "a direct federal responsibility."

On Thursday, October 26, Kerry joined seventy-eight other senators to support the death penalty for the terrorist murder of U.S. nationals abroad. Kerry had always opposed the death penalty, even for terrorists. In his 1996 campaign against Governor William Weld, he said capital punishment for terrorists would "amount to a terrorist protection policy" because countries that ban capital punishment would refuse to extradite captured terrorists to the United States. After 9/11, Kerry altered his position "because terrorists have declared war" on America. He remained opposed to the death penalty applied inside the criminal justice system, raising concerns about the fairness of its application.

Kerry also backed Bush's decision to establish an Office of Homeland Security as part of the executive branch to coordinate America's war against domestic terrorism. But he also expressed doubts about its effectiveness. "Washington has a long history of moving the deck chairs and trying to rearrange the pieces, but it just doesn't work unless someone has the line of authority and the ability to hold people accountable," said Kerry.

One year later, Kerry said it was imperative that Congress vote to establish a new cabinet-level Department of Homeland Security: "Since September 11, I, along with several colleagues, have believed that a reorganization of the federal government is critical to improving the security of this country."

In January 2002, with U.S. forces still fighting in Afghanistan, President Bush made his first public suggestion of the next war America would face. In his first State of the Union address since the 9/11 attacks, the president labeled Saddam Hussein's regime part of an "axis of evil, arming to threaten the peace of the world."

Administration officials warned that Iraq's weapons of mass destruction could be used in terrorist attacks far worse than the airline hijackings that damaged the Pentagon and destroyed New York's World Trade Center. They also posited an unsubstantiated link between Hussein and the 9/11 hijackers.

For Kerry, this would become an excruciating test. Despite his antiwar activism when he returned from Vietnam and his later opposition to the Vietnam War, he voted in favor of military action in Panama in 1989 and Kosovo in 1999. In the case of Kosovo, Kerry said "the choice of doing nothing" to stop the murderous sprees of Serbian leader Slobodan Milosevic "is absolutely unacceptable."

There is "no moral equivalency," he argued, between deaths that would result from bombing raids and the human destruction being mounted by Milosevic and his forces, "the murder, rape, organized rape, pillage, plunder, decimation of ethnicity, robbing of identities, the wholesale destruction of villages, the killing of teachers and parents in front of their children."

We are "at war," he said. "The question we must ask ourselves is whether or not we are prepared to win." After the Republican-led House narrowly voted to withhold U.S. approval of the NATO bombing campaign there, Kerry said in an interview, "I will never forget the perfidy, the callow crassness, of the vote in the House on Kosovo," which he described as a despicable move that undercut U.S. servicemen by making it "Clinton's war." Added Kerry: "I think that was a disgrace."

During this March 23, 1999, floor speech, Kerry turned again to his lessons from Vietnam: "If you are going to commit American forces, you make the decision at the outset about what you are trying to achieve, and you make the decision at the outset that if you are going to send those soldiers—airmen, seamen, all of them—into battle, you do so with the understanding that you are committed to achieving the goals that you have set out."

But Kerry's thinking on Iraq would never be so clear-cut. And Kerry's personal decisionmaking style made it even murkier. For John Kerry, all major decisions were

Socratic exercises. He would seek advice from many quarters, examine all the angles, and raise every doubt. Over the years, a number of aides have privately described the approach as methodical to the point of excruciating.

On policy matters, these exercises provided him a lawyerly command of the arguments pro and con, and gave him great peripheral vision in the political arena. But this due diligence often manifested itself in Kerry's propensity for windy explanations, with nuance layered upon nuance. He often sounded as if he were talking himself out of the decision he had just made.

To critics, this is Kerry the straddler, trying to create a record so broad that it becomes one big Rorschach inkblot in the minds of the electorate. Never would Kerry become more vulnerable to this charge than in his gyrations over the October 10, 2002, resolution authorizing President Bush to use military force against Iraq.

Kerry made clear during a TV interview just weeks after 9/11 that he considered Saddam Hussein a threat. "Saddam Hussein has used weapons of mass destruction against his own people, and there is some evidence of their efforts to try to secure these kinds of weapons and even test them," he said on *Face the Nation*. But in 2002, the Bush administration began talking about war as the means to stop him.

A month after his "axis of evil" speech, President Bush began including military force among the options available to remove Hussein and the threat of outlawed weapons of mass destruction. By spring, the Pentagon had finalized invasion plans, and by midsummer, the Senate Foreign Relations Committee was hearing testimony by specialists who described "an active and growing Iraqi program to manufacture weapons of mass destruction." The war drums were beating, but the president, on August 21, called growing speculation about an invasion a "frenzy" and said he was a "patient man" who would consult international allies and Congress before taking action.

Back home in Boston, the heat was on Kerry. Nine days later, about eighty antiwar protesters demonstrated outside the senator's office. Kerry issued a statement saying that "while I want us to arrive at a policy that eliminates the threat that Saddam Hussein represents, I want us to arrive at a policy that does that and advances the cause of America." Within days, President Bush said he would seek congressional approval, as his father had more than a decade earlier, before any military assault.

Bush on September 12 addressed the United Nations Security Council, setting conditions on Hussein that the president later said he doubted the Iraqi leader would meet. Following Bush's remarks, Kerry said he was "very supportive of the president," but two days later, after Bush had urged immediate action by Congress, Kerry, on national television, termed the Bush speech "a slap in the face" of the United Nations. Kerry also said there were still "unanswered questions."

For John Kerry, whose ambivalence toward war was symbolized by his past history, Iraq was a conundrum. He had voted against a popular war eleven years earlier. Now, with a presidential campaign all but certain, he would be asked to vote on war again. He criticized Bush but was still on the fence.

Events were moving rapidly. Leaders of other nations

were declaring their support or opposition to military action. The administration's quick timetable was forcing congressional action before the crucial midterm elections in November that could affect the balance of power in both houses of Congress.

Furious bipartisan negotiations with the White House continued for weeks, with congressional leaders pushing for a stricter resolution on the use of force. On October 1, with Congress preparing to debate the resolution's wording, Bush criticized efforts to "weaken" the resolution in a way that "ties my hands." He said he wanted to be able to act even if the United States failed to win broad international support.

At issue was a bipartisan measure crafted by Senators Richard G. Lugar, Republican of Indiana, and Joseph R. Biden Jr., Democrat of Delaware. Their alternative would have made the disarmament issue the principal goal of the threat of force. With a showdown looming, Kerry, a harsh critic of the Bush foreign policy, called a new draft of the resolution "an improvement" because it included advance notification to Congress. But he was still uncommitted and seemed to be wavering.

A few days later, in a speech in Cincinnati, Ohio, the president said: "Saddam Hussein is harboring terrorists and the instruments of terror, the instruments of mass death and destruction, and he cannot be trusted. The risk is simply too great that he will use them or provide them to a terror network."

"Facing clear evidence of peril, we cannot wait for the final proof—the smoking gun—that could come in the form of a mushroom cloud," said Bush. "Approving this resolution does not mean that military action is imminent or unavoidable," he stated. "The resolution will tell the United Nations, and all nations, that America speaks with one voice and it is determined to make the demands of the civilized world mean something."

Among Kerry supporters, a debate raged over the upcoming vote. Some advisers warned him that a yes vote could mean dangerous political fallout. "There were voices in the room that said, 'John, you'll never be the Democratic nominee,' and, 'John, you're alienating your base,'" said his former counsel, Jonathan Winer.

Two days later, Kerry, despite months of criticism of Bush's foreign policy, declared his support for the resolution in a forty-five-minute address on the Senate floor. "The vote that I will give to the president is for one reason and one reason only, to disarm Iraq of weapons of mass destruction if we cannot accomplish that objective through new, tough weapons inspections in joint conference with our allies," Kerry said in his address. "I expect him to fulfill the commitments he has made to the American people in recent days—to work with the United Nations Security Council . . . and to 'act with our allies at our side' if we have to disarm Saddam Hussein by force."

The next day, October 10, both houses of Congress voted overwhelmingly to give Bush the leverage he sought. The bipartisan Senate vote was 77-23, with Ted Kennedy among the opponents.

Within days, Kerry was answering his critics, suggesting it was a vote for peace not war. His circumlocutory explanations, however, were confusing. For example, speaking at a

Democratic Party dinner in Arizona four days after the vote, Kerry responded to charges that the Democratic majority had caved in the Senate.

"Wrong," he said. "What's happened is every single member of the United States Senate moved to take it to the U.N. with a willingness to enforce through the United Nations if that is the will of the international community."

He went on to say he would oppose unilateral U.S. force. "There is no justification whatsoever for sending Americans for the first time in American history as the belligerent, as the initiator of it, as a matter of first instance, without a showing of an imminent threat to our country."

In Massachusetts, Kerry had only a Libertarian Party candidate, Michael E. Cloud, facing him on the ballot. There was no Republican. Suddenly, however, an antiwar write-in candidacy had sprung up. Randall C. Forsberg of Cambridge, an arms control specialist and peace activist, said her candidacy "won't only send a message to Kerry, but also sends a message nationally that there are an awful lot of people who are opposed to war in Iraq."

Coincidentally, Forsberg was a national leader of the nuclear freeze movement Kerry had embraced twenty years earlier. In the November 5 election, Kerry took 80.3 percent of the vote to Cloud's 18.5 percent. Forsberg, whose campaign was brief and known almost exclusively by word-of-mouth communication, nevertheless tallied 24,898 votes, 1.2 percent of the total.

Chapter 18

THE SEARCH FOR THE PRESIDENCY

BY THE TIME terrorists attacked the World Trade Center and Pentagon, John Kerry was already taking steps toward an official candidacy for president. Publicly, the senator said he was only a candidate for reelection in 2002, but many of his actions were consistent with those of a man eyeing the White House. Indeed, there were signs even before the inauguration of George W. Bush. By early January 2001, Kerry allies in New Hampshire were asking activists not to commit to other potential presidential hopefuls. New Hampshire's first-in-the-nation presidential primary was still more than three years away.

By the end of June, Kerry was in Iowa, the first caucus state, and in August, he made a high-profile visit to New Hampshire. He'd also been to Texas and was augmenting what was already a national fund-raising network with trips to California, Washington state, Colorado, and Georgia.

Kerry would take his first public steps toward making it

official in mid-December, two months after the terrorist attacks, when he established the Citizen Soldier Fund, a political action committee to support other Democratic candidates for office, including those at the local level in Iowa and New Hampshire.

For someone known to deliberate endlessly on major issues, the Kerry decision on when to run for president spanned years. Within the Democratic Party, Kerry was a member of a distinct class, one of the five freshmen Democrats who entered the Senate in January 1985, after surviving the Ronald Reagan tsunami that sank Walter Mondale in the presidential race.

There were no lightweights in this group, each of whom had presidential ambitions. Preceding Kerry as presidential candidates were Albert Gore Jr. of Tennessee in 1988 and 2000, Paul Simon of Illinois in 1988, and Thomas Harkin of Iowa in 1992. The fifth member of the club, John D. (Jay) Rockefeller IV of West Virginia, had been an undeclared candidate for several months in 1991, visiting twenty-two states before backing out.

Kerry did not seriously consider running in 1992, but as the end of the Clinton era approached, he conducted some soundings. In late February of 1999, he said no. "My heart loves the battle. My heart loves these issues. My heart said go out and fight for these things," Kerry explained. "My head said the day after I make an announcement, I have to raise an exorbitant amount of money and do it all in ten months."

He might have added that the odds were long and the hill to climb steep. Gore, the vice president, was the presumptive favorite for the nomination. Former senator Bill Bradley of New Jersey was all but in the race at that point. If beating Gore in a head-to-head matchup would be difficult, it would be virtually impossible in a three-way contest. In his second term as Clinton's No. 2, Gore enjoyed a quasi-incumbency. Kerry would later endorse Gore in the nomination fight, campaign hard for him, and be among those considered as a running mate after the vice president swept aside the Bradley challenge.

Kerry's unfolding presidential candidacy was helped by the fact that in 2002, Bay State Republicans, for the first time ever, failed to recruit a challenger for Kerry's Senate seat. This freed the senator to raise his national profile, amass an enormous war chest, and travel freely to states that were potential battlegrounds in the nomination process.

In May, he visited South Carolina, making his ninth trip to a Southern state in the past fourteen months. The Palmetto State had already moved its presidential primary date into the pack of states that would have contests soon after New Hampshire.

The first stages of the race for the 2004 Democratic presidential nomination were shaped by an event of a Republican's making—President Bush's decision to invade Iraq. Kerry voted in support of Bush's resolution requesting authority to "use all means he determines to be appropriate, including force," to push Saddam Hussein into compliance with the U.N. resolution demanding that Iraq disarm. That vote left the Massachusetts senator on the defensive with liberal activists.

For a burgeoning antiwar movement, Vermont governor Howard Dean became an intriguing alternative. Dean, an obscure figure even in New England, was the first candidate to establish a presidential campaign committee, Dean for America, on May 29, 2002. By October of that year, he was moving toward a position in opposition to the war.

On the eve of the October 10 and 11 congressional votes on Bush's war resolution, Dean was described in a *Philadelphia Inquirer* story as sounding "like a dove one minute, a hawk the next." "Why do we have to do everything in a unilateral way?" Dean complained, adding, two sentences later: "We clearly have to defend the United States, and if we must do so unilaterally, we will."

Kerry, meanwhile, was answering charges that he had caved in to the Republican White House. The many explanations and defenses that followed his vote were alternately tortured, confusing, or opaque. Four days after he voted for the resolution, he said the resolution didn't actually give Bush a "free hand" to wage war, though in reality it did. "We've given him the opportunity to work with the international community and to try to bring the world together on something that is a concern," Kerry told a group of Democrats in Arizona.

Ironically, Kerry began offering as his own defense the argument that a "yes" vote would give the White House needed leverage to pressure Saddam Hussein into disarmament. He had expressly rejected the leverage argument eleven years earlier, when Bush's father, George H.W. Bush, wanted to go to war against Hussein.

In 1991, when he voted against the senior Bush's war resolution, Kerry said: "For us in Congress now, this is not a vote about a message. It is a vote about war because whether or not the president exercises his power, we will have no further say after this vote." In 2002, when he voted in favor of George W. Bush's war resolution, Kerry declared he would support the resolution only as a means to pressure Hussein to disarm through "tough weapons inspections in conference with our allies."

Heading into the first presidential campaign of his long political career, Kerry was in full straddle mode. He had always taken the long view, worrying that in a general election campaign, Republicans would paint him as weak on defense. But now, he had given Dean an opening, which he seized, hardening his opposition to the Iraq war and drawing sharp distinctions between himself and Kerry and many of the other Democrats who were moving toward presidential bids. Dean also attracted attention for his groundbreaking use of the Internet as a fund-raising and organizing tool.

Despite his Iraq vote, Kerry was drawing good notices as a national candidate. An October 24, 2002, a story in the *Wall Street Journal* carried the headline "A War Hero Moves to the Front of the Pack." A few days earlier in Columbia, in South Carolina's largest newspaper, the *State*, influential columnist Lee Bandy called Kerry "an early favorite among S.C. Democratic leaders." In late November, *New Yorker* writer Joe Klein, whose coverage of Kerry dated back three decades, weighed in with an in-depth and mostly positive profile. Kerry was on his way to becoming, in the minds of the great mentioners, a leading contender in an unformed but potentially large field.

That fall, Kerry breezed to a fourth term in the Senate,

reaping 80 percent of the vote in a contest against a Libertarian and a write-in peace activist who was protesting Kerry's Iraq vote. On December 4, 2002, Kerry took the leap and filed a statement of candidacy with the Federal Election Commission, enabling him to raise and spend money specifically for a presidential run. He used $2.6 million remaining in his Senate campaign account to launch the effort and immediately embarked on a multistate fundraising swing. The Kerry campaign would be built on the theory that financial superiority determines the winner.

At the same time, Kerry began to publicize his post-9/11 shift on the death penalty, noting that he now supported the punishment, but only for terrorists. As always, Vietnam was a reference point. "We're not talking about American citizens in the American criminal justice system, by and large," he said. "We are talking about people who have declared war on our nation, and just as I was prepared to kill people personally and collectively in Vietnam ... I support killing people who declare war on our country."

Gore, who had been considering another run, withdrew from contention on December 15. Two days later, Kerry met with a group of about twenty high-powered Democratic campaign financiers in New York City. At the Park Avenue office of equity fund manager Alan Patricof, the senator confidently predicted he could raise at least $30 million before the first primaries, which were about thirteen months away. The goal was ambitious—overly so, it turned out.

The American Research Group in January 2003 conducted its first monthly poll of likely candidates in the

New Hampshire primary. Kerry led Dean, 27-15, with no other candidate registering significant support.

Late that month, Kerry sat with three *Boston Globe* reporters for an interview in the senator's "hideaway" office in a remote section of the Capitol building. The windowless space served as a sort of retreat from the bustle of congressional life. During the interview, Kerry was shown the results of research into his ancestry, conducted as part of a lengthy profile on the candidate.

Years earlier, he had been told that his paternal grandmother had probably been Jewish. What he did not know was that his paternal grandfather was born Jewish as Fritz Kohn in what is now the Czech Republic. "Amazing . . . fascinating to me," he responded. "This is incredible stuff. I think it is more than interesting; it is a revelation."

Kerry's grandfather had changed his name to Frederick Kerry, converted to Catholicism to avoid persecution, and immigrated to the United States. The revelation would also jolt many in Massachusetts who for decades had assumed that their Catholic senator with the Celtic-sounding surname had strong Irish roots. Kerry himself had never claimed the Kerrys were Irish, but the impression had been left uncorrected in numerous news accounts.

A second piece of new information left Kerry stunned and, for a time, silent. He had known that this same grandfather had committed suicide. What he did not know were the circumstances: in the washroom of the Copley Plaza Hotel in Boston on November 23, 1921, by a single gun shot to the head. The senator was shaken. "How many times have I walked into that hotel?" Kerry said, staring in disbelief at the copy of a news clipping. "God, that's awful ... That is kind of heavy."

During the interview, Kerry had been shifting uncomfortably in his chair, sipping, from time to time, a protein drink. He wore a dark blue suit but seemed wan and thinner than usual. The reason for his appearance would soon become public. Five weeks earlier, on Christmas Eve, Kerry learned that he had prostate cancer.

Even at age fifty-nine, Kerry was a vigorous, athletic man who could lace up his skates and play hockey; he had recently taken up the somewhat perilous new sport of kiteboarding and remained an accomplished windsurfer. As recently as 1998, he had windsurfed about twenty-five miles between Cape Cod and Nantucket Island with the editor of *American Windsurfer* magazine, a feat that took six and a half hours.

But now he was on the shelf, with prostate cancer, the disease that had claimed the life of his father, Richard Kerry, two and a half years earlier, shortly after his eighty-fifth birthday. After receiving the news, Kerry began to research treatment options, spending much of his holiday season on the Internet collecting information.

On February 12, 2003, at Johns Hopkins Hospital in Baltimore, Kerry's prostate gland was removed during surgery by Dr. Patrick C. Walsh, a renowned urologist. Walsh said Kerry had "very early, curable prostate cancer," and the surgery was highly successful. There was no sign the malignancy had spread and the patient would not require chemotherapy or radiation. Kerry could return to the campaign trail in two weeks, the surgeon said.

Months later, Kerry said he remained optimistic after the diagnosis; after all, he had survived combat in Vietnam. "I just had a sense of confidence. 'I'm going to get through this. I'm going to be okay,'" he told the *Boston Globe*. The candidate was eager to portray the cancer surgery as a minor setback. He could have chosen a more conservative treatment—radiation therapy, for example—but that would have left him weakened for months and restricted his ability to campaign.

In late February, as he recovered, Kerry was too weak to cross town to attend the winter meeting of the Democratic National Committee in Washington. Instead, he invited some activists to his Georgetown home. Dean, meanwhile, lit up the room at the Hyatt Regency Hotel on Capitol Hill. With a series of "What I want to know" questions, the former Vermont governor ripped his own party's leaders for failing to stand up to the Bush administration on Iraq, tax cuts, prescription drug coverage, and education reform. "I'm Howard Dean, and I'm here to represent the Democratic wing of the Democratic Party," he said, appropriating the signature line of the late Senator Paul Wellstone.

The surgery had broken Kerry's front-runner-like momentum. He soon resumed a heavy campaign schedule, much of it devoted to fund-raising around the country. Kerry may have had his doctor's permission to return to the road in two weeks, but a month later, during an interview at his Boston office, he was still wincing from the pain.

As Kerry returned to the stump in early 2003, President Bush escalated the pressure on Iraq and full-scale war seemed imminent. That helped Howard Dean build more support from the vociferous antiwar wing of the Democratic Party.

Over opposition led by France at the United Nations, the United States, Britain, and Spain on March 7 said they would give Hussein ten days to surrender banned weapons. As that deadline passed, Bush issued an ultimatum: If Saddam Hussein and his sons didn't flee within forty-eight hours, the United States would invade. The defiant dictator said Iraq was girding for the "last battle," which began on March 20 with air strikes, followed by 60,000 U.S. and British troops crossing into the desert of southern Iraq from their positions in Kuwait.

The American public was transfixed by around-the-clock, and often spectacular, televised coverage of the invasion's progress. The onset of war widened the fissure among Democrats—and among the candidates campaigning for the presidential nomination. For Kerry, the rapid success of the American invasion, contrasted with continued public fears about its aftermath and a newly energized antiwar wing of Democrats, produced a zig-zagging of his position that lasted for months.

Before the invasion, Kerry had criticized President Bush for his failure to assemble a larger international alliance against Iraq. Two days after the shooting began, Kerry said: "I am completely supportive of our troops over there, and I am not going to make critical comment about the war in any way. The country needs to be united with respect to our troops." It was an echo of his stance during the 1991 Gulf War.

Dean, however, remained an outspoken opponent, and

in a March 27 speech in Iowa, he hammered Kerry's war posture. "To this day I don't know what John Kerry's position is," Dean said. "If you agree with the war, then say so. If you don't agree with the war, then say so, but don't try to wobble around in between."

Backpedaling less than a week later, Kerry abandoned his pledge to tone down the anti-Bush rhetoric—with words that would dog his candidacy for weeks. "What we need now is not just a regime change in Saddam Hussein and Iraq, but we need a regime change in the United States," he told a gathering in Peterborough, New Hampshire.

Kerry's comment, which appeared calculated to appeal to the antiwar voters whom Dean had galvanized, lit up radio talk-show switchboards and drew stern rebukes from Republicans. With U.S. troops closing in on Baghdad, Kerry's patriotism and judgment were questioned by critics. They accused him of equating Bush with Hussein. For nearly a month, Kerry was forced to defend his call for a "regime change" in Washington. At one point, he acknowledged, his remark may have been "too harsh." At another, he said the comment was "a quip," made in the context of the political campaign, not the war.

On April 9, a crowd of cheering Iraqis, helped by American Marines, tore down the statue of Hussein in Baghdad's Firdos Square. The dictator's regime had fled. On May 1, President Bush landed in a Navy S-3B Viking jet on the deck of an aircraft carrier near San Diego and, standing on the flight deck, declared that the end of major combat was a "turning of the tide" in the war on terror. A large banner, saying "Mission Accomplished," hung across the tower of the carrier, the USS *Abraham Lincoln.*

Meanwhile, Kerry was still losing points for his "regime change" comment, and he suffered a setback when John Edwards, a lesser known first-term senator from North Carolina, raised more money—$7.4 million to Kerry's $7 million, during the first quarter of the year. As usual, Kerry's aides put a positive spin on the numbers, noting that their candidate had more cash on hand than Edwards.

The ability to raise money, and the perceptions it created, would radically alter the race in a field that had grown to nine. Along with Kerry, Edwards, and Dean, the candidates included Senators Robert Graham of Florida and Joseph I. Lieberman of Connecticut, Representatives Richard A. Gephardt of Missouri and Dennis J. Kucinich of Ohio, former senator Carol Moseley Braun of Illinois and activist minister Al Sharpton of New York.

Fund-raising figures for the second quarter were a shocker: Dean, with a $7.6-million infusion, led the field by a wide margin. Kerry was second with $5.8 million. Again, Kerry's spinmeisters portrayed the news in the most positive light: Two second-place finishes in the fund-raising derby had demonstrated his consistency. But it was Dean who was fast becoming a media darling; his campaign's clever innovations and gimmicks made news, day after day.

From the outset of the Kerry campaign, producing an aura of inevitability had been a cornerstone of the strategy: Raise big money, grab establishment endorsements, and the nomination would follow. But by the middle of 2003, the money and attention were starting to flow the way of the little-known former governor of Vermont.

Worse, Kerry's campaign was undergoing an identity crisis. The basis of his candidacy was his biography—the Vietnam hero who came home and led the antiwar effort. Kerry looked and sounded presidential. He had foreign policy experience, an asset in a time of war.

But his message was faint. In a field where the Iraq war became a defining characteristic of each candidate early in the contest, other policy differences among the leading Democrats were reduced to nuance. They all had health care plans, the details of which were incomprehensible to the average voter. They all favored civil rights and legal abortion. Each offered something to improve the environment. Every candidate had fallen in behind Gephardt's call for fair trade agreements to protect American jobs. Each of the candidates even had agriculture plans appealing to Iowa farmers, who would be voting in the nation's first contest for the Democratic nomination.

John Kerry had his bio and a slogan: "The courage to do what's right." The problem was, it wasn't clear to voters what exactly Kerry thought was right. Dean, meanwhile, was drawing support by ratcheting up the antiwar rhetoric against Bush. Dean's clear stance against the U.S. invasion of Iraq "made him the anti-Bush," said Steve Murphy, Gephardt's campaign manager. "It came to symbolize opposition to Bush across the board."

Indeed, the combative Vermonter went after the president hard on a range of issues. He blasted away on the Patriot Act, which Kerry had supported, accusing the administration of trampling civil rights. He was an early and vocal critic of No Child Left Behind, another Bush priority that Kerry had supported. The education initiative required annual testing for students in grades 3–8 and sanctions for schools that did not make annual progress in their results. But the funding fell short of what the act allowed and educators were complaining about one-size-fits-all standards.

Dean's campaign, much like that of Republican John McCain's four years earlier, was being marketed as the straight-talk express; the media signed on to this refreshing departure from the usual canned speech making. But, like McCain, Dean was already displaying a lack of campaign discipline that would lead to his undoing. (At the height of Dean's popularity, McCain predicted to *Boston Globe* reporters that Dean's bursts of anger, like his own, would hurt his candidacy.)

At the same time, Kerry's campaign was hamstrung by a top-heavy decisionmaking structure, with two pollsters and two media consultants. His campaign manager, Jim Jordan, had put in place many of the organizational and political pieces Kerry needed to win. But Kerry's old friends in Boston were complaining bitterly that Jordan and his Beltway friends had cut them out of decisionmaking. Kerry wasted time refereeing disputes between Jordan and Bob Shrum, a sharp-elbowed Democratic message-shaper, who had long ties to Ted Kennedy and whose tough TV ads helped Kerry beat Bill Weld in the epic 1996 Senate contest.

Jordan was also often at odds with Cameron Kerry.

Seven years the senator's junior, Cam had been by his brother's side in every political battle, dating back to the 1970 citizens' caucus at Concord-Carlisle High School. He was the candidate's most trusted counselor.

In early July, Kerry summoned top aides—twenty-one of them—to his Nantucket home to discuss strategy. The advisers were split. Should he start attacking Dean (Jordan's advice) or hold his fire (Shrum's view)? Kerry sided with Shrum. Dean then launched an early TV ad campaign in both Iowa and New Hampshire that paid quick dividends. (Kerry's famously blunt-speaking wife, Teresa, would later tell reporters that the failure to immediately counter Dean's ads was one of the campaign's early blunders.)

A *Des Moines Register* poll, conducted in late July, showed Dean inching ahead of Gephardt, 23 to 21, in the Hawkeye State. Gephardt, who had won the Iowa caucuses in 1988 but pulled out of the nomination process two months later, had been the presumptive favorite in this must-win state that bordered his home in Missouri. New Hampshire, bordering Massachusetts, held similar significance for Kerry, and a mid-August poll by the American Research Group showed Dean—who had recently been featured on the covers of *Time* and *Newsweek*—leading Kerry there by 28 to 21.

By summer's end, Kerry's campaign had decided to move its ceremonial campaign kickoff from Boston to South Carolina, a critical Southern state with a primary just one week after New Hampshire. The campaign, which appeared to have two of everything, also had two announcement speeches. Jordan, the campaign manager, and Chris Lehane, the campaign's communications director, were working on one speech. But Kerry had also asked his media consultant Shrum to write an alternate version. The candidate chose Shrum's, a decision that crystallized the campaign's internal schism: Jordan and Lehane wanted Kerry to sharpen the contrast to the insurgent Dean; Shrum believed Kerry should ignore Dean, sound more presidential, and focus on the ultimate target—Bush.

On September 2, with the aircraft carrier USS *Yorktown* as a backdrop in Charleston, Kerry tried to give his sagging candidacy a fresh start by assailing Bush's "radical new vision of government." With casualties mounting in Iraq in the months following the invasion, Kerry also chided the president for appearing on the flight deck of an aircraft carrier months earlier and declaring the end of major combat in Iraq. "Being flown to an aircraft carrier and saying 'Mission accomplished' doesn't end a war," Kerry said.

But the candidate drowned out the day's hoopla with an acknowledgment later in Iowa that a shake-up of his campaign team was possible. And on the stump, Kerry continued to stumble. On a good day, his remarks tended toward windy senator-speak. His justification for his war vote at times was unintelligible, never more so than in this explanation during the Democratic debate in Baltimore on September 9: "If we hadn't voted the way we voted, we would not have been able to have a chance of going to the United Nations and stopping the president, in effect, who already had the votes and who was obviously asking serious questions about whether or not the Congress was going to be there to enforce the effort to create a threat."

This obfuscation on an issue that was dividing the country didn't help Kerry's bid for the presidency. Voters had strong views about the war, and Kerry apparently didn't. Despite the public relations offensive surrounding the official announcement, Kerry's campaign seemed dead in the water. Dean had widened his lead in New Hampshire to twelve points in a *Boston Globe* poll, and on September 15, Lehane quit. Kerry had rejected not only the advice of Lehane and Jordan to take the fight to Dean, he'd tossed aside their campaign kickoff speech.

Two days after Lehane's departure, more bad news arrived when retired four-star army general Wesley K. Clark grabbed headlines by jumping into the race. With his military background, which included combat decorations from Vietnam, Clark was perceived as an instant threat to Kerry.*

Kerry's campaign lurched into the fall, wheels wobbling. Yet there were some mildly encouraging signs. Although a mid-September American Research Group poll showed Dean's lead over Kerry in New Hampshire at ten points, voters still thought highly of their Massachusetts neighbor. Kerry was viewed favorably by 64 percent of respondents. Only 13 percent had an unfavorable view.

In Iowa, Gephardt was locked in a similar duel with Dean. Kerry was running a consistent but distant third, though he was well regarded in the September focus group sessions assembled by Gephardt's campaign. "They thought he looked presidential and sounded presidential," said Steve Murphy of the Gephardt campaign. "They liked

---

* Lehane, who had been spokesman for Al Gore's presidential campaign in 2000, would join Clark's campaign in late October.

his Vietnam story and they liked his foreign policy experience. He just wasn't making a connection."

The Kerry campaign was stagnant, but reinforcements were on the way. On September 23, Jeanne Shaheen, the former governor of New Hampshire, brought her formidable skills to the Kerry team, signing on as national campaign chair. The next day, the 200,000-member International Association of Fire Fighters endorsed Kerry. This was the candidate's first major labor endorsement, but it was less about union issues than Kerry's gestures on behalf of brother firefighters. In 1999, Kerry was on an Asian fact-finding trip when he learned that six firefighters in Worcester, Massachusetts, had perished in a terrible warehouse blaze. He cut short the trip and returned home so he could be in Worcester.

Shaheen and her husband, Bill Shaheen, were a well-established political team. Jeanne was battle hardened. She had managed Gary Hart's upset of Walter Mondale in the 1984 presidential primary and had won three elections to the state Senate and three more for governor. In 2002, she had lost a bruising U.S. Senate fight to Representative John E. Sununu, son of the senior president Bush's chief of staff.

Shaheen's role with Kerry was ill-defined. But she quickly realized that the gears weren't meshing in his campaign, and it was taking a toll on fund-raising. For the quarter ending September 30, Dean raised a record $14.8 million. By comparison, Kerry's $4-million take seemed measly.

Through October and November, Kerry split most of his time between New Hampshire and Iowa. He tried to draw contrasts with Dean on taxes. Dean favored a repeal of all of the Bush tax cuts to pay for health care and start balancing the budget. Kerry advocated repeal of only those cuts that benefited the wealthy and supported retaining cuts for the middle class and the poor. Kerry also echoed Gephardt's attacks on Dean for supporting deep cuts in Medicare in 1995.

But the Massachusetts senator was spending too much time in small living rooms, expounding on subjects through endless disquisitions that seemed to lack periods, or even commas. Agenda-setting speeches and soaring moments of vision were missing. It was, as one Iowa adviser recalled, "days after days of events that didn't amount to anything."

Aboard Kerry's van in New Hampshire, over dinner with him in Nashua, New Hampshire, and inside his Louisburg Square mansion on Boston's Beacon Hill, the Shaheens made their case that the campaign was veering dangerously off course. People who knew Kerry best, like Bostonians Thomas Kiley, the pollster, and longtime adviser John Marttila, didn't feel their input was welcome by the Washington staff. And Shaheen herself began to believe that the Washington office was unresponsive. "There were a lot of people who did not feel included, and there were a lot of ideas that were not acted on," she said.

Tension was growing between Jordan and Kerry. "John felt real uneasiness about it," said Bill Shaheen. "You had a senator who was working hard, but a campaign that wasn't in sync with him. The horses weren't pulling the wagon with the same weight and intensity, so the wagon wasn't going anywhere."

Kerry was frustrated. "There were a lot of days when I would read something in the paper, or show up at a day of events, and I came away feeling that this campaign wasn't going the right way," Kerry told the *Boston Globe* in late 2003. "I'd feel the need to be on my cell phone, calling Washington, making sure things were getting done, concerned that they weren't."

On the night of Sunday, November 9, with the Iowa caucuses ten weeks away, Kerry told campaign manager Jordan he was fired. He had considered making the move since September. It was not an easy decision; Jordan was a friend who had talent. But he was a source of constant conflict. Taking the advice of Jeanne Shaheen, Kerry replaced Jordan with Mary Beth Cahill, Ted Kennedy's chief of staff and a tough, efficient veteran of the Clinton White House and many campaigns. The Cahill hiring was clear evidence of the increasingly important role Kennedy was taking in the Kerry effort. For nearly twenty years, Kerry had labored in the long shadow of Ted Kennedy. Now Kennedy was pushing his junior seatmate toward the presidency—a goal Kennedy himself had once pursued.

At 5 A.M. the next day—about two hours before Jordan's firing would be made public—Jeanne Shaheen was en route to Washington to calm nerves at the campaign's headquarters. But the bigger worries were in Iowa, where Kerry was arriving that morning. Some Kerry aides in Des Moines were already awake and bracing for the fallout.

At a 9 A.M. meeting at Des Moines headquarters, John Norris, director of Kerry's Iowa campaign, tried to steady the staff. People were frightened. "We have a focus here, and we're going to do our jobs," Norris told the troops.

The mood in the office was lightened by the presence of several Vietnam veterans who were meeting Kerry at the airport that morning to accompany him on the maiden voyage of his new campaign bus, the Real Deal Express. Twenty reporters—quadruple the usual complement—sat a few seats back from Kerry, waiting to pounce on the Jordan news. Yet the candidate was joking easily and reminiscing with the vets. "I love having these guys here," Kerry told the *Boston Globe* reporter on board that day. "Guys who really get me, you know?"

The day's only "press availability" with Kerry lasted about five minutes in a gentle rain outside a Des Moines center for paralyzed veterans. Ten times Kerry repeated that he had to "change the dynamics" of the campaign. Eight times he said, "We're moving forward."

Privately, advisers said, he was sick of not trusting his own campaign manager, ready to take a leap of faith that Cahill could turn things around. He was weary of reading the media's "process stories" about his faltering campaign's internal problems. He was tired of worrying about what was going on back in Washington. "I wanted this to be a real Kerry campaign," he would say later. "Fighting to win, fighting with my heart, fighting for every last vote. I didn't feel we were fighting."

If the campaign was "moving forward" after the shake-up, it was not immediately apparent. For days, news accounts focused on turmoil inside his headquarters and the resignations of three Jordan loyalists. One story particularly grated on the candidate—that he could be heard munching on his dinner during a conference call with top advisers to announce Jordan's departure.

In retrospect, Jordan said of his firing: "I think I served

John well for a long time. But I think it's also true that the inevitable infighting and jockeying for position had gotten nasty and personal enough that it'd turned into a real distraction for the candidate. He made the only choice he could."

But Kerry's campaign manager wasn't the sole source of problems. Kerry himself had contributed to the drag with long, dreary stretches on the stump. This fit a pattern of Kerry's campaign style. In virtually all of his earlier contests, he would perform listlessly for long periods. But when his candidacy was in danger and he suddenly feared losing, he would—like a racehorse rounding the track—transform and burst toward the finish line.

Cahill began to recruit new staff, some of whom felt they were coming in to salvage Kerry's reputation as much as to right the course toward the nomination. Stephanie Cutter, who had been Ted Kennedy's press secretary, was hired to hone Kerry's day-to-day message and prepare a fusillade of attacks against Dean when opportunities arose. "The communications shop was the most obvious example of what needed to change," Jeanne Shaheen said. "There was almost no system in place. There was little strategy about what John Kerry should be saying, or how to push back against what others were saying."

And the difficult news cycles were not over. Four days after announcing Jordan's firing, Kerry disclosed on November 14 that he would loan his campaign the money needed to compete against Dean, who had capitalized on his record-breaking fund-raising by deciding to refuse federal matching funds, thus freeing the campaign from spending caps in early, battleground states. A career-long advocate of public funding and campaign finance reform, Kerry nevertheless followed suit. The message conveyed by his decision to use his own money, however, was unmistakable: Kerry's fund-raising was drying up. But it was also a signal that Kerry was putting his money where his mouth was. He borrowed $6.4 million, mortgaging his half interest in the Louisburg Square manse he owned with his multimillionaire wife.

The week of Jim Jordan's firing became a turning point, Kerry's senior advisers later said. Although Kerry never gave up believing in himself, the change gave him renewed faith in his campaign. And he found some new footing with a rally and a speech at Iowa's Jefferson Jackson Day dinner on November 15, where he energized thousands with his most direct challenge yet to President Bush.

Outside the event at Veterans Memorial Auditorium in Des Moines, Dean's campaign created a spectacle, a half-mile-long caravan of forty-three school buses, bearing hundreds of Deaniacs, many from out of state. But inside the hall, Kerry was in top form. "Iowa Democrats, it's time to get real," he began, in a speech that culled some of the toughest language developed by Jordan, speechwriter Andrei Cherny, strategist Bob Shrum, and Kerry himself over a period of weeks.

For the next ten minutes, Kerry painted Bush as an enemy of veterans, firefighters, and farmers, of teachers, children, and soldiers. In a line that became a defining theme of his campaign, Kerry turned Bush's well-known war cry into the evocation of a Vietnam veteran's resolve to challenge the president on his signature issue, the war on terror. "I know something about aircraft carriers for real. And if George Bush wants to make this election about national security, I have three words for him he'll understand: Bring . . . it . . . on."

Notwithstanding the quality of Kerry's performance, the bad news continued. Dean was widening his lead in New Hampshire and, three days before the dinner in Des Moines, had scored a coup—the joint endorsement of the two largest unions in the AFL-CIO, the Service Employees International Union and the American Federation of State, County, and Municipal Employees.

In late November, Kerry's campaign hit a new low when three Massachusetts newspapers published the results of separate polls, all showing Dean leading Kerry in the senator's own state, albeit within the margin of error in two of the surveys. At the same time, Kerry was twenty-one points behind Dean in New Hampshire. On December 9, Al Gore bestowed his endorsement on Dean, making him the undisputed front-runner. Within two weeks, Dean would shoot to the top of the field in independent polls in five more states, raising to at least seventeen the number of states in which polls showed him ahead. In newspapers and on television talk shows, pundits were speculating that the race was all but over.

For Team Kerry, it was decision time. On December 10, the eve of Kerry's sixtieth birthday, pollster Mark Mellman argued persuasively—if counterintuitively—that the campaign should roll the dice and devote most of its time and resources in Iowa. A fast finish might provide a post-Iowa bump for the return to New Hampshire, a state famous for springing surprises in presidential primaries. Kerry had built a solid organization in Iowa, rivaling the field operations of Dean and Gephardt. The nature of caucus politics—in which citizens gather and debate before voting—required sophisticated communication with voters. Campaigns needed to identify supporters in advance, make sure they arrived on time, and knew what to do once there.

"At an absolute minimum, we were always better positioned to make a run at the end," said Kerry's Iowa chairman Jerry Crawford, a force in caucus politics for three decades. Kerry's campaign was all set with the first part of the formula for winning in Iowa—organize, organize, organize. Now, the challenge was the second part—get hot at the end.

Iowa opinion polls and newspaper reports rarely if ever reflected Kerry's assets in the state. Cahill and Kerry dispatched to Iowa one of their longtime allies, veteran Democratic operative Michael Whouley, who had played an important role in Kerry's first two statewide campaigns in Massachusetts and had served on his staff in the lieutenant governor's office. The Boston native had earned a reputation as something of a magician in the Clinton and Gore campaigns. If there was a problem, he could fix it. With that reputation, he would have no problem getting what the Iowa operation needed from Kerry's Washington headquarters. "Christmas every day," he called it.

*

On Sunday morning, December 14, Americans awoke to the television image of a doctor examining the mouth and mangy hair of Saddam Hussein. The fugitive dictator had been captured the night before by U.S. troops in a cramped pit, "a spider hole," under a building near his hometown of Tikrit. He surrendered quietly.

The next day, in Los Angeles, Dean declared: "The capture of Saddam Hussein has not made America safer." It was a line he personally penciled into the text of what was supposed to be a major foreign policy speech. His aides were flabbergasted. For days, Dean was on the defensive. It was another gaffe, and they were piling up. Another problem for Dean was the fact that though many Democrats remained opposed to the war, anger was subsiding. On the campaign trail, voters were less interested in candidates' stances on the invasion itself than in what should be done to stabilize Iraq and bring American troops home.

This was good news for Kerry and bad for Dean.

In Iowa, Dean and Gephardt had been banging away at each other for months, running one-two, two-one in poll after poll. After a Christmas hiatus, when campaigns shut down phone banks to avoid antagonizing weary voters, both campaigns began to notice a subtle shift. When they resumed their voter identification calls, Kerry, and, to a lesser degree, Edwards, were starting to pick up more undecideds and even peeling away some Dean and Gephardt supporters. On the night of January 4, after the *Des Moines Register* debate, Tricia Enright, Dean's communications director, was at Centro, a trendy restaurant in Des Moines. Dean's campaign was seeing signs that Kerry was emerging as a serious threat, she said. Edwards was moving too, but there probably wasn't enough time for him to close the gap.

On January 8—eleven days before the caucuses—the Kerry campaign rolled out a new ad that would describe the Kerry Vietnam story in personal, compelling terms. In virtually every campaign, his Vietnam experience became an asset at the end. The first test of his presidential candidacy would be no different. Production of the 30-second spot actually began in the fall of 2001, when Kerry was gearing up for his Senate reelection effort the next year. The candidate's advertising team, with an eye toward a presidential bid, had filmed a tribute to Kerry by his Vietnam crewmate, Del Sandusky.

Sandusky's praise was eloquently succinct: "He had unfailing instinct and unchallengeable leadership." Crafted by adman Jim Margolis and his team, the spot compressed into a half minute a story line familiar in everything from *The Odyssey* to *The Matrix*. A protagonist overcomes conflict, discovers a truth, and is transformed.

"There's a sense, after Vietnam, that every day is extra," Kerry said in the ad.

It was a powerful ad, rival campaigns acknowledged. Iowa poll numbers started to reflect what the phone banking was showing: Kerry was gaining. At the same time, all the campaigns were nervously watching New Hampshire, where polls showed another military veteran, Wesley Clark, was starting to gain voter support, passing Kerry to move into second place. He, like Lieberman, had skipped Iowa to focus on the Granite State. It seemed to be paying off for

Clark. "While we're all out here running around Iowa, Clark is shooting free throws in New Hampshire," said David Plouffe, a Gephardt strategist. When some Kerry advisers, in an early January conference call, argued for more candidate time in New Hampshire, Cahill shut the door. "We're in Iowa. That's it." If the campaign was better, so was the candidate. Gone were the circumlocutions. He was listening to voters and connecting with them, said Ted Kennedy, who spent four days stumping with Kerry in Iowa.

Meanwhile, Dean was becoming an unwitting ally to the Kerry campaign. His gaffes were mounting, and media reports were unearthing inconsistencies and controversial remarks from his past. Kerry's campaign issued "Daily Straight Talk" e-mails, a collection of both snarky cheap shots and substantive comparisons of conflicting Dean quotes. The e-mails found their way into the political water supply and became subjects of press conferences and news stories.

After rising to the top of the polls in late fall, Dean's campaign never found the theme for a second act. He was still pushing the outsider, anti-Washington rhetoric. Yet his campaign kept running the same play—endorsements from the party mainstream. On December 6, it was Bill Bradley, Gore's old foe. Three days later it was Tom Harkin, the influential Iowa senator. On January 15, after securing a pledge from Dean to hire her as a consultant and help retire her campaign debt, Carol Moseley Braun withdrew from the race and endorsed Dean.

None of it made any difference. The questions about Dean's temperament and electability, the daily stories about his missteps and misstatements, had reached critical mass. Dean was coming down fast in daily tracking polls in Iowa, and also in New Hampshire.

Gephardt was also stalled. He had never been able to overcome the perception that he was a retread or that, as former minority leader in the House, he was a symbol of the party's fading power in Congress. Labor unions airlifted nearly 1,000 organizers to help him in Iowa. They had rousing rallies, but there were few other signs of spark in Gephardt's campaign. In the week before the caucuses, he and Dean hurt themselves further with a three-day exchange of negative TV ads in Iowa. Gephardt's media consultant, Bill Carrick, would call it "a murder-suicide," but the erstwhile leaders had other problems that were eroding support.

Among all the candidates, Kerry maintained the most consistent strength across every demographic group. When he lost support, it was across the board. When he gained, the support came from every segment of the Democratic electorate. Kerry was also a candidate whom many voters settled on by the process of elimination, the research showed. For those who thought Dean too erratic, Gephardt too stale, or Edwards too inexperienced, Kerry became an alternative.

Then, three days before the caucuses, James Rassmann of Oregon contacted Kerry's campaign. He wanted to help.

Rassmann was no ordinary volunteer. On March 13, 1969, the Army Special Forces officer was foundering in a canal off the Bai Hap River when swift boat skipper John Kerry heard a cry of "Man overboard!" Already bleeding from a wound suffered after his boat had struck a mine, Kerry directed the craft through enemy gunfire, reached into the water, and pulled Rassmann to safety.

Their next encounter was on January 17, 2004, at a campaign event at a Des Moines community center. Kerry's campaign had flown Rassmann to Iowa. The candidate learned of his arrival about ninety minutes before their emotional reunion. Speaking to reporters after he heard the news, Kerry looked ashen and stunned. He had an unusually hard time sharing even minor details about his feelings. Kerry said he was "very emotional," amazed, touched. But his face had a vacant look, as if he was recalling those events thirty-five years ago. At the community center, Kerry called it "a stunning story . . . It's extraordinary. I'm grateful to him for calling." Rassmann wept.

"John didn't have to, but he came to the front [of the boat] under fire, the bow, pardon me, sir, I always had a problem with navy terminology," Rassmann said as the audience broke into laughter. "He pulled me over. Had he not, there's no question in my mind that I would have fallen back into the river . . . He could have been shot at any time. I figure I owe him my life."

"Anybody would have done what I did," Kerry said. "That is not a big deal."

The reunion was a major news event, creating a great Kerry buzz in the campaign's final hours. For the Iowa endgame, he was finally hot.

Two days later, Kerry convincingly won the Iowa caucuses, with 38 percent of the votes. Edwards was second at 32 percent. Dean trailed with 18 percent. Gephardt suffered a crushing fourth-place finish at 11 percent, and dropped out.

Just a few weeks earlier, Kerry's campaign had appeared doomed and the media was treating Dean as the presumptive nominee. By the end of December, Dean had raised a whopping $41 million and seemed to have a commanding lead in the polls. But in his first test, after all the buildup, Dean ran a distant third. Then, on caucus night, he dealt a deadly blow to his own campaign.

Ignoring his aides' advice to make a traditional concession speech, Dean bounded to the platform of the Val Air ballroom in West Des Moines, ripped off his coat, rolled up his shirtsleeves, and launched into what would later be called his "I Have a Scream" speech, or "the yell."

Dean would say later that he merely wanted to boost the spirits of the many young volunteers inside the rink with a rousing exhortation. Those present said later that the candidate didn't seem out of control and had to holler over his screaming supporters. On television, however, with Dean's mike blocking the background cheering, it came across as a ranting, roaring yell. Dean strutted around in front of 1,500 supporters with an eerie half-smile frozen on his face. His eyes were blazing. Dean began shouting the names of thirteen states they would take the campaign to. "And then we're going to Washington, D.C., to take back the White House." Then came the coup de grâce. His voice became hoarser and he growled a long low "yeeehhaaaaaaaagghh." After some more chanting, Dean then delivered a normal concession speech. Most of the country, however, never saw that part. They only saw the rant—many times.

It was a pivotal moment in the campaign's history. At the worst possible time, Dean, for a moment, looked unhinged, feeding already existing doubts about his temperament. The fallout was catastrophic as the video was replayed over and over on the news, TV talk shows, late-night comedy shows, and Web sites. Jay Leno joked that cows feared "getting mad Dean disease" one night, and on the next said: "It's a bad sign when your speech ends with your aides shooting you with a tranquilizer gun."

In New Hampshire, Dean's twenty-five-point lead had been shrinking for days. By the time he left Iowa for Manchester, he was leading Kerry, who rebounded past Clark, by eight and Clark by nine according to the American Research Group's tracking poll. Dean's campaign tried to stanch the bleeding by recruiting his long-invisible wife, Dr. Judith Steinberg Dean, to appear on national television with her husband and soften his image. The candidate himself tried to change the subject back to the Iraq war.

Kerry was riding above it all, trying to act presidential. Democrats were desperate for a winner who could beat President Bush in November. Kerry was the only candidate who had proven he could win, and he did it dramatically and against odds and expectations in Iowa. Electability became the watchword in New Hampshire where, unlike Iowa, Independents could vote. And Kerry at last found a concise response to criticisms about his vote on Iraq. "If you think I would've gone to war as George Bush did, don't vote for me," Kerry now said.

The Massachusetts senator was stealing Dean's momentum—and poaching his message. In New Hampshire, Kerry promised to "break the grip of the powerful interests in this country and put the people in charge." These paraphrased the themes Dean had ridden to the top of the polls in the late fall of 2003. (Pilferage by Edwards was even less subtle, as when he told supporters at one rally, "You have the power." It was Dean's tag line, verbatim, but with a Southern accent.)

Throughout his career, Kerry had been prolific in raising funds from special interests, particularly from the telecommunications and financial services sectors. His presidential campaign had collected $227,950 in contributions from lobbyists, some of whom were his key fund-raisers. Dean would later call him on it, but it was too late. Kerry was starting to break away. In tracking polls conducted during the eight days between the Iowa caucuses and the New Hampshire primary, he was jumping three or four points most nights, while Dean was losing two or three percentage points.

After Iowa, the Edwards campaign made a strategic decision to make a full commitment to New Hampshire, hoping that a good showing there would build the same ball of momentum that Kerry had in Iowa. It was a risk: Just a week after New Hampshire, seven states were holding primaries and caucuses, including South Carolina, the state of his birth and a must-win contest for Edwards.

Edwards had invested early and heavily in New Hampshire television advertising but was still mostly in high single digits. Clark, meanwhile, had plateaued. The former NATO commander's standing in the state was hurt when Kerry's top strategist—and former New Hampshire governor—Jeanne Shaheen questioned his party loyalty, noting his past votes for Richard M. Nixon, Ronald Reagan, and George H.W. Bush. Clark was new to politics, and it showed: At one point he claimed there would be no more terrorist attacks under his watch. At another, he all but defended filmmaker Michael Moore's slanderous assertion that President Bush was a "deserter" because of his spotty attendance in the Air National Guard three decades earlier.

A record number of voters turned out on January 27, as Kerry triumphed with 39 percent of the New Hampshire primary vote. Exit polls showed that voters were most interested in tapping a candidate capable of beating Bush. Dean was a distant second with 26 percent, while Clark edged Edwards to finish a remote third. Joe Lieberman was fifth but vowed to continue.

The wheels came off Dean's once-vaunted campaign the next day with the resignation of Joe Trippi, the tech-savvy campaign manager who had revolutionized politics by using the Internet. Trippi quit after Dean told him Roy Neel, a former Gore aide, would become the campaign's CEO. But with the departure of the "mad scientist," as Trippi was known internally, much of the spirit went out of the campaign.

The next week would be an expensive one for all the candidates as they faced campaigning in seven states for the February 3 contests. Dean had raised an astounding $45 million to that point, but he had also spent it. Nearly broke, he was forced to take his TV ads off the air in South Carolina and other states.

The February 3 scramble would be a test of Kerry's

momentum. His campaign moved aggressively to pick up Missouri, now in play with favorite-son Gephardt out. And, unlike the other candidates, his two big wins meant an influx of cash that enabled him to actively compete in all the other states as well.

At a debate in Greenville, South Carolina, two nights after his New Hampshire win, Kerry came under attack, mostly from Dean, who accused him of being a Washington insider and an ineffective one at that. "Kerry sponsored nine bills having to do with health care, and not one of them passed," Dean asserted.

"One of the things you need to know as president is how things work in Congress if you want to get things done," was Kerry's retort. For most of the night, however, Kerry did not respond directly to his rivals' jabs, hoping to offer voters a candidate who looked presidential enough to beat Bush.

On February 3, Kerry won Missouri, Delaware, New Mexico, Arizona, and North Dakota, finished second to Edwards in South Carolina, and a close third behind Clark and Edwards in Oklahoma. Kerry won three of the states with more than 50 percent of the vote. Dean finished no better than third in any of them. Lieberman was wiped out and quit.

"It's a huge night," Kerry declared.

Only now, after seven wins out of nine states could the Kerry campaign claim the aura of inevitability it had hoped to establish early in the campaign. The following weekend, Kerry swept caucuses in Michigan, Washington, and Maine, and the following Tuesday, February 10, he knocked Clark out of the race with double wins in Virginia and Tennessee. Kerry had now won twelve of fourteen contests, and in every region of the country.

As he became the undisputed leader, Kerry came under increasing fire from the Republicans. Bush-Cheney '04, the president's reelection committee, rolled out pieces of its prodigious opposition research in e-mails to journalists. The "Kerry Line," with selected Kerry votes, outlined the incumbent's lines of attack in the fall.

Kerry had voted to cut weapons systems "that today are winning the war on terror," said one. Kerry backed gay civil unions and opposes Bush's "principled stand" for a constitutional amendment to define marriage as between a man and a woman, said another. Kerry's advocacy for higher auto fuel efficiency standards would cost thousands of jobs, contended a third.

Meanwhile, Kerry cruised to victory in the District of Columbia and Nevada before snuffing out the Dean candidacy in Wisconsin on February 17. Dean had vowed to make a stand there. He finished third, behind Edwards, who had closed fast on Kerry. Edwards had taken aim at Kerry's past support of free trade agreements, but his own record was similar. Still, a relatively close finish kept his candidacy alive. With Edwards now his only real competition, Kerry easily swept three minor contests on February 24 in Hawaii, Idaho, and Utah.

After Kerry's early victories, much of the party establishment had fallen in behind the front-runner. The AFL-CIO, Walter Mondale, and former rivals Gephardt and Clark led a long list of new endorsers.

A week before Super Tuesday, Kerry now seemed bulletproof. On March 2, contests in ten states, led by California and New York, could decide the nomination. One-fourth of the convention delegates were on the table. Polls showed Kerry ahead in every state, by insurmountable margins in many.

Edwards made a final stand, selling his soft populism and optimistic message. He poured most of his time and resources into Georgia and Ohio, the third-biggest delegate prize.

Exit polls eliminated much of the suspense on election night. On Super Tuesday, Kerry knew fairly early that he would win a resounding victory, end the Edwards candidacy, and effectively earn his party's nomination. Ultimately, Kerry won nine states, most by huge margins. In Vermont, voters gave their former governor, who was no longer a candidate, a sentimental victory.

At the Old Post Office Pavilion on Washington's Pennsylvania Avenue, scene of Kerry's election-night party, a phone rang. It was President George W. Bush, calling to congratulate Kerry on his primary victories. He expressed the hope for "a spirited campaign." Kerry said he looked forward to "a great debate about the issues before our country."

As he put the finishing touches on his victory speech, John Kerry sat five blocks west of the White House. Three blocks away was the National Mall, where thirty-three years earlier Kerry had camped with fellow Vietnam veterans before delivering the electrifying speech before the Senate Foreign Relations Committee, the first step on a path to national prominence and the *60 Minutes* interview asking if he wanted to be president someday.

The Mall encampment was also where he first met Senator Ted Kennedy of Massachusetts, the youngest brother of a president who had inspired a student at an exclusive prep school in New Hampshire to chart a course in politics. Kennedy was also at the Pavilion to share the triumphal moment with his junior colleague, now a good friend. Kennedy had turned seventy-two years old just two weeks earlier. He was grayer and much stouter now, but the liberal lion had walked with Kerry for much of this journey.

The senior and junior senators from Massachusetts walked down to the floor of the Pavilion. Kerry and his family stood behind a curtain as Kennedy stepped to the podium. Inside the hall, with its soaring arched ceilings, a crowd of about 2,000 erupted at the sight of "Old Ted," as he called himself in his travels on the Kerry bus. He embodied and evoked so much political history, much of it painful; the youngest of three brothers who had run for president, two of them assassinated, one after attaining the goal, the other while reaching for it.

Now, he was here to help Kerry achieve the goal. "He's a super nominee, and he'll be a super president of the United States," Kennedy thundered. "He takes his mission out across the country to make sure we send George Bush back to Texas and put this country back on the right road."

After Kennedy introduced Kerry and his family, the two senators shared a firm handshake and pats on the back.

"When I first led veterans to the Mall here in Washington to stop the Vietnam War, it was a time of doubt and fear in this land," Kerry told cheering onlookers. "It was a time when millions of Americans could not trust or believe what their leaders were telling them. Now, today, many Americans are once again wondering if they can trust and believe the leadership of our country.

"My campaign is about restoring that faith, about speaking plainly and honestly to the American people—about leading America in a new direction, guided by the enduring values that this nation has held to for the last 200 years," Kerry said. "Our campaign is about building a fairer, safer, more prosperous America—the nation that is again the great light to all the world."

APPENDIX

When the *Boston Globe* reported in January 2003 that John Kerry's grandparents on his father's side of the family were originally Jews from the old Austrian Empire, not Irish Catholics as some may have assumed, Kerry said he was "excited about learning the full measure" of his family's heritage. What follows is some of the background research, including much done by Austrian genealogist Felix Gundacker, who was hired by the *Boston Globe* to research and translate records.

Kerry said that although he knew his grandmother, Ida Löwe, had been born Jewish, he did not know that his father, the former Fritz Kohn, had also been Jewish. He said that though some people may have assumed that the Kerry family was Irish, he always knew his family came from Austria and hadn't tried to mislead anyone. The *Boston Globe*, among other publications, had incorrectly called Kerry "Irish-American" for many years. Kerry's spokesman said that if Kerry had been aware of the misstatement, he would have corrected it. In 2004, Gundacker also tracked down relatives named Kerry still living in Vienna, including Michael Kerry, who shares a great-grandfather with Senator Kerry. The Kerrys in Vienna said they had never talked to Senator Kerry, but they followed his campaign and wished him well.

Kerry's grandmother, the former Ida Löwe, returned to Europe at least twice, according to Ellis Island records. Gundacker's research found that two of Ida's siblings, John Kerry's great-uncle and great-aunt, Otto and Jenni Löwe, died in the Theresienstadt and Treblinka concentration camps, respectively. Thus, it is likely that the decision by Fred and Ida Kerry to immigrate to the United States saved their lives, as well as making possible the life of John F. Kerry.

In filing his intention to become a U.S. citizen on June 21, 1907, Frederick Kerry said he was 6 feet, 2 inches tall, had brown hair and gray-brown eyes, and weighed 195 pounds. He declared that he was born in Bennisch, Austria, and, as required, swore that he was not an anarchist. Bennisch has been renamed Horni Benesov in today's Czech Republic, where town officials say they hope to celebrate Kerry's heritage.

It is not possible to say whether the Kerry family legend about how the name Kerry came to be chosen is true. But there is no doubt the legend has been passed down over the years. Frederick's brother, Otto, changed his name to Kerry several years before Frederick, according to genealogist Gundacker's examination of Austrian records. Whatever the reason for choosing the name Kerry, the evidence is conclusive that the name was changed from Kohn to Kerry and the religion changed from Jewish to Catholic, according to Gundacker's research.

The description of Frederick Kerry's time in Chicago came largely from records examined for the *Boston Globe* by genealogist Jeanne Larzalere Bloom. Frederick Kerry lived in Chicago initially on Lake Avenue. He filed a petition for naturalization on February 6, 1911, at the time he was working as a business counselor and living on Sheridan Road, in the uptown area.

The Brookline home in Boston that was previously occupied by the Kerry family still exists, and the gracious current owner allowed the author to visit.

As noted in the text, Frederick Kerry's assets are described in probate records, filed November 15, 1921. His personal estate is listed as follows: "Automobile—Cadillac Touring—Model 59—Number 59N832—$1,500; Clothing, jewelry and minor personal effects—$350; 2 shares Boston Chamber of Commerce—$200; Cash—$25; Shares of stock in J.L. Walker Co. and Spencer Shoe Manufacturing Co.— Worthless."

The house is not listed among the assets, which suggested the possibility that he had recently had to sell it. Property records located by *Boston Globe* librarian Richard Pennington provide some clues. They show that the Downing Road land (the house was apparently built a couple of years later) was originally acquired in 1911 "in consideration of one dollar and other valuable considerations paid by Ida Kerry, formerly of Chicago, in the State of Illinois, now Brookline, Massachusetts (wife of Fred A. Kerry)." In 1915, Fred and Ida Kerry took out what appears to be a three-year $10,000 loan at 5 percent per year, apparently for the newly built house, and that is probably about the time they moved in. But in July 1920, property records show that Fred and Ida Kerry sold the property, with a notation that they still owed $8,000 and that the interest rate had risen to 6 percent per year. Although it is impossible to say with certainty what happened, the documents suggest that Kerry had financial problems and was unable to repay the loan. This is in keeping with his notation that he held shares of worthless stock.

Frederick Kerry's death was front-page news in the *Boston Evening Globe*, November 23, 1921. His death certificate lists him as a shoe merchant, although that seemed to be an understatement, given his role in reorganizing major businesses. It lists his father as Benedict Kerry of Austria (it had actually been Kohn), and his mother as Mitaldia Franckel (also spelled as Mathilde Frankel) of Austria. There are conflicting reports about whether Fred Kerry joined his wife on the trip to Europe a few weeks before his death; Ellis Island records do not show him on the trip, but one newspaper report said he went.

A story in the *Boston Herald* said, in a tone that suggested a lack of confirmation: "Mr. Kerry is reported to have made the statement to [a business associate] at the time that they became associated in business, that his father was born in Ireland and that his mother was an Austrian woman, a native of Vienna, which city was also his birthplace." The tone suggests that there was some question about the statement. In fact, the birth certificate of Frederick Kerry's father, Benedict Kohn, states that he was born in Troubky, Moravia, in the former Austrian Empire, according to genealogist Gundacker. Benedict Kohn subsequently moved to Bennisch, in the former Austrian Empire, where Fritz Kohn (later Fred Kerry) was born. In addition, Fred Kerry's Boston death certificate states that his father's birthplace was "Austria."

The *Boston Herald* story also said that Fred Kerry "had been quite active in the reorganization of upwards of 100 (department stores) in various parts of the country . . . following the Siegel company failure, he became vice president and general manager of the rejuvenated institution."

A story in the *Evening Transcript* said that Kerry's wife, Ida, came to the Copley Plaza Hotel to identify her husband. The story also said that Kerry, a frequent visitor to the hotel, "was said to have sent a letter to his mother just before taking his life." The *Boston Telegram* reported that when Kerry drew his gun in the washroom, "several bystanders rushed to intercept him but arrived too late. Still others fled at the sight of the revolver and caused a great commotion through the lobby and the corridors of the hotel." The *Boston American,* with what seems like some embellishment, reported that Kerry "unobtrusively entered the room and sat down. He seemed engaged in deep thought. Suddenly he reached into his pocket. Gleaming nickel flashed. A moment later came a roar which brought hotel attendants and guests to the room . . . before the attendants could reach his side the body had fallen to the carpet." Descriptions of Kerry ranged from "shoe merchant" to "wealthy shoe manufacturer."

The *Boston Globe* listed Kerry's home address as 10 Downing Road in Brookline and his business as 487 Boylston Street in Boston, but some other papers said his residence was at 487 Boylston Street in Brookline and his business elsewhere in Boston.

Property records confirm that the Kerrys lived at 10 Downing Road for at least five years, but given the fact that the Kerrys sold the property in 1920, it is possible that the *Boston Globe* in 1921 misstated Kerry's home address at the time of the suicide. Whatever the case, there is no question that the Kerrys did live on Downing Road for most of their time in Brookline, from at least 1915 to 1920.

A NOTE ON THE SOURCES

Portions of this book were previously published in different form in June 2003 as part of the *Boston Globe*'s seven-part series, "Candidate in the Making: John Kerry."

This book includes interviews conducted for the original series as well as many new interviews undertaken for this book. Unless alternative sources are cited, interviews with Senator Kerry and others were conducted by the authors.

Much of the material for Chapter 8, about Kerry's failed run for Congress in 1972, was gleaned from microfilm copies of the *Lowell Sun* and, to a lesser extent, the *Lawrence Eagle-Tribune*. Also providing source material were clippings from the archives of the *Boston Globe*, and other publications, including this journalistic artifact: a story in the *Real Paper*, a now-long-defunct alternative weekly in Boston, written by Joe Klein. Similarly, the *Sun* was a major source of information about Kerry's years as first assistant district attorney in Middlesex County, a major component of Chapter 9.

Kerry's official papers from his two years as lieutenant governor, contained in seventeen large boxes at the Massachusetts State Archives, were the basis of much of the material in Chapter 10. They include his daily schedules, correspondence, and quite a bit of inside information about his first campaign for the U.S. Senate, the subject of Chapter 11.

Some records of Kerry's aborted tax shelter investment are also in these files. In addition to interviews, details of Kerry's Senate career were drawn from the archives of the *Boston Globe* and other publications, the *Congressional Record*, and transcripts of congressional committee hearings.

Chapter 1

"Fritz Kohn": Michael Kranish, "Search for Kerry's Roots Find Surprising History," *Boston Globe*, February 2, 2003; Ellis Island immigration records, Chicago naturalization records, and Austrian records translated by genealogist Felix Gundacker.

"well off in Vienna": On Jewish life in Austria, see Marsha L. Rozenblit, *The Jews of Vienna, 1867–1914* (Albany: State University of New York Press, 1983); interview with Rozenblit.

"moved to Chicago": Genealogist Jeanne Larzalere Bloom's examination of Chicago records for the *Boston Globe; Chicago Sun-Times*, February 10, 2003.

"moved to Brookline": City of Boston records; U.S. Census reports, 1920.

"shift . . . in America's view": On the Emergency Quota Act of 1921 and annual immigration limits from any country to 357,000, see Gerald A. Danzer, *The Americans* (Boston: McDouglas Littell, 2003).

"Around 11:30 A.M.": For Copley Plaza history, see the hotel's Web site; author visit to the Copley Plaza.

"story was front-page news": "Shot Himself in Copley Plaza—F. A. Kerry, Merchant, Died Very Soon," *Boston Evening Globe*, November 23, 1921.

"one of Kerry's granddaughters": Interview with Nancy Stockslager, daughter of Eric Kerry, the oldest child of Frederick Kerry.

"explanation makes sense": Probate court records, Dedham, Mass., filed November 15, 1921.

"In 1763, the Reverend John Forbes": Sources used by *Boston Globe* librarian Richard Pennington: Forbes Papers, Massachusetts Historical Society, Boston; Twenty-Fifth Anniversary Class Notes, Harvard Class of 1901. For Forbes and Winthrop family histories, author interviews with two of Senator Kerry's siblings, Cameron and Diana. Letter from James Grant Forbes to Cameron W. Forbes, April 22, 1928, Forbes Papers.

"Winthrop family history": Winthrop family Web site; the "City upon a hill" speech has been described in many histories of the Puritans.

"Robert Charles Winthrop": *Biographical Dictionary of the U.S. Congress*.

"much-celebrated marriage": "Miss Winthrop to Wed—Her Marriage to J.G. Forbes Will Unite Two Noted Boston Families," *New York Times*, August 17, 1906.

Chapter 2

"letter to her future husband": Letter from Rosemary Forbes to Richard Kerry, July 14, 1940, provided by the Kerry family; portions originally published in "Candidate in the Making," *Boston Globe* series, June 2003.

"Nazis had taken over": Interviews with the Kerry family.

"The couple was married": Alabama marriage certificate, January 1941.

"life-threatening case of tuberculosis": Interviews with the Kerry family. In his 2003 book, *A Call to Service* (New York: Viking), John Kerry described his father's service in a passage about the generation that served in World War II: "In that conflict my father flew DC-3s in the Army Air Corps."

"large farmhouse in Millis": Interviews with the Kerry family; visit to the home formerly occupied by the Kerrys by researcher Richard Pennington.

"Forbes family estate in Saint Briac": Interview with John Kerry, who vividly recalled seeing the burned-out remains around 1947.

"Chevy Chase ... divided city of Berlin": Interviews with family members.

"boarding school ... Montana": Interviews with family members.

"St. Paul's School": Information from promotional material, interviews with school officials, and an author visit to St. Paul's. On St. Paul's activities: interview with Herbert Church; school archives; and classmate interviews.

"The Electras ... Peter Wyeth Johnson": The Electras' record jacket, including the liner notes, has been reproduced as a result of an on-line auction sale. Information on the trip from Bermuda and Johnson's death in Vietnam: interview with John Kerry; Vietnam War records.

"Clara Winthrop": Interviews with John Kerry and Diana Kerry.

"Kennedy's last speech before the election": Reported in the *New York Times*, the *Boston Globe*, and other publications, as well as in Theodore H. White, *The Making of the President, 1960* (New York: Atheneum, 1962).

"Janet Auchincloss": Interviews with John Kerry, David Thorne, and other classmates from Yale.

"Kennedy was visiting": Photos and letters documenting Kerry's meetings with President Kennedy from John F. Kennedy Library, Boston, Mass.

Chapter 3

"Yale University": Interviews with many of Kerry's classmates, especially fellow members of Skull and Bones, including: David Thorne, Fred Smith, Alan Cross, Dr. George Brown, Michael Dalby, and William Stanberry.

"Jonathan Edwards College": Author visit; *A Collegiate Way of Living* (Jonathan Edwards Trust, 2001); interviews with Kerry and his two roommates, Daniel Barbiero and Harvey Bundy.

"Yale Political Union": Yale yearbook; and the Yale Political Union Web site.

"champion debater": Interview with former Kerry Senate aide Jonathan Winer; debate team description is from the Yale yearbook.

"Kerry and Bush ... encounter": Interview with Kerry classmate David Thorne. Kerry said in an interview that he didn't recall the meeting, but in an interview with *Vogue* magazine in March 2003, Kerry said of Bush: "I know this guy. He was two years behind me at Yale, and I knew him, and he's still the same guy." Bush, asked on NBC's *Meet the Press* on February 8, 2004, whether he knew Kerry, responded: "No," and said Kerry's statement in *Vogue* was "politics."

"Skull and Bones": Interviews with Kerry and his two roommates, Daniel Barbiero and Harvey Bundy; Alexandra Robbins, *Secrets of the Tomb* (New York: Little, Brown and Company, 2002).

"Richard Pershing": Gene Smith, *Until the Last Trumpet Sounds* (New York: John Wiley and Sons, 1999); interview with Fred Smith.

"Naushon Island": Interview with Diana Kerry.

"William Bundy": Interviews with John Kerry, Harvey Bundy, and Daniel Barbiero. Further information on William Bundy is in Kai Bird, *The Color of Truth* (New York: Simon and Schuster, 2000).

"class oration": Original written version published in the Yale yearbook of 1966; the actual oration delivered by Kerry was provided by the senator's office.

Chapter 4

"flew for kicks": Interviews with John Kerry and David Thorne; Thorne produced a photo of Kerry in the cockpit, taken just before the incident. Kerry remembered: "I used to rent the T-34 a lot, I'd fly to Las Vegas, San Francisco, out West, learned to do aerobatics."

"Thorne's twin sister, Julia": Interview with Julia Thorne at her Montana home, by *Boston Globe* columnist Alex Beam. Thorne has spoken publicly in many forums over the years, in articles, interviews, and books; many of these sources were used.

"U.S. personnel killed in Vietnam": Statistics from James S. Olson, ed., *Dictionary of the Vietnam War* (New York: Peter Bedrick Books, 1987).

"protesters halted in front of the Century Plaza": Interviews with John Kerry and David Thorne; *New York Times*, June 24, 1967.

"Pershing was rushed ... into action": On Pershing's mission before the one that cost him his life, see Smith, *"Until the Last Trumpet Sounds* (New York: John Wiley and Sons, 1999).

"he wrote anguished letters": Letter from John Kerry to his parents, provided by Kerry to the *Boston Globe*, 2003.

"Kerry was heading to Vietnam": On the events of early 1968, see Stanley Karnow, *Vietnam: A History* (New York: Viking, 1983). On Kerry's initial disinterest in combat, see Edward Doyle and Samuel Lipsman, eds., *The Vietnam Experience—A War Remembered*, (Boston: Boston Publishing Company, 1986).

"Senator Eugene McCarthy": The Fenway rally is described in Robert L. Turner, "45,000 Overflow Fenway Park for McCarthy," *Boston Globe*, July 26, 1968.

Chapter 5

"December 2, 1968": On the incident for which Kerry won the Purple Heart: Interview with John Kerry; Douglas Brinkley, *Tour of Duty* (New York: William Morrow, 2004); interviews with crewmates Patrick Runyon and William Zaladonis.

"Lieutenant Commander Grant Hibbard": Interviews with Hibbard.

"The Purple Heart regulation in effect": The Purple Heart criteria come from Presidential Executive Order 11016.

"The letter was stamped": Letter of February 28, 1968, to John Kerry from Donald A. Still, chief staff officer, U.S. Naval Support activities, Saigon.

"Referring to the notation": Kerry's press secretary allowed a reporter on March 6, 2004, to view, but not copy, a transcription of Kerry's medical treatment in Vietnam, which included the notation that shrapnel was removed on December 3, 1968. The campaign said it was still considering a request to release all of Kerry's medical and military records.

"Kerry had written a memo": Kerry's letter to chief of naval personnel, written while Kerry was serving on the USS *Gridley* in early 1968; this letter and the response from Slifer were provided by the Kerry campaign.

"Elmo Zumwalt Jr.": On navy operations in Vietnam, see the co-autobiography by Elmo Zumwalt Jr. and Elmo Zumwalt III, *My Father, My Son* (Old Tappan, NJ: Macmillan, 1986).

"Captain Howard Kerr": The oral history was conducted by the U.S. Naval Institute, Annapolis, Maryland, 1989.

"Zumwalt's Wild Ideas": On ZWIs and the background on swift boat patrols, see Lieutenant Commander Thomas J. Cutler, *Brown Water, Black Berets* (New York: Pocket Books, 1989).

"Michael Bernique": Interviews with Bernique; and the documentary film *Swift Boats, Brave Sailors*.

"in an oral history, Zumwalt": Zumwalt's oral history, conducted by U.S. Naval Institute historian Paul Stillwell from 1982 to 1986. The interviews were released publicly in 2003.

"the spraying of Agent Orange": In 2003, Kerry was diagnosed with prostate cancer, a disease that had afflicted his father, so he believed his condition was genetic. He is also aware that some studies say Agent Orange can cause prostate cancer, thus he has wondered whether he was affected by spraying in Vietnam: "I don't have recollection of being 'sprayed' ... I wondered because of Elmo Zumwalt.... I think a lot of us have wondered. There are problems with kids, problems with pregnancies. I haven't obsessed, but I've wondered."

"James Wasser": Interviews with Wasser.

"Of all his 'War Notes'": Senator Kerry provided several entries from his diarylike War Notes to the *Boston Globe* in 2003, including his dramatic description of Christmas Eve, 1968. Separately, in a review of the movie *Apocalypse Now* for the *Boston Herald* on October 14, 1979, he wrote: "I remember spending Christmas Eve of 1968 five miles across the Cambodian border being shot at by our South Vietnamese allies who were drunk and celebrating Christmas. The absurdity of almost being killed by our own allies in a country in which President Nixon claimed there were no American troops was very real." As for the movie, Kerry panned it. Tellingly, he said that it "missed the life of the villages and the confusion between enemy and ally."

"Steven Michael Gardner": Interviews with Gardner. Unlike most other Kerry crewmates, Gardner has not appeared at campaign events with Kerry and does not support him for president. He said he had never talked with a reporter about his experiences with Kerry until he was contacted in regard to this book.

"the killing of a boy": Kerry had never spoken publicly about the incident until asked by reporter John Aloysius Farrell during a January 2003 meeting with three *Boston Globe* reporters; the incident was described in print for the first time in the *Boston Globe*'s June 2003 series, "Candidate in the Making." Kerry spoke at length about the event but could not pinpoint either the date of the incident or which crewmates were with him at the time. It appears similar to one described as taking place on January 20, 1969, in a naval report, and that date coincides with the memories of some crewmates. Kerry is quoted in Brinkley's *Tour of Duty* amid a passage that suggests this incident happened on swift boat No. 94, but crewmates of No. 94 interviewed by the *Boston Globe* said they don't recall such an incident; however, several of those on swift boat No. 44 do recall an incident similar to that described in the naval report.

"extraordinary meeting with Zumwalt ... and General Abrams": The meeting was confirmed by a notation in Zumwalt's appointment log for January 22, 1968. Although memories vary about whether it was mostly a pep rally or a discussion of the problem of free-fire zones, there is no question that the skippers met with Zumwalt and General Creighton Abrams.

"the *Dick Cavett Show*": On the June 30, 1971, show, Kerry debated a fellow swift boat sailor, John O'Neill, who defended the views of the Nixon administration.

Chapter 6

"Navy swift boat No. 94": The experiences of swift boat No. 94 were described in detail during interviews with most of Kerry's surviving crewmates, as well as by some of those who were on his boat for brief training sessions. Crewmates interviewed include: Michael Medeiros, David Alston, Del Sandusky, Charles Gibson, and Fred Short. Medeiros kept a log of events. All the events described were checked against official navy records, most in "spot reports" filed by commanders just after action, many of them written by Kerry. The records are on file at the Naval Historical Center in Washington, where archivist Michael Walker proved immensely helpful. Other sources of background information include a video documentary, *Brothers in Arms;* and Brinkley's *Tour of Duty.*

"Edward Peck": Interviews with Peck. Months after Peck returned from Vietnam, while he was still recovering from his wounds in New York City, he ran into Kerry, who had returned to the United States in spring 1969. Peck said that over a beer, Kerry asked him to join in opposing the war, but Peck refused. "That is how I left John Kerry," Peck said.

"Tommy Belodeau": Belodeau's support of Kerry was recollected in interviews with several crewmates.

"On February 20, 1969": From a description in a naval report written by someone on the scene. The contents of the report, in which someone criticized the way "targets of opportunity" were being fired upon, was read to Kerry in 2003, and at that time he dismissed the criticism as unfair. The Kerry campaign was sent a copy of the report in 2004 and asked to double-check with Kerry to see if there was any chance he wrote the report, but the campaign did not respond.

"Lieutenant Doug Reese": Reese provided a copy of an army commendation medal for his actions on February 28, 1969, "for heroism in connection with military operations against a foreign force." In an interview, Michael Medeiros, one of Kerry's crewmates, recalled the role of army advisers, saying they were "extremely important" in the operation that day.

"Ten Vietcong had been killed": The Silver Star day events have become part of the Kerry lore; most renditions include the essential fact that Kerry killed a Vietcong carrying a rocket launcher. However, it is less well known that seventy South Vietnamese forces also crowded onto the three swift boats, and many went ashore during the action. Naval reports say that the U.S.-led forces, including South Vietnamese troops working with army advisers, were responsible for at least six of the ten Vietcong killed that day.

"Zumwalt, who had listened": Kerry followed Bernique's lead in beaching his boat, and Elmo Zumwalt Jr., the overall naval commander, had made clear that he approved of this technique, even though skippers were usually instructed not to put themselves in such a potentially dangerous situation.

"James Rassmann": Interview with Rassmann. Rassmann did not reconnect with Kerry until the presidential campaign in Iowa in January 2004. Rassmann's whereabouts were a mystery to Kerry because his name was misstated in the official navy report as "Rassman," with no first name. In searching for Rassmann, the Kerry campaign posted a notice on its Web site in November 2003, to no avail. Rassmann said he contacted the campaign after watching the documentary *Be Good, Smile Pretty*, about the death of swift boat skipper Don Droz, which included some people whom Rassmann remembered from Vietnam, and after seeing his name mentioned in Brinkley's *Tour of Duty*. Rassmann said he had written Kerry a letter years earlier, but Kerry said he never got it. Several of Kerry's crewmates similarly said they had lost touch with Kerry, only to reunite either in an earlier Senate campaign or during the presidential bid.

"naval policy permitted waivers": The regulation that enabled Kerry to leave after receiving three Purple Hearts includes a waiver provision: "Personnel desiring to waive reassignment under the purview of this Instruction must forward a written request to that effect to the Chief of Naval Personnel for final determination." Jim Galvin of Kerry's division also got three Purple Hearts and left early. In an interview, Galvin said he could have stayed if he wanted to, and he wound up returning for two additional combat tours. He said no one ever suggested he could not return to Vietnam after having earned three Purple Hearts.

"the infant daughter ... left behind": Tracy Tragos showed her documentary film, *Be Good, Smile Pretty*, to Kerry and other swift boat sailors at an emotional reunion in Norfolk, Virginia, in 2003. Later that year, as part of a feature story on the *60 Minutes* television program, Tracy and her mother returned to the spot in Vietnam where Don Droz was killed, where she found a memorial had been erected to commemorate the day's battle. Her film was named best documentary at the Los Angeles Film Festival.

Chapter 7

"secretly recorded dialogue": The White House tapes are available for public listening at National Archives II in College Park, Maryland. Headsets are available; visitors bringing their own audio equipment are allowed to make copies. Some tapes are transcribed, but many still remain untranscribed; some have a subject index. Material used in this book comes from the lesser-known pre-Watergate tapes.

"Adam Walinsky": Interview with Walinksy.

"Judy Droz": Interview with Judy Droz; news accounts from United Press International; and other sources. Kerry said he did not hear Droz speak, but he became aware of her views and said they had an influence on antiwar activities. Droz's daughter, Tracy Tragos, worked briefly for Senator Kerry and interviewed him for her documentary, *Be Good, Smile Pretty.*

"told the *Harvard Crimson*": Samuel Z. Goldhaber, "John Kerry: A Navy Dove Runs for Congress," *Harvard Crimson*, February 18, 1970.

"citizen's caucus": Interviews with Jerome Grossman and Reverend Robert F. Drinan; and Jerome Grossman, *Relentless Liberal* (New York: Vantage Press, 1996).

"Kerry married": "John Kerry Weds Miss Julia Thorne," *New York Times*, May 24, 1970.

"During Labor Day weekend": On the Valley Forge speech, see Brinkley's *Tour of Duty;* interview with Jane Fonda.

"Winter Soldier hearings": *Detroit News* stories; *The Winter Soldier* film; transcript of hearings collected by the University of Virginia–Charlottesville "60s Project"; and interviews with Jane Fonda and George Butler. The *Life* magazine with Fonda on the cover appeared the week of April 23, 1971.

"Video footage": The video was viewed through the generosity of filmmaker George Butler, who provided access to archival footage.

"Thomas Oliphant": Interview with Oliphant.

"a band of 800 or so Vietnam veterans": The Mall protest rally was described in author interviews with John Kerry, David Thorne, George Butler, and Scott Camil. A valuable history of the antiwar movement is Gerald Nicosia's *Home to War: A History of the Vietnam Veterans' Movement* (New York: Crown Publishers, 2001).

"At the White House": Colson described his memory of Kerry, John O'Neill, and Richard Nixon in an interview.

"Vice President Spiro T. Agnew": Agnew's description of Kerry was quoted in numerous news accounts.

"Lexington, Massachusetts": Bruce McCabe and Gerald F. Mahoney, "500 Antiwar Vets Arrested on Lexington Green, *Boston Globe*, May 30, 1971.

"a better way to go after Kerry": Chuck Colson memo to Van Shumway, June 15, 1971: "I have read a copy of your memo to Al Snyder regarding the UPI request for a Kerry/O'Neill debate. This is fine but the major story that should be pushed here is that Kerry has avoided every invitation for a debate: the Frost show, the Cavett show, "Face The Nation," it is now a consistent pattern. I think we have Kerry on the run, he is beginning to take a tremendous beating in the press, but let's not let up, let's destroy this young demagogue before he becomes another Ralph Nader. Let's try to move through as many sources as we can the fact that he has refused to meet in debate, even though he agreed to do so and announced to the press he would." The memo is quoted on p. 275 in Bruce Oudes, ed., *From: The President: Richard Nixon's Secret Files* (New York: HarperCollins, 1990).

"*The Dick Cavett Show*": Broadcast on June 30, 1971. John O'Neill stated his view of Kerry in an interview.

"As quickly as Kerry's star": Kerry's encounter with POW wives is described in several places, including Mary McGrory, "Kerry Clash Shows Rift Among POW Kin," July 24, 1971.

"dogged by apathy": On Kerry's view of antipathy toward war protest: David Cook, "Antiwar Vet Says Issue Is Fading," *Christian Science Monitor*, December 10, 1971. On the Bryant Park protest rally: Robert Lenzner, "Thousands March in N.Y. to Protest Vietnam War," *Boston Globe*, April 23, 1972.

"James McCord": McCord's testimony was brought to the attention of the author by Robert S. Weiner; interview with Bernard Barker.

Chapter 8

"Framingham": Interview with Ronald Rosenblith.

"baggage": Interview with John Kerry.

"told two journalists": Interview with Frank Phillips.

"Julia put down $6,000": Deed in Worcester, Mass., registry.

"hired a reporter": Frank Phillips, *Lowell Sun*, October 27, 1972.

"never moved into": Interview with John Kerry.

"Even Kerry's seat-searching": Nigel Hamilton, *JFK: Reckless Youth* (New York: Random House, 1992), p. 738.

"lived in the area": Interview with Cameron Kerry.

"Groton School": Interview with Cameron Kerry

"unemployment to around 12 percent": Rachelle Patterson, "Polls Put Kerry Ahead, but 2 Rivals Reap Defectors," *Boston Globe*, October 26, 1972.

"goodwill" and "young activists": Rachelle Patterson, "Crowded Field of 15 in 5th District Free-for-All," *Boston Globe*, August 27, 1972; "John Kerry's Service Record," campaign brochure.

"Plimpton . . . at Bishop's": Interview with Frank Phillips.

"*Sun* . . . an afternoon paper": Interviews with Kendall M. Wallace and Frank Phillips.

"Charges . . . dropped a year later": "Judge Drops Charges in Kerry 'Break-In,'" *Boston Globe*, October 24, 1973.

"haunted look . . . gaping hole . . . pigeons": Interviews with Frank Phillips and John H. Costello Jr.

"Kerry's platform called for": Kerry campaign ads and position papers.

"Costello . . . changed the editorial": Interviews with Robert Kennedy, Paul Sheehy, Frank Phillips, and Kendall Wallace.

"Kerry one night bought the house a round": Frank Phillips, "Kerry Breaks the Ice in Lowell Bar," *Lowell Sun*, October 5, 1972.

"abortion . . . jog to the center": "John Kerry on the Issues," *Lowell Sun*, October 11, 1972. During this interview, Kerry gave a full explanation of his position on abortion. His quote, "I think the question of abortion is one that should be left for the states," directly contradicted his remarks five months earlier to Massachusetts PAX, an liberal interest group: "I believe that the decision for or against abortion must be one made between a woman and her physician. It is not an area of concern for either the federal or state governments." Kerry said he did not recall the "left for the states" remark to the *Lowell Sun*. In that 1972 interview, Kerry also expressed his personal opposition to abortion. "On abortion, I myself, by belief and upbringing, am opposed to abortion but as a legislator, as one who if called on to pass a law, I would find it very difficult to legislate on something God himself has not seen fit to make clear to all the people on this earth."

"la Professoressa": Interview with Julia Thorne; Joe Klein, "John Kerry: They Loved Him in Lowell," *Real Paper*, October 1972.

"Oklahoma, Indiana, Michigan, and New York": Kerry campaign ad "Some People Have Already Decided."

"They called me un-American:" Kerry letters, November 30, 1972, to Engineers Political Education Committee et al., Massachusetts Archives.

"Julia was outraged": Interview with Alex Beam.

"I'd be in Washington with the veterans": Stephen Wermiel, "In Defeat, Kerry Calm, No Regrets About Fight," *Boston Globe*, November 8, 1972.

Chapter 9

"$51,000 home": Deeds in the Middlesex North Registry indicate that Julia closed on the property about three weeks after her husband's defeat in the congressional race. In a complex transaction, she paid $86,000 for a house and two lots totaling about five acres, and on the same day sold one of the lots, about 2.8 acres, for $35,000.

"CARE Inc.": Kerry application for admission to Massachusetts bar, June 10, 1976.

"Kerry … commissioned a poll": "Poll to Decide If Kerry Runs," *Boston Globe*, September 13, 1973.

"But Paul Tsongas": Interview with Kerry.

"traumatized by the 'negativity'": Interview with Julia Thorne by Alex Beam of the *Boston Globe*.

"We couldn't make ends meet": Thorne-Beam interview.

"radio talk-show host": Kerry bar application.

"MassAction": Kerry bar application; interviews with David Harmon and Samuel Tyler; "MassAction Claims State Losing Millions," *Boston Globe*, July 29, 1974; "Kerry Resigns MassAction Post," *Boston Herald*, October 28, 1974.

"Once a hot political property": Crocker Snow Jr., *Boston Globe*, November 3, 1974.

"father, a prosecutor": Interviews with John and Cameron Kerry.

"winning all of the ... cases": Kerry interview.

"William Homans": Kerry interview.

"I never lost a case": Interview with C. David Nyhan.

"salary of $12,900": Paul Merry, "Ex-Congress Candidate Kerry Named First Assistant DA," *Lowell Sun*, January 24, 1977.

"3.8 million infusion": "Kerry's Resignation Didn't Surprise Droney," *Lowell Sun*, May 23, 1979.

"many of the new hires were women": Massachusetts Lawyers Diary, 1975–1979.

"Kerry was directing the investigation": Interviews with Kerry and J. William Codinha.

"Winter was sentenced": "Attorneys for Winter, Sperlinga Ask for New Pinball Case Trial," *Lowell Sun*, May 27, 1978.

"Kerry ... took responsibility for the full-page newspaper ad": Alberta Cook, "Judge Criticizes Droney for Controversial Ad," *Lowell Sun*, November 4, 1978.

"hitchhike murderer": Richard Gaines, "The DA and the Gag Order," *Boston Phoenix*, October 24, 1978.

"hinted at a wider conspiracy": Paul Merry, "Indictment Expected as County Probe Widens," *Lowell Sun*, August 29, 1978.

"A defense lawyer ... accused Kerry": Alberta Cook, "Lawyer Charges Kerry with Probe Misconduct," *Lowell Sun*, September 7, 1978.

"neither went to prison": Alberta Cook, "Gets Suspended Term, Fine in Job-Selling Case," *Lowell Sun*, May 8, 1979; Middlesex Superior Court dockets 77-3124 and 78-3971.

"Staged media events": "Harshbarger Charges DA 'Timing' Indictments," *Lowell Sun*, September 1, 1978.

"first time the two had ever met": Alberta Cook, "A Party Atmosphere in the DA's Office," *Lowell Sun*, September 22, 1978.

"inventory of 12,000 criminal cases": Kerry interview.

"closer to 3,800": "The Inside Story on How John Droney Cracked Some of Massachusetts' Most Famous Crimes," *Lowell Sun*, September 14, 1976.

"eliminating 2,772": Alberta Cook, "Kerry's Resignation Didn't Surprise Droney," *Lowell Sun*, May 23, 1979.

"raised that number to 10,772": Kerry announcement of candidacy for lieutenant governor, February 26, 1982.

"never exceeded 7,265": annual reports of the Massachusetts Trial Court, fiscal years 1976 through 1979.

"Another exaggerated claim": Kerry announcement of candidacy for lieutenant governor, February 26, 1982; interviews with Kerry and J. William Codinha.

"not even 'Number Two'": "A Contest That Has Something for Everyone," *Boston Globe*, September 8, 1982.

"Roanne Sragow, an assistant DA": Alberta Cook, "Kerry's Departure Signals Shift in Office Politics," *Lowell Sun*, May 27, 1979; *Boston Globe*, David Farrell column, June 3, 1979, *Focus* section.

"bout of undiagnosed clinical depression": Thorne-Beam interview.

"flirtation with suicide": Patti Doten, "Defying Depression for Years, Julia Thorne Suffered in Silence," *Boston Globe*, May 8, 1994.

"I functioned": Thorne-Beam interview.

Chapter 10

"Kerry was among the speakers in ... Central Park": Interviews with Larry Carpman and Kerry.

"competency, experience, and vision": Ben Bradlee, "A Lieutenant Governor Debate," *Boston Globe*, August 30, 1982.

"Kerry campaign tried to make policy appeals to both camps": Interview with Cameron Kerry.

"his floor troops artfully maneuvered delegates": Chris Black, "Evelyn Murphy Edges Rotondi on 5th Lieutenant-Governor Ballot," *Boston Globe*, May 23, 1982.

"65 percent didn't know enough about him": "Poll on Lieutenant Governor Race Finds Most Democrats Undecided," *Boston Globe*, August 29, 1982.

"politely made their points and avoided conflict": Ben Bradlee, "A Lieutenant Governor Debate," *Boston Globe*, August 30, 1982.

"personal loan to his campaign": Kerry campaign report, filed January 10, 1983, in the Massachusetts Office of Campaign and Political Finance.

"did not formally concede": Andrew Blake, "Kerry Emerges as Dukakis' Running Mate," *Boston Globe*, September 16, 1982.

"quietly separated that summer": Julia Thorne interview with Alex Beam of the *Boston Globe*.

"Frankly, the governor": Chris Black, "Kerry Task: Deal with US," *Boston Globe*, December 9, 1982.

"Kerry's public schedule was a blur": This and other references to events on Kerry's schedule are based on an examination of Kerry's official papers at the Massachusetts Archives.

"threw his deputy a curve": Kerry interview.

"Kerry played an important role": files in Massachusetts Archives; interview with Jonathan Winer.

"Dukakis sent Kerry to testify": Eileen McNamara, "Dukakis Urges Repeal of Capital Punishment," *Boston Globe*, April 12, 1983.

"February 1984 resolution of the National Governors Association": Jerry Ackerman, "Politicians Hit Acid Rain Stand," *Boston Globe*, March 16, 1984.

Chapter 11

"upended the money edge": Interview with Ronald F. Rosenblith.

"he would disavow": "State Race and PAC funds," *Boston Globe*, March 28, 1984.

"clear pattern": Chris Black, "Senate Candidates Criticize Shannon's Position on PACs," *Boston Globe*, April 26, 1984.

"first to blink": Chris Black, "Money for Politicking," *Boston Globe*, April 17, 1984.

"$51,400": Chris Black, "Shannon Gives Up PAC Funds," *Boston Globe*, April 30, 1984. Interview with James M. Shannon.

"cold feet": Chris Black, "Markey Abandons Bid for Senate," *Boston Globe*, May 2, 1984.

"liberal twins ... litmus-test liberals": Eileen McNamara and Laurence Collins, "Countdown to Senate Primary," *Boston Globe*, September 2, 1984.

"Rosenberg wrote in an internal memo": Memo dated May 23, 1984, Massachusetts Archives.

"Kerry revised his answers": Chris Black, "Kerry Attacks Shannon on Arms, PACs," *Boston Globe*, May 31, 1984.

"internal memo": Michal Regunberg to John Marttila, Ron Rosenblith, Paul Rosenberg, June 19, 1983, Massachusetts Archives.

"B-1 bomber; B-2 stealth bomber": Kerry responses to Freeze Voter '84 questionnaire.

"he also advocated reductions": Chris Black, "Kerry Asks Cuts in Defense Outlay," *Boston Globe*, May 30, 1984.

"Kerry as lieutenant governor made use of cars": The section about the Bob Brest lease was based on interviews with Kerry, Frank Phillips, Kerry aide Chris Greeley, state campaign finance reports; Brian McGrory, "Kerry Leased Cars from Brest, Did Not Pay for 16 Months," *Boston Globe*, September 26, 1992; and Frank Phillips, "Car Dealer Back in Spotlight due to Deal with Kerry," *Boston Globe*, October 25, 1996.

"had visited Brest's dealership": Kerry daily schedules in 1983 for April 16, August 19, September 17, and September 23, Massachusetts Archives.

"$225,105": Kerry Senate Financial Disclosure Report, filed June 25, 1984.

"known as a 'straddle'": Interviews with attorney Joe Vaulx Crockett III, who represented Sytel investors, and Larry Sylvester, a founder of Sytel Traders.

"met all public disclosure requirements": Interviews with Ronald Rosenblith, Jonathan Winer, and Marc Elias.

"Both companies were registered in the Caymans": Records of the Office of the Register of Companies, Cayman Islands.

"On December 13, 1983": Promissory Note & Agreement, Sytel Traders Ltd.; and Pledge Agreement, Sytel Traders Ltd., Massachusetts Archives.

"Some Sytel investors": Interview with Joe Vaulx Crockett III, the investors' lawyer.

"major overhaul of the tax structure": Transcript of "Eyewitness News Conference," WBZ-TV, Boston, May 6, 1984.

"Flynn introduced ... helping Kerry was Raymond C. Dooley": Interview with Raymond L. Flynn.

"In late tracking polls": Interview with John Marttila.

"proud that you changed your mind": Eileen McNamara, "4 Senate Rivals Use Debate to Toss Their Windup Pitches," *Boston Globe*, September 12, 1984.

"You impugn the service ... that dog won't hunt": Chris Black, "Kerry, Shannon Stand Ground During Tense Television Debate," *Boston Globe*, September 14, 1984.

"John Birch Society": Chris Black, "2 Issues Unresolved: On-Site Inspection, Name Calling," *Boston Globe*, October 31, 1984.

"left the impression—and resulted in press reports": John E. Mulligan, "Hawk and Dove—John F. Kerry Has Been Both," *Providence Journal*, March 23, 2003; "Black Task Force Endorses Kerry," *Boston Globe*, September 11, 1984.

"Grenada invasion": Kerry remarks April 10, 2003, caucus room of Cannon House office building, Washington, D.C.; transcript, NBC News, *Meet the Press*, June 23, 2002.

"Boston College playing football": Eileen McNamara, "Acrimony Accentuates Last Shamie, Kerry Debate," *Boston Globe*, October 31, 1984.

"the Reagan policy of substituting": "1984 State Primary," *Cape Codder*, September 12, 1984.

Chapter 12

"must not break faith": Ronald Reagan, State of the Union Address, January, 1985.

"mercenary army": *Congressional Record*, April 23, 1985.

"cocky smooth operator": Lois Romano, "John Kerry, Coming Full Circle," *Washington Post*, February 21, 1985.

"perception of me as a showboat": Walter V. Robinson, "Kerry Adds Substance to Style," *Boston Globe*, April 23, 1985.

"warm, caring person": Rosemary Kerry quoted in Louise Sweeney, "Swept to Senate via Vietnam, Kerry Takes On US Policy," *Christian Science Monitor*, July 18, 1895.

"The same lushness ... a businessman": Myra McPherson, "Harkin & Kerry, Back in a War Zone," *Washington Post*, April 23, 1985.

"way without violence": Walter V. Robinson, "Mother Tells Kerry, Harkin of Contra Ambush," *Boston Globe*, April 20, 1985.

"We asked for ... great opportunity": Walter V. Robinson, "Nicaragua Offers Truce If US Halts Contra Aid," *Boston Globe*, April 21, 1985.

"time and again": Walter V. Robinson, "Kerry Adds Substance to Style," *Boston Globe*, April 23, 1985.

"We have to learn": CBS's *Face the Nation*, April 21, 1985.

"I am willing": *Congressional Record*, April 23, 1985.

"Disney World": Eileen McNamara, "Ortega's Trip to Moscow Looms Large on Capitol Hill," *Boston Globe*, June 9, 1985.

"I'm as mad as anyone": George Gedda, "US to Bar Trade with Nicaraguans," *Boston Globe*, Associated Press, May 1, 1985.

"Kerry issued his own response": Mary McGrory, "Two Leaders on Trips to the Wrong Places," *Washington Post*, May 1, 1985. McGrory recounts that Ortega "told two recent sympathetic visitors, Democratic Sens. Tom Harkin and John Kerry, that he was going to Moscow to get a $200 million loan for seed and fertilizer—the United States blocked his request to the Inter-American Development Bank. In keeping his schedule, he profoundly embarrassed those members of Congress who went bail for him last week."

"our view of world order": Richard Kerry, *The Star-Spangled Mirror: America's Image of Itself and the World* (New York: Rowman and Littlefield Publishers, 1990); on the Nicaragua discussion, see pp. 109–112.

"national security in a nuclear environment": *Congressional Record*, March 19, 1985.

"impressive leadership role": Kennedy letter to the editor, "Amendment Responds to Crippling US Deficits," *Boston Globe*, October 24, 1985.

"linking RR [Ronald Reagan] to La Penca": Oliver North Notebooks, National Security Archives.

"I can say that while": For the Abrams-Kerry exchange, see Hearing Before the Senate Foreign Relations Committee, October 10, 1986.

"show some evidence and stop leaking out information": Stephen Kurkjian and Walter V. Robinson, "Bush Denies Arms-Drug Tie, Blasts Kerry," *Boston Globe*, May 17, 1988.

Chapter 13

"Already on conservative hit lists": For conservative attacks on Kerry and Kerry's defense, see David Shribman, "The Right Sees Sen. Kerry as a Leftist Demon But He Says He's Just a Mainstream Politician," *Wall Street Journal*, March 27, 1987.

"John started off behind ... if the mix": John Robinson, "Kerry Lauded for Strong Effort in Support of Democrats," *Boston Globe*, August 5, 1987.

"An aide later assured reporters": Scot Lehigh, "Fund-Raising by Survey," *Boston Globe*, June 7, 1990.

"a convoluted transaction": Walter V. Robinson, "Kerry Borrows $473,313 for House, Debts," *Boston Globe*, March 1, 1985; interviews with Kerry and Ronald Rosenblith.

"Back in Boston": The chronicling of Kerry's many addresses was gleaned from the stories by *Boston Globe* reporters Stephen Kurkjian and Michael Rezendes that appeared in October 1996, in addition to a transcript of Kurkjian's interview with Kerry on October 9, 1996. Their initial story, "Friends Gave Kerry Cut-Rate Lodging Deal," on October 18, provided many of the details, including the information that wealthy Kerry friends were known to pick up the check when they had dinner with him. The "gypsy period" remark, based on an interview with Teresa Heinz, also appeared in this story. Kerry's statement that he sometimes spent weekends with Roanne Sragow was in the Kurkjian interview.

"Kerry sold the unit for $445,000": Unit deed, Book 16968, p. 331, Suffolk County Registry of Deeds.

"a semi-regular at Yvonne's": Brian McGrory, "Kerry and Heinz Are Eyeing Slice of Storied Locke-Ober," *Boston Globe*, April 10, 1998.

"having a love affair with suicide": Patti Doten, "Defying Depression," *Boston Globe*, March 8, 1994.

"Kerry was winning high marks": John Robinson and Robert L. Turner, "Kerry Is Building Image as a Worker" *Boston Globe*, February 16, 1986.

"senator of the world": "Short Circuits," *Boston Globe*, March 2, 1996.

"from the far end of his district, Nicaragua": Sarah V. Snyder, "Bulger's Roast Jokes Draw Blood and Laughs," *Boston Globe*, March 17, 1986.

"Most of the honoraria": Kerry's Senate Public Financial Disclosure Reports, 1985 through 1990.

"had seats on three committees": *Congressional Quarterly*'s "Politics in America," 1990.

"low-risk real estate deal": Frank Phillips, "Kerry, Aide Profited in Deal with Fund-Raiser," *Boston Globe*, June 2, 1988.

"Finch boasted": Michael Grunwald, "Dealings Draw Questions But No Proof That Kerry South to Aid Developer," *Boston Globe*, October 23, 1996.

"sweetheart deal in Faneuil Hall": Kurkjian interview.

"reputation as the Senate's bon vivant": On Oxenberg and other relationships, see John Robinson, "The Senate's New Romeo," *Boston Globe*, February 22, 1989.

"Israeli Air Force fighter jet": Curtis Wilkie, "Kerry Gets Airborne View of Mideast," *Boston Globe*, May 29, 1986.

"Ferrari of motorcycles": Andrew Miga, "Exotic Bike Cost Kerry $8,600; Says He Was Too Strapped to Give Much to Charity," *Boston Herald*, June 14, 1996.

"The economy fell apart": Charles Stein, "The '80s: A Decade That Didn't Know When to Quit," *Boston Globe*, December 31, 1989.

"Jerry Rappaport ... Charles River Park": Peter Anderson, "West End Story," *Boston Globe Sunday Magazine*, May 24, 1987; Michael Rezendes, "City Wins Suit Against Rappaport," *Boston Globe*, November 2, 1990.

"Metamorphosis": Michael Rezendes, "Rappaport Won't Stray from Course in Campaign Year Full of Negatives," *Boston Globe*, October 29, 1990.

"marijuana": Frank Phillips, "Among Politicians, a Variety of Views," *Boston Globe*, March 2, 1990.

"Kerry's campaign responded" and "wink spots": Michael Rezendes and Steve Marantz, "Kerry Easily Tops Rappaport for Senate Seat," *Boston Globe*, November 7, 1990.

"Hot Heir": Michael Rezendes, "Kerry, Rappaport Intensify Fight in New Negative Television Ads," *Boston Globe*, October 19, 1990.

Chapter 14

"the most important vote": *Congressional Record*, January 11, 1991.

"My greatest fear": Tom Ashbrook, "US Should Allow Iraq Room to Back Off, Kerry Says," *Boston Globe*, August 28, 1990.

"anger, treachery": Michael K. Frisby, "Kerry, Returning from Gulf, Says PLA Is Losing Its Allies," *Boston Globe*, September 5, 1990.

"I'm disturbed": Hearing before the Senate Foreign Relations Committee, December 5, 1990.

"we are talking about war": *Congressional Record*, January 11, 1991.

"not a pacifist": Michael K. Frisby, "Activists Hit Kerry's Stand on Salvador Aid," *Boston Globe*, October 16, 1989.

"green light for aggression": *Congressional Record*, January 11, 1991.

"We must not repeat": Julia Stimson Thorne, "How to Prevent Another Vietnam," *Boston Globe*, February 2, 1991.

"mistakenly mailed letters to constituents": On contradictory letters from Kerry's office, see Nancy Walser, "Politics Inconsistent," *Boston Globe*, February 28, 1991. Kerry's response appeared Thursday, Feb. 28, 1991, p. 14.

"courage and optimism": Elizabeth Neuffer, "Senators Doubt US Will Intervene in Iraqi Strife," *Boston Globe*, March 17, 1991.

"one single soldier or airman": Bush quoted in Michael Duffy and Dan Goodgame, *Marching in Place* (New York: Simon and Schuster, 1992).

"given the nature of Saddam Hussein": John Laidler, "Kerry Walks Gulf Tightrope," *Boston Globe*, May 26, 1991.

"backhanded intervention": Michael Kranish, "Failure to Aid Rebels Called Policy Retreat," *Boston Globe*, April 7, 1991.

"misguided policy": Michael Kranish, "Democrats Blame Bush for Iraq Refugee Crisis," *Boston Globe*, April 18, 1991. Chafee quoted in same.

"You knew it was wrong": Hearing before Senate Select Committee on POW-MIA Affairs, June 25, 1992.

"flat-out lie": Hearing before Senate Select Committee on POW-MIA Affairs, September 22, 1992.

"no compelling evidence . . . hopes have not been realized": Report of the Select Committee on POW/MIA Affairs, January 13, 1993.

"litigious society": Stockdale appearance before Senate Select Committee on POW/MIA Affairs, December 3, 1992.

Chapter 15

"For the next few minutes": Excerpts of Kerry's speech were published in the *Boston Globe*, April 2, 1992. A version of Kerry's speech also appeared in the *Congressional Record*, April 2, 1992.

"chafed under the stigma": John Aloysius Farrell, "Kerry Stands by Yale Speech; He Says Politics Wasn't Involved," *Boston Globe*, April 19, 1992.

"David Duke": John Aloysius Farrell, "Democratic Debate Comes to Light: Power v. Purity," *Boston Globe*, April 3, 1992.

"ruffled feathers": Teresa M. Hanafin, "Kerry to Meet with Minority Leaders," *Boston Globe*, April 3, 1992.

"It's a speech": WCVB, *Five on 5*, April 5, 1992.

"get rid of the perception": Bob Hohler, "Kerry: Defining Voice, Vision While Looking Ahead to 1996," *Boston Globe*, December 11, 1994.

"get ahead of John Kerry": John Aloysius Farrell, "Rumor Mill Is Cranking Up on Kerry," *Boston Globe*, May 31, 1992.

"sparring match": Hearing before Senate Armed Services Committee, May 8, 1993.

"Seven years later": John Ellement, "Kerry Criticizes Gore, Bradley for Position on Gays in Military," *Boston Globe*, January 7, 2000.

"Kerry wrote a commentary": John F. Kerry, "Keep the Cuts Coming," *Boston Globe*, August 6, 1993.

"ostriches": Adrian Walker, "Kerry Announces He Will Back Pact," *Boston Globe*, November 14, 1993.

"Founding Fathers": Jill Zuckman, "Kerry Opposes Balanced Budget Effort," *Boston Globe*, March 1, 1994.

"socialist threats": Kerry appearance on CNN's *Crossfire*, January 25, 1994.

"delighted by the shakeup": Bob Hohler, "Kerry Faults Clinton on Losses," *Boston Globe*, December 1, 1994. Moakley quoted in same.

"intense and aloof": For description of Senator John Heinz, see Michael Barone and Grant Ujifusa, *Almanac of American Politics, 1990* (Boston: Gambit, 1990), p. 1026.

"spirit and wildness": Susan Stiles Dowell, "Her Private World: Teresa Heinz, Interview," *Town & Country*, January 1, 2000.

"sustainable development ... not pro-choice 100 percent": Harry Stoffer, "Teresa Heinz: A Woman on a Mission," *Pittsburgh Post-Gazette*, November 7, 1993.

"fundamentally ugly": Bob Hohler, "Senate OK's Bar on Gay Marriages," *Boston Globe*, September 11, 1996.

"hypocritical, anti-family": Frank Phillips, "Kerry Ex-Wife Assails Annulment Process," *Boston Globe*, April 10, 1997.

"pet wolf": Joe Klein, "The Long War of John Kerry," *New Yorker*, December 2, 2002.

"ridiculous": Ellen J. Silberman, "Kerry's wife calls his presidential ambitions 'ridiculous,' *Boston Herald*, October 24, 1998.

Chapter 16

"Butchy Cataldo": "Sen. Kerry gets a crash course in state Legislature-type humor," *Boston Globe*, April 14, 1996; Alan Sheehan, "After Three Trials, Reinstein Is Acquitted," *Boston Globe*, February 10, 1982.

"Many had no relationship with him": Brian C. Mooney, "An Image of Aloofness Shadows Kerry," *Boston Globe*, January 16, 2003.

"barnstormed for a week or two": Interview with Christopher Greeley.

"2,000 pounds of gold": Charles M. Sennott, "The Making of the Candidates/William Floyd Weld," *Boston Globe*, October 6, 1996.

"Dodge City": Frank Phillips, "Cellucci, Weld Join Forces," *Boston Globe*, September 30, 1989.

"the first media-savvy (baby) boomer": Don Aucoin and Frank Phillips, "Bill Weld: It Was Not Hard to Like Him," *Boston Globe*, April 28, 1997.

"apparently got drunk": Scot Lehigh and Frank Phillips, "Scrutiny of Weld Will Rise with Profile," *Boston Globe*, January 16, 1995.

"In his formal announcement": Michael Grunwald, "Yes, He's (Still) Running for Senate," *Boston Globe*, March 28, 1996.

"a couple of fishwives": Mike Barnicle, "One Columnist's Dream Come True," *Boston Globe*, December 3, 1995.

"Robert L. Turner": "Kerry vs. Weld," *Boston Globe Sunday Magazine*, January 14, 1996.

"governor made news almost daily": Meg Vaillancourt, "Weld Savors Headlines as Kerry Seeks His Own," *Boston Globe*, January 14, 1996.

"important check point": Frank Phillips, "Kerry, Weld Primed for St. Pat's Events," *Boston Globe*, March 15, 1996.

"Weld ... stole the show": Geeta Anand, "Weld's Blarney Steals the Day," *Boston Globe*, March 11, 1996.

"blocking a fire hydrant": Nathan Cobb, "Just Another Zillionaire on the Square," *Boston Globe*, March 27, 1996.

"Kerry 'shredded' Weld": Geeta Anand, "Bulger Hosts with Flair," *Boston Globe*, March 18, 1996.

"opposition to an increase in the federal minimum wage": Frank Phillips, "Weld Voices Opposition to Minimum Wage Hike," *Boston Globe*, March 23, 1996.

"National restaurant chains": Brian C. Mooney, "PACs Bolster Weld Campaign with $700,000 in Contributions," *Boston Globe*, November 1, 1996.

"I know something about killing": "Kerry and Weld Strike Sparks in Lively First Debate," *Boston Globe*, April 9, 1996.

"Weld jabbed Kerry": Frank Phillips and Don Aucoin, "Kerry, Weld Put Focus on Voter Anxiety in Round 2," *Boston Globe*, June 4, 1996.

"rented the billboard": Associated Press, May 22, 1996.

"Jeff Jacoby": "Kerry's Charity Gap," *Boston Globe*, May 16, 1996.

"Kerry bristled": Frank Phillips, "Irked Kerry Defends His Donation Record," *Boston Globe*, June 5, 1996.

"Ducati": Andrew Miga, "Exotic Bike Cost Kerry $8,600," *Boston Herald*, June 14, 1996.

"Imus in the Morning": "Kerry Pledges on Radio Show to Give to Charity," *Congress Daily*, June 17, 1996.

"Metalbanc": Stephen Kurkjian and Frank Phillips, "2 in Money Laundering Contributed $7,000 to Kerry," *Boston Globe*, June 28, 1996.

"thousands of boisterous supporters": Frank Phillips and Meg Vaillancourt, "Kerry, Weld Tussle over Workers, Taxes," *Boston Globe*, July 3, 1996.

"Kerry's campaign polls had continually shown": Interviews with Chris Greeley and pollster Tom Kiley.

"including $70,000 in credit card debt": Brian C. Mooney, Gerard O'Neill, and Daniel Golden, "Cellucci Amasses Huge Debt," *Boston Globe*, July 26, 1996.

"Weld stood by his lieutenant": Daniel Golden and Bruce Mohl, "Democrats Taking Aim at Cellucci's Finances," *Boston Globe*, July 27, 1996.

"an important change": Chris Black, "Election-Year Mood Propels Bills," *Boston Globe*, August 2, 1996.

"Clintonesque": Doris Sue Wong, "Advocates Blast Kerry for Voting for Welfare Bill," *Boston Globe*, August 3, 1996.

"still quotes almost verbatim": Charles Sennott, "Finding 4 Generations Sustained by Welfare," *Boston Globe*, February 20, 1994"; Weld e-mail, February 20, 2004.

"the campaigns issued a joint statement": Meg Vaillancourt, "Kerry, Weld Will Limit Spending to $6.9 Million," *Boston Globe*, August 8, 1996.

"dove into the Charles River, fully clothed": Don Aucoin and Meg Vaillancourt, "Weld Goes to New Depths for Publicity," *Boston Globe*, August 8, 1996.

"46–38 percent": "Weld Soars Ahead of Kerry in Poll," *Boston Herald*, August 12, 1996.

"he was losing a popularity contest": Frank Phillips and Don Aucoin, "Kerry, Weld Show Voters Softer Sides," *Boston Globe*, August 20, 1996.

"changed the tone almost immediately": Michael Grunwald, "It's Clear: Ad Spots Tarnish Reputations," *Boston Globe*, November 3, 1996.

"Ray delays": Scot Lehigh and Don Aucoin, "Aides Say Controversy Took Toll on Kennedy," *Boston Globe*, August 30, 1997.

"duplicitous and brazen distortion": Meg Vaillancourt, "Addiction Experts Say Weld Ad 'Misleading,'" *Boston Globe*, September 27, 1996.

"Sleazy": Meg Vaillancourt, "Weld, Kerry Press Issue of Benefits," *Boston Globe*, September 18, 1996.

"Boston Police Patrolmen's Association": Don Aucoin and Frank Phillips, "Boston Patrolmen Endorse Kerry," *Boston Globe*, September 25, 1996.

"Johnny Chung": relies primarily on two stories in the *Boston Globe* (Brian McGrory, "Kerry Is Alleged to Help Donor with SEC Contact," December 24, 1997; and Aaron Zitner, "Kerry, SEC Defend Contributor's Visit," December 25, 1997).

"children's health insurance bill": Michael Grunwald, "Kerry Files Health Bill After 3-Month Delay," *Boston Globe*, October 2, 1996.

"Kennedy who did all the heavy lifting": Adam Clymer, *Edward M. Kennedy: A Biography* (New York: William Morrow and Company, 1999), pp 585–589.

"free or reduced-price housing": relies on several *Boston Globe* stories, primarily Stephen Kurkjian and Michael Rezendes, "Friends Gave Kerry Cut-Rate Lodging Deal; Senator Says Disclosure Not Required," October 1, 1996; and Frank Phillips and Michael Rezendes, "Weld Asks Probe of Kerry and His Rent-Free Housing," October 2, 1996.

"neglecting to mention that Kerry had belatedly paid": Michael Rezendes and Michael Grunwald, "A New Topic, but Candidates up to Old Tricks," *Boston Globe*, October 24, 1996.

"contract made no mention of fees": "Report: Kerry Spent $1.7 m on Election," *Boston Globe*, December 6, 1996.

"a darker version of events": David Warsh, "Behind the Hootch," *Boston Globe*, October 27, 1996.

"Kerry reacted with outrage": Brian MacQuarrie, "Senator Hits Column Hard, Defends His War Record," *Boston Globe*, October 28, 1996.

"battle of the titans": Michael Grunwald, "Kerry Crusaders Take Center Stage on the Sidewalks," *Boston Globe*, October 29, 1996.

Chapter 17

"healing and a reconciliation," Susan Milligan, "Healing on Vietnam an Honor for Senators," *Boston Globe*, September 10, 2001.

"People were concerned": Susan Milligan, "Congress Gives Bush Power to Hunt Terrorists," *Boston Globe*, September 15, 2002.

"more comfortable": Scot Lehigh, "Why Is Kerry So Secretive About 2004 Race?" *Boston Globe*, August 8, 2001.

"critique to include": Anne E. Kornblut, "Kerry Hits Bush, Democrats on Education," *Boston Globe*, September 22, 1999.

"Free the Senate!": Michael Kranish, "Senate's Would-Be Candidates Can't Wait for the Trial to End," *Boston Globe*, February 11, 1999.

"decided not to run": Jill Zuckman and Michael Kranish, "Suspense Is Over: Kerry Won't Run for President," *Boston Globe*, February 27, 1999, *Globe* staff.

"globalization of terror": Senator John Kerry, *The New War: The Web of Crime That Threatens America's Security* (New York: Simon and Schuster, 1997), pp. 109–132.

"those who strike": Mark D. Preston, "Mass Lawmakers Support Terrorist Strike," States News Service.

"came within yards": NBC *Nightly News*, January 18, 1999.

"The president does not control": John Hall, "As Bombs Rain on Iraq, Some Question President's Motive," *Richmond Times Dispatch*, December 17, 1998.

"buy that car": CBS's *Face the Nation*, September 23, 2001.

"intelligence apparatus": *Congressional Record*, May 1, 1997.

"exceedingly careful and thoughtful": Glen Johnson, "Kerry Backs Action, but Warns of Possible Diplomatic Pitfalls," *Boston Globe*, October 9, 2001.

"some players": Ibid.

"ground forces are going to be necessary": Ronald Brownstein, "Response to Terror," *Los Angeles Times*, November 9, 2001.

"not for a prolonged bombing ... farm system": Stephen Kurkjian, "Kerry Praises Bush but Questions US Policies," *Boston Globe*, October 21, 2001.

"Patriotism isn't blind": Joan Vennochi, "Will This Jolt Put Vietnam Behind Us?" *Boston Globe*, September 20, 2001.

"very tight straits": Thomas Grillo, "Kerry Underlines Law of Probability," *Boston Globe*, October 14, 2001.

"failed military operation": NBC's *Meet the Press*, June 23, 2002.

"trust government": *Congressional Record*, October 11, 2001.

"contract out": John Kerry, "Security Should Be Our Only Priority," *Boston Herald*, November 4, 2001.

"terrorists have declared war": NBC's *Meet the Press*, December 1, 2002 .

"moving the deck chairs": Ann Scales, "America Prepares," *Boston Globe*, September 28, 2001

"reorganization of the federal government": *Congressional Record*, November 19, 2002.

"no moral equivalency": *Congressional Record*, May 3, 1999.

"never forget the perfidy": David Nyhan, "Kerry's Big Leap Forward," *Boston Globe*, June 30, 1999.

"one reason only": *Congressional Record*, October 9, 2002.

Chapter 18

"By early January 2001": Glen Johnson, "Kerry Likely to Get Spot on Finance Panel," *Boston Globe*, January 11, 2001.

"Kerry was in Iowa": Glen Johnson, "Kerry in Key States, Finds the Spotlight," *Boston Globe*, June 25, 2001; "With Travels, Kerry Hints Presidential Run," *Boston Globe*, July 21, 2001.

"He'd also been to Texas": Scot Lehigh, "Why Is Kerry So Secretive About 2004 Race?" *Boston Globe*, August 8, 2001; Glen Johnson, "Kerry in Key States, Finds the Spotlight."

"Citizen Soldier Fund": Filings with Federal Election Commission and Internal Revenue Service; Glen Johnson, "In a Switch, Kerry Is Launching PAC," *Boston Globe*, December 15, 2001.

"Rockefeller": David Wilkison, "Rockefeller Decides Against Presidential Bid," Associated Press, August 1, 1991.

"for the first time ever": Frank Phillips and Stephanie Ebbert, "Romney Plans Agenda of Jobs, Health Care," *Boston Globe*, April 6, 2002.

"he visited South Carolina": Wayne Washington, "Kerry Courts Southern Skeptics," *Boston Globe*, May 4, 2002.

"Dean became an intriguing alternative": Susan Milligan, "Dean to Form Committee for 2004 Run," *Boston Globe*, May 30, 2002.

"a dove one minute, a hawk the next": Dick Polman, "Democrats All Over Map on Iraq War," *Philadelphia Inquirer*, October 9, 2002.

"everything in a unilateral way?" CBS interview with Dean, September 29, 2002.

"group of Democrats in Arizona": Glen Johnson, "Senator Stands By Iraq Vote," *Boston Globe*, October 15, 2002.

"this is not a vote about a message": *Congressional Record*, January 11, 1991 (legislative day of January 3, 1991).

"tough weapons inspections": Glen Johnson, "Kerry Backs Bush on Resolution," *Boston Globe*, October 10, 2002.

"A War Hero": Albert R. Hunt, "A War Hero Moves to the Front of the Pack," *Wall Street Journal*, October 24, 2002.

"Joe Klein": Joe Klein, "The Long War of John Kerry," *New Yorker*, December 2, 2002.

"filed a statement of candidacy": Glen Johnson, "Kerry Files as a Candidate, Will Explore Fund-Raising," *Boston Globe*, December 5, 2002.

"shift on the death penalty": Anne E. Kornblut, "Kerry Traces His Shift on the Death Penalty," *Boston Globe*, December 18, 2002.

"confidently predicted he could raise": Walter Shapiro, *One-Car Caravan: On the Road with the 2004 Democrats Before America Tunes In*, (New York: Public Affairs, 2003), pp. 60–61.

"Kerry led Dean": New Hampshire Poll, American Research Group, Inc., January 2003.

"Cape Cod and Nantucket": John Chao, "A Windsurfer in the White House?" *American Windsurfer* magazine, vol. 5, iss. 5 (1998).

"holiday season on the Internet": John Kerry, "A Response to Cancer Forged by Vietnam," *Boston Globe*, January 1, 2004.

"Prostate gland was removed": Glen Johnson, "Prostate Cancer Surgery for Kerry Today," *Boston Globe*, February 12, 2003.

"return to the campaign trail": Glen Johnson, "Surgeon Says Kerry Can Campaign in Two Weeks," *Boston Globe*, February 13, 2003.

"I'm going to get through this": John Kerry, "A Response to Cancer Forged by Vietnam."

"I am completely supportive of our troops over there": "Kerry Says Education Must Become a Priority," Associated Press, March 23, 2003.

"Dean ... hammered Kerry's war posture": Nedra Pickler, "Dean Says Kerry Is Wobbling on War," Associated Press, March 28, 2003.

"regime change in Saddam Hussein": Glen Johnson, "Kerry Says U.S. Needs Its Own 'Regime Change,'" *Boston Globe*, April 3, 2003.

"too harsh": Glen Johnson, "Kerry Says His Bush Remark Was Quip," *Boston Globe*, April 30, 2003.

"Mission Accomplished": Anne E. Kornblut, "Bush Proclaims a Victory," *Boston Globe*, May 2, 2003.

"In early July, Kerry summoned top aides ... to his Nantucket home": Michael Kranish, "In a Shift of Strategy, Kerry Takes on Dean," *Boston Globe*, September 14, 2003.

"twenty-one of them": Glen Johnson, "Kerry Campaign Opts to Pick Up Pace in Fall," *Boston Globe*, July 8, 2003.

"Kerry's famously blunt-speaking wife": Glen Johnson, "Kerry Heinz Offers a Critique of Husband's Rivals," *Boston Globe*, November 21, 2003.

"Kerry had also asked his media consultant": Paul Farhi, "In Kerry Campaign, Overlaps Chafee; Staffs in Washington and Boston Have Different Visions," *Washington Post*, October 9, 2003.

"Kerry was on an Asian fact-finding trip": Brian C. Mooney, "Kerry's About-Face Wins Over Mayors," *Boston Globe*, December 11, 1999.

"dangerously off course": Patrick Healy and Michael Kranish, "Bold Strategy Sparked Campaign's Turnaround," *Boston Globe*, February 8, 2004.

"At 5 A.M. the next day ... Guys who really get me": Ibid.

"munching on his dinner": Mike Glover, "Sen. Kerry Changes Campaign Manager," Associated Press, November 10, 2003.

"Jordan ... He made the only choice he could": Patrick Healy and Michael Kranish, "Bold Strategy Sparked Campaign's Turnaround."

"forty-three school buses": Thomas Beaumont, "Clinton, Democrats Fire Up Crowd," *Des Moines Register*, November 16, 2003.

"Mellman argued persuasively": Patrick Healy and Michael Kranish, "Bold Strategy Sparked Campaign's Turnaround."

"tribute to Kerry by his Vietnam crewmate, Del Sandusky": Ibid.

"Cahill shut the door": Ibid.

"Rassmann ... contacted ... Kerry's campaign": Patrick Healy, "Past Resurfaces in Unusual Day for Kerry," *Boston Globe*, January 18, 2004.

"raising to at least seventeen": "State by State Primary Matchups," *National Journal* Web site.

"after securing a pledge from Dean": Lynn Sweet, "Braun Drops Out, but Wins Anyway," *Chicago Sun-Times*, January 16, 2004.

"poaching his message ... Pilferage by Edwards": Thomas Fitzgerald, "In Rhetoric Race, Dean Has It All Over His Rivals," *Philadelphia Inquirer*, January 27, 2004.

"$227,950 from lobbyists": Center for Responsive Politics Web site, opensecrets.org.

"claimed there would be no more terrorist attacks": Annmarie Timmins, "Clark Says He Can Keep U.S. Safe from Attacks," *Concord Monitor*, January 9, 2004.

"mad scientist": Howard Kurtz, "Schmooze-Makers; Howard Dean's Campaign Team Charms His Way into Print," *Washington Post*, December 18, 2003.

ACKNOWLEDGEMENTS

This biography of John F. Kerry had its genesis in a decision by the *Boston Globe*'s editor, Martin Baron, to push for a comprehensive series on the life and career of the junior senator from Massachusetts. He instructed his reporting team to "leave nothing on the table" in terms of information about Kerry, and he matched that assignment by leaving nothing on the table in terms of his support and enthusiasm for the project. The result was a seven-part, 14-page series that ran in the newspaper in June 2003.

Kerry is a seemingly well-known figure, having spent more than thirty years in the public eye, but also something of an enigma, perpetually in the shadow of the senior senator from Massachusetts, Edward M. Kennedy. Kennedy and his two older brothers and the rest of the Kennedy family have been the subject of countless books, but no complete biography had been written about Kerry. The view at the *Boston Globe* was that if Kerry became the likely Democratic nominee, the newspaper was ideally positioned to be the first to tell the full story of Kerry's life. Thus, when it became increasingly apparent in January 2004 that

Kerry would be the nominee, the decision was quickly made to expand the series into a book. As a result, those who participated in the series, as well as the book, deserve much credit.

John Aloysius Farrell, who was one of the co-authors of the original series, left the *Boston Globe* around the same time the series was published to become Washington bureau chief of the *Denver Post*. He spent hours in outlining and coordinating the project from the beginning.

Among the editors who worked many hours on the project in Boston were deputy managing editor John Yemma and national editor Kenneth J. Cooper, both of whom provided countless invaluable suggestions for improving the articles. Peter Canellos, the Washington Bureau chief, provided valuable editing input for the series and the book. Head librarian Lisa Tuite contributed significant resources, and librarian Richard Pennington provided first-rate research assistance at every stage of the series and the book. David Schutz of editorial design and Thea Breite of the photo department also spent many hours on the original series, and Catherine Aldrich, the director of photography, coordinated photos for the book.

Among the others at the *Globe* who provided support, assistance and advice throughout were Helen W. Donovan, the newspaper's executive editor; Walter V. Robinson, the spotlight team editor and a valuable resource on Vietnam issues; Stephen Kurkjian, the assistant metro editor who provided tapes of his own key interviews with Kerry; and, reporter Frank Phillips, who has covered Kerry for many years. The *Globe*'s political reporters, who spent countless hours on the campaign trail while we worked on the series and book, provided support as well; these include Glen Johnson and Patrick Healy, who were especially helpful in writing the last chapter of this book. At some point, every member of the *Globe*'s political team and Washington bureau, including national political reporter Anne E. Kornblut, provided helpful suggestions. Washington Bureau office manager Cynthia Taylor calmly sorted through faxes and phone calls and many requests for help. Alex Beam of the *Globe* contributed by interviewing Julia Thorne.

Felix Gundacker, an Austrian genealogist, spent many hours in remote archives and helped find much of the information about Kerry's ancestry. Brian Whitmore, a *Globe* correspondent in Europe, interviewed Kerry ancestors in Austria. While Senator Kerry did not provide interviews for the book project, he did agree to ten hours of interviews for the series, and his staff and many of his friends and family members spent countless hours providing recollections and documents about the senator's life.

Peter Osnos, the publisher of PublicAffairs, was enthusiastic about the possibility of this book within days of the publication of the original series. As soon as Kerry won the New Hampshire primary, he made good on that enthusiasm, committing himself to publishing the book. The editor of the book, Robert Kimzey, worked at lightning pace with grace, as did his associate, Melanie Peirson Johnstone, and copy editor Michele Wynn.

Finally, the production of this book under an unusually tight deadline would not have been possible without the love, understanding, enthusiasm and support of our families, to whom we give our most heartfelt thanks.

MICHAEL KRANISH, NINA J. EASTON
AND BRIAN C. MOONEY

The authors can be reached at kerrybook@globe.com

INDEX

PublicAffairs is a publishing house founded in 1997. It is a tribute to the standards, values, and flair of three persons who have served as mentors to countless reporters, writers, editors, and book people of all kinds, including me.

I. F. STONE, proprietor of *I. F. Stone's Weekly*, combined a commitment to the First Amendment with entrepreneurial zeal and reporting skill and became one of the great independent journalists in American history. At the age of eighty, Izzy published *The Trial of Socrates*, which was a national bestseller. He wrote the book after he taught himself ancient Greek.

BENJAMIN C. BRADLEE was for nearly thirty years the charismatic editorial leader of *The Washington Post*. It was Ben who gave the *Post* the range and courage to pursue such historic issues as Watergate. He supported his reporters with a tenacity that made them fearless and it is no accident that so many became authors of influential, best-selling books.

ROBERT L. BERNSTEIN, the chief executive of Random House for more than a quarter century, guided one of the nation's premier publishing houses. Bob was personally responsible for many books of political dissent and argument that challenged tyranny around the globe. He is also the founder and longtime chair of Human Rights Watch, one of the most respected human rights organizations in the world.

For fifty years, the banner of Public Affairs Press was carried by its owner Morris B. Schnapper, who published Gandhi, Nasser, Toynbee, Truman and about 1,500 other authors. In 1983, Schnapper was described by *The Washington Post* as "a redoubtable gadfly." His legacy will endure in the books to come.

Peter Osnos, *Publisher*

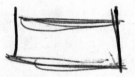